Founded in 1921 to foster 'interest in the history and traditions of British and Commonwealth armies, and to encourage research in these fields', the Society for Army Historical Research is one of the oldest societies of its kind, dedicated to 'serving scholars, enthusiasts and soldiers'. In 2021 the Society celebrated its centenary year with a series of events including a research conference, which, due to the ongoing COVID pandemic, took place partly online and partly at the National Army Museum. This volume contains a selection from the proceedings of that conference, as well as a short history of the Society's first 100 years.

Topics covered comprise: a personal microhistory of service in the Restoration army; a new narrative of the Battle of Lincelles, 1793; a study of the Fencible regiments during the French Revolutionary War; analysis of medical aspects of Wellington's campaigns in India; fashion and satire in the aftermath of Waterloo; relations with friends and foes during the Salonika campaign, 1915; the evolution of identity discs during the Great War and afterwards; the Motor Machine Gun Corps in India 1915-1919; civil relations during the invasion of Sicily, 1943; British and Canadian combat engineers during operations to clear the Scheldt estuary, 1944; and the changing role of Army chaplains in the past century.

Dr Andrew Bamford is a military historian whose research focusses on the British Army during the eighteenth century and Napoleonic era. After completing a PhD at the University of Leeds, subsequently published by the University of Oklahoma Press as *Sickness, Suffering, and the Sword*, he worked for some years as a freelance historian and author producing a number of titles with Frontline Books as well as working as a researcher and in the museum sector. In 2016 he was invited to set up and manage the 'From Reason to Revolution 1721-1815' series for Helion & Company; the first title appeared the following year and to date nearly 100 books have been published under the series brand. A member of the Society for Army Historical Research since 2012, he joined its Council in 2015 and was elected Hon. Secretary at the 2022 Annual General Meeting.

One Hundred Years of Army Historical Research

Proceedings of the SAHR Centenary Conference

Edited by Andrew Bamford

 Helion & Company Limited

Helion & Company Limited
Unit 8 Amherst Business Centre
Budbrooke Road
Warwick
CV34 5WE
England
Tel. 01926 499619
Email: info@helion.co.uk
Website: www.helion.co.uk
Twitter: @helionbooks
Visit our blog at http://blog.helion.co.uk/

Published by Helion & Company 2022
Designed and typeset by Mach 3 Solutions Ltd (www.mach3solutions.co.uk)
Cover designed by Paul Hewitt, Battlefield Design (www.battlefield-design.co.uk)
Printed by Henry Ling Limited, Dorchester, Dorset

Text © Individual Contributors 2022
Illustrations and maps as individually credited

ISBN 978-1-804512-86-9

British Library Cataloguing-in-Publication Data.
A catalogue record for this book is available from the British Library.

For details of other military history titles published by Helion & Company Limited, contact
the above address, or visit our website: http://www.helion.co.uk

We always welcome receiving book proposals from prospective authors.

Contents

List of Plates

List of Maps

Foreword by HRH the Duke of Kent

Having been a member and then Patron of the Society for Army Historical Research for many years, it is a pleasure to introduce this collection of essays, which were used to mark the Society's centenary.

The Society's first members would be delighted to see that the organisation which they launched is flourishing, and that its members deemed its centenary worth marking and celebrating.

The Society proudly serves soldiers, scholars and enthusiasts. Whether you are within the United Kingdom, in the Commonwealth, or one of our many supporters from abroad, as long as you have an interest in the land forces of the Crown, you will find something to interest you here.

Let us hope that the Society's first centenary was not a destination but, rather, only a waypoint on a long and healthy journey!

H.R.H. The Duke of Kent, K.G.
Patron of the Society for Army Historical Research

Preface – The Society at One Hundred

Sir Barney White-Spunner

I think our founding fathers would have been very proud, and possibly not a little surprised, had they known that we would be celebrating the centenary of the Society they founded in 1921. Their purpose, in the aftermath of a World War that had fundamentally changed the character and practices of the British Army, was to establish a Society that encouraged the study of its history and traditions. I like to think that we have remained true to their vision, but I would also suggest that they would have been impressed by how widely that vision has been interpreted over the last century. We have extended the range of the Society both in terms of historical span and subject matter. A quick glance at the contents of this book illustrates that, with articles covering topics ranging from the British Civil Wars to contemporary soldiering and from military fashion to engineering tactics. The Society, quite apart from being one of the oldest organisations dedicated to military research, now offers the very widest perspective of the British Army and its soldiers.

Beyond that, one of the Society's great strengths is that it offers a forum for historians, from A level students to much-published professionals, to contribute their thoughts whether through our lecture programme or the Journal. This is a hugely valuable contribution to research both in terms of encouraging individuals and in exposing interesting and often over-looked aspects of army history. I can think of few other disciplines which have such a well-managed method of publishing research.

Two most important aspects of the Society's work are the Templer Medal and the Student Essay Prize, both of which have done such an enormous amount to encourage people to write military history. The ever-increasing number of entries for both categories shows just how much they are valued and for me one of the greatest pleasures at the annual prizegiving is to see young school historians receiving prizes alongside national figures.

The way that the Society has embraced technology, both in terms of handling archives and in promulgating lectures has been truly inspirational as have the ever-closer links to the National Army Museum. None of this would be possible without all the long hours put in by our dedicated volunteers who run the Society, as well as by our members. It is this enthusiasm and energy that makes it such a huge pleasure to be your President and, although sadly I fear I will not be there to see it, makes me sure that we will see a similar celebration for our bicentenary.

Lieutenant-General Sir Barney White-Spunner KCB, CBE
September 2022

Introduction

Andrew Bamford

One could be forgiven for thinking that the Society for Army Historical Research is cursed to have its key dates upstaged by major world events. In 1914, as Peter Howson tells us in his contribution to this book, plans to form what would become SAHR were delayed by the outbreak of the First World War. The Society's eventual foundation in 1921 placed its Centenary in 2021, giving the Society's Centenary Subcommittee the challenge of organising commemorative events as the nation struggled through the COVID pandemic. In the grand scheme of human suffering caused by the virus outbreak, the imposition of extra work upon a group of military historians is scarcely worthy of a mention, but it would be remiss not to open this introduction by recording the hard work of Major-General Ewan Carmichael, Dr Andrew Cormack, Charles Street, and in particular my conference co-organiser Eamonn O'Keeffe, in creating – and then continually recasting – the programme of Centenary events of which the conference on which this book is based formed a part.

Within that programme, the research conference from which the bulk of the material contained in this volume is drawn was originally envisaged as forming the second day of a two-day in-person event planned for April 2021. Day One would have involved keynote lectures by leading figures in the field and would have concluded with a dinner. That, by our way of thinking, would serve to sum up and commemorate the first 100 years of the Society's history; Day Two, by contrast, was to look ahead and give a spotlight to the next generation of historians who are leading the way into the Society's second century. As Eamonn and I began to receive proposals for papers, however, it quickly became apparent that those responding were far more numerous than we had expected, came from a far more diverse set of backgrounds, and were representative of a much wider age range than the early career researchers who had been our expected target. Some years ago, the Society adopted as its tagline 'Serving Scholars, Enthusiasts and Soldiers', so it was to our great delight that all these groups were strongly represented both in the range of proposals that were submitted for the conference and in those eventually selected. We had students just beginning postgraduate work, and we had senior professors; regulars and reservists from non-commissioned right up to field rank; enthusiasts of every stamp. As we worked through the proposals, it quickly became clear that even the employment of parallel panels would not enable us to get all of the worthy contenders into a single day. Thus, the plan shifted to having a day of papers in April as part of the main Centenary celebration, and a second day in the Autumn of 2021 by way of a second bite – and, even then, there were still excellent proposals that it was simply impossible to incorporate.

In the event, of course, our plans for in-person events in April 2021 proved to be wildly overoptimistic, and instead this entire portion of the programme was shifted to an online format. With the technical help of Colonel Dudley Giles, without whose patient assistance we would have been floundering, the two-day event programme was converted into six evening sessions hosted via the Demio conferencing platform and each consisting of one of the Day One keynote lectures followed by one of the Day Two conference panels. This arrangement proved a great success, and has since formed the model for a programme of online lectures which the Society continues to host. It did prove possible, however, to go ahead with the plan for an in-person event during the autumn of 2021 and this took place at the National Army Museum on 22 September of that year. As well as four regular panels, this session included two additional keynote presentations by Drs Sarah Ashbridge and Patrick Watt, recipients respectively of the Society's 2019 Independent Research Grant and of a special additional Centenary Research Grant. Due to the ongoing restrictions on travel, however, a number of overseas speakers were obliged to join us on the day via video-links, while a further four contributors, unable to avail themselves of that option due to conflicting time zones, instead gave their papers as part of a final online session later in the autumn.

By the conclusion of that last, extra, online session, we had heard a total of 33 research papers and thoughts turned towards the options for publishing them. The original expectation had been that those speakers who wished to write up their research could do so as contributors to the Society's Journal, and, indeed, several speakers who felt unable to deliver a written-up version of their paper in time for inclusion in this work have indicated their intention to do just that in the fullness of time. However, with so much of the planned Centenary programme cancelled due to the pandemic – although it did prove possible to resurrect the Centenary Dinner on a somewhat smaller scale – sufficient funds were available to finance the publication and distribution to members of the book that you are now reading. Clearly, it was never going to be possible to include all the papers, and, in any case, there were several that for one reason or another did not lend themselves to publication – some because they discussed research that was still being developed, others because the work drew on material already being published elsewhere. The chronological balance of the eventual selection owes more to luck than good management, but the 11 research-based chapters have ended up being pleasingly representative of the conference as a whole in terms of the range of topics covered and the range of backgrounds of the contributors. To these 11 has been added a twelfth chapter written specially for this work by my predecessor as the Society's Hon. Secretary, giving an account of the history of the Society's first 100 years. It came as something of a surprise realisation, underscored by a recent research enquiry relating to the early years of the Society, that our own foundation and activities are themselves now part of history, but this is of course the case. Peter's chapter places SAHR's first century in historical context and shows how much the Society has evolved and changed over the years in parallel with changes both in military history and historiography, and in society more generally.

Turning to the 11 chapters arising from the Centenary Conference, the reader will find a variety of topics and approaches. Some are unashamedly representative of 'old' military history, with a narrative focus on the course of battles and campaigns; others pick up some of the trends in 'new' military history, looking at social and cultural factors or employing the techniques of microhistory to explore events from the perspective of a single individual. They are, of course, entirely self-contained pieces intended to be read as such, but they have been presented in as close to a chronological order as is possible when one makes allowance for a certain amount of overlap, and, as such, provide an overview of the four centuries of British military history that is at the core of SAHR's remit.

All chapters have been through peer-review, and I would like to take the opportunity to thank – without compromising anyone's anonymity by naming names – all those who gave their time and expertise to facilitate that process. More publicly, I would like to repeat my thanks to the Centenary Subcommittee for all their support, and also add my thanks to my colleague on the Society's Council Dr Phil McCarty for his assistance with the checking of the proofs; needless to say, any errors that have made it into print remain my responsibility. I am honoured that our Royal Patron, HRH the Duke of Kent, a stalwart supporter of the Society for over half of its history, and our President Lieutenant General Sir Barney White-Spunner have agreed to furnish this work with a Foreword and Preface respectively and I thank them both for agreeing to do so. Duncan Rogers, Managing Director of Helion & Company and a former member of the SAHR Council, has been supportive throughout the evolution of this project, and the technical support of George Anderson with the cartography and Kim McSweeney with the typesetting is also greatly appreciated. Lastly, I must thank the 12 contributors, without whose efforts we would not have a book: I hope that you enjoy reading their work as much as I have done.

Dr Andrew Bamford
October 2022

Contributor Biographies

Dr Sarah Ashbridge is a Research Fellow in Military Sciences at the Royal United Services Institute for Defence and Security Studies (RUSI). Sarah's research into identity discs began during her MSc in Forensic Archaeology, ultimately leading to an AHRC funded PhD thesis focusing on the discs and their role in the identification of soldiers from the First World War. Sarah's historical research has been informed by archaeological practice, having supported the recovery of soldiers with archaeological organisations including Operation Nightingale (DIO), Breaking Ground Heritage, and Ruben Willaert BVBA. Sarah continues to focus on mortuary affairs and identification practice in her current research.

Captain Philip Brazier completed a PGCE in 2000 and has taught in New Zealand and the United Kingdom. He has Reservist service with the British and New Zealand Royal Engineers. A Graduate Diploma in Defence and Security Studies (Massey, 2012) was followed by an MA in Military History (Birmingham, 2016). He is an active member of the Royal Engineers Historical Society and has guided military and private studies in New Zealand, the USA, Belgium, France, the Netherlands and Malta. He enjoys making cross-curricular links to history.

Rory Butcher has been a doctoral student at the University of Leeds since 2021. His primary field of research, and the subject of his thesis, is the Fencible regiments in Britain during the French Revolutionary Wars. He completed his MA at the University of Kent, with his dissertation serving as introductory research into the Fencibles and the home defence apparatus during this period. His wider interests include questions of military, regional, and national identity within both auxiliary and combat troops. He currently serves as the Student Representative on the Council of the Society for Army Historical Research and is a Postgraduate Lead for the War and Peace Research Cluster at the University of Leeds. This is his first contribution to an edited collection.

Jake Gasson is a History DPhil student at the University of Oxford specialising in the Macedonian Front of the First World War. His doctoral research investigates how the men of the British Salonika Force experienced and endured the psychological challenge posed by boredom. Prior to this, he earned an MSt in the History of War at Oxford and a BA in History from King's College London.

Martin Howard is a former hospital consultant and honorary visiting professor at the University of York. He is a Fellow of the Royal Colleges of Physicians and Pathologists, and of the Royal Historical Society. His main interest is in eighteenth- and nineteenth-century warfare, with a particular focus on the human dimension of these conflicts and the lesser-known campaigns. He is the author of *Wellington's Doctors* (2002), *Napoleon's Doctors* (2006), *Napoleon's Poisoned Chalice* (2009), *Walcheren 1809* (2012), *Death Before Glory* (2015), and *Wellington and the British Army's Indian Campaigns 1798–1805* (2020). He has recently contributed the chapter on military medicine to the *Cambridge History of the Napoleonic Wars* and is currently researching the medical history of the American Revolution.

The Rev. Dr Peter Howson was the Secretary of the Society for Army Historical Research from 2014 to 2022. He had previously served two periods as a member of the Society's Council, having become a member whilst a serving chaplain. During his 25 years in the British Army he saw service in BAOR and it successors, as well as Cyprus and Hong Kong with detachments to various other countries. After leaving the Army he became the Methodist Minister in Inverness and completed a PhD at the University of Aberdeen. His interests are in military chaplaincy and post-conflict military occupations, and he has published monographs in both areas.

Lieutenant-Colonel Paul Macro is a serving Royal Tank Regiment officer, currently posted in the NATO Joint Force Command HQ at Brunssum. His early career was spent on regimental duty. Subsequently he held various staff appointments largely concerned with equipment acquisition and training. He has devoted spare time to the study of regimental history and his family's military history. The latter resulted in publishing *Action at Badama Post* (Casemate, 2019). Paul holds a MSc in Defence Technology and a MA in Defence Studies.

Dr Linda Parker is an author and independent scholar. Her main historical interests research areas are twentieth and twenty-first century military history, particularly military chaplaincy. Since 2009 she has been writing for Helion & Company and has published five books on British Army chaplaincy in the two World Wars. Her most recent book is *Nearer My God to Thee: Airborne Chaplains in the Second World War* (2020) She has also contributed to several volumes of collected essays on military and polar topics. She is a member of the Western Front Association and the Second World War Research Group, and a founder member of the British Modern Military History Society.

Dr Ismini Pells is a Departmental Lecturer in the Department for Continuing Education at the University of Oxford. She is also the Project Manager of the Civil War Petitions project (www.civilwarpetitions.ac.uk). She is a military and medical historian of the early modern period, with a particular interest in the seventeenth-century British Civil Wars. She is the author of *Philip Skippon and the British Civil Wars* (Routledge, 2020) and editor of *New Approaches to the Military History of the English Civil Wars* (Helion, 2016).

Dr Luke Reynolds received his PhD from the City University of New York's Graduate Center in 2019 and also holds degrees from Cambridge University, Hunter College, CUNY, and Trinity College, Dublin. His first book, *Who Owned Waterloo? Battle, Memory, & Myth in British History, 1815-1852* was published by Oxford University Press in the summer of 2022. Currently a Visiting Assistant Professor at the University of Connecticut's Stamford Campus, he is a native New Yorker and a Fellow of the Royal Historical Society.

Dr Fabio Simonetti is Lecturer in European History and Warfare at Brunel University London. Prior to that, he taught Italian History and Culture at the University of Reading, where he earned his PhD in Italian Studies as part of an AHRC Collaborative Doctoral Partnership in collaboration with the Imperial War Museums. Fabio is a social and oral historian specialising in Italian and European modern history, intercultural and gendered encounters in conflict zones, and occupation studies. He has recently completed his research on the dynamics of the Second World War encounter between British soldiers and Italian civilians in Italy. Fabio has presented papers at a number of international conferences and has published on both the Allied and German Second World War occupations of Italy as well as on intercultural encounters in war zones.

Garry David Wills has been interested in the Napoleonic Wars since he started wargaming the period in 1971. In 2011, Garry self-published his first book, *Wellington's First Battle*, about the battle of Boxtel in 1794. Garry also contributed a series of articles to the *Smoothbore Ordnance Journal* relating to British artillery in Flanders 1793–1795. In 2020, Helion published Garry's latest book, *Wellington at Bay, the Battle of Villamuriel, 25 October 1812*. Subsequently, he provided an acclaimed chapter in Helion's *Glory is Fleeting* entitled Maucune's Division at Salamanca. Most recently Garry has presented a paper to the second NRWGC 'War and Peace in the Age of Napoleon' conference entitled 'Where did Wellington fight his first battle?' Garry is currently writing *Throwing Thunderbolts: A Wargamer's Guide to the War of the First Coalition, 1792–7*, to be published by Helion in 2023.

1

A History of the Society for Army Historical Research

Peter J. Howson

Contemplating the centenary of the Society for Army Historical Research prompts the question, 'Why is it only ONE hundred years old?' Elements of the British Army can trace their origin back to 1485 when, following the accession of Henry VII to the throne of England in the aftermath of the Battle of Bosworth, the Yeomen of the Guard were formed. The Royal Monmouthshire Royal Engineers can claim a continuous existence from 1539; the Honourable Artillery Company (HAC), which curiously follows it in the order of precedence of the British Army, from 1537. The concept of an 'army' as an organised body came to be recognised after the Restoration of Charles II in 1660. There was no lack of interest in the history of fighting men but a curious disinclination to research the history of the British Army as a single entity.

The Society should have celebrated its centenary in 2014. Colonel Cyril Field, of the Royal Marine Light Infantry, recorded the origins of the formation of the Society in an article in the Society's Journal that marked the tenth anniversary of the formation.[1] He had been a member of the Society for Naval Research and had, in 1910, been impressed by the way that that body helped those interested in the history, traditions and customs of seafaring. As someone with an interest in both naval and military matters there was, he thought, a place for a similar society that would do the same for the army. As he noted:

> It occurred to me that a similar Society and Journal, dealing with Military traditions and antiquities, would have at least the same interest, and

---

1 C. Field, 'The Society for Army Historical Research', in the *Journal of the Society for Army Historical Research*, Vol.10 (40) Oct. 1931, pp.235-236.

perhaps an even greater scope, both on account of the larger numbers to whom it might be expected to appeal and the many different branches, Corps and Regiments of the land service, each with its more or less separate relics, history and tradition.'[2]

Herein perhaps lies the answer to the question. There had not been any shortage of curiosity about the history of those 'departments, Corps and Regiments'. There has been no lack of books about battles and soldiering. More limited though have been the works that dealt with the British Army as a whole. The most comprehensive was that of John Fortescue.[3] Another work had been that by the former Secretary of State for War in Balfour's government, Arnold-Forster's 'The Army in 1906'.[4] The first decade of the twentieth century had been a time of reconstruction and change for the whole of the land forces following the apparently inept showing of the Army in the Second Anglo-Boer War of 1899 to 1902, and the looming threat of a potential European conflict. If it appears strange that it had taken so long to show any interest in the Army as an organisation it might be noted that almost 70 years after the creation of the current Ministry of Defence, there still is no learned group dedicated to the consideration of its history.

Colonel Field garnered interest and a provisional committee was formed, in early 1914, to further the aim of the creation of such a society to be concerned with military history. Sufficient responses had been received to list 138 potential members and to propose names for a committee to take the plan forward. Field took it upon himself to act as Secretary. A circular letter, giving the names of those who had subscribed already, was to be issued on 1 August 1914. At that point events took an unforeseen course and most of those interested were to be involved in the making of history rather than the recording of it.

The war meant that progress stopped until the idea was again raised in 1919. Lieutenant Colonel J.H. Leslie, one of the pre-war provisional committee, became involved again. The idea for a Society was duly discussed at a meeting which was held in London at the Royal United Services Institution on 3 June 1921, and at which 22 people were present. The meeting decided to create a Society which would aim to publish a quarterly magazine. It estimated the cost of each edition to be around £20 thus, if 80 subscribers could be found, the annual membership fee would be 10 shillings. It was agreed to publish two editions without charge and then to hold a meeting to review whether the plan could be progressed. A committee was formed to oversee the production of the two editions. The Chairman was to be Colonel Sir Arthur Leetham, the Secretary of the Royal United Services Institution and

2   Field, 'The Society for Army Historical Research', pp.235-236.
3   John William Fortescue, *History of the British Army from the Norman Conquest to the First World War* (London: Macmillan, 1899-1930), in 13 volumes with six separate map volumes.
4   H.O. Arnold-Forster, *The Army in 1906* (London: John Murray, 1906).

a former Royal Engineer. Major H.G. Parkyn was to act as both Treasurer and Secretary. Professor Charles Oman, a noted military historian,[5] together with Lieutenant Colonel J.H. Leslie, who was to become the Editor of the Journal, W.Y Baldry, from the War Office Library, and A.S. White, the latter two names that were to figure large in the early years of the Society, were the remaining members.

The report of the meeting also included the outline of the Society's aims.[6] The Object of the Society was:

> To encourage research into Army Antiquities, into matters connected with Regimental History, Uniform Dress and Equipments of the past. Old Military Customs and Traditions, the Art of War in bygone days, Pictures, Prints, Medals, relics and other objects of similar interest.[7]

Membership was open to 'any person', subject to the approval of the Committee. In addition, 'Libraries, Clubs, Societies and Regiments, may, through their representatives, be admitted to Membership.'[8] This distinction between individual and corporate membership was to trouble the Society at various times during its history. One solution was to separate them into 'members' and 'subscribers'. Even in 2021 there remains a certain ambiguity as to how the 'representative' of an organisation might participate in the Society's governance and activities.

The first copy of the Society's Journal, which contained a report of the June meeting, was dated September 1921. It had an elaborate cover design and a list of those who had recently joined and who had thus brought the number of members to 227. It is worth noting that at its formation the Society was known as The Society *of* Army Historical Research, the 'of' only becoming 'for' in 1929. As the Chair had noted, the Society's Journal would, 'contain original articles, extracts from rare and not easily accessible military works, prints and drawings, notes, questions and answers, and generally to serve as a medium of inter-communication between members of the Society'.[9] Many of those aims remain as important in 2021 and have been reflected in the pages of the Journal over the last 100 years.

The Council of the Society was pleased that it was able to report, as indicated above, that by the end of 1921 it had 227 members. Analysis of the names of 'new members' for the period September to November of that year has shown that of the 74 listed, 40 used military titles, the most senior being Major General A.E. Sandbach CB DSO, a former Royal Engineer. There were also 10 institutional

---

5   Sir Charles William Chadwick Oman, KBE, FBA (12 January 1860 – 23 June 1946) was immediate Past President of the Royal Historical Society and Chichele Professor of Modern History at Oxford as well as at the time being Member of Parliament for the University of Oxford constituency.

6   *JSAHR*, Vol.1 (1) September 1921, pp.3-5.

7   *JSAHR*, Vol.1 (1) September 1921, pp.3-5.

8   *JSAHR*, Vol.1 (1) September 1921, pp.3-5.

9   *JSAHR*, Vol.1 (1) September 1921, pp.1-2.

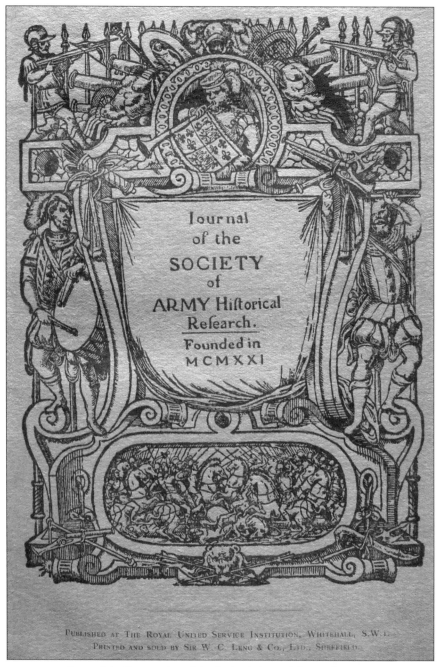

Cover of the first number of the Society's Journal, September 1921.
(Courtesy of Andrew Cormack)

members. Four were regimental Officers' Messes: the Cheshire Regiment Depot, the 1st Battalion the Gloucestershire Regiment, and the Depots of the Royal Welch Fusiliers and Worcestershire Regiment. Others included the Public Record Office (now The National Archives), which may well be able to claim the longest continuous subscription, and the New York Historical Society. It is likely that many of the individuals who gave no military title might well nevertheless have served in the army during the First World War. Only one of the names on the list gave any indication of possible academic connection: Dr A.A. Payne, and even he might have been a medical doctor.

The second number of the Journal, issued in December 1921, indicated that the Society's postal address was care of the Royal United Services Institution (RUSI) in Whitehall. The link would remain strong until the early 1930s when a change of Secretary saw the address move to care of the War Office Library and Annual General Meetings being held at the War Office. The Society maintained a link with RUSI and shared in a joint project to create a directory of information on old uniforms, equipment and colours.[10] Sadly, there was no acknowledgement of the former association when the Society returned to RUSI to hold its 2017 Annual Members Meeting. The choice of the location on that occasion was part of a policy by the Society's Council to meet in a different location each year, and if possible one likely to be unfamiliar to members.

The second edition also included a notice of a 'General Meeting' to be held at RUSI on Thursday 13 December 1921. The meeting was to formally constitute the Society and to elect the Committee and Officers.[11] The notice was signed H.G. Parkyn, who described himself as the Hon. Secretary. Colonel Field was unable to attend, and Lieutenant Colonel Leslie assumed the role of editor of the Journal. The first President was Harold Arthur Dillon-Lee, 17th Viscount Dillon, a noted authority on the history of arms and armour and medieval costume.[12]

The history of the formation and earliest days of the Society has been gleaned from what appeared in the pages of the Society's Journal. The Society's own records are sadly non-existent for most of its history: as will be discussed later, a hiatus in the governance of the Society in 2012 may have been responsible for the loss of much documentation. There has also never been a policy for the proper archiving of the records, always a problem for organisations administered by part-time officers. Thus, for the period until the mid-1990s, from when some records are available, this chapter has had to rely on what can be found in the Journal. In some years the decision was taken the publish the minutes of the Annual General

---

10 *JSAHR*, Vol.13 (51) Autumn 1934. Notice in unpaginated front matter.
11 *JSAHR*, Vol.1 (2) December 1921, 'Notice to Members' on the inside back cover.
12 Harold Arthur Lee-Dillon, 17th Viscount Dillon CH FBA (24 January 1844–18 December 1932) was a leading authority on the history of arms and armour and medieval costume. He had served in the Rifle Brigade and then in the Oxfordshire Militia.

Meeting, giving a good insight into the state of the Society at that time. For others only the barest information about the Council and Officers can be found in the pages of the Journal. Further records are likely to exist in private collections. If these become available, it will then be possible to write a fuller account of the history of the Society.

The Society continued to develop throughout the 1920s. The financial predictions had proved inaccurate, possibly due to the economic problems of the period. The subscription had, by 1924, been raised to one guinea, or £1.05 in modern currency.[13] It would remain at that rate until 1959, when it was doubled:[14] a remarkable period of stability lasting 35 years. During that period individual numbers of the Journal were available for six shillings. The subscription would not be raised again until the winter of 1972 when, in the world of post-decimal currency, the subscription was increased to £3.00.[15] The inflationary spiral of the next 40 years saw a steady and continual rise in the cost of subscription until it reached the current level of £37.50. Since then, the Society has been able to keep costs under control and has not needed to raise the subscription to members living in the United Kingdom. At the same time, it has also been able to introduce new benefits such as the grants that have been made available to students and to members.[16]

It was clear from the early days of the Society that it was not going to concentrate merely on the Army as an organisation. The interest of many members appears to have been in the constituent parts of the army rather than the whole. There was not, and still is not, a 'Royal Army' to set alongside the other two services. Land Forces, which fight under the Union Flag and the Colours of their own part of the force, have no direct equivalent of the White Ensign or the RAF Standard. The Army flag seems more of a brand to be used in advertising rather than a rallying point to lift morale. The Editor of the Journal recognised the centrality of the individual cap badges. In 1924 J.H. Leslie invited 'members of the Society and others' to contribute articles on:

Early Colonial and Dominion Expeditions
Old Traditions, Customs and Mottoes of Regiments.
Military Bibliography
Disbanded Regiments
Old Indian Regiments
Regimental Colours, Drum-banners, Standards and Guidons

13   *JSAHR*, Vol.3 (11) January 1924, front cover.
14   *JSAHR*, Vol.37 (151) September 1959, p.1.
15   *JSAHR*, Vol.50 (204) Winter 1972, inside back cover.
16   The references to the rate of subscription are to the amount paid by an ordinary member based in the United Kingdom. The rates for some categories such as students and those living overseas have differed.

Army and Regimental Medals and Decorations
Arms, Clothing and Equipment
Historical Mess Plate
Plate, Swords of Honour, etc., presented to Distinguished Commanders
Regimental Buttons, Badges and Uniform generally
Early Militia, Fencible, Local Militia and Volunteer Regiments[17]

Perhaps a Society with a committee, and many members, whose military experience came from before the reforms that had created the new army identity in the period between 1902 and 1910 could be forgiven for concentrating on the historical minutiae of the 'old' Army. Perhaps too it was a way of not needing to deal with the experiences of the army in the First World War, still too recent for many to view as 'history'. Current readers will recognise that many of the themes listed still remain well represented in the articles published each year.

After the first tentative editions the Journal began to take a definite shape. There was a move away from the elaborate cover, used in the first editions, to a plainer design. That created a format which has remained largely unaltered to the present although the Centenary year editions for 2021 returned to a more pictorial cover, partly in homage to the original ones. As already noted, the Society made a small, but significant, change to its name at the start of 1929 substituting 'for' for 'of' to become The Society for Army Historical Research. An attempt, in the following year to abbreviate what some members felt was a cumbersome title, and replace it with SofAHR, was defeated. A similar attempt to rename the Society as 'The Army Historical Society' was also defeated in the following year. The tension about the main focus of the Society was reflected in a contribution to the Journal by B.H. Liddell-Hart entitled 'Some Proposals'.[18] What he proposed was the creation of an index of sources for British Army history. He was conscious that it would not find favour with everyone but pointed out that it was in line with the aim of the Society. 'It would seem that, as a guiding principle, any scheme of research should fulfil the title of the Society. Hence it should be of an historical and not merely an Antiquarian nature.'[19]

This was indicative of what those responsible for the organisation of the Society, and especially the selection of articles for the Journal, believed came under the heading of 'history'. There have been occasional hints as to what was felt to count. As late as 1962 there was a comment in a book review that 'the official preserve' of the Society effectively ended in 1914.[20] There were some exceptions, possibly not seen as 'history'. Thus, the Summer 1936 edition contained an article on

17 *JSAHR*, Vol.3 (12) April 1924, p.1.
18 B.H. Liddell-Hart, 'Some Proposals', in *JSAHR*, Vol.9 (38) October 1930, p.244.
19 Liddell-Hart, 'Some Proposals', p.244.
20 *JSAHR*, Vol.40 (162) June 1962, p.88.

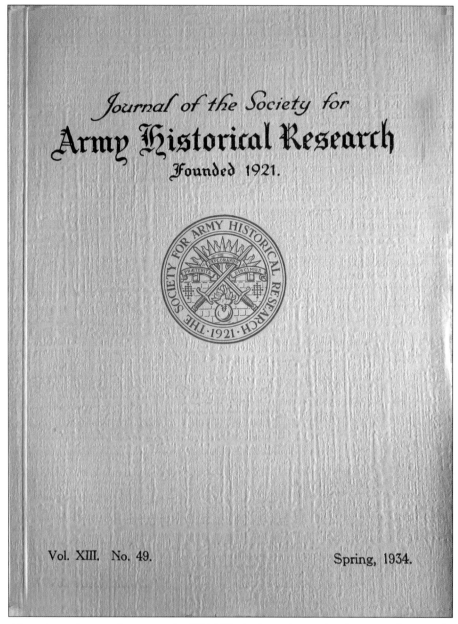

After using an intermediate paper size 1926-1933, the Journal moved to the current format with the Spring 1934 number, which also adopted a much less ornate cover design. (Courtesy of Andrew Bamford)

the badges of the Canadian Expeditionary Force.[21] Ten years later another book review dealt with the Second Anglo-Boer War, the first historical consideration of a twentieth century topic.[22] Occasionally even contemporary subject matter could be included. The Summer 1945 edition contained an article on the uniforms of the women's services that used 1945 as its end date.[23] It was about the forms of dress rather than what would be considered by many as an historical analysis. The inclusion of such pieces reminds the Society that there is a place not just for learned articles about the long ago past but also for observations on the recent era that will help inform the historian of the future.

Another change took place in 1929. The Journal included a photograph of Prince Arthur, the Duke of Connaught, who had agreed to become the Patron of the Society.[24] Prince Arthur was the last surviving son of Queen Victoria. He was commissioned into the Royal Engineers but spent most of his 40 years in the army serving in the Rifle Brigade. The Duke served until his death on 16 January 1942. He was to be the first of the three members of the Royal Family to have served as Patrons. He would be followed by the Princess Royal, Mary Countess of Harwood, who became Patron in 1951 and served until her death on 28 March 1965. The following year the Duke of Kent, at that time a serving office in the Royal Scots Greys, became Patron beginning his unbroken spell of association with the Society that happily continues to the present day.[25]

The Duke of Connaught presided at a 'Festival Dinner' held on 14 July 1930 at Armoury House, home of the Honourable Artillery Company, to mark the beginning of the Society's tenth year of existence. The published account of the evening that appeared in the Journal showed the continuing importance to many of what might be described as an 'Antiquarian' approach to military history.[26] Fifty members of the Society were joined by 18 from the HAC. The photographs show that the order of dress for the evening was 'white tie'. The report has a distinctly archaic quality which becomes wearisome with reading and may well have seemed out of place even at the time. This was 'Merrie England' and had little to do with any study of the recent history of the Army. It may, though, have reflected the custom of the HAC, who hosted the event. The description of the menu provides a good illustration of the whole:

21 Major Louis Keene, 'The Badges of the Canadian Expeditionary Force', in *JSAHR*, Vol.15 (88) Summer 1936, pp.72-82.
22 *JSAHR*, Vol 24 (100) Winter 1946, p.201.
23 Lieutenant Ernest J. Martin, 'Women's War Work with the Army', in *JSAHR*, Vol.23 (94) Summer 1945, pp.54-65.
24 *JSAHR*, Vol.8 (31) January 1929, p.1.
25 *JSAHR*, Vol.44 (179) September 1966, p.177.
26 'The Society's Festival Banquet – 14 July 1930', in *JSAHR*, Vol.10 (39b) July 1931, pp.173-194.

FOODES TO BEE SERVYD
A Brave Fyshe called a Salmon, from North Britain – cold.
Varietyes of Vegetables, mixed and dressed with a sawce.
Some rare Sir Loynes of Beefe – rosted – To bee eaten
Wyth a sawce made from rootes of horse-radysh,
and with a Pudding of Elmet.
Young Byrdes, called Capons, boyled, and served with some greene
peas and bergamots sliced.
Raspes with Raysens of Corinthe, in a mixture, covered with a
layer of paste, and baked in the oven.
A Gelley, flavoured with wyne from Xeres, *vulgo* Sherry.
Byskets made from flour and cheese, formed lyke dryed
straws of wheate, called 'straw'.
Coffee – and some fruits.[27]

It might be that the Duke of Connaught felt a need to counter-balance the tendency to such faux medievalism. In the last of the five speeches made that evening he referred to the need to understand military history:

> I have, ever since I have been in the Army, taken a very deep interest in its history, and when I heard that it was proposed to get up a Society for Army Historical Research, I was delighted. I thought that what had been a loss before, would be made good. Whether we shall have time to make up all that we might have known, had we had our Society years ago, we cannot say, but in the present day I think that the interest taken in the Army by the country is so great that any assistance from civilians in working out many historical points that we are anxious to learn, will be freely given.[28]

The next 50 years was to see the growth in the influence of the 'civilians' to whom he referred. For some years now the Society's Council has mostly comprised those without direct military experience. The evening ended shortly after 11.00 p.m. when the Duke departed for his home at Bagshot Park.

The Society's membership had increased steadily throughout its first decade. The 227 reported at the end of 1921 had become approximately 300 by the summer of 1925. The number increased further until by 1930 there were 'over 500' members with 94 having joined in the previous year.[29] There were regular appeals for members to recommend the Society to their friends and colleagues. More members meant the possibility of increasing the size of the Journal. That

27   'The Society's Festival Banquet – 14 July 1930', p.178.
28   'The Society's Festival Banquet – 14 July 1930', p.188.
29   *JSAHR*, Vol.9 (35) January 1930, inside back cover.

had been achieved with the summer 1925 edition when it had doubled from 48 to 96 pages. At this point it is appropriate to comment on the numbering of the Journal. Each year has seen a separate Volume with four editions: the exceptions are Volume One, with six issues across 1921 and 1922, and Volume 22 with eight issues covering the whole of 1943 and 1944 at a time when wartime restrictions had greatly reduced the number of pages per issue.

However, the description of the timing of the editions has varied, and cannot always be relied upon as an accurate reflection of their actual publication. Volume One began with issues scheduled to appear in June, September and December. For Volume Two the dates had been altered to January, April, June and October. From the start of Volume Four a change was made to listing the first number as Jan-March, and likewise for the remainder of the year. The change may have reflected problems encountered by the editor in ensuring publication in the month that had been on the cover. The system lasted until Number 23, January 1927, when the old practice was reintroduced. A further change was made with Volume 12 when No. 45 was labelled 'Spring'. Issues were then seasonal until 1956 when Volume 34 No. 137 reverted to the use of March, June, September and December. Eleven years later the system changed back to the quarterly titles and has remained so until the present. As well as the regular numbers, members received occasional 'Special' editions. The first of these had appeared in December 1921.[30] Additional copies of these were printed, and continued to be available for as long as stocks lasted.[31]

Not long after the tenth anniversary celebrations the Society saw a year of change. The Autumn edition of the Journal in 1933 contained an apology for its late appearance.[32] The Editor, Lieutenant Colonel J.H. Leslie, who lived in Sheffield, had been ill but had concealed the severity of his condition from the committee, who were London based. After various delays a letter, dated 4 October 1933, was received in which he resigned his membership of Society, thus automatically ceasing to be the Editor. Swift action had to be taken to ensure that further editions could be published. The next edition noted that W.Y. Baldry, who had been the Honorary Auditor since the inception of the Society was to take on the role of Editor.[33] The autumn edition had also noted the deaths of Viscount Dillon, the President, and Sir John Fortescue, who had been a Vice-President.

A major initiative was taken by the Society during the 1930s, to encourage and support the work of Army museums. A Museums Committee was created to promote this aim.[34] It had official support as the Journal recorded that details

---

30 JSAHR, Vol.1 December 1921 Special Number, 'TANGIER 1630 – The Diary of Sir James Halkett edited by Captain H.M. McCance'.
31 A list of the 'Special' editions of the Journal can be found at Annex to this chapter.
32 JSAHR, Vol.12 (47) Autumn 1933, p.130.
33 JSAHR, Vol.12 (48) Winter 1933-1934, p.194.
34 JSAHR, Vol.16 (61) Spring 1937, announcement in unpaginated front matter.

of it had been published in an Army-wide notice.[35] Details of museums were to appear in the Journal before eventually a 'Museum Supplement' appeared alongside the regular numbers. The Autumn 1937 Journal included a note from the Museums Committee. It indicated that the committee was willing, 'to give advice on any objects in, or general arrangement of, the Regimental Museums'. It noted that visits had already been made to the museums of the Lincolnshire Regiment, the Border Regiment, the King's Own Yorkshire Light Infantry and the York and Lancaster Regiment.[36]

As the 1930s progressed it became increasingly obvious that the Army would be adding to its history. Quite how that would happen was as yet unseen. Throughout this period the running of the Society remained under the control of a settled team. Colonel Lord Cottesloe, someone with an interest in small arms, and a Territorial with a lifelong interest in the Army, had taken over as President and Brigadier General Sir James Edmonds, noted for his involvement in the 28 Volume *History of the Great War*, was Chairman. A.S White acted as both Secretary and Treasurer with W.Y Baldry continuing as Editor. There were an additional 11 members of Council, including Major H.G. Parkyn, who had been involved with the Society since the start. One member, Lieutenant Colonel H. Bullock, was designated as 'Indian Representative', presumably to see that the interests of the Indian Army and its predecessors were safeguarded.

The Society was able to maintain publication of its Journal throughout the Second World War, announcing in the Winter 1939 edition 'that it would continue to be published in 1940'.[37] It was reduced in size and began to carry advertisements, some of which used military themes in a variety of humorous ways to promote their wares. One specific war related notice appeared. An appeal was made to members to help Sir Herbert Creedy's *Services Libraries and Book Fund* with the supply of reading matter for the troops.[38] The Spring 1942 edition carried a full obituary for the Duke of Connaught, the Society's Royal Patron.[39] It would be nine years before The Princess Royal became the new Patron. With other distractions, many potential contributors to the Journal were too busy to write articles. The editor came to rely on a faithful few. One such was the Reverend Percy Sumner, a long serving member of the Council. Writing in 1950 to announce his death, W.Y. Baldy the editor of the Journal noted his, 'ready willingness at all times to contribute articles to the Journal as the need arose.'[40]

The Society was determined to revive its activities once the war was over. The 1947 Annual General Meeting appointed a Museums Committee to develop the

35   Army Council Instruction (ACI) 338/36 issued by the War Office.
36   *JSAHR*, Vol.16 (63) Autumn 1937, p.182.
37   *JSAHR*, Vol.18 (72) Winter 1939, announcement in unpaginated front matter.
38   *JSAHR*, Vol.19 (75) Autumn 1940, announcement in unpaginated front matter.
39   *JSAHR*, Vol.21 (81) Spring 1942, pp.1-2.
40   *JSAHR*, Vol.28 (114) Summer 1950 p.58, obituary for the Reverend Percy Sumner.

work that had been started before the outbreak of war. Colonel R.G.J. Ogilby, a member of Council and a name still perpetuated in the Army Museums Ogilby Trust (AMOT) created after his death from a generous legacy, chaired a committee of five that initially included the Revered Percy Sumner. The first report noted that the committee's terms of reference were, 'To investigate how best to encourage and extend regimental museums and to consider how a National Army Museum might be organised.' [41] The committee proposed the formation of 'local federations' of regimental museums where information could be shared, and which could form a link with the Society. It noted at the end of the report that, 'It was not considered an opportune time to discuss how a National Army Museum might be organised.'[42] The idea was, however, not going to go away.

It is possible to obtain a fuller picture of how the Society was operating in 1951 as the calling notice for the 24th Annual General Meeting appeared in the Spring Journal.[43] It was to be held on 30 March 1951 at RUSI, and to be followed by a lecture given by James Laver of the Victoria & Albert Museum and entitled *The Meaning of Military Uniforms*. The Minutes of the meeting appeared in the same edition,[44] suggesting that the seasonal date on the cover of the Journal bore little resemblance to when the members received it. By 1950 the President of the Society had become the Marquess of Cambridge. He had replaced Field Marshal Earl Wavell whose death in that year, after only three years as President, had denied the Society a long association with a noted military scholar.

The 1951 meeting was attended by 41 members out of a total of 650. Some of the items have remained a familiar topic at such meetings. Details were given of membership, a healthy increase of 56, of whom 15 were Life Members at a subscription of fifteen guineas. (£15.75) There were also details of the accounts. There had been a loss of £444. The Society's credit balance had thus been reduced to £1,390, less than a single year's expenditure. The income had been bolstered by a grant of £150 from the Army Council, important when subscription only contributed £679. There had been five nominations for three posts on Council and a ballot had had to be held, whether of all members or solely of those at the AGM was not indicated. The three retiring members were re-elected. There then followed a detailed report of work of the Museums Committee. It had provided a member to the War Office Military Museum Committee. As a part of its own work towards considering how an Army Museum might be established it noted that a Museum at the Royal Military Academy, Sandhurst had been established. It commented, 'So far, the Indian Army room has been opened, but plans are going ahead for the

---

41   *JSAHR*, Vol.26 (105) Spring 1948, p.iii.
42   *JSAHR*, Vol.26 (105) Spring 1948, p.iii.
43   *JSAHR*, Vol.29 (117) Spring 1951. Report of the 24th Annual General Meeting, unpaginated.
44   *JSAHR*, Vol.29 (117) Spring 1951. Report of the 24th Annual General Meeting, unpaginated.

disbanded Irish Regiments and the Cavalry to have rooms.'[45] Elsewhere meetings had been held with various Regimental Museums. The lecture which followed was hoped to be the first in a series. The text of the lecture was, however, published in RUSI's Journal, rather than that of the Society.

The Autumn 1951 edition printed the details of the Officers and Council of the Society.[46] As indicated the Princess Royal was Patron. The Marquess of Cambridge was the President, and there were four Vice-Presidents, all retired officers with an interest in military history.[47] The Council was chaired by Colonel Ogilby, with W.Y. Baldry remaining as Editor and A.S. White as Secretary and Treasurer. There were an additional 12 members of the Council, including the now Brigadier H. Bullock who remained the 'Indian Representative.'

The following years were to see changes in the Old Guard. By the Summer of 1953 a new team was in charge still, for a while, under the chairmanship of Colonel Ogilby. The editor was now T.H. McGuffie, the Secretary was R.T. Eldridge, and a new post of Treasurer had been filled by Lieutenant Colonel P.L. Binns.[48] Council had been reduced to 10 in addition to the Chair, with Brigadier Bullock still a member but no longer annotated as the 'Indian Representative.' There was also a new queen on the throne, and, as with other previous new monarchs, the Society published the Royal Cypher on a single page in the Journal.[49] It also marked significant moments in the reigns of King George V and the present queen by publishing 'Jubilee' editions of the Journal. Deaths of monarchs were noted with mourning bands on the front cover of the next issue of the Journal. There were also editions designated as 'Coronation Numbers'.

Another glimpse of the state of the Society in the 1950s comes from the 27th AGM, held once more at RUSI, on 21 May 1954 at 4.00 pm, and again followed by a lecture, minutes of which appeared in the Winter 1954 edition of the Journal.[50] Membership had increased to 779. But there had been deaths, including that of Captain H. Oakes-Jones who had been a founder member and on Council for many years. It was noted that the Army Council grant was to increase to £200. There was good news in that the Society had been recognised as a Charitable Institution. Deeds of Covenant signed for seven years would now mean that the Society could claim back money in respect of those who were taxpayers. The Museums Committee reported that the Museum at Sandhurst would see the sections devoted to the Cavalry and the disbanded Irish Regiments opened on 26 June 1954.

---

45 JSAHR, Vol.29 (117) Spring 1951. Report of the 24 Annual General Meeting, unpaginated.
46 JSAHR, Vol 29 (119) Autumn 1951, inside back cover.
47 The four were, Lieutenant General Sir James Brown, Brigadier General James Edmonds, Major Lord Carnock and Lieutenant General Sir George MacMunn.
48 JSAHR, Vol.31 (126) Summer 1953, inside back cover.
49 JSAHR, Vol.31 (126) Summer 1953 includes a page with the cypher of Queen Elizabeth the Second.
50 JSAHR, Vol.32 (132) Winter 1954. Minutes of the 27th Annual General Meeting, unpaginated.

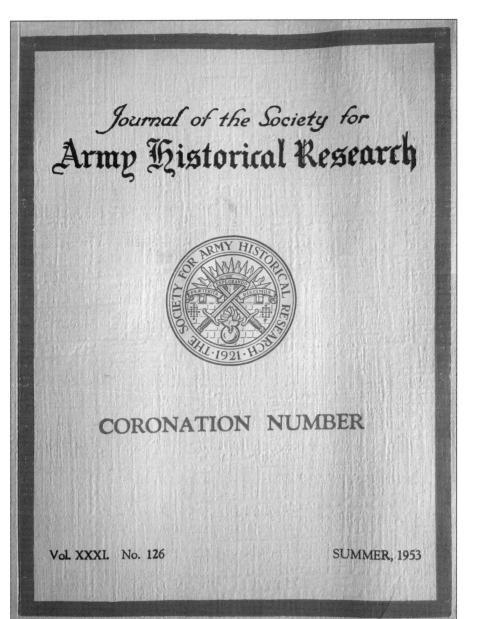

The Summer 1953 number of the Journal, with special cover to mark the coronation of Queen Elizabeth II. (Courtesy of Andrew Bamford)

The Annual General Meeting for 1960 was to be held at the Royal Commonwealth Society in Northumberland Avenue on 26 May 1960. The calling notice was signed by Captain C.R. Hurley who had become Secretary in 1958.[51] There was to be no lecture, but members were invited to a soiree after the meeting, 'during which light refreshments will be available at a charge of 3s [15p] per head'. Sadly, Captain Hurley was unable to continue as Secretary; Major N.P. Dawnay, an existing member of Council, took on the role.[52]

Reports of Annual General Meetings appeared in a number of years during the 1960s. The Annual General Meeting for 1962 saw Brigadier B.W. Webb-Carter in the chair and 28 members present.[53] Field Marshal Sir Claude Auchinleck, who had become President the previous year, was unable to attend. There were 577 members and 244 subscribers which, with honorary and life members (33) and institutions (eight), totalled 862. It is not clear what the distinction was at that time between the members and the subscribers. This was a reduction in the total of 59. The next available Minutes are for the 1965 meeting.[54] By this time both Colonel Ogilby and Lieutenant Colonel Binns had died, the latter being replaced by J.M.A Tamplin. Field Marshal Sir Gerald Templer had become President in place of Field Marshal Auchinleck whose term of office had expired and not been renewed. Templer was associated with the project to create a National Army Museum, about which he spoke at the meeting, and had had a long interest in military history. He hoped that room could be found for offices of both the Society and of AMOT once the new museum was opened. The meeting also heard that there were now 904 members, an increase of 21.[55]

The deaths of older members were noted during the 1960s. W.Y. Baldry, who had served for many years as Editor, died in January 1966.[56] He had joined the War Office Library in 1904 and served within it until his retirement in 1947. He had been the second editor of the Journal, taking over in difficult circumstances in 1933 and continuing for 19 years. It was acknowledged that he had been able to keep publishing editions throughout the war, no mean feat. The following year saw the death of his successor, T.H. McGuffie.[57] He had been a schoolmaster and had also been based outside London. David Erskine was appointed as an interim replacement, an arrangement that lasted until 1968 when Major G.J. Flint-Shipman took over the post.

One of the innovations that Flint-Shipman made was to introduce an Editorial although the practice did not last long. The first editorial did hint that changes were

51   *JSAHR*, Vol.36 (147) September 1958, inside front cover.
52   *JSAHR*, Vol 39 (157) March 1961, inside front cover.
53   *JSAHR*, Vol.40 (162) June 1962. Report on the 35th Annual General Meeting, unpaginated.
54   *JSAHR*, Vol 43 (174) June 1965. Report of the 38th Annual General Meeting, unpaginated.
55   *JSAHR*, Vol 43 (174) June 1965. Report of the 38th Annual General Meeting, unpaginated.
56   *JSAHR*, Vol.44 (177) March 1966, p.18, obituary for W.Y. Baldry.
57   *JSAHR*, Vol.45 (182) Summer 1967 p.121, obituary for T.H. McGuffie.

needed to the Journal, including the following that indicated that all was not well, 'I shall firmly eschew the *cult of personality* and resist the temptation to air any personal whims or fancies'.[58] That first editorial, in the Spring of 1969, was informative about the history of the Society. The Society was approaching its half-century. There were three remaining members from the original 153. One of them was A.S. White, who had been Secretary from 1921 to 1952. Flint-Shipman noted that he was the fifth Editor. The Society was in good heart with a membership of 950.

With the 50th anniversary approaching Flint-Shipman's second editorial suggested a repeat of the 1930 celebration dinner, possibly after the Annual General Meeting, 'If there was sufficient interest'.[59] There evidently was as a 'Jubilee Dinner' was held on 15 October 1970 at the United Services Club. Some 40 members attended with A.S. White as a guest. Field Marshal Templer proposed the health of the Society. In his speech he deplored the use of the word *militaria* that was currently in vogue.[60]

The Society at 50 appeared to be in a healthy condition. It had an active and interested President in Templer, a membership hovering around 1,000, a reputation for the quality of its publications, and an interest in military museums which was about to be recognised by the opening of the first stage of the National Army Museum on a site in Chelsea, adjacent to the Royal Hospital. In the same year Major Dawnay retired as Secretary to be replaced by Mr B. Mollo who was a member of staff at the National Army Museum.[61] However, the initial connection with the National Army Museum was an illusory success. The Society was to become disconnected from army museums, losing contact with AMOT and watching the National Army Museum develop as a stand-alone institution. The late 1970s were to see the start of a gradual decline in the number of members as first the veterans of the First World War and then of the Second ceased to be members. The small volunteer Army of the post 1960s did not appear to have the same interest in its history. Templer died in 1979 and was succeeded as President by General Sir David Fraser. Huge changes in British society in the 1960s and 1970s made organisations such as the Society less relevant to many who no longer had any links to the British Army.

By the mid-1970s the subscription had begun to rise. For 1973 it was to be £3.00 with a rate of £3.50 for what were described as 'Subscribers'.[62] The previous year A.L. Kipling had become the sixth Editor. The subscription could not be held at £3.00 in the face of rising inflation, and in 1975 was raised to £5.00.[63] That year also

58 *JSAHR*, Vol.47 (189) Spring 1969, p.1.
59 *JSAHR*, Vol.47 (190) Summer 1969, p.63.
60 *JSAHR*, Vol.48 (196) Winter 1970, p.249.
61 *JSAHR*, Vol 49 (200) Winter 1971. Minutes of the 44th Annual General Meeting held on 2 June 71, unpaginated.
62 *JSAHR*, Vol.52 (212) Winter 1974, inside back cover.
63 *JSAHR*, Vol.53 (215) Autumn 1975, inside back cover

saw the first Annual General Meeting to be held at the National Army Museum. The Duke of Kent attended his first meeting with 35 other members present. The Society seemed to be strong with the meeting told that the membership had reached 1,067 on 1 June 1975. What was not reported was how many of those had not yet paid their subscription for the year, a common problem faced by the Society at that time. The extent of the problem was revealed two years later. The membership was then given as 1,182 but 147 had not paid their 1978 subscription and 237 were underpaid.[64] The following year there were 119 in arrears and 70 who had underpaid.[65] The figures given were from the report of the Annual General Meeting, the last to be reproduced in the Journal. In 1981 the subscription had risen to £10.00.[66]

One innovation in the 1970s had been the appointment of Michael Cane as advertisement manager for the Journal.[67] He was successful in bringing in much-needed revenue with up to 10 pages and the back cover being used for advertising. He would eventually, in 1979, become the Editor.[68] Another innovation in the 1980s was the introduction of 'Corresponding Members of Council'. The Autumn 1981 Journal listed nine, in Australia (1), South Africa (2), Canada, (3), and the United States of America (3).[69] The aim was to promote knowledge of the Society in as many countries as possible and to encourage the interchange of ideas and information. Although an excellent idea there is little to indicate that it produced anything of value. As the original people ceased to carry out the role they were rarely replaced until the numbers reduced to zero.

Following the appointment, in 1978, of Major General J.D. Lunt as Chair of Council, another innovation was introduced. A prize was instituted for the author of the book which had made the most notable contribution to the history of the British or Commonwealth Land Forces in the previous calendar year. It was to be known as the 'Templer Medal' in honour of the previous President of the Society, Field Marshal Sir Gerald Templer. The first winner was a Canadian historian, John Houlding, who continues to be a distinguished contributor to the Journal, for his book, *Fit for Service*. The award was presented by the Society's Patron at a ceremony at the National Army Museum held in November 1982.[70] There has been a shortlist for the Templer Medal in every subsequent year although in some years no award was made. The increasing prestige of the Medal, and consequent increase

---

64   *JSAHR*, Vol.57 (228) Winter 1978. Minutes of the 51st Annual General Meeting held on 11 October 78, unpaginated.

65   *JSAHR*, Vol.57 (232) Winter 1979. Minutes of the 52nd Annual General Meeting held on 16 October 79, unpaginated.

66   *JSAHR*, Vol.58 (236) Winter 1980, inside back cover.

67   *JSAHR*, Vol.54 (217) Spring 1976, inside back cover.

68   *JSAHR*, Vol.57 (231) Autumn 1979, contents page.

69   *JSAHR*, Vol.59 (239) Autumn 1981, inside back cover.

70   *JSAHR*, Vol.62 (245) Spring 1983, p.38,

in the number of entries, resulted in a second award, that for the best first book published by an author, being instituted in 2014.

Whilst from the outset the Journal had carried sections where questions could be posed and replies given, it had not included any 'Letters'. It must therefore have been a surprise to members when the Spring 1982 edition reached them. It carried a long letter from John Terraine who had taken issue with a review by Hew Strachan of his book about the First World War, *The Smoke and the Fire*, published by Sidgwick & Jackson two years previously, noting that Strachan had accused the book of being 'fundamentally illiberal' and 'amoral'. Terraine's response was that he was telling the truth.[71] There was a further letter from Correlli Barnett whose name had been coupled with that of John Terraine by Strachan. Barnett described the review as 'frankly polemical'.[72] The Editor included a letter from Hew Strachan, to whom who Barnett had sent a copy of his own letter and the Editor a copy of Terraine's. After a detailed analysis, Strachan indicated that had he footnoted his review with what he described as 'the pompous academic machinery of footnoted authorities'.[73] There was also a letter from Brigadier Shelford Bidwell, a retired Gunner and military historian, commenting on Strachan's review.[74] To this letter Strachan again replied arguing that he had not been opposed to the views of the letter writers; in reality he was seeking a middle way.[75] The correspondence was illustrative of the passions that could develop about or over interpretations, particularly of aspects of the First World War. It has remained as a rare example of such a difference of opinion appearing so openly in the Society's Journal.

The next 30 years saw things continuing much as before in the affairs of the Society. Little new activity was chronicled in the pages of the Journal. It did note though, the regular change of officials. Field Marshal Sir John Chapple, who had become the Chair of the Council in 1986,[76] moved to be the Society's President following the retirement, in 1993, of General Sir David Fraser.[77] He would be succeeded by Lieutenant General Sir Barney White-Spunner in 2012. Sir John was followed as Chair by Brian Robson.[78] Robson was then followed, in 1998, by Professor Brian Holden-Reid,[79] and in 2004 Paul Cornish became Chair.[80] Cornish did not complete his term of office due to increasing academic duties and was

---

71 *JSAHR*, Vol 60 (241) Spring 1982, pp.50-52.
72 *JSAHR*, Vol 60 (241) Spring 1982, pp.52-53.
73 *JSAHR*, Vol 60 (241) Spring 1982, pp.53-54.
74 *JSAHR*, Vol 60 (241) Spring 1982, pp.54-55.
75 *JSAHR*, Vol 60 (241) Spring 1982, pp.55-56.
76 *JSAHR*, Vol.64 (258) Summer 1986, inside back cover.
77 *JSAHR*, Vol.71 (286) Summer 1993, inside back cover.
78 *JSAHR*, Vol.71 (287) Autumn 1993, inside back cover.
79 *JSAHR*, Vol.76 (307) Autumn 1998, inside back cover.
80 *JSAHR*, Vol.82 (332) Winter 2004, inside back cover.

replaced, in 2008, by Major General Sebastian Roberts.[81] Roberts was followed in 2014, by Major General Ashley Truluck,[82] who in turn was replaced at the end of his term of office by Major General Ewan Carmichael.

Things were less clear with the office of Secretary. Peter Boyden had become Secretary in 1991.[83] He was followed in 2000 by George Evelyn.[84] When, in 2009, ill-health forced Evelyn to stand aside the post remained vacant until 2012 when Ismini Pells, the then Student Member of Council, became the Meetings Secretary.[85] Her resignation in 2014 saw the Reverend Doctor Peter Howson become the Honorary Secretary.

The difficulty, at the end of the first decade of the twenty first century, with the post of Secretary masked a problem for the Society. Colonel Guy Sayle had joined Council in 2002, becoming Treasurer and Membership Secretary in succession to Arthur Bailey.[86] When George Evelyn ceased acting as Secretary and was not replaced, Colonel Sayle became the sole point of contact for the Society as the only 'Officer' listed in the Journal.[87] This concentration of authority was not properly regulated and resulted in a difficult period for the affairs of the Society. Colonel Sayle's name abruptly disappeared from the list of Council members between the Spring and Summer 2012 editions of the Journal.[88] The latter edition showed Lieutenant Colonel D. Saunders as Membership Secretary and C. Street as Treasurer; both had been co-opted onto Council. The posts of Treasurer and Membership Secretary then continued as separate appointments, and an attempt was made to find a new Secretary for the Society. That moment was probably the low point in the history of the Society. It had in retrospect been unwise to allow insufficient separation of key roles and thus lose oversight of the day-to-day governance of the Society.

There had also been a number of changes in the role of Editor. Michael Cane had become Editor in 1979,[89] and remained so until replaced by Major Alan Harfield in 1994.[90] In due course he was replaced by Mark Nicholls,[91] who would in turn be succeeded by Matthew Hughes.[92] Andrew Cormack, the current Editor, was first recorded as such in 2009.[93]

81   *JSAHR*, Vol.86 (348) Winter 2008, inside back cover.
82   *JSAHR*, Vol.92 (371) Autumn 2014, inside back cover.
83   *JSAHR*, Vol.69 (277) Spring 1991, inside back cover.
84   *JSAHR*, Vol.78 (323) Spring 2000, inside back cover.
85   *JSAHR*, Vol.90 (364) Winter 2012, inside back cover.
86   *JSAHR*, Vol.80 (323) Autumn 2002, inside back cover.
87   *JSAHR*, Vol.88 (356) Winter 2010, inside back cover.
88   *JSAHR*, Vol.90 (361) Spring 2012, inside back cover; *JSAHR* Vol.90 (362) Summer 2012, inside back cover.
89   *JSAHR*, Vol.57 (231) Autumn 1979, contents page.
90   *JSAHR*, Vol.72 (289) Spring 1994, contents page.
91   *JSAHR*, Vol.78 (313) Spring 2000, contents page.
92   *JSAHR*, Vol.82 (331) Autumn 2004, contents page.
93   *JSAHR*, Vol.87 (351) Autumn 2009, contents page.

The appointment, in 2014, of Major General Truluck saw the Council reorganised to meet the challenges that the Society faced. Each member was now responsible for an area of the Society's activities. Among changes introduced was the inclusion of a new strap line to indicate the Society's aims. The website now proclaimed that it was, 'Serving Scholars, Enthusiasts and Soldiers'. The categories, and the order in which they were placed, indicated how much the Society had changed since its foundation. Other initiatives included the First Book Prize already mentioned, essay prizes for both Sixth Form Students and Undergraduates, and a prize for the best work of fiction to use the life of the British Army as a background. Competitions have received entries from around the world, indicating the recognition given to the Society.

Council, having stabilised the finances of the Society after the 2012 problems, felt able to offer grants to those studying the history of the British Army. These were, initially, for anyone undertaking research into the areas of interest of the Society for a higher degree at university but have more recently been joined by an additional grant restricted to members of the Society.

In an age of easy communication, the Council of the Society has recognised that it needs to be more in touch with its members. Activities are now circulated as part of a quarterly newsletter, which is also made available on the Society's website. The Society's online presence began in a small way as a voluntary effort before the decision was taken to employ a firm of website designers. One advantage of the professionally-built site has been that it has been able to become a portal for accessing the back numbers of the Society's through JSTOR. The decision to digitalise the back numbers has made them available to a much wider readership, bringing both awareness of the Society and also generating some valuable income to fund the various projects. The quarterly newsletter has highlighted, amongst other things, battlefield tours that the Society has arranged for its members. There had been occasional such tours before but the first of the current series took place in 2018 and was to Spain and Portugal in the footsteps of Wellington. That was followed a year later by a visit to Malta to view the long military history of the island. Further tours were planned but had to be cancelled as a result of the COVID pandemic.

Along with other such organisations, 2020 and 2021 were difficult years for the Society. It has been especially hard as planning had moved into high gear for the Centenary when it became necessary to alter what was able to be offered. The 2020 Annual General Meeting had to be moved to an electronic platform. It was to be the first use of new forms of meeting that were to become more commonplace over the succeeding months. The first half of the Centenary Conference, planned to be held at the National Army Museum in April 2021, became a series of six Wednesday evening online presentations. Each began with a lecture on an aspect of the history of the British Army. That was then followed by presentations by those engaged in various areas of research, leading to spirited discussions to close the evening. It was possible to hold the second half of the planned Conference at the National Army Museum in September 2021. That day concluded with a Reception at which

Society members at Ciudad Rodrigo on the 2018 battlefield tour to the Iberian Peninsula.
(Andrew Bamford)

delayed presentations were made to those who had been awarded prizes by the Society. Such a ceremony has, in more ordinary recent years, become a feature of the Annual General Meeting.

Towards the end of 2020 the Society entered into a working agreement with the National Army Museum. The agreement reflected that the Museum and the Society shared a common history. Field Marshal Templer, honoured in the name of the Museum's Research Centre, had been a driving force in the creation of the Museum. He had also been President of the Society. The annual award for the best book covering the area of interest of the Society was also named The Templer Medal in his honour. The Museum has also been able to help the Society increase the value of the financial award that accompanies the medal. It is hoped that further co-operation between the Society and Museum can add further to the development of the study of the British Army.

A dinner to mark the hundredth anniversary of the Society had been an aim for the Centenary. Circumstances made it seem that it might not be able to take place. Eventually, in November 2021, a dinner was held at the Army and Navy Club in London. Those present heard greetings from the Society's Royal Patron. Whilst not on the scale of previous dinners, it allowed those present to toast the health of the Society. With the publication of this selection of the papers given to the Society in its Centenary, the expectation is that the next hundred years will offer as much to members as has the last.

Journal of the Society for
ARMY HISTORICAL RESEARCH

SERVING SCHOLARS,
ENTHUSIASTS AND
SOLDIERS
FOR 100 YEARS

Spring 2021

Volume Ninety-Nine Number 396

ISSN 0037-9700 (Print)
ISSN 2516-7146 (On-line)

The four Journals published during the Centenary year all contained extra content, as well as adopting a new temporary cover design. (Courtesy of Andrew Bamford)

Annexe I: Royal Patrons of the Society for Army Historical Research

1929-1944, Prince Arthur, Duke of Connaught (died in office)
1951-1965, Princess Mary, Countess of Harwood, the Princess Royal (died in office)
1966 to date, Prince George, Duke of Kent

Annexe II: Presidents of the Society for Army Historical Research

1921-1932, The Rt Hon. the Viscount Dillon
1933-1947, Colonel the Rt Hon. Lord Cottesloe
1947-1950, Field Marshal the Rt Hon. the Earl Wavell
1950-1961, The Most Hon. the Marquess of Cambridge
1961-1965, Field Marshal Sir Claude Auchinleck
1965-1979, Field Marshal Sir Gerald Templer
1980-1993, General Sir David Fraser
1993-2012, Field Marshal Sir John Chapple
2012 to date Lieutenant General Sir Barney White-Spunner

Annexe III: Chairs of the Council of the Society for Army Historical Research

1921-1923, Lieutenant Colonel A. Leetham
1923-1926, Major General Sir G. Aston
1926-1948, Brigadier General J. Edmonds
1948-1951, No Chair listed in Journal
1951-1960, Colonel R.J.L. Ogilby
1960-1978, Brigadier B.W. Webb-Carter
1978-1986, Major General J. Lunt
1986-1993, Field Marshal Sir John Chapple
1993-1998, B. Robson
1998-2004, Professor B. Holden-Reid
2004-2008, P. Cornish
2008-2014, Major General S. Roberts
2014-2020, Major General A. Truluck
2020 to date, Major General Ewan Carmichael

Annexe IV: Editors of the *Journal of the Society for Army Historical Research*

1921, Editorial Committee
1922-1932, Lieutenant Colonel J.H. Leslie
1932-1952, W.Y. Baldry
1953-1967, T.H. McGuffie
1967-1968, Hon. D. Erskine (acting editor)
1968-1972, Major G.J. Flint-Shipman
1972-1979, A.L. Kipling
1979-1996, M.A. Cane
1996-2004, M. Nicholls
2004-2008, M. Hughes
2008 to date, A.E. Cormack

Annexe V: Special Publications of the Society for Army Historical Research

No. 1 *Tangier 1660; the Diary of Sir James Halkett* (ed. Captain H.M. McCance), 1922.

No. 2 *The Orderly Book of Lord Ogilvie's Regiment in the Army of Prince Charles Edward Stuart* (ed. Brevet-Colonel Sir Bruce Seton, Bt), 1923.

No. 3 *The Army List of 1740* (ed. Lieutenant-Colonel J.H. Leslie), 1931.

No. 4 *Cavalry in the Corunna Campaign (from the diary of the Adjutant of the 15th Hussars)* (ed. Major Lord Carnock, MC), 1936.

No. 5 *A Royal Dragoon in the Spanish Succession War* (ed. C.T. Atkinson), 1938.

No. 6 *Badges of Rank of Warrant and Non-Commissioned Rank in the British Army* (Major N.P. Dawnay), 1949.

No. 7 *Distinctions of Rank of Regimental Officers 1684-1855* (Major N.P. Dawnay), 1960.

No. 8 *Reminiscences of William Verner (1782-1871) 7th Hussars* (ed. Ruth W. Verner), 1965.

No. 9 *"To Mr. Davenport", being letters of Major Richard Davenport (1719-1760) to his brother during service in the 4th Troop of Horse Guards and the 10th Dragoons, 1742-1760* (ed. WOII C.W. Frearson), 1968.

No. 10 *The Hawley Letters, The Letters of Captain R.B. Hawley, 89th, from the Crimea, December 1854 to August 1856* (ed. S.G.P. Ward), 1970.

No. 11 *The Succession of Colonels of the British Army from 1660 to the Present Day* (N.B. Leslie), 1974.

No. 12 *A Journal of Marlborough's Campaigns during the War of the Spanish Succession 1704-1711 by John Marshall Deane* (ed. David Chandler), 1984.

No. 13 *Nobles, Gentlemen and the Profession of Arms in Restoration Britain 1660-1688* (John Childs), 1987.

No. 14 *… By Dint of Labour & Perseverance … A journal recording two months in northern Germany kept by Lt-Col James Adolphus Oughton, commanding 1st battalion, 37th Regiment of Foot, 1758* (ed. Stephen Wood), 1997.

No. 15 *The British Army in Cape Colony: Soldiers' Letters and Diaries, 1806-1858* (ed. Peter Boyden), 2001.

No. 16 *Victorians at War: New Perspectives* (ed. Ian F.W. Beckett), 2007.

No. 17 *'… a damn nice thing … the nearest run thing you ever saw in your life …'. A Peninsular and Waterloo Anthology* (ed. A.E. Cormack) 2015.

No. 18 *A Long, Long Trail A-Winding. Centenary Perspectives on the Great War* (ed. A.E. Cormack) 2018.

2

John Woodward, the British Civil Wars and the History of the British Army

Ismini Pells

To the R[igh]t hon[oura]ble and R[igh]t wors[hi]p[fu]ll the Justices of the
   peace for the County of North[amp]ton[shire].
The humble petic[i]on of John Woodward of Easton neare Tociter in this
   County of North[amp]ton[shire]
Humbly Sheweth
That your petic[i]oner served his late majesty of euer blessed memory as a
   Leiftennant in the Regiment of the R[igh]t hono[ura]ble James Earle
   of Northampton and receiued divers wounds in the said service; and
   since his Majesties happy restaurac[i]on hath continued to serve His
   s[ai]d majesty in the troope of the hono[ura]ble S[i]r Francis Compton,
   untill about a yeare last past, at w[hi]ch time he was forced to leaue
   the said troope, being, by reason of his said wounds become unable to
   performe any further service, whereupon your petic[i]oner is reduced
   to a very poore and low condic[i]on
Your petic[i]on[e]r therefore humbly praies that your hon[ou]rs will please
   to grant him an annuall pention for his life, and he shall every pray &c.
<January ye 9th 1676>
<*It is desired* thatt ye peticoner haue a penc[i]on of foure pounds by ye
   yeare to be paid by ye Treasurer of the west division.>
<Will[iam] Washbourne>
<[Several illegible words]>
<Rob[er]t Clerke>

Ord[ere]d yt 4 li. p[er] ann[um] bee allowed to ye pet[ition]er to be paid
him quarterly by ye Tr[easur]er of the ~~West~~ West Division of ye first
paym[en]t to be at this p[re]sent Sessions.
Jo[hn] Willughby[1]

These are to certifie all whom it may concerne that John Woodward of
Easton neare Toister in this County of Northampton[shire] serued his late
Majesty in ye times of Rebellion as a Leiftenant in my Regiment where
he receiued many wounds whereby he is utterly disabled for doeing any
further service, and is now become very Indigent, and as I conceiue a very
fitt object to receiue ye charity of ye County as a pentioner. Wittness my
hand this ninth day of January 1676.
Northampton[2]

On 9 January 1677, John Woodward of Easton Neston in Northamptonshire petitioned the court of Quarter Sessions in his home county for a military pension.
He was one of several thousand veterans who applied in the second half of the
seventeenth century to the first military pension scheme and whose petitions have
been collected by the Civil Wars Petitions project.[3] Woodward had recently been
discharged from the Army on account of past wounds, which (combined with his
age) made him no longer fit for service. Woodward had served the royalist cause
during the British Civil Wars in the regiment of James Compton, third Earl of
Northampton. At the Restoration, Woodward enlisted in the Royal Regiment of
Horse (The Blues), serving in the troop commanded by the Earl of Northampton's
younger brother, Sir Francis Compton.

   Woodward had joined one of the four newly formed 'guards' regiments, the two
units of infantry and two units of cavalry established in England in 1661 by Charles
II. The formation of Charles II's army is commonly viewed as the beginnings of
the modern British Army, though it is worth noting that Charles raised separate
standing forces in Scotland which remained independent from those in England
until they were combined in 1707. However, the first centrally-organised standing
army in Britain had in fact been raised in Scotland in 1639 for the so-called
'Bishops' Wars' of 1639–1640 against England, which are viewed as a precursor to
the Civil Wars in England and part of the wider conflict across the British Isles.
The Scottish Army of the Covenant, as it was known, subsequently intervened in

1   Northamptonshire Archives: QSR 1/84, fol. 61: The Petition of John Woodward of Easton Neston,
    Northamptonshire, 9 January 1677.
2   Northamptonshire Archives: QSR 1/84, fol. 62: The Certificate for John Woodward of Easton Neston,
    Northamptonshire, 9 January 1677.
3   Andrew Hopper, David Appleby, Mark Stoyle, Lloyd Bowen and Ismini Pells (eds), *Civil War Petitions:
    Conflict, Welfare and Memory during and after the English Civil Wars, 1642–1710*, <www.civilwarpeti-
    tions.ac.uk>, accessed 29 April 2022.

the Civil Wars in England on the side of Parliament in 1644–1646. England quickly followed suit in raising its own first standing army when Parliament formed the New Model Army in 1645.

When Charles II was restored to his throne in 1660, he inherited the New Model Army as well as his own army of exiled royalists who had been allied with Spain and were engaged in war in Flanders against the forces of the Cromwellian government. Although the New Model had publicly sworn allegiance to the King, Charles remained rightly suspicious of this formidable army. Public sentiment, fuelled by discontent at nearly two decades of repeated military interference in civilian government and spiralling taxation to pay for the armed forces, was no more enthusiastic than their monarch about the New Model Army. As we will see in this chapter, the Restoration government worked quickly to disband the New Model Army but did not wish to be rid of a standing force altogether. The units of foot and horse guards were Charles's solution to maintaining a permanent body of troops while circumventing contemporary sensibilities about standing armies. The new regiments were ostensibly designed to be a small household force for royal protection and were comprised of elements drawn from both the royal army from Flanders and the New Model Army. The Royal Regiment of Horse that John Woodward joined was largely drawn from a regiment originally raised in 1650 by the Interregnum government for service in the New Model Army, though it had a new officer corps of men loyal to the King and was supplemented by new recruits – some of whom may, like Woodward, have also fought for the King's father during the Civil Wars.

This chapter will use Woodward's petition to provide an insight into his military career as one who fought at this pivotal time for the foundations of the British Army and whose service spanned the divide between the Civil War years and the Restoration period. As well as outlining the details of the units in which Woodward fought and the men who commanded them, this chapter will emphasise the strength of the continuity between the forces raised during the Civil Wars, especially the New Model Army, and the army which was established at the Restoration. The chapter will then move on to use the evidence that can be reconstructed from Woodward's petition to reflect upon the trends in military historiography that have influenced the history of the British Army since the formation of the Society for Army Historical Research in 1921. Finally, this chapter will conclude with some brief observations on the value of scholarship on the British Civil Wars to a better understanding of the history of the British Army from the perspective of these different historiographical trends.

Woodward's petition informs us that he began his military career during the Civil Wars, serving on the royalist side in 'the Regiment of the R[igh]t hono[ura]ble James Earle of Northampton'. This unit was Northampton's Regiment of Horse, which was originally raised in late 1642 under the command of James Compton's father, Spencer Compton, the second Earl of Northampton. When Spencer was killed at the Battle of Hopton Heath on 19 March 1643, James succeeded his father as third Earl of Northampton and colonel of the regiment. The majority of the regiment was raised around Oxfordshire and Warwickshire. Woodward himself was, of course, from Northamptonshire but the regiment was based at Banbury Castle, situated only 23 miles from his home village of Easton Neston. Northampton's men fought in several notable encounters during the Civil Wars, including the First Battle of Newbury, Cropredy Bridge, Lostwithiel and Naseby. Banbury Castle did not surrender until 9 May 1646 and the regiment was subsequently disbanded.[4]

Within Northampton's regiment, Woodward served as a lieutenant in the troop commanded by Captain Flammock Colborne.[5] In 1645, Colborne was promoted to major and, like Woodward, he was to resume his military career again after the Restoration in the Royal Regiment of Horse.[6] Colborne joined the same troop as Woodward in the Blues, being appointed Quartermaster to Sir Charles Compton's (later Sir Francis Compton's) troop in February 1661, shortly after the regiment's formation the previous month.[7] The continued association with the Compton family suggests that Northampton's Regiment had enjoyed a strong corporate ethos that endured long after the Civil Wars, something that will be explored in more detail below. Colborne was a Warwickshire man, a county where Northampton exercised a strong influence and from which (as indicated above from Stuart Reid's research) a large proportion of the regiment was recruited. His family seems to have hailed from around the village of Ashorne, though Colborne was a resident of the village of Willington by the time of his death in 1664.[8]

It is possible that Woodward was recruited closer to his own place of residence by Sir William Fermor. In 1642, Fermor was appointed a commissioner of array, entrusted by the King with raising men for the royalist armies from Northamptonshire.[9] Fermor also owned the estate at Easton Neston and served as a captain in Northampton's Regiment, before being commissioned as a colonel of

4   Regimental history summarised from Stuart Reid, *Officers and Regiments of the Royalist Army* (Leigh-on-Sea: Partizan Press, 1985), Vol.3, p.135.

5   Anon., *A List of Officers Claiming to the Sixty Thousand Pounds, &c. Granted by His Sacred Majesty for the Relief of His Truly-Loyal and Indigent Party* (London: Henry Brome, 1663), p.101.

6   Peter R. Newman, *Royalist Officers in England and Wales, 1642-1660: A Biographical Dictionary* (London: Garland Publishing, 1981), p.76.

7   Charles Dalton (ed.), *English Army Lists and Commission Registers, 1661-1714* (London: Eyre & Spottiswoode, 1892), Vol.1, p.4; The Lord Cottesloe, 'The Earliest "Establishment"—1661—of the British Standing Army', *Journal of the Society for Army Historical Research*, Vol. 9, No.37 (July 1930), pp.147–161, at p.151.

8   The National Archives (TNA): PROB 11/260/296: Will of Amias Colborne of Ashorne, Warwickshire, 26 July 1654; TNA: PROB 11/316/164: Will of Flammucke Colburne of Willington, Warwickshire, 29 September 1664.

9   E.T. Bradley, revised by S.L. Sadler, 'Fermor [Farmer], Sir William, first baronet', *Oxford Dictionary of National Biography*, <https://doi.org/10.1093/ref:odnb/9347>, accessed 18 February 2021.

his own regiment of horse.[10] After the Civil Wars, he contented himself in defeat with low-level skulduggery against the various Interregnum regimes. Firstly, he concealed the fact that when he married in September 1646, his new wife, Mary Perry, brought him an estate worth £300 in Rutland. This was problematic because, as a royalist, Fermor was forced to compound for his estates – that is, his estates had been seized and he had only been able to recover them by paying a fine calculated on their value. When, in 1651, the Commonwealth government discovered the existence of Fermor's Rutland estate, he was forced to compound for those lands also.[11] Four years later, he was hauled before Oliver Cromwell's Council of State for poaching the Lord Protector's deer and encouraging deer stealers in Whittlewood Forest, Warwickshire, as well as ordering his keepers to shoot the Protector's officers if they came near his lands.[12] Finally, he was summoned to Whitehall in 1653, probably on suspicion of royalist scheming, alongside James Compton's younger brother, Sir Charles Compton.[13] It seems that like Woodward and Colborne, Fermor had maintained close relations with the Compton family after the Civil Wars had ended. Fermor just lived long enough to welcome the Restoration, his last public appearance being the coronation of Charles II, before his death on 14 May 1661.[14]

Sir Charles Compton was the second son of Spencer Compton and the original commander of the troop in which Woodward served in the Royal Regiment of Horse.[15] Sir Francis Compton, who succeeded to the Troop, was the fifth son of Spencer Compton. Born around 1629, Francis was a mere 13 years of age when civil war broke out in England and he played little part in public affairs until after the Restoration.[16] He was commissioned a lieutenant in Charles Compton's troop in the Royal Regiment of Horse at the regiment's formation.[17] Francis succeeded his elder brother as captain on 30 November 1661, after the latter had died falling from his horse.[18] By the time that Woodward left the regiment in 1676, Francis

---

10 Reid, *Officers and Regiments*, Vol.3, p.135; Anon., *List of Officers*, p.46.

11 Mary Anne Everett Green (ed.), *Calendar of the Committee for Compounding* (London: H. M. Stationery Office, 1890), Part 2, pp.1063–1064.

12 TNA: SP 18/99/78 fol. 188: Charge against Sir William Farmer, 24 July 1655; TNA: SP 18/99/79 fol. 192: Order by the Lord Protector that Sir William Farmer, John Urlin, John Hathway, William Taylor and William Perry appear before Council of State, 24 July 1655.

13 TNA: SP 25/69 fol. 190: Order that Sir Charles Compton and Sir William Farmer appear before the Council of State, 2 June 1653.

14 E.T. Bradley, revised by S.L. Sadler, 'Fermor [Farmer], Sir William, first baronet', *Oxford Dictionary of National Biography*, <https://doi.org/10.1093/ref:odnb/9347>, accessed 18 February 2021.

15 Dalton, *English Army Lists*, Vol.1, p.4.

16 A.M. Mimardière, 'COMPTON, Sir Francis (c. 1629–1716), of Hamerton, Hunts. and Kew, Surr', *History of Parliament Online*, <http://www.historyofparliamentonline.org/volume/1660-1690/member/compton-sir-francis-1629-1716>, accessed 18 February 2021.

17 Dalton, *English Army Lists*, Vol.1, p.4.

18 TNA: SP 44/4 fol. 3: Note of Commission for Francis Compton to be Captain in Lord Oxford's Regiment, 30 November 1661.

had been promoted to major and two years later, he rose to lieutenant-colonel.[19] Francis's dedication to the Crown and the army attracted criticism in some quarters from some contemporary observers.[20] He seems to have been a committed officer and, with the exception of a brief interruption following the Glorious Revolution, served constantly throughout the period and was still in command at the time of his death in 1716, aged 87. During his parliamentary career as an MP for Warwick, Francis was associated with the 'Court Party' and was entrusted with whipping in support for the party's policies in 1675, although, thereafter, he began to drift away from supporting royal policy.[21]

Given the Compton family's royalist commitment, something that Woodward seems to have shared (as will be discussed in more detail below), it is perhaps ironic that the origins of the Royal Regiment of Horse are to be found in Parliament's New Model Army. On 29 August 1650, the Commonwealth Council of State granted a commission to form a regiment of horse for 'The 4 Northerne Countyes' under Sir Arthur Hesilrige as colonel. The regiment was originally raised as a militia unit to safeguard the border region while Oliver Cromwell led the New Model Army in an invasion of Scotland, where the Prince of Wales (the future Charles II) had been declared King.[22] Following Cromwell's victory at the Battle of Dunbar on 3 September 1650, the regiment was deployed to garrison Linlithgow in West Lothian and it remained in Scotland until 1653. Throughout 1655, the regiment, now under the command of James Berry, was instrumental in defeating the royalist insurrection known as Penruddock's Uprising, but it was back in Scotland by spring 1657 and continued as part of the occupation forces until winter 1658–1659.[23]

Even histories of the British Army that begin in 1660 commonly acknowledge the role of the New Model Army as an important forerunner to the modern establishment. However, the strength of the connection between the two often remains understated. As Malcolm Wanklyn argued, whilst 'It has been customary to see the New Model Army's story coming neatly to an end in the winter of 1660/1', with only General George Monck's Regiment of Foot (later the Coldstream Guards) and his Lifeguard of Horse surviving, while the rest of Charles II's army was made

19 Dalton, *English Army Lists*, Vol.1, pp.190 and 240.

20 Andrew Marvell, *A Seasonable Argument to Perswade all the Grand Juries in England to Petition for a New Parliament* (Amsterdam: Publisher unknown, 1677), p.19; Andrew Marvell (ed. Sir N.H. Nicolas), *Flagellum Parliamentarium: being sarcastic notices of nearly two hundred Members of the first Parliament after the Restoration A.D. 1661 to 1678* (London: J. B. Nichols, 1827), p.23.

21 A.M. Mimardière, 'COMPTON, Sir Francis (c. 1629–1716), of Hamerton, Hunts. and Kew, Surr.', *History of Parliament Online*, <http://www.historyofparliamentonline.org/volume/1660-1690/member/compton-sir-francis-1629-1716>, accessed 18 February 2021.

22 TNA: SP 25/119 fol. 87: Militia Commission granted to Sir Arthur Hesilrige, 29 August 1650.

23 Charles Firth and Godfrey Davies, *The Regimental History of Cromwell's Army* (Oxford: Clarendon Press, 1940), Vol.1, pp.239–246.

up of forces which had served him on the Continent. However, as Wanklyn went on to argue, 'any idea that the New Model Army was dead by 1661… must be hit firmly in the head'.[24]

As far as what had been Berry's Regiment of Horse was concerned, a series of changes were made to the officer corps in February and July 1660 to ensure that the regiment was in the hands of men loyal to the King. Berry had been cashiered by Parliament the previous October for supporting Major General John Lambert's struggle against the New Model Army's political masters. Major Unton Croke had taken command of the regiment and was appointed colonel on 10 January 1660.[25] In February 1660, the month that he arrived in London as a precursor to the Restoration, General George Monck made alterations amongst the junior officers of Croke's Regiment. In July of the same year, following Charles II's return, an entirely new officer corps was appointed under Colonel Daniel O'Neill [O'Neale].[26] O'Neill had been lieutenant-colonel of Prince Rupert's Regiment of Horse on the royalist side during the Civil Wars.[27] He served Charles II as Groom of the Bedchamber during the King's exile on the Continent and it was a post in which he continued at the Restoration. Upon O'Neill's death, Charles described him as 'an honest man as ever lived' and 'a very good servant'.[28] Although the officers of Croke's Regiment had been replaced by summer 1660, the vast majority of the rank-and-file continued to serve in the regiment.[29]

At that time, the regiment was transferred to the King's service and – perhaps due to the relationship between Charles and O'Neill – became styled 'The Royal Regiment'. It was one of the last regiments of the New Model Army to be disbanded, officially being paid off in December 1660.[30] Yet in January 1661, it was 'mysteriously, still intact' at Bath.[31] The fact that the regiment did not actually disperse at Bath has led to speculation that the King and his brother, James, Duke of York, had been determined to keep it as part of the permanent forces that they had been planning since August 1660.[32] On 6 January 1661, a riot broke out in London led by Thomas Venner. His adherents were all Fifth Monarchists, who rejected earthly monarchy and only recognised the authority of 'King Jesus'. The riots were quickly suppressed, but the threat to the King was the opportunity that

24 Malcolm Wanklyn, *Reconstructing the New Model Army Volume 2: Regimental Lists 1649 to 1663* (Solihull: Helion and Company, 2016), pp.26–27.

25 Firth and Davies, *Regimental History of Cromwell's Army*, Vol.1, pp.250–251.

26 Wanklyn, *Reconstructing the New Model Army Volume 2*, pp.174–175.

27 Reid, *Officers and Regiments*, Vol.4, p.151.

28 Jerrold I. Casway 'O'Neill, Daniel (c. 1612–1664)', Oxford Dictionary of National Biography, <https://doi.org/10.1093/ref:odnb/20768>, accessed 26 February 2021.

29 Barney White-Spunner, *Horse Guards* (Basingstoke: Macmillan, 2006), p.44.

30 Firth and Davies, *Regimental History of Cromwell's Army*, Vol.1, p.252.

31 White-Spunner, *Horse Guards*, p.22.

32 White-Spunner, *Horse Guards*, p.39.

the royal brothers had been waiting for to implement their plans for a permanent force of royal 'guards'.[33]

In spite of the New Model's role in the downfall of his father, Charles II could see the benefits of maintaining at least some military forces – as long as they could be kept strictly under the Crown's control. He had also been inspired by the *Mousquetaires de la Garde* which he had witnessed while in exile in France at the court of Louis XIV.[34] However, the King had to tread carefully. Popular opinion had long feared permanent forces as a tool for royal tyranny, and opposition to a standing army, fuelled by two decades of war-weariness and unprecedented levels of taxation, had reached peak levels by 1660.[35] The Convention Parliament, which facilitated the Restoration process, had been no less eager to be rid of an army that meddled in politics and drained the public purse, hurrying through the legislation that aimed to disband the New Model Army as quickly as possible.[36] Therefore, when Charles signed an order creating two regiments of horse and two regiments of foot on 26 January 1661, these units were labelled 'guards'.[37]

The Royal Regiment that had been under O'Neill's command formed the basis of one of the new regiments of horse guards and was now called the Royal Regiment of Horse. This regiment was placed under the command of Aubrey de Vere, 20th Earl of Oxford, but O'Neill was made captain of the King's own troop and thus the effective lieutenant-colonel of the regiment.[38] It is not known exactly when Woodward enlisted in the Royal Regiment of Horse. Yet since he claimed to have served in this unit 'since his Majesties happy restarac[i]on', it is possible that Woodward joined the regiment from the moment of its formation in early 1661, perhaps as part of a recruitment drive to fill vacancies in the rank-and-file left by natural wastage and by those former New Model Army men for whom military service in the name of the Crown was unpalatable.[39]

It seems unlikely that Woodward would have been the only ex-royalist to have rubbed shoulders with the ex-parliamentarians in the ranks of the Royal Regiment of Horse. John Childs certainly claimed that when Oxford was commissioned colonel of the regiment in February 1661, 'he recruited his regiment from loyal volunteers', though Childs does not substantiate this claim and he mistakenly

---

33   White-Spunner, *Horse Guards*, p.20.

34   White-Spunner, *Horse Guards*, pp.22–23.

35   For more on this, see: Lois G. Schwoerer, *'No Standing Armies!': The Antiarmy Ideology in Seventeenth-Century England* (London: John Hopkins University Press, 1974).

36   David J. Appleby, 'Veteran Politics in Restoration England, 1660–1670', *The Seventeenth Century*, Vol.28, No.3 (2013), pp.323–342, at p.327.

37   TNA: SP 29/29/45 fols 92–96: Establishment of forces to be raised for the safety of His Majesty's person and government, 26 January 1661.

38   Dalton, *English Army Lists*, Vol. , p.4; White-Spunner, *Horse Guards*, pp.22 and 45–46.

39   Northamptonshire Archives: QSR 1/84, fol. 61: The Petition of John Woodward of Easton Neston, Northamptonshire, 9 January 1677.

asserts that these new recruits were to augment troops drawn from Cromwell's Life Guard of Horse (command of which had passed to Monck).[40] Monck's Life Guard, in fact, went on to be one of three troops which formed the Life Guards in the Restoration army, not the Royal Regiment of Horse.[41] Such mistakes help explain why the extent of the continuity between the New Model Army and the Restoration army have been overlooked. It is unclear how well former foes may have mixed in the Royal Regiment of Horse but tensions certainly persisted along past fault lines elsewhere in the King's forces. For example, the force of 4,500 soldiers which were sent to the Iberian Peninsula between 1662 and 1668 in support of Portugal's war of independence against Spain drew on troops from both sides of the Civil Wars, which resulted in a number of politically motivated confrontations despite official attempts to clamp down on these frictions.[42]

The continuities in the Royal Regiment of Horse from the Civil War years were not just limited to its personnel. The regiment was known more familiarly as 'The Blues'. This nickname, derived from the colour of the regiment's uniform, was first used in 1661 but it is notable that they had worn blue coats since the time they had been first raised by Haselrige, when they had also carried a blue standard fringed with gold.[43] The structure of the regiment was directly taken from that which had been in place under the New Model Army, although this was a structure that was largely ubiquitous during this period and, as the regiment's historian and SAHR President Sir Barney White-Spunner has described, 'was to endure well into the next century as the most efficient method of running a regiment of horse'.[44]

Having used Woodward's career to argue for a close connection between the Restoration army and its Civil War predecessors, the second half of this chapter will demonstrate how Woodward's career might be used to engage with some of the trends in military historiography that have influenced the history of the British Army since the formation of the Society for Army Historical Research in 1921. Undoubtedly the biggest development in the last 100 years came with the arrival of what has been dubbed the 'new military history'. This is the branch of military history that moved away from the study of campaigns and battles and focused instead on the impact on society of warfare and the institutional arrangements for supporting armed forces.[45] Subjects of interest to the 'new military history', or 'war and society' studies as it has also been known, have included the social composition

40   John Childs, *The Army of Charles II* (London: Routledge, 1976), p.16.
41   Dalton, *English Army Lists*, Vol.1, pp.1–3; Wanklyn, *Reconstructing the New Model Army Volume 2*, p.176; Firth and Davies, *Regimental History of Cromwell's Army*, Vol.1, p.57.
42   Appleby, 'Veteran Politics in Restoration England', pp.331–332.
43   White-Spunner, *Horse Guards*, pp.39–40.
44   White-Spunner, *Horse Guards*, p.41.
45   Stephen Morillo and Michael F. Pavkovic, *What is Military History?* (Cambridge: Polity Press, 2018), pp.41–42.

of armies and officer corps, civil-military relations and the interconnections between war and race, class and gender.[46] As Robert Citino summarised:

> Once controversial, and still the occasional subject of grumbling from a traditionalist old guard, the new military history is today an integral, even dominant, part of the parent field from which it emerged. It has been around so long, in fact, and has established itself so firmly, that it seems silly to keep calling it "new".[47]

The 'new military history' has been around since the 1950s, although it was not until the era between the mid-1970s and early 1980s that it became widespread and accepted. It was the result of an increasing diversity amongst students studying at university from the 1960s onwards, who became interested in the neglected voices of those who shared their ethnicity, class or gender. They were drawn to social history, which was flourishing at this time. Social history enabled scholars to study warfare – the influence of which on history could not be denied – at a time when pacifism had led to a suspicion of military history as glorifying war.[48]

Woodward's story provides the 'new' military historian with multiple avenues through which to explore questions prompted by this trend. One of the most influential works in the emergence of the 'new military history' was the publication in 1976 of John Keegan's *The Face of Battle*. This book moved away from examining battles from the viewpoint of generals and attempted instead to recover the experiences of ordinary soldiers, whose voices had hitherto largely been neglected in military history. Although Woodward served as a lieutenant during the Civil Wars, he was not the type of senior officer that dominated military histories in 1921 but instead is a prime example of more recent studies, inspired by Keegan, that have sought to understand what it was like for ordinary soldiers on the battlefield and how they influenced the fighting capacity and identity of armies.[49]

Even prior to the Civil Wars, it seems that Woodward was not a man of substantial means. He does not appear to have owned any property in Easton Neston before the conflict, making it unlikely that he, by the time of the Restoration, conformed to the stereotype of the loyal cavalier as an impoverished gentleman who had suffered for his loyalty to the Crown. Nowhere in his petition does Woodward claim to have ever held social status. He certainly no longer maintained

---

46   Robert M. Citino, 'Military Histories Old and New: A Reintroduction', *American Historical Review*, Vol.112, No.4 (2007), pp.1070–1090, at p.1071.

47   Citino, 'Military Histories Old and New', p.1071.

48   Morillo and Pavkovic, *What is Military History?*, pp.41–43.

49   See, for example, Charles Charlton, *Going to the Wars: The Experience of the English Civil Wars, 1638–1651* (London: Routledge, 1992). Although riddled with factual errors, Carlton's study openly acknowledges the influence of Keegan and is a good illustration of how Keegan's approach can be applied to the Civil Wars.

any substantial possession in Easton Neston by the 1660s, as he was absent from the Hearth Tax returns (and exemption certificates) for his village.[50] This was the levy imposed between 1662 and 1689 on occupants of dwellings according to the number of hearths they had in (each of) their properties. Those who inhabited a property worth less than 20 shillings a year, had assets worth less than £10 or were exempt from the parish poor rate did not have to pay the tax.[51] By the Restoration, Woodward was living in Westminster and he was possibly the John Woodward who was rated for seven hearths in the north end of Petty France in 1664.[52] If this John Woodward was the same man as the subject of this chapter, then this indicates that he inhabited a dwelling befitting a man of moderate means though less considerable than that in which a gentleman probably expected to reside.

Officers originating from lower down the social scale have been traditionally associated with the New Model Army, rather than royalist armies. For example, Ian Gentles revealed 'the exceptional opportunities' which the New Model Army presented to 'men from conventionally subordinate social groups'. Gentles noted that the most spectacular examples of social advancement were reserved for New Model Army officers who went on to obtain large quantities of confiscated royalist land and/or loyally served the Protectorate regime.[53] Conversely, all of the officers from the rank of captain upwards in Charles I's main 'Oxford Army', the army in which Northampton's Regiment served, were of gentry status or higher.[54] This does not suggest that Woodward was necessarily exceptional amongst his fellow lieutenants in the Oxford Army and neither was Woodward especially unusual amongst officers from across the royalist armies more widely. Peter Newman maintained that 'far from active royalism being dominated by grandees and greater gentlemen, the real muscle of the royalist army lay with minor gentry and their

---

50 TNA: E179/254/11 rot. 2: Easton Neston Hearth Tax returns, c. 30 September 1662; TNA: E179/157/468 Part 1: Easton Neston Hearth Tax returns, c. 17 May 1664; TNA: E179/157/468 Part 2 fol. 5: Easton Neston Hearth Tax returns, c. 17 May 1664; TNA: E179/157/468 Part 6 fol. 21: Easton Neston Hearth Tax returns, c. 17 May 1664; TNA: E179/157/468 Part 7 fol. 4v: Easton Neston Hearth Tax returns, c. 17 May 1664; TNA: E179/157/468 Part 9 fol. 17: Easton Neston Hearth Tax returns, c. 17 May 1664; TNA: E179/266/16 fol. 168: Easton Neston Hearth Tax returns, c. 25 March 1666; TNA: E179/352/3 Part 2 fol. 11: Certificates of exemption from the Hearth Tax for Easton Neston, 1670; TNA: E179/157/446 rot. 6v: Easton Neston Hearth Tax returns, c. 1670; TNA: E179/254/14 rot. 27v: Easton Neston Hearth Tax returns, 30 May 1674.

51 For more information, see 'A brief introduction to the hearth tax', *Centre for Hearth Tax Research*, <https://www.roehampton.ac.uk/research-centres/centre-for-hearth-tax-research/the-hearth-tax>, accessed 24 August 2021.

52 Anon., *A List of Officers Claiming to the Sixty Thousand Pounds*, p.101; 'Hearth Tax: Westminster 1664, St Margaret's Westminster, Petty France North', *London Hearth Tax: Westminster 1664* <http://www.british-history.ac.uk/london-hearth-tax/westminster/1664/st-margarets-westminster-petty-france-north>, accessed 24 March 2021.

53 Ian Gentles, 'The New Model Officer Corps in 1647: A Collective Portrait', *Social History*, Vol.22, No.2 (1997), pp.127–144, at pp.136 and 144.

54 Gentles, 'The New Model Officer Corps in 1647', p.143.

social inferiors'.[55] Newman calculated that even amongst those who held the rank of major and above across the royalist armies, 89 percent were drawn from below the social rank of knights and of this 89 percent only 23 percent were gentlemen or esquires.[56] However, the extent to which lesser royalists like Woodward might have translated military office into social status had the King's men ended up winning the war has been a disputed point and one which, in any case, can never be anything other than speculative.[57]

In contrast to its antecedents in the Civil War years, Royal Regiment of Horse of the Restoration period was, as White-Spunner's history of the regiment highlighted, commanded by men of wealth and property, many of whom had purchased their commissions.[58] Technically, the sale of commissions was illegal but the practice suited the King. The officer corps of the Restoration army was a way of finding a position that gave status, prestige and patronage – not to mention an income – to former cavaliers whose families had suffered financially for their support for the Crown during the Civil Wars. The sale of commissions added to the rewards and made officer service even more attractive. It was not unusual for men who had commanded regiments for Charles I to hold a captaincy or even lieutenancy in the regiments raised by Charles II.[59] This might explain why Woodward appears never to have been commissioned in the Blues. His exact position amongst the other ranks unfortunately remains uncertain, as no nominal rolls beyond the officer corps exist for the regiment prior to the eighteenth century.[60] The sale of commissions had the effect of excluding from the officer corps those like Woodward who were men of military experience but lacked funds.

We should exercise caution in either taking Woodward's later statement that he was in a 'very poore and low condic[i]on' entirely at face value or in backdating this prior to the time of his petition in 1677. It was, of course, in a petitioner's interests to assert straightened circumstances in order to be successful in their claim for a military pension. Even if Woodward's claims to poverty in 1677 were sincere, he made it clear that this was a direct result of his discharge from the Army and consequently being cut off from his source of income. Therefore, from what has been pieced together from Woodward's financial circumstances, it seems unlikely that he was in abject poverty at the time he joined the Restoration army but almost certain that he would not have been able to have afforded a commission. According to John Childs, although information on the average prices paid for commissions is scarce, 'the cost of commissions were generally very high' with captain's

55   Peter R. Newman, 'The Royalist Officer Corps, 1642–1660: Army Command as a Reflexion of the Social Structure', *Historical Journal*, Vol.26, No.4 (1983), pp.945–958, at p.945.
56   Newman, 'The Royalist Officer Corps', p.950.
57   Newman, 'The Royalist Officer Corps', p.956; Gentles, 'The New Model Officer Corps in 1647', p.143.
58   Dalton, *English Army Lists*, Vol.1, *passim*.
59   Childs, *Army of Charles II*, pp.18–19 and 44–45.
60   White-Spunner, *Horse Guards*, p.72.

commissions usually fetching around £1,000.[61] Presumably lieutenants' commissions would have been cheaper, though for a man such as Woodward who appears to have been dependent on his army salary and lacked independent means, even a commission costing in the hundreds of pounds would have stretched his means.

The purchase of commissions was the flip-side of having a permanent army: whilst a standing army might be regarded as more professional, its permanence meant that commissions were a good investment because officers were secure in the knowledge that the regiment would not be disbanded and they would therefore be able to sell their commission when they wished to retire.[62] The presumed equation between permanent armies and higher professional standards has sometimes, as Barbara Donagan has argued, led historians to dismiss the quality of the Civil War forces that preceded the Restoration army because the former had more permeable boundaries between military and civilian life. Donagan contended that 'The self-conscious professionalism of civil war officers has been underestimated, in part because so many came from and returned to civilian life'.[63] Woodward did not enjoy an unbroken military career, returning to civilian life in 1646 and not re-entering the armed forces again until after the Restoration. The royalist army in which he fought was never intended to be a permanent institution. Indeed, neither were the forces of his adversaries, including the New Model Army. Yet, Northampton's Regiment was, in royalist opinion, 'esteemed the best Regiment the King had', suggesting that the level of military skill amongst Woodward and his colleagues was high.[64]

Furthermore, Donagan claimed that even though it was common for contemporaries to pass between civilian and military lives, military standards were maintained because, when in service,

> they knew that there were professional codes that applied to their relations with the enemy and with each other. So they knew that there were rules to be observed in, for example, taking and exchanging prisoners, in negotiating and celebrating surrenders, in controlling their own troops and killing or saving the enemy's, and that their honour as soldiers depended on adherence to them. It behoved a soldier to 'understand … his profession', a formulation that covered its rules of conduct as well as its killing skills.[65]

---

61 Childs, *Army of Charles II*, p.45.

62 White Spunner, *Horse Guards*, pp.29–30.

63 Barbara Donagan, 'The Web of Honour: Soldiers, Christians, and Gentlemen in the English Civil War', *Historical Journal*, Vol.44, No.2 (2001), pp.365–389, at pp.367–368.

64 George Payne, *A Late Victory Obtayned by the Parliaments Forces Neere Farrington, Aprill the third 1646* (London: Edward Husband, 1646), p.3: Thomason Tracts E.330[21].

65 Barbara Donagan, 'The Web of Honour: Soldiers, Christians, and Gentlemen in the English Civil War', *Historical Journal*, Vol.44, No.2 (2001), pp.365–389, at pp.367–368.

The codes of military professionalism that underpinned military relations during the Civil Wars were common across Europe at this time. These combined traditional chivalric concepts with shared moral and cultural traditions. They were based on a sense of reciprocity and reinforced by a soldier's reputation in honouring his word.[66] This sense of military professionalism strengthened soldiers' confidence in their own worth and enhanced their public standing.[67] Woodward would have witnessed the professional codes Donagan referred to in action, such as in the articles of surrender following the Battle of Lostwithiel, which took place from 21 August to 2 September 1644.[68]

The efficacy of such military codes should obviously not be exaggerated. As Donagan herself acknowledged, while the literature of atrocities linked to the British Civil Wars is small-scale in comparison with the horrifying accounts of the contemporaneous Thirty Years War, 'England knew atrocities, as well as marginally permissible cruelties'.[69] Scholars such as Mark Stoyle have demonstrated that atrocities in the Civil Wars could be particularly brutal when English troops faced 'strangers', especially the Welsh, Cornish and Irish.[70] Yet, as Donagan reiterated, atrocities 'also occurred on home ground against the home-grown'.[71] Indeed, Woodward may have witnessed the attempted implementation of military codes in the articles of surrender following the Battle of Lostwithiel, but he would have also witnessed the failure to enforce these: as the surrendering parliamentarians marched out from their quarters, supposedly under safe conduct, royalist troops set about plundering their vanquished foes.[72] In short, 'laws were acknowledged although practice was imperfect'.[73] That said, as Donagan pointed out, modern wars have demonstrated that the 'tigers of cruelty and revenge have changed little since the seventeenth century and are still at large' today.[74]

Lostwithiel marked a high point in Woodward's military career. Within less than two years the fortunes of war had completely reversed and the royalist defeat in the 'First Civil War' in 1646 resulted in the complete disbandment of the King's army. Woodward's enforced return to civilian life is a reminder to military

66   Donagan, 'The Web of Honour', pp.367 and 389; Barbara Donagan, *War in England, 1642–1649* (Oxford: Oxford University Press, 2008), pp.129 and 167.
67   Donagan, 'The Web of Honour', p.388.
68   British Library: Sloane MS 1983B fol. 14: Articles of agreement between the royalist and parliamentarian forces at Fowey, 2 September 1644.
69   Barbara Donagan, 'Atrocity, War Crime, and Treason in the English Civil War'. *American Historical Review*, Vol.99, No.4 (1994), p.1137–1166, at p.1137.
70   See, especially: Mark Stoyle, *Soldiers and Strangers: An Ethnic History of the English Civil War* (London: Yale University Press, 2005)
71   Donagan, 'Atrocity, War Crime, and Treason', p.1137.
72   Richard Symonds (ed. Charles Long and Ian Roy), *Richard Symonds's Diary of the Marches of the Royal Army*, (Cambridge: Cambridge University Press, 1997), pp.66–67.
73   Donagan, 'Atrocity, War Crime, and Treason', p.1151.
74   Donagan, 'Atrocity, War Crime, and Treason', p.1166.

historians that they should not disregard the 'old military history'. This is the traditional operational history which was common in 1921 and is mainly concerned with campaigns and battles. In 1975, as the 'new military history' was beginning to flourish, Dennis Showalter bemoaned that it was 'distinctly unfashionable to suggest that historical watersheds can actually be crossed on the battlefield'.[75] Six years later, Walter Kaegi was in agreement and perceived what he termed a 'Crisis in Military Historiography', in which the 'old military history' was too readily written off as:

> [M]ediocre, boring, without methodological interest, a historiography that sometimes seemed to be impregnated with a false and perhaps dangerous chauvinism and naivete, a historiography that seemed to them to be concerned solely with minute and uninspired details of narrative and chronology and that failed to demonstrate any genuine comprehension of events or basic developments.[76]

At the heart of these military historians' dissatisfaction was the loss of appreciation of timing, of how critical decisions and events (intentional or unexpected) can have a pivotal impact on the course of historical change. In any era in history 'there are instances in which military decisions, events, technology, combats, and developments have significantly altered reality and have reshaped the very context in which economic, social, and cultural processes have existed, developed, or disappeared'.[77] Military historians who neglect the study of armies and operational history were likened to historians of science choosing to disregard Newton's laws or students of modern politics overlooking the conduct of elections.[78]

Yet, by the early 1990s, there was a consensus that the 'new' military history should not ignore the 'old' military history or try to 'escape from war'.[79] Likewise, the best operational military histories today integrate political, sociological and cultural questions.[80] Acknowledging the interaction between events on the battlefield and the broader political, sociological and cultural developments is essential to understanding Woodward's story. To begin with, the reason why Woodward had to wait until the second half of the seventeenth century to claim a military pension can be directly traced back to the battlefield. Woodward's petition

---

75 Dennis E. Showalter, 'A Modest Plea for Drums and Trumpets', *Military Affairs*, Vol.39, No.2 (1975), pp.71–74, at p.72.

76 Walter Emil Kaegi Jr, 'The Crisis in Military Historiography', *Armed Forces & Society*, Vol.7, No.2 (1981), pp.299–316, at p.300.

77 Kaegi Jr, 'The Crisis in Military Historiography', p.302.

78 Showalter, 'A Modest Plea', p.71.

79 John Whiteclay Chambers, 'The New Military History: Myth and Reality', *The Journal of Military History*, Vol.55, No.3 (1991), pp.395–406, at p.405.

80 Citino, 'Military Histories Old and New', p.1079.

makes it clear that his injuries were sustained during the Civil Wars. Woodward explained that he 'served his late majesty of euer blessed memory as a Leiftennant in the Regiment of the R[igh]t hono[ura]ble James Earle of Northampton and receiued divers wounds in the said service'.[81] Wounded soldiers had been able to claim military pensions from the state since 1593.[82] During the Civil Wars, first Parliament and then the King reaffirmed their commitment to the Elizabethan legislation, which entitled wounded soldiers to pensions.[83] However, in 1647, after victory in the First Civil War the previous year, Parliament prohibited anyone who had been in arms for the King from accessing the pension scheme.[84] It was not until the Restoration that royalist veterans felt emboldened to begin to petition for pensions, and it was not until 1662 that an Act of Parliament officially entitled royalists to submit pension claims.[85] If Woodward had been on the winning side at the decisive Battles of Naseby (14 June 1645) and Stow-on-the Wold (21 March 1646), he would have been able to make his claim for a military pension much sooner.

At the same time, wounded veterans could have an impact on the way in which armies operated both on and off the battlefield. John Lynn once claimed that subjects like wounded veterans and prisoners of war are 'topics that are marvelously [sic] off the point [to military history] most of the time, since pensioners and prisoners have ceased to be involved in combat. But since the individuals were suffering by then, it was somehow more admirable to study them'.[86] In fact, this could not be further from the truth. Andrew Hopper demonstrated, using the aftermath of the Battle of Seacroft Moor on 30 March 1643 as an example, how wounded and captive soldiers should not be considered tangential to military studies as soon as they ceased to be combatants but could continue to shape the strategy of senior commanders and military events.[87] Moreover, Woodward's case highlights how wounded veterans might seek to return to service and could

---

81   Northamptonshire Archives: QSR 1/84, fol. 61: The Petition of John Woodward of Easton Neston, Northamptonshire, 9 January 1677.

82   Geoffrey L. Hudson, 'Disabled Veterans and the State in Early Modern England', in David A. Gerber (ed.), *Disabled Veterans in History* (Ann Arbor: University of Michigan Press, 2003), pp.117–144, at pp.118–119.

83   Charles H. Firth and Robert S. Rait (eds), *Acts and Ordinances of the Interregnum, 1642-1660* (London: H. M. Stationery Office, 1911), Vol.1, p.36; *Mercurius Aulicus*, 18th Week (Oxford: William Webb, 6 May 1643), p.226: Thomason Tracts E.102[1].

84   Firth and Rait, *Acts and Ordinances*, Vol.1, pp.938–940.

85   Hudson, 'Disabled Veterans and the State', p.122; John Raithby (ed.), *Statutes of the Realm: Volume 5, 1628–80* (London: Dawsons, 1819), pp.389–390.

86   John A. Lynn, 'The Embattled Future of Academic Military History', *The Journal of Military History*, Vol.61, no.4 (1997), pp.777–789, at p.784. I am very grateful to Andrew Hopper for this reference.

87   Andrew Hopper, 'The Story after the Battle Before: The Wounded Prisoners of Seacroft Moor', *Civil War Petitions*, <https://www.civilwarpetitions.ac.uk/blog/the-story-after-the-battle-before-the-wounded-prisoners-of-seacroft-moor/>, accessed 24 August 2021.

still play an integral role to the functioning of their regiment. It is likely that the impact of Woodward's injuries was initially not that severe, which is why he was able to re-enlist after the Restoration. The disabling effects of his wounds would have become worse with increasing age, possibly exacerbated further by his military career after 1660. The Blues' responsibilities consisted in the main of policing duties and the preservation of the peace across the country.[88] For example, very few men from the Blues volunteered for the forces raised for service in the Netherlands in 1672-1674 during the Third Anglo-Dutch War (possibly because of the strength of Protestant sentiment in the regiment) and instead, their contribution to the war effort was in rounding up deserters from the army and navy.[89] Nevertheless, Andrew Cormack has illustrated the severe toll that even these types of duties could have on the bodies of soldiers in the early years of the standing army and the additional risks specifically faced by cavalry units.[90]

At least some of Woodward's service with the Blues may have been in itself a type of military welfare. Several men in the Royal Regiment of Horse who had served in the Civil Wars were kept on the books and continued to be paid until they died as a form of a pension. The Commissary-General gave the regiments in Charles II's army an allowance for these payments, which ranged between 6 d. and 2 s. per day, depending on rank and service of the intended recipients.[91] It is thus possible, though it cannot be proven, that Woodward was maintained in the Blues after he was largely no longer capable to perform active duties in recognition for his service to the Crown during the Civil Wars.

This does not necessarily mean, however, that Woodward did not continue to serve any useful purpose in the Blues or that his regiment no longer valued his presence. Cormack's research on the Chelsea Out-Pensioners in the early eighteenth century revealed that even soldiers with serious wounds or disablement that resulted in a reduction of capability were maintained within their regiments.[92] During times of reductions made in the size of the Army during peacetime, prompted either by re-organisation and/or Parliament's unwillingness to continue to fund the Army's existing numbers, many regiments released younger and fitter men whilst maintaining older men who would have qualified for pensions through injuries or ailments. The explanation given was that officers were reluctant to lose the experience of senior servicemen who did not wish to leave the regiment.[93] It is not unreasonable to suggest that the officers in the Blues in the later seventeenth century felt much the same way and that Woodward was maintained in the

---

88   White-Spunner, *Horse Guards*, p.48.
89   White-Spunner, *Horse Guards*, p.57.
90   Andrew Cormack, *'These Meritorious Objects of the Royal Bounty': The Chelsea Out-Pensioners in the Early Eighteenth Century* (London: Andrew Edward Cormack, 2017), pp.36–39 and 103–104.
91   White-Spunner, *Horse Guards*, p.72.
92   Cormack, *'These Meritorious Objects of the Royal Bounty'*, p.104.
93   Cormack, *'These Meritorious Objects of the Royal Bounty'*, pp.72–74 and 78.

musters in spite of his incapacities because his superiors valued the extensive military experience he brought to the regiment. Indeed, it is notable that the timing of Woodward's discharge from the Blues was, according to his petition, sometime around 1676. A general reduction in the Army was ordered following the conclusion of the Third Anglo-Dutch War, which was to include 10 men from each troop in the Blues. It was stipulated that these should not be 'effective men'.[94] It is possible that it was only as a result of this reduction that Woodward was, perhaps reluctantly, forced from the Army and was therefore obliged to apply for a pension from his county of origin. The Royal Hospital at Chelsea was not set up until 1682 and did not become operational for a decade.

Finally, the language used in Woodward's petition when he eventually filed his claim for a military pension before the Northamptonshire Quarter Sessions in 1677 leads to a consideration of a third and most recent development in military historiography that has influenced the history of the British Army: that which emphasises the impact of cultural attitudes on the conduct and memory of war. Amongst other concerns (and of particular relevance to this chapter), this branch examines the way in which the memory of conflicts is affected by political concerns past and present, and the way in which contemporary values lead to some conflicts being memorialised and others forgotten. Although cultural analyses of war predate the 1990s, it was not until that decade that such studies became commonplace. This was in line with developments in the field of history more broadly and has tied military history in closer with its parent discipline.[95]

In his petition, Woodward was at pains to stress his attachment to the Crown, as well as his long years in its service. For Woodward, Charles I was 'his late majesty of euer blessed memory', whilst the Restoration of Charles II was a 'happy' event.[96] Of course, it must be acknowledged that this language was in keeping with that used in the 1662 Act entitling royalists to claim pensions. This Act declared that pensions were to be reserved for those of

> His Majesties Loyal and Faithfull subjects who out of the sense of theire Duty and Allegiance to His Majesties Royal Father of ever blessed and glorious Memory and to His Majesty that now is[,] have during the late Wars wherein they have been imployed both by Sea and Land as Officers Souldiers and Mariners in the said Service exposed themselves to the utmost hazard of their Lives losse of theire Limbs and utter ruine of theire Fortunes...[97]

---

94   White-Spunner, *Horse Guards*, p.57.
95   Citino, 'Military Histories Old and New', p.1082; Morillo and Pavkovic, *What is Military History?*, p.45.
96   Northamptonshire Archives: QSR 1/84, fol. 61: The Petition of John Woodward of Easton Neston, Northamptonshire, 9 January 1677.
97   Raithby, *Statutes of the Realm*, p.389.

This was also the language used in official proclamations and a vibrant popular print culture throughout the Restoration, which, as historians such as Matthew Neufeld and Erin Peters have recently shown, sought to obliterate the memory of what the parliamentarian cause had stood for and frame the Civil Wars simply as a rebellion that had resulted in the barbarous murder of the saintly king.[98] By including all the politically appropriate phraseology, Woodward would have maximised his chances of obtaining a pension. He may also have been assisted in drafting his petition by a scribe. Most veterans, even those who were literate, had their petitions written out for them by a scribe. As well as producing a neater document, scribes could help petitioners formulate their case into a coherent argument that included targeted language that the officials to whom the petition was addressed would wish to hear.[99]

Nevertheless, we should not be too hasty to dismiss Woodward's engagement with this language as merely a cynical ploy to obtain his pension. Lloyd Bowen's research has demonstrated the strength and sophistication of popular royalism amongst the lower orders using cases of 'seditious speech' amongst Interregnum legal records, whilst Mark Stoyle's analysis of royalist maimed soldiers' petitions from Devon maintained that the evidence that 'many ordinary royalist soldiers had felt a genuine commitment to the cause in which they fought' is reinforced by the fact that many of the King's men 'retained links with their former officers and comrades for decades after the conflict had come to an end'.[100] On this basis, it seems that the Earl of Northampton's Regiment enjoyed a particularly strong *esprit de corps* and affinity with the royalist cause. No less than 12 certificates issued by James Compton in support of the pension claims of his former soldiers (including Woodward's) have survived – more than any other regimental commander.[101]

The attachment of the Compton family to the Crown has been noted above and this manifested itself in the two Earls' leadership of their regiment. Spencer Compton set the ultimate example of loyalty to his cause in the manner of his death at the fateful Battle of Hopton Heath, an example which became enshrined in royalist folklore. According to the Earl of Clarendon, during the heat of the battle, Spencer Compton was unhorsed and surrounded by the enemy. Upon

98   Matthew Neufeld, *The Civil Wars after 1660: Public Remembering in Late Stuart England* (Woodbridge: The Boydell Press, 2013); Erin Peters, *Commemoration and Oblivion in Royalist Print Culture, 1658-1667* (London: Palgrave Macmillan, 2017).

99   David J. Appleby, 'Unnecessary Persons? Maimed Soldiers and War Widows in Essex, 1642-1662', *Essex Archaeology and History*, Vol.32 (2001), pp.209–221, at pp.211 and 213.

100 Lloyd Bowen, 'Seditious Speech and Popular Royalism, 1649–60', in Jason McElligott and David L. Smith (eds), *Royalists and Royalism during the Interregnum* (Manchester: Manchester University Press, 2010), pp.44–66; Mark Stoyle, '"Memories of the Maimed": The Testimony of Charles I's Former Soldiers, 1660–1730', *History*, Vol.88, No.2 (2003), pp.204–226, at p.225.

101 A larger number of certificates issued by Oliver Cromwell have survived but most of these are in his capacity as Commander-in-Chief of the New Model Army.

having his helmet knocked off with a musket butt, he refused to surrender himself and had his head shattered by a halberd.[102] James Compton (as his father had before him) demonstrated his commitment to the Royalist cause by spending such a substantial proportion of his personal wealth in supporting his regiment that he found himself financially ruined by the time the Civil Wars were over.[103] The continued association of men like Woodward and Colborne with the Compton family long after the Civil Wars suggests that some of those who had fought in the Earl of Northampton's Regiment fully shared their colonels' values. In turn, James Compton's certificate, in which he declared that Woodward was 'a very fitt object to receiue ye charity of ye County as a pentioner', could be construed as a public testament to the Earl's belief that his former lieutenant fulfilled the required criteria of the 1662 Act that pensions only be awarded to 'Loyal and Faithfull subjects'.[104]

This chapter has used the military career of John Woodward of Easton Neston in Northamptonshire, as uncovered through his petition for a military pension, to argue for a close relationship between the British Civil Wars and the origins of the British Army and to consider the trends in military historiography that have influenced the history of the British Army since the formation of the Society for Army Historical Research in 1921. It thus remains for this chapter to tie these two themes together and make the case for the value of scholarship on the British Civil Wars in the further development of scholarship on the history of the British Army from the perspective of all three historiographical approaches highlighted in this chapter.

Firstly, as Robert Citino pointed out, whilst modern historians were relative latecomers to the new military history, historians of the early modern period have been interested in the relationship between war and society for decades.[105] For example, Charles Firth considered issues such as medical care and welfare, religion, and political activism in his study of the New Model Army as far back as 1902.[106] Analyses of such topics have developed exponentially since the days of Firth to provide a rich scholarship that historians of the British Army's later periods might draw upon for illuminating comparisons. Likewise, and as a consequence of this longstanding interest in the sociological questions surrounding Civil War armies, Civil War scholarship has provided an enduring model for

---

102 Edward Hyde, Earl of Clarendon (ed. William Dunn Macray), *The History of the Rebellion and Civil Wars in England* (Oxford: Clarendon Press, 1888), Vol.2, p.476.

103 Peter R. Newman, *The Old Service: Royalist Regimental Colonels and the Civil War, 1642–46* (Manchester: Manchester University Press, 1993), pp.85–86.

104 Northamptonshire Archives: QSR 1/84, fol. 62: The Certificate for John Woodward of Easton Neston, Northamptonshire, 9 January 1677; Raithby, *Statutes of the Realm*, p.389.

105 Citino, 'Military Histories Old and New', p.1077.

106 Charles H. Firth, *Cromwell's Army: A History of the English Soldier During the Civil Wars, the Commonwealth and the Protectorate* (London: Methuen, 1902).

combining these questions with the more traditional operational questions that can be dated back to Samuel Rawson Gardiner's magisterial *History of the Great Civil War* published in 1893. This interwove examinations of the tactical and strategic details of the military campaigns and scrutiny of the capabilities of the leading commanders not just with the high politics that influenced the war's course but also with topics such as female petitioners to parliament, local civilian sentiments and the licensing of the press. Thirdly, the politics surrounding the commemoration and oblivion of the Civil Wars have endured to this day in aspects of the modern Army. Most famously, the Coldstream Guards are placed second in seniority to the Grenadier Guards, despite the former having been raised in 1650, some six years before the latter. The Grenadiers were given seniority due to their continuous service to the Crown, having been raised by Charles II in exile, whilst the Coldstreamers were originally raised by George Monck for the New Model Army in 1650. The Coldstream Guards, of course, responded to this with their motto *Nulli Secundus* [Second to None]. Simultaneously, the Grenadiers' story of their origins remains to this day one of 'loyal men who had followed their King into exile rather than live under tyranny' during 'the military dictatorship of Cromwell, the Lord Protector'.[107] A greater appreciation of the lasting legacy of the Civil Wars is central to understanding the cultural history of the British Army.

Finally, returning to John Woodward himself, what does his story specifically contribute to the history of the British Army? Above all, it is a reminder that a reciprocal obligation of service exists between the British State and its Army. In return for a soldier's service in hazarding his or her life for the State, the State has a duty of care to ensure the welfare of its soldiers and veterans. Those soldiers and veterans do not have to be high-ranking officers, nor must they have led exclusively military lives. But this reciprocal obligation of service has been at the heart of what it ought to mean to be a soldier in the British Army from its very earliest days to the present.

Bibliography

Manuscript Sources

British Library:
　Sloane MS 1983B fol. 14: Articles of agreement between the royalist and parliamentarian forces at Fowey, 2 September 1644

---

107 'A Short History of the First or Grenadier Regiment of Foot Guards', *The Grenadier Guards*, <https://www.grengds.com/history>, accessed 24 August 2021.

Northamptonshire Archives:
>   QSR 1/84, fol. 61: The Petition of John Woodward of Easton Neston, Northamptonshire, 9 January 1677.
>
>   QSR 1/84, fol. 62: The Certificate for John Woodward of Easton Neston, Northamptonshire, 9 January 1677.

The National Archives (TNA):
>   E179/157/446 rot. 6v: Easton Neston Hearth Tax returns, c. 1670
>
>   E179/157/468 Part 1: Easton Neston Hearth Tax returns, c. 17 May 1664
>
>   E179/157/468 Part 2 fol. 5: Easton Neston Hearth Tax returns, c. 17 May 1664
>
>   E179/157/468 Part 6 fol. 21: Easton Neston Hearth Tax returns, c. 17 May 1664
>
>   E179/157/468 Part 7 fol. 4v: Easton Neston Hearth Tax returns, c. 17 May 1664
>
>   E179/157/468 Part 9 fol. 17: Easton Neston Hearth Tax returns, c. 17 May 1664
>
>   E179/254/11 rot. 2: Easton Neston Hearth Tax returns, c. 30 September 1662
>
>   E179/254/14 rot. 27v: Easton Neston Hearth Tax returns, 30 May 1674
>
>   E179/266/16 fol. 168: Easton Neston Hearth Tax returns, c. 25 March 1666
>
>   E179/352/3 Part 2 fol. 11: Certificates of exemption from the Hearth Tax for Easton Neston, 1670
>
>   PROB 11/260/296: Will of Amias Colborne of Ashorne, Warwickshire, 26 July 1654
>
>   PROB 11/316/164: Will of Flammucke Colburne of Willington, Warwickshire, 29 September 1664
>
>   SP 18/99/78 fol. 188: Charge against Sir William Farmer, 24 July 1655
>
>   SP 18/99/79 fol. 192: Order by the Lord Protector that Sir William Farmer, John Urlin, John Hathway, William Taylor and William Perry appear before Council of State, 24 July 1655
>
>   SP 25/69 fol. 190: Order that Sir Charles Compton and Sir William Farmer appear before the Council of State, 2 June 1653
>
>   SP 25/119 fol. 87: Militia Commission granted to Sir Arthur Hesilrige, 29 August 1650
>
>   SP 29/29/45 fols 92–96: Establishment of forces to be raised for the safety of His Majesty's person and government, 26 January 1661
>
>   SP 44/4 fol. 3: Note of Commission for Francis Compton to be Captain in Lord Oxford's Regiment, 30 November 1661

Printed Primary Sources

Anon., *A List of Officers Claiming to the Sixty Thousand Pounds, &c. Granted by His Sacred Majesty for the Relief of His Truly-Loyal and Indigent Party* (London: Henry Brome, 1663).

Dalton, Charles (ed.), *English Army Lists and Commission Registers, 1661-1714* (London: Eyre & Spottiswoode, 1892).

Firth, Charles H. and Rait, Robert S. (eds), *Acts and Ordinances of the Interregnum, 1642-1660* (London: H. M. Stationery Office, 1911).

Green, Mary Anne Everett (ed.), *Calendar of the Committee for Compounding* (London: H. M. Stationery Office, 1890).

Hyde, Edward, Earl of Clarendon (ed. William Dun Macray), *The History of the Rebellion and Civil Wars in England*, ed. William Dunn Macray (Oxford: Clarendon Press, 1888).

Marvell, Andrew, *A Seasonable Argument to Perswade all the Grand Juries in England to Petition for a New Parliament* (Amsterdam: Publisher unknown, 1677).

Marvell, Andrew (ed. Sir N.H. Nicolas), *Flagellum Parliamentarium: being sarcastic notices of nearly two hundred Members of the first Parliament after the Restoration A.D. 1661 to 1678* (London: J. B. Nichols, 1827).

Payne, George, *A Late Victory Obtayned by the Parliaments Forces Neere Farrington, Aprill the third 1646* (London: Edward Husband, 1646): Thomason Tracts E.330[21].

Raithby, John, (ed.), *Statutes of the Realm: Volume 5, 1628–80* (London: Dawsons, 1819).

Symonds, Richard (ed. Charles Long and Ian Roy), *Richard Symonds's Diary of the Marches of the Royal Army* (Cambridge: Cambridge University Press, 1997).

Mercurius Aulicus, 18th Week (Oxford: William Webb, 6 May 1643): Thomason Tracts E.102[1].

Secondary Sources

Appleby, David J., 'Unnecessary Persons? Maimed Soldiers and War Widows in Essex, 1642-1662', *Essex Archaeology and History*, Vol.32 (2001), pp.209–221.

Appleby, David J., 'Veteran Politics in Restoration England, 1660–1670', *The Seventeenth Century*, Vol.28, No.3 (2013), pp.323–342.

Bowen, Lloyd, 'Seditious Speech and Popular Royalism, 1649–60', in Jason McElligott and David L. Smith (eds), *Royalists and Royalism during the Interregnum* (Manchester: Manchester University Press, 2010), pp.44–66.

Carlton, Charles, *Going to the Wars: The Experience of the English Civil Wars, 1638–1651* (London: Routledge, 1992).

Chambers, John Whiteclay, 'The New Military History: Myth and Reality', *The Journal of Military History*, Vol.55, No.3 (1991), pp.395–406.

Childs, John, *The Army of Charles II* (London: Routledge, 1976).

Citino, Robert M., 'Military Histories Old and New: A Reintroduction', *American Historical Review*, Vol.112, No.4 (2007), pp.1070–1090.

Cormack, Andrew, *'These Meritorious Objects of the Royal Bounty': The Chelsea Out-Pensioners in the Early Eighteenth Century* (London: Andrew Edward Cormack, 2017).

Cottesloe, Lord, 'The Earliest "Establishment"—1661—of the British Standing Army', *Journal of the Society for Army Historical Research*, Vol. 9, No.37 (July 1930), pp.147–161.

Donagan, Barbara, 'Atrocity, War Crime, and Treason in the English Civil War'. *American Historical Review*, Vol.99, No.4 (1994), p.1137–1166.

Donagan, Barbara, 'The Web of Honour: Soldiers, Christians, and Gentlemen in the English Civil War', *Historical Journal*, Vol.44, No.2 (2001), pp.365–389.

Donagan, Barbara, *War in England, 1642–1649* (Oxford: Oxford University Press, 2008).

Firth, Charles H., *Cromwell's Army: A History of the English Soldier During the Civil Wars, the Commonwealth and the Protectorate* (London: Methuen, 1902).

Firth, Charles H. and Davies, Godfrey, *The Regimental History of Cromwell's Army* (Oxford: Clarendon Press, 1940).

Gentles, Ian, 'The New Model Officer Corps in 1647: A Collective Portrait', *Social History*, Vol.22, No.2 (1997), pp.127–144.

Hudson, Geoffrey L., 'Disabled Veterans and the State in Early Modern England', in David A. Gerber (ed.), *Disabled Veterans in History* (Ann Arbor: University of Michigan Press, 2003), pp.117–144.

Kaegi Jr, Walter Emil, 'The Crisis in Military Historiography', *Armed Forces & Society*, Vol.7, No.2 (1981), pp.299–316.

Lynn, John A., 'The Embattled Future of Academic Military History', *The Journal of Military History*, Vol.61, no.4 (1997), pp.777–789.

Morillo, Stephen and Pavkovic, Michael F., *What is Military History?* (Cambridge: Polity Press, 2018).

Neufeld, Matthew, *The Civil Wars after 1660: Public Remembering in Late Stuart England* (Woodbridge: The Boydell Press, 2013).

Newman, Peter R., *The Old Service: Royalist Regimental Colonels and the Civil War, 1642–46* (Manchester: Manchester University Press, 1993).

Newman, Peter R. 'The Royalist Officer Corps, 1642–1660: Army Command as a Reflexion of the Social Structure', *Historical Journal*, Vol.26, No.4 (1983), pp.945–958.

Newman, Peter R., *Royalist Officers in England and Wales, 1642-1660: A Biographical Dictionary* (London: Garland Publishing, 1981).

Peters, Erin, *Commemoration and Oblivion in Royalist Print Culture, 1658-1667* (London: Palgrave Macmillan, 2017)

Reid, Stuart *Officers and Regiments of the Royalist Army* (Leigh-on-Sea: Partizan Press, 1985)

Showalter, Dennis E., 'A Modest Plea for Drums and Trumpets', *Military Affairs*, Vol.39, No.2 (1975), pp.71–74.

Schwoerer, Lois G., *'No Standing Armies!': The Antiarmy Ideology in Seventeenth-Century England* (London: John Hopkins University Press, 1974).

Stoyle, Mark, '"Memories of the Maimed": The Testimony of Charles I's Former Soldiers, 1660–1730', *History*, Vol.88, No.2 (2003), pp.204–226.

Stoyle, Mark, *Soldiers and Strangers: An Ethnic History of the English Civil War* (London: Yale University Press, 2005).

Wanklyn, Malcolm, *Reconstructing the New Model Army Volume 2: Regimental Lists 1649 to 1663* (Solihull: Helion and Company, 2016).

White-Spunner, Barney, *Horse Guards* (Basingstoke: Macmillan, 2006).

Online Sources

Anon., 'A brief introduction to the hearth tax', *Centre for Hearth Tax Research*, <https://www.roehampton.ac.uk/research-centres/centre-for-hearth-tax-research/the-hearth-tax>.

Anon., 'A Short History of the First or Grenadier Regiment of Foot Guards', *The Grenadier Guards*, <https://www.grengds.com/history>

Anon., 'Hearth Tax: Westminster 1664, St Margaret's Westminster, Petty France North', *London Hearth Tax: Westminster 1664* <http://www.british-history.ac.uk/london-hearth-tax/westminster/1664/st-margarets-westminster-petty-france-north>.

Hopper, Andrew *et al* (eds), *Civil War Petitions: Conflict, Welfare and Memory during and after the English Civil Wars, 1642–1710*, <www.civilwarpetitions.ac.uk>.

Hopper, Andrew, 'The Story after the Battle Before: The Wounded Prisoners of Seacroft Moor', *Civil War Petitions*, <https://www.civilwarpetitions.ac.uk/blog/the-story-after-the-battle-before-the-wounded-prisoners-of-seacroft-moor/>.

History of Parliament Online, <www.historyofparliamentonline.org>.

Oxford Dictionary of National Biography, <www.oxforddnb.com>.

3

An Affair of Posts: Mapping the Battle of Lincelles, 18 August 1793

Garry Wills

Introduction

In popular histories, on 18 August 1793 the three battalions of the Guards Brigade assaulted the hill on which stood the village of Linselles, taking two redoubts by coup de main through a hail of case shot from a force of French republican defenders three times their own number. In so doing the Guards regiments earned the earliest battle honour of the French Revolutionary and Napoleonic Wars, LINCELLES. However, there are difficulties with the histories of the battle that need to be addressed. This chapter aims to address three such difficulties: firstly, the spelling of the battle honour relative to the spelling of the place name, secondly to place the Guards Brigade's attack in the full context of the day, and thirdly to discuss some serious problems with the mapping of the battle.

The Spelling of Linselles

Linselles rather than Lincelles is the correct spelling of the place name; this spelling is that shown on modern maps, the *Carte d'État Major* (1818-1835),[1] Cassini's map (1758) and Bodenehr's map (1716).[2] The spelling Lincelles, which features in the

---

1   The *Carte d' État-major* is available online at <https://www.geoportail.gouv.fr/>, accessed 15 August 2021. The dates relate to the surveys for the Lille region.
2   The Cassini map is available online at <https://www.geoportail.gouv.fr/>, accessed 15 August 2021. Gabriel Bodenehr's map '*Menin in Flandern*', naming it 'Linsele', is available at <https://www.david-rumsey.com/luna/servlet/detail/RUMSEY~8~1~283819~90056454:Menin-in-Flandern>, accessed 15 August 2021.

Guards battle honour, has been blamed on the Duke of York's campaign map on which the 's' was obscured, so that the Duke of York read it as a 'c' when writing his dispatch of 19 August 1793 to the King.[3] However, the reports of the French commanders Jourdan, Béru and Levasseur all also spell it Lincelles.[4] Furthermore the Prince of Orange's own account uses both spellings.[5] The Le Rouge map of the area around Lille, dated 1744, spells it Lincelles, which perhaps provides an alternative explanation for the confusion. This map is in George III's topographical, rather than his military, map collection.[6]

Campaign Background

In August 1793, Great Britain had been at war with France for six months, as a partner in the First Coalition with Prussia, Austria and the Holy Roman Empire, Spain, Portugal, Sardinia, the Two Sicilies, and the United Provinces. The Guards Brigade had left England on 25 February 1793.[7] After the 1792 French invasion of the Austrian Netherlands and then Holland in February 1793, the French armies had been pushed back to the borders of France by May 1793. After the successful siege of Valenciennes in July 1793, rather than advance on Paris directly, the British Government chose to divert the Duke of York's army towards the coastal objective of Dunkerque. For the British government Dunkerque had always been a primary objective of the expedition.[8] Prime Minister Pitt's view was that the attack on Dunkerque would create additional stress that might cause the collapse of the French, although his critics point to the unwarranted dispersion of the allies in pursuit of individual goals, at a time when a united stroke was required. Similarly, the Austrians preferred to besiege Le Quesnoy.[9]

3   Alfred Higgins Burne, *The Noble Duke of York* (London: Staples Press, 1949), p.67.

4   *Service Historique de la Défense* (SHD), Paris, SHD B1 17, *Armée du Nord Correspondence, 16 –31 Août*, pp.134, 136 and 141.

5   Anon., *Nieuwe Nederlandsche Jaarboeken* (Leiden: P. van der Eyk and D. Vygh, and Amsteldam: J. van der Burgh, 1793), vol.II, pp.1401, 1409.

6   George Louis Le Rouge, *La chatellenie de Lille et le bailliage de Tournay*, British Library, BLL01004876659, available online at <https://www.flickr.com/photos/britishlibrary/50263216008>, accessed 18 October 2021.

7   Frederick William Hamilton, *History and Origins of the First Regiment of Foot Guards* (London: J. Murray, 1874), vol.II, pp.271–272.

8   Steve Brown, *The Duke of York's Flanders Campaign: Fighting the French Revolution 1793-1795* (Barnsley: Frontline Press, 2018), p.60.

9   Harry Verney, *The Journals and Correspondence of General Sir Harry Calvert* (London: Hurst & Blackett, 1853), p.101; Burne, *Noble Duke*, p.66.

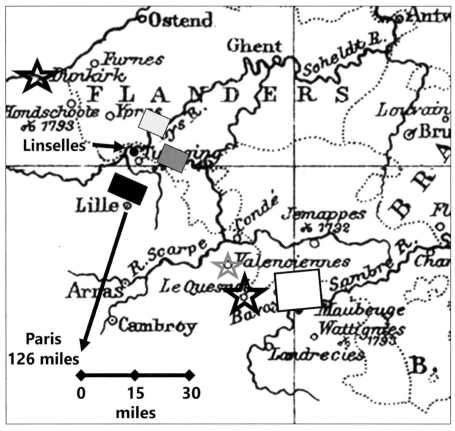

Map One: Campaign Map, Austrian Netherlands. (© Garry Wills 2022)

The Dutch Attack and then Defend Linselles

On 18 August 1793, the Duke of York was marching from Tourcoing to Menen. At dawn, covered by the Duke's march, Willem, Erfprins van Orange-Nassau,[10] with some 5,000 men including the Dutch Guards, had expelled the French outposts from the village of Linselles, six-and-three-quarter miles to the northwest of Lille, and the hamlet of Le Blaton.[11] In his memoirs, the future *Maréchal* Étienne Jacques

---

10   William, Hereditary Prince of Orange-Nassau, who became King William I of the Netherlands in 1815.
11   The *Carte d'État-major* records two hamlets of similar names, Blaton, three-quarters of a mile from Linselles and Le Blaton, one-and-three-quarter miles therefrom. The Cassini map only shows Blaton but calls it Le Blaton, while Le Rouge's map only shows Blaton. Modern maps refer just to the nearer hamlet and call it Le Blaton.

Macdonald, then a *chef de brigade*, stated that he was 'sent to command the frontier from Menen to Armentières' and had command of the French outposts.[12] The French sources do not record the initial French garrisons of Linselles and Le Blaton, but an Austrian bulletin states that 3,000 or 3,600 men initially held Linselles and its environs, although Levasseur implies that the garrison of Linselles itself was only one battalion.[13]

During this initial assault on Linselles, the Dutch lost approximately 100 men in total.

Having driven off the French, the main Dutch force then retired leaving garrisons in both Le Blaton and Linselles. The garrison of Linselles comprised the Van Breydenbach and Van Plettenberg grenadier battalions and the single battalion of the De Schepper Infanterie Regiment No.1, with two 3-pounder battalion guns, two 12-pounder and two 6-pounder guns, as well as two squadrons of the Garde Dragonders.[14] These troops were all under the command of *Generaal-Majoor* Frederik Willem van Nostitz, who had been promoted to this rank earlier in 1793; he was approximately 70 years old.[15] Van Nostitz had a total strength of approximately 1,275 infantry and 165 cavalry.[16] At Le Blaton, the garrison comprised two battalions, the Waldeck Infanterie Regiment No.1, and the Nassau-Usingen Infanterie Regiment Walsche (Walloon) with their battalion guns, plus two 12-pdr cannon and two howitzers, together with one squadron of the dragoon regiment Hessen-Kassel, and one of the cavalry regiment van's Gravemoer (van der Duijn), approximately 1,000 men (880 infantry and 175 cavalry), all commanded by *Generaal-Majoor* van Drachstadt.[17]

Général de Brigade Antoine Anne Lecourt de Béru and *Général de Division* Jean Baptiste Jourdan (the future *maréchal*) met at Wambrechies and resolved on a counterattack with a large and overwhelming force. Consequently, while *Chef de Brigade* Macdonald marched from Quesnoy-sur-Deûle, with 2,300 men, to attack

---

12 Camille Rousset (ed.), *Recollections of Marshal Macdonald, Duke of Tarentum* (London: Bentley, 1893), pp.30–31.

13 SHD B1 40, p.144; R. Levasseur, *Mémoires de R. Levasseur* (Paris: Rapilly, 1829), vol.II, p.34.

14 For the Dutch Army in 1793, see Geert van Uythoven, '*Intermezzo 1787–1793: The Dutch during the Revolutionary Wars –5*', pp.24–30, *First Empire*, 56, 2001, pp.25–30. The infantry regiments, while originally comprising two battalions, were each reorganised into a single battalion of eight companies.

15 Anon., *Jaarboeken*, pp.1400–1401; Hendrik van der Deyster, *Naamregister der heeren militaire officieren…* (Leiden: Publisherd by the Author, 1742 and 1746), pp.50, 59; van Nostitz was an ensign in 1742 and a lieutenant in 1744, for a discussion of van Nostitz's age and career see <https://www.thewargameswebsite.com/forums/topic/generaal-majoor-frederik-willem-van-nostitz-1723-1793/>, accessed 16 August 2021.

16 Geert van Uythoven, 'The Dutch Army of 1793-1794', available on the *Napoleon Series*, at <https://www.napoleon-series.org/military-info/organization/c_dutch.html>, accessed 16 August 2021. Strengths estimated from the returns for 21 September 1793 (Geert van Uythoven, personal communication) and the losses for 18 August given by the Prince of Orange on the 22 August, deducting the losses of the Dutch guards (Anon., *Jaarboeken*, pp.1409–1410).

17 Anon., *Jaarboeken*, p.1404; this total of eight guns (four 3-pounders, two 12-pounders and two howitzers) differs from Macdonald's account in which he claimed to have taken 10 guns.

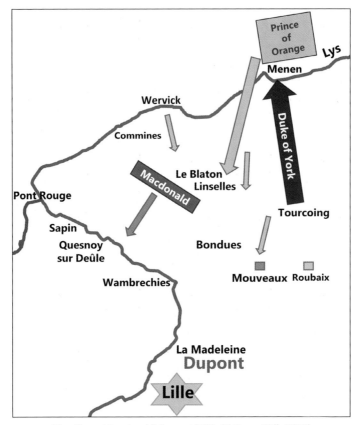

Map Two: Morning 18 August 1793. (© Garry Wills 2022)

the Dutch in Le Blaton,[18] Jourdan attacked Linselles from Wambrechies and Béru from Bondues, with approximately 4,600 men.[19]

The French infantry was largely organised into *demi-brigades* formed by the *embrigadement,* comprising a regular battalion of the old army combined with two volunteer battalions. These *demi-brigades* were named after the battalion and regiment of the regular army unit.[20]

Macdonald's men comprised his own *demi-brigade,* the 5e Volontaires de l'Aisne, 2/2e Régiment d'Infanterie and 40e Volontaires Nationaux. Also present were the

---

18   Camille Rousset, *Recollections of Marshal Macdonald, Duke of Tarentum,* 1893, p.31.

19   Victor Dupuis, *La campagne de 1793 à l'armée du Nord et des Ardennes, De Valenciennes à Hondtschoote* (Paris: R. Chapelot et Cie, 1906), p.14.

20   Terry E. Crowdy, *Napoleon's Infantry Handbook* (Barnsley: Pen and Sword Military, 2015), p.4; the *embrigadement* began 21 February 1793, but was then adjourned 31 March 1793. The order of battle in Dupuis, *Valenciennes,* pp.14–15, shows its impact in the *Camp de Madeleine.*

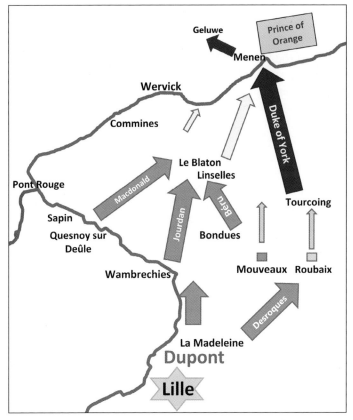

Map Three: Afternoon 18 August 1793. (© Garry Wills 2022)

2e Volontaires du Finistère. Jourdan himself led the *demi-brigade* comprising the 1/45e Régiment d'Infanterie, 5e Volontaires des Vosges and 10e Volontaires de Paris, together with a half company of *artillerie légère* (horse artillery). The 2/12e Régiment d'Infanterie and the 1er Volontaires de l'Allier were also sent by *Adjudant-Général* Pierre Dupont de l'Étang from the *Camp de la Madeleine*, although the third battalion of this *demi-brigade* was elsewhere. Béru led the *demi-brigade* comprising the 10e Volontaires de Seine-et-Oise, 1/47e Régiment d'Infanterie and 2e Volontaires de la Vienne, together with the 2e Volontaires de Paris. The French sources thus suggest that Macdonald led four battalions to Le Blaton and that Jourdan and Béru took nine battalions to Linselles, or 13 battalions in all. [21]

21   Dupuis, *Valenciennes*, pp.14–15, 199–202.

At Linselles, despite being outnumbered almost three to one and assailed from two different directions, there is clear evidence from the French accounts that the Dutch put up a fight to defend the position.[22] The Prince of Orange's casualty return suggests that the Dutch lost an estimated 220 men at Linselles, some 17 per cent of their starting strength.[23] Nevertheless both Linselles and Le Blaton were re-captured by the French.

As a footnote to these attacks, *Représentant du Peuple en Mission* Pierre Louis Bentabole reported that amongst the Dutch retiring from Le Blaton, there were two companies of emigrants who wore the livery of the house of Orange with a red cross on the coat. In the pursuit a large number of them were killed, 'the soldiers of the Republic did not take any prisoners'.[24] The Dutch column that had taken Le Blaton did indeed include a company of Béon's emigres, but this unit was not left behind as part of the Le Blaton garrison, which was attacked by Macdonald. Neither is Béon's *Légion* included in the Prince of Orange's casualty list.[25]

The Guards March to Linselles

When the French attacked Linselles, *Generaal-Majoor* van Nostitz wrote to Menen, four-and-a-half miles away, to appeal for help. The Duke of York recorded receiving the request at 3:00 p.m., which suggests that the French appeared before Linselles at approximately 1:30 to 1:45 p.m.[26] In his memoirs, Levasseur stated that the French attacked at 3:00 p.m., however in his despatch Jourdan stated that the French attack was at 4:00 p.m.[27] The French attacks recaptured both villages before any help could arrive.

In response to the Dutch request for help, the Duke of York dispatched the Guards Brigade from Geluwe under the command of Major General Gerard Lake, a veteran of the Battle of Yorktown in 1781, to assist them. On his arrival Lake found that the Dutch were not able to participate in the retaking of the villages, having retired by a different route. Undaunted, 'a firm believer in the attack', he decided to

---

22   L. Chassin and L. Hennet, *Les Volontaires Nationaux pendant la Revolution* (Paris: Cerf, Noblet and Quantin, 1902), vol.II, p.114; referencing the archives of the 79e Demi-brigade.

23   Anon., *Jaarboeken*, pp.1409–1410; estimates based on named officer casualties using Oman's proportional method.

24   Dupuis, *Valenciennes*, p.212.

25   Anon., *Jaarboeken*, p.1404.

26   John Hussey, *Waterloo: The Campaign of 1815 from Elba to Ligny and Quatre Bras* (London: Greenhill Books, 2017), pp.302–303; cites measured courier speeds based on the Prussian staff logs of two miles an hour normally and 3.6 miles an hour in a crisis.

27   Levasseur, *Memoires*, vol.II, p.34; SHD B1 17, 134 & 136; Jourdan has MacDonald attacking from Le Quesnoy which is 38 miles SE of Lille, but Béru has him attacking from Commines. Quesnoy-sur-Deûle is the most likely point of departure.

launch an assault himself.[28] Awaiting the British, MacDonald still held Le Blaton, while Béru and Jourdan held Linselles.[29] The National Convention's *Représentant du Peuple en Mission*, René Levasseur was also present at Linselles; 'to study the spirit of the soldier and maintain the sacred fire in his soul'.[30] Major Jesse Wright, Royal Artillery, who commanded Lake's battalion guns, reported that 'the action began about 6 o'clock in the afternoon and lasted until it was quite dark'.[31]

The identification of the actual site of the fighting is not as straightforward as might be expected.

The maps included in the histories of the Grenadier Guards and the Scots Guards (Map Four) both show the Guards attacking from the west of Linselles having apparently advanced via Commines. These maps appear to be based on a contemporary map in the Royal Collection (Map Five).[32]

The map from the Royal Collection has neither scale nor compass rose but is a very detailed map showing a stream flowing from left to right through the village on the opposite side to the redoubts. The Royal Collection map shows the three Guards battalions in three positions, firstly the approach march from the bottom right, secondly the assault on the redoubts and finally the positions for the evening attempt of the French to retake the village. The Coldstreams are on the left, the Third Guards in the centre and the First Guards on the right, according to the usual precedence, as shown in the version in the *History of the Scots Guards*. The map published in the history of the Scots Guards includes a scale which suggests that the Royal Collection map represents an area approximately 1,615 metres wide and 1,330 metres high.

However, these maps are all poor matches, especially with respect to the wider road layout, to the nineteenth century *Carte d'État Major*. The versions in the histories of the Guards regiments have the left of the royal map as the north, with the Guards attacking from the west or southwest.

To understand these maps, it is important to consider the route taken by the British Guards in their march to Linselles. On 17 August the Guards Flank Battalion, comprising all the light and grenadier companies of the brigade, had marched through Menen to the village of Geluwe, just over two miles to

28 Hugh Wodehouse Pearse, *Memoir of the life and military services of Viscount Lake, Baron Lake of Delhi and Laswaree, 1744–1808* (London: William Blackwood, 1908) p.77.

29 Dupuis, *Valenciennes*, p.211.

30 Levasseur, *Memoires*, vol.II, p.34; he was a doctor and a member of the *Montagnards*. 'Sacred Fire' as in *'feu sacré de la liberté'* (sacred fire of freedom) or *'feu sacré de l'amour de la patrie'* (sacred fire of love for the homeland); see Marco Marin, 'The Sacralization of Politics in the Political Catechisms of the French Revolution', p.10, available at <https://www.academia.edu/8547499/The_Sacralization_of_Politics_in_the_Political_Catechisms_of_the_French_Revolution>, accessed 13 September 2018.

31 Francis Arthur Whinyates, *The Wright Letters: being a collection of letters written by Major J. Wright, R.A., and others, during the Duke of York's campaigns in the Low Countries, 1793–4* (London: Eyre, 1902), p.19, Letter 18.

32 Hamilton, *First Guards*, opp. p.278; Fredrick Maurice, *The History of the Scots Guards …* (London: Chatto and Windus, 1934), vol.I, p.207; Royal Collection Trust, Windsor, RCIN 735016.a, *Attack of Lincelles, 18th Augt. 1793.*

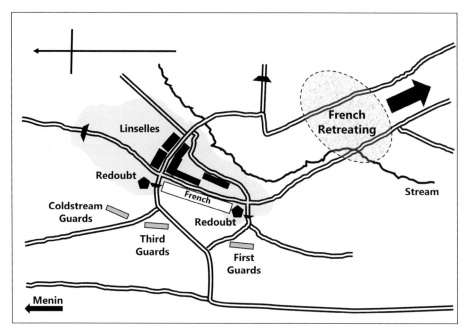

Map Four: Sketch based on the maps in the histories of the Guards. (© Garry Wills 2022)

the northwest. The battalion camped near this village, about three miles from Wervick.[33] On 18 August they were joined there by the rest of the Guards Brigade, although the history of the Grenadier Guards and Corporal Robert Brown of the Coldstream Guards refer to the village as Ghelins and Gheluis respectively.[34]

From Geluwe, there were five potential routes to Linselles.

- Route One, back towards Menen, crossing the river Lys across a pontoon bridge between Bousbecque and Halluin, about a mile from Menen, and then via Colbra and La Vignette, a march of six miles (approximately 2½–3¾ hours), attacking Linselles from the northeast.[35] This road through Colbra is described as the *Chemin de Linselles à Menen* on the *Carte d'État Major.*

33 Peter Harrington (ed.), *With the Guards in Flanders, the Diary of Captain Roger Morris 1793–1795* (Solihull: Helion, 2018), p.36; Verney, *Calvert*, p.106.

34 Hamilton, *First Guards*, p.284; Robert Brown, *An impartial journal of a detachment from the brigade of Foot Guards commencing 25th February 1793 and ending 9th May 1795* (Godmanchester: Ken Trotman 2006), p.64.

35 Anon., *Jaarboeken*, p.1402; Johann Gottfried von Hoyer, *Neues Militarische Magazin*, (Leipzig: Baumgärtnerischen Buchhandlung, 1801), vol.II, pt.2, plate 2; Verney, *Calvert*, p.106; Anon., *Jaarboeken* describes the pontoons as being stored at Bousbecque, while the *Neues Militarische Magazin* map shows it closer to Halluin and Calvert places it 'about a mile above Menin', which situates it at Le Malplaquet.

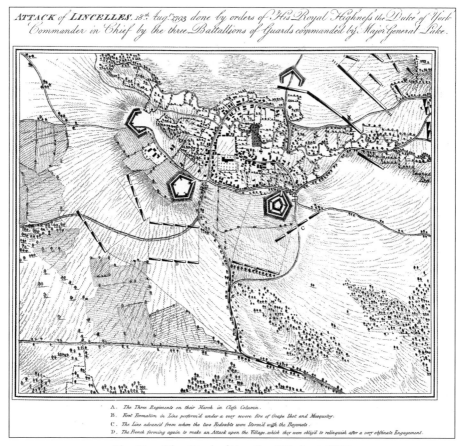

ATTACK of LINCELLES, 18th Aug.r 1793. done by orders of His Royal Highnefs the Duke of York Commander in Chief by the three Battallions of Guards commanded by Major General Lake.

A. The Three Regiments on their March in Close Column.
B. First Formation in Line perform'd under a very severe fire of Grape Shot and Musquetry.
C. The Line advanced from where the two Redoubts were Storm'd with the Bayonets.
D. The French forming again to make an Attack upon the Village, which they were obliged to relinquish after a very obstinate Engagement.

Map Five: 'The Attack of Lincelles, 18th Augt. 1793'.
(Royal Collection Trust/© His Majesty King Charles III 2022)

- Route Two, back to Menen then along the major *Route de Lille à Menen* through Roncq, turning off at La Roussel onto the *Pavé de la Vignette* through Vicourt, a march of eight miles (approximately 3½–5 hours), attacking Linselles from the east.
- Route Three, directly through Wervick over the high ground and through Le Blaton, a march of six miles (approximately 2½– 3¾ hours), attacking Linselles from the northwest.
- Route Four, to Wervick then southwest along the river Lys to Commines and then to Linselles via La Beau Chêne, Le Long Champ and Ste Barbe, thus bypassing Le Blaton, a march of nine miles (approximately 3¾–5½ hours), attacking Linselles from the west. This route is that implied by the histories of the Guards.

- Route Five, back to Menen then via Halluin, Roncq, Bondues, Les Boudins and La Vignes, attacking Linselles from the southwest, a march of 12-and-a-quarter miles (approximately 5–7¾ hours). This is the route implied by the map in the Royal Collection, if the top of that map is north.[36]

For the times these marches would have taken, we have the evidence of the diary of Captain Roger Morris of the Coldstream Guards to help us. He recorded 23 marches complete with start point, destination and marching time. These records suggest an average marching speed of 1.6 miles per hour, with a maximum of 2.4 miles per hour. Scharnhorst's later *Military Field Pocket Book* gives a similar figure of 1½ miles/hour. The ranges of marching times given above use the average speed and the maximum speed, as recorded by Morris.[37]

Brown (Coldstream Guards) describes the march of the Guards as beginning at 2:00 p.m. and reaching Linselles at 6:00 p.m., or four hours in total.[38] While 'an Officer of the Guards' related that 'regardless of their former fatigues, the brigade advanced so rapidly, that in little more than an hour [clearly an exaggeration] from the time they had received their orders, they were at their place of destination, distant nearly 6 miles from encampment.'[39]

In contrast to the histories of the Guards, the evidence suggests that they attacked Linselles from the northeast, having followed the itinerary outlined in Route One above. The fortifications themselves are the clue that resolves the dilemma as to which route the Guards took. The Prince of Orange's account is clear that the Dutch attacked Linselles in the early morning, from the northeast via the road through La Vinage and that the Hollandische Gardes stormed a redoubt on their way into the village while the Zwitzer Gardes went to the right and entered the village from the north. Map Six is an interpretation of the Prince of Orange's account.[40]

The prince also left an engineer (*Capitein Ingenieur* Frans Jacob Alexander Berg)[41] and some labourers with van Nostitz. The engineer was 'to erect entrenchments to the enemy's side [of Linselles], and to demolish those on our side', to prepare for attacks from the direction of Lille. Berg was later killed during the

---

36   Royal Collection Trust, Windsor, RCIN 735016.a.

37   Harrington (ed.), *With the Guards*, pp.42, 47, 55, 62, 71, 72, 83, 86, 87, 90, 104, 111, 116, 124, 127, 146, 147, 158; J.Haverfield and H.Hofmann, *Scharnhorst's Military Field Pocket Book*, 1811 (Uckfield: Naval and Military Press, 2009), Appendix p.7.

38   Brown, *Impartial Journal*, p.65, 67; Harrington (ed.), *With the Guards*, p.36; Brown also refers to the return march taking five hours between 10:00 p.m. and 3:00 a.m. Morris has the Guards leaving at 4:00 p.m.

39   Anon., *An accurate and impartial narrative of the war by an officer of the Guards in 2 volumes* (London: Cadell and Davies, 1796), vol.I, p.69.

40   Anon., *Jaarboeken*, pp.1401–1406.

41   A.J. van der Aa, *Biographisch woordenboek der Nederlanden* (Haarlen: J.J. van Beederode,1854), Deel 2, Eerste en tweede stuk, pp.360-361.

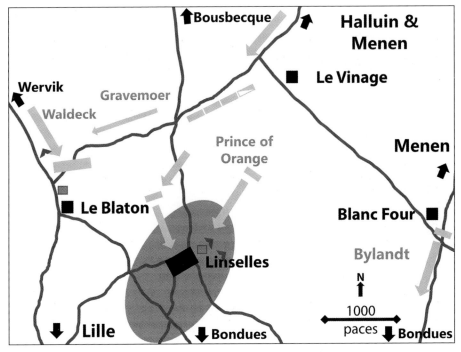

Map Six: The Dutch dawn attack. (© Garry Wills 2022)

French assault.[42] Similarly, although Levasseur did recall that 'the English [i.e., the Dutch] had already established a redoubt on the French side [of the village]',[43] the French reports of their afternoon assault on Linselles do not mention frontally assaulting the redoubts during their approach from the southwest, while later accounts refer to capturing the redoubts via their gorges; that is, by way of the entrances at the rear of the redoubts.[44]

Thus, the Guards brigades would have assaulted the same redoubts, also from the northeast, having advanced from Geluwe via the pontoon bridge (Route One). This conclusion is supported by a map that was published in 1801 which showed the British Guards battalions attacking Linselles from the northeast having marched directly from Geluwe via Halluin and La Vignette.[45]

42 Anon., *Jaarboeken,* p.1404.
43 Levasseur, *Memoires,* vol.II, p.34.
44 Levasseur, *Memoires,* vol.II, p.34; Antoine Henri Jomini, *Histoire Critique et Militaire des Campagnes de la Révolution, Campagne de 1793 — Seconde Période* (Paris: Magimel, Anselin et Pochard, 1819), vol.IV, p.42.
45 Hoyer, *Neues Militarische Magazin,* 1801, vol.II, pt.2, p.38 and plate 2.

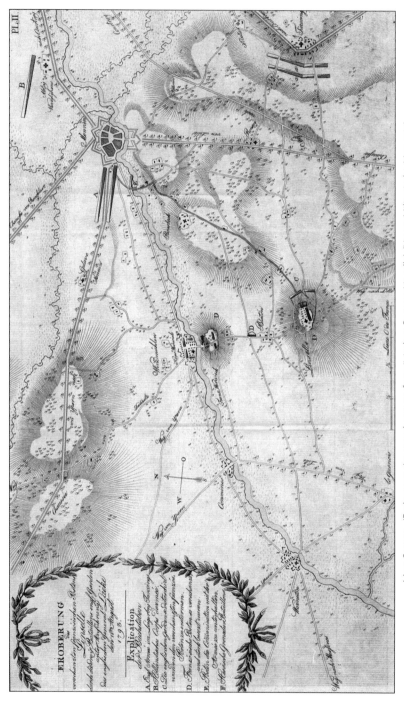

Map Seven: 'Eroberung das verschantzen französischen Postens Linselle'. (Neues Militairische Magazin)

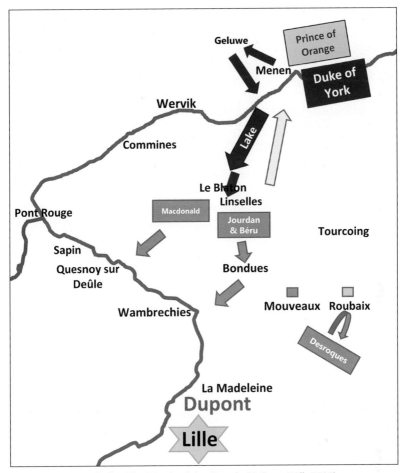

Map Eight: The March of the Guards. (© Garry Wills 2022)

Route Two can be eliminated as the Guards did not, during their march, meet the Dutch garrison as it retired from Linselles presumably along the most direct route to Menen, via the *pavé* towards Vicourt and then the main road from Lille to Menen. The Dutch garrison did, however, meet the 14th Foot marching from Menen, as part of the reinforcements sent later by the Duke of York.[46]

---

46   National Army Museum (NAM), London, Accession: 1976–07–45; diary of Lieutenant (later Captain) Thomas Powell (14th Foot).

Route Three is ruled out because the Guards did not meet Macdonald at Le Blaton. Macdonald was not attacked, and only withdrew after Linselles was taken by the Guards.

Route Four can be eliminated on two counts. Firstly, the accounts from both sides confirm that the Guards pursued the French towards Bondues to the south-southeast of Linselles having passed through the village, which would not have been necessary in an attack from the direction of Commines. Secondly, *Lieutenant* Jean-Pierre Dellard tells us that he and a detachment of his battalion, the 23e Volontaires des Réserves, were sent at midday the three-and-a-half miles from Commines to Le Blaton, where they arrived after Macdonald's success against the Dutch there. The Guards brigade did not meet a French garrison at Commines during their march to Linselles.[47]

Route Five can also be eliminated on two counts. Firstly, the route is the longest and unlikely to have been completed in the time given by Brown. Secondly it required the Guards to march towards the centre of the French position, within one-and-a-quarter miles of the French outpost at Mouveaux and marching more than half a mile further south before marching to Linselles through the French outpost at Bondues.[48]

Taking all the evidence together the most likely battlefield is as represented by Map Nine, with the Dutch defending the southwestern approaches to the village in the afternoon against the French assault and the French defending the north-eastern and eastern approaches in the early evening when the British Guards attacked. Map Nine is based on the *Carte d'État Major*. In 1783 Linselles had 2,840 inhabitants.[49] The streams are based on more modern maps. In the absence of stronger evidence, the redoubts have been placed in positions which are those most likely, given the requirements of an open field of fire from higher ground. The two to the east of the village are the more permanent ones constructed some-time after September 1792 when the Austrians first threatened Lille.[50] The Duke of York's Adjutant General, Sir James Murray, described them as being 'upon a height adjoining the high road in front of the village of Linselles'; that is, the pavé heading to Vicourt and Menen.[51] Each redoubt covered one of the two roads from

47   Jean-Pierre Dellard, *Mémoires Militaires du Général Baron Bellard* (Paris: Libraire Illustrée, 1892), p.18; Dellard's account suggests he would have arrived after approximately 2:30 p.m. His unit is shown in Dupuis's order of battle with its original name, 3e Volontaires du Lot (p.9). Dellard was a general under Napoleon.

48   Dupuis, *Valenciennes*, pp.207, 210, 211; the Dutch had also made an attack on Mouveaux but were repulsed and retired to Tourcoing.

49   Theodore Leuridan, *Histoire de Linselles* (Lille: L.Danel, 1883), p.113; available at <http://www.caue-nord.com/SPASSDATA/ALGEDIM/QOKQWR/D325/D32525.pdf>, accessed 15 August 2021.

50   Eugène Cruyplants, *Dumouriez dans les ci-devant Pays Bas Autrichiens* (Bruxelles: A. de Boeck, 1912), vol.I, p.309–311.

51   The National Archives (TNA), WO1/166 p.755; *Letter dated Menin 19th August 1793*.

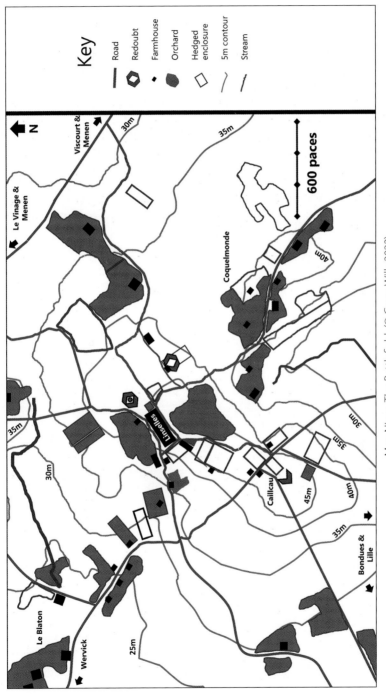

Map Nine: The Battlefield. (© Garry Wills 2022)

Menen. The Royal Collection map suggests that the redoubts to the northeast of the village were closed but the French and other accounts suggest that they were completely open to the rear, more like redans than redoubts.[52]

An editorial comment appended to Murray's account in the *London Gazette* stated, 'the redoubt taken by the First Regiment [that is, the one to the northeast] was a double redoubt, in the centre of which was a second work much more elevated, similar to a cavalier surrounded by a parapet on which one piece of cannon was placed.'[53] Ditfurth, inspired by the *Neues Militarische Magazin*, described Linselles as being surrounded by an 'an enceinte [enclosure] and forward ditch, but from the back quite open', but this is difficult to verify from other sources.[54]

The work shown to the west of the village is that erected during the six to eight hours available to the engineer Berg, after the early morning assault by the Dutch, before the arrival of the French. This redoubt was probably built to protect two to four of Nostitz's six guns (the 6- and 12-pounders, not the battalion pieces) and is positioned on the map facing the most likely line of approach from Lille and with the most commanding field of fire. Given the time available, Berg's redoubt would most likely have been a simple ditch surrounding an unrevetted earthen parapet. The parapet would have been six feet thick, proof against musket shot, and probably covered an area of approximately 88 feet by 14 feet and six feet high.[55] The hedged enclosure to the northeast of Linselles alongside the road to La Vignette is a candidate for the 'bean field', which obstructed the Guards Brigade, as mentioned in the account of 'An officer of the Guards'.[56]

This analysis suggests that the map in the Royal Collection in fact has north as the bottom left corner, with the French retreating towards the south towards Wambrechies rather than southeast onto the roads to Bondues as reported by Jourdan. This apparently odd alignment in fact reflects the established eighteenth-century practice of drawing maps facing the direction of action of whichever army was the mapmaker's, regardless of the compass.[57]

Together the various Dutch, British and French accounts enable the construction of the following approximate timeline;[58]

---

52   Hoyer, *Neues Militarische Magazin*, 1801, vol.II, Part 2, p.37; Jomini, *Histoire*, vol.IV, p.42.

53   Royal Collection Trust, Windsor, RCIN 735016.b.

54   Maximilian Joseph Carl von Ditfurth, *Die Hessen in den Feldzügen von 1793, 1794 und 1795 in Flandern* (Kassel: J.Bohné, 1893), vol.I, p.79.

55   Ralph Willett Adye, *The Bombardier and Pocket Gunner* (London: T. Egerton, 1813), p.169–71; Haverfield and Hofmann; *Pocket Book*, p.248; approximately 3,750 cubic feet of earth would have been moved in this work taking 34 man-days or by 100 men in eight hours.

56   Anon., *An Officer of the Guards*, p.69.

57   Dr Yolande Hodson, personal communication.

58   USNO is the United States Naval Observatory, available at <https://www.usno.navy.mil/USNO/astronomical-applications/data-services/data-services>, accessed 3 March 2018.

Table 1: Chronology of Events

	Time	Source
Twilight begins, i.e., dawn	4:15 a.m.	U.S.N.O.
Prince of Orange attacks Linselles	5:00 a.m.	Prince of Orange
Sunrise	5:40 a.m.	U.S.N.O.
French attack Linselles	12:00 Noon 1:00 p.m. 3:00 p.m. 4:00 p.m.	Ditfurth Austrian bulletin Levasseur Jourdan
Dellard arrives at Le Blaton	2:30 p.m.	Dellard/Scharnhorst
Duke of York receives request for help	3:00 p.m.	Duke of York
British Guards leave Geluwe	2:00 p.m. 3:30 p.m. 4:00 p.m.	Brown Duke of York + courier time Morris
British Guards attack Linselles	6:00 p.m.	Wright and Brown
Allied reinforcements leave Menen	7:00 p.m. 7:30 p.m.	Powell *Neues Militarische Magazin*
Sunset	8:00 p.m.	U.S.N.O.
End of Twilight/full dark; fighting ends	9:23 p.m.	U.S.N.O., Wright
Allied reinforcements arrive Linselles, and Guards leave	11:00 p.m. 1:00 a.m.	Brown (based on arrival) Powell
Guards arrive back in Geluwe	3:00 a.m.	Brown

The Guards Attack

Prior to the attack of the British Guards, three officers offer evidence that the French at Linselles had received some small reinforcements to the nine battalions that evicted the Dutch. David Hendrik Chassé, then a *capitaine* in the Légion Franche Étrangère, 'was so absorbed by the sight of the fine movement of the English that he was about to be taken captive by their skirmishers; the cry of one of his chasseurs alerted him and awoke him as if from a dream'.[59] A small detachment of the Légion Franche Étrangère (146 men) was stationed on the River Lys, presumably on the stretch from Commines to Wervick.[60] Another Dutch officer from the Légion Franche Étrangère was the then *Lieutenant Colonel* Hermann Willem Daendels, commander of the Légion, was also almost captured by 'his Dutch [sic] compatriots'

---

59 Willem Jacobus Del Campo, *Het leven en de krijgsbedrijven van David Hendrik Baron Chassé, in leven Generaal der Infanterie, oud lid der Staten-Generaal, Grootkruis der Militaire Willemsorde, Officier van het Legioen van Eer van Frankrijk* ('s Hertogenbosch: Muller, 1849), p.11; none of the British accounts mention the Guards deploying skirmishers and the flank battalion, including the light companies, was left at Geluwe.

60 Dupuis, *Valenciennes*, p.14–15; Geert van Uythoven, 'Legion Franche Étrangère', *First Empire*, 76, 2004, p.23.

at Linselles.[61] The third officer, like Chassé of Waterloo fame, was the Belgian, Joannes Baptista van Merlen, who, as a *capitaine* in the Légion Belge, 'while leading his men into battle, had two of his ribs shattered by a bullet'.[62] Dupuis shows this unit as the Bataillon Belge in his order of battle for 30 July 1793 based on the Lys. At that time, the unit had 184 men present under arms.[63]

Dupuis does not include the Légion Franche Étrangère or Bataillon Belge amongst the units that Jourdan and Béru led to Linselles, however both Béru and Levasseur reported that some unidentified French infantry retired from Linselles on Commines. This suggests that like Dellard's unit, which arrived in Le Blaton after the French assault, the Légion Belge/Bataillon Belge and the Légion Franche Étrangère arrived in Linselles after it had been retaken by Jourdan and Béru. These units probably arrived from posts along the Lys from Commines to Wervick.

As mentioned above, Jourdan was accompanied by half of a company of *artillerie légère*, comprising two 8-pounder cannon and one 6-inch howitzer.[64] The 8-pdr cannon were placed in the redoubt on the French right.[65] Some of the French infantry would have had their two 4-pounder battalion guns with them. Given the average for the Armée du Nord at the time, we might expect 11 such guns.[66] Although we know that the French retreated with some of their guns, the British Guards captured seven of these battalion guns plus the two 8-pounders. Together the evidence suggests that the French at Linselles had the two 8-pounders and one howitzer from the *artillerie légère* plus from eight to eleven 4-pounders.[67] The French also had four guns taken from the Dutch that

61   François de Bas, *Prins Frederik der Nederlanden en zijn tijd* (Schiedam: Roelants, 1887), vol.I, p.202; Geert van Uythoven, *Dutch Generals of the Napoleonic Wars, Herman Willem Daendels, Marshal of Holland, First Empire*, 39, p.5; The Chassé and Daendels stories are similar and raises the question as to whether François de Bas confused his source.

62   *Biografisch Woordenboek van Nederland: 1780-1830*, available at; <http://resources.huygens.knaw.nl/bwn1780-1830/lemmata/data/Van%20Merlen>, accessed 10 May 2020.

63   Dupuis, *Valenciennes*, p.14; Laurent Brayard and Didier Davin, *Les troupes Belges et Liégeoises sous la Révolution, 1792–1803* (SEHRI, 2017), pp.15, 34, available at <http://assosehri.fr/bibliothequemili/les-troupes-belges-de-1792-1803.pdf>, accessed 30 August 2021; Dupuis names another unit the *1e bataillon belges* but this appears to be the *1e battalion chasseurs belges*.

64   Dupuis, *Valenciennes*, pp.201, 211; Arthur Chuquet, *Les Guerres de la Révoluion XI Hondschoote* (Paris: Léon Chailley, 1896), p.137.

65   Hamilton, p.285; Royal Collection Trust, Windsor, RCIN 735016.b; both sources refer to them as four 9-pounders.

66   Dupuis, *Valenciennes*, p.48; cites a report showing that 37 per cent of the 4-pounders guns were missing, which suggests 11 guns, while Béru's report to the Minister of War confirms that the division had insufficient guns (SHD B1 17, 134).

67   Ditfurth, *Die Hessen*, vol.1, p.79; Abel Hugo, *France Militaire. Histoire des Armées de Terre et de Mer, 1792–1832* (Paris: Delloye, 1835), vol.I, p.116; in 1801 *Neues Militarisch Magazin* (p.37) described the guns as 12- to 16-pounder cannon, then *France Militaire* and Ditfurth later reported them as twelve 16-pounder cannon, but neither description tallies with Congreve's return of the captured guns as published in the *London Gazette*.

morning, although it appears that two had subsequently been removed as the British liberated only two of these when they captured the redoubts.

Thus, the French garrisoned Linselles with some 5,000 men and from 11 to 14 guns. Although Jourdan and Béru had difficulty stopping their troops from looting the village, they nonetheless offered a tough nut for Lake to crack.

Against this force, Lake led just the three Guards battalions, the First Foot Guards, the Coldstream Foot Guards, and the Third Foot Guards,[68] without their flank battalion, in all 1,122 rank and file.[69] The battalions were supported by their six light 6-pounder battalion guns, commanded by Major Jesse Wright, First Battalion, Royal Artillery.[70] Sir James Murray described how the Guards 'were instantly formed and advanced under a very heavy fire, with an order and intrepidity for which no praise can be too high. After firing three or four rounds, they rushed on with their bayonets, stormed the redoubt and drove the enemy through the village'.[71] The *History of the Grenadier Guards* includes the following account of the fighting in the redoubts:

> [I]n physique there is no doubt that at this time the French troops were inferior, for the better part of the population had not yet been drawn into the ranks. The Guards, instead of killing them when they got into the redoubt, rather treated them as a mob in London, striking them with their fists, and frequently calling out, "Let him alone, the little animal can't do much harm".[72]

Major Jesse Wright provided the following account of the action, from his perspective on the right of the British line:

> The troops sent on this service were the 3 regiments of the Guards under General Lake, and the 6 guns belonging to them, which I command. The [Royal Artillery] officers with me are De Ginkle [attached to First Guards], De Peyster [attached to Third Guards] and Watson [attached to Coldstream Guards], the whole number of us altogether did not amount

---

68   The Scots Guards, although originally raised as the Scottish Regiment of Guards, is described in the 1793 *Army List* as the Third Regiment of Foot Guards. In 1830, the regiment was renamed the Scots Fusilier Guards.

69   Maurice, *Scots Guards*, pp.232–233; the total for all ranks would have been approximately 1,300–1,350 men, the balance being officers, staff, sergeants, and drummers.

70   Garry David Wills, 'British Battalion Guns', pp.81–96, in Stephen Summerfield (ed.), *Smoothbore Ordnance Journal*, 6, pp.82–3. Wright was killed in action in May 1794.

71   *London Gazette*, 22 August 1793, p.710.

72   Hamilton, *First Guards*, p.285; the source for this is obscure, the account is not in any of the other available accounts. It is therefore likely to have been from Sergeant George Darby's *Account of the Battle of Lincelles*, which was not included when the archives of the Grenadier Guards Museum (Accession A03/03) were transferred to the National Army Museum.

to more than 1,300 men, and the enemy were more than 3 times the number, strongly intrenched in and about the village of Lincelles. The action began about 6 o'clock in the afternoon and lasted until it was quite dark. The Guards gallantly stormed the intrenchments under a dreadful fire and retook the village, together with 12 pieces of cannon, with their horses, and many prisoners. They lost about 12 officers and near 200 men killed and wounded, among the former is Colonel Bosville [Coldstream Guards]. De Peyster is killed; he behaved with a great deal of bravery and spirit. He was wounded by a grapeshot that hit him in the temple and died very soon afterwards. There are about 6 artillerymen killed and wounded, and 6 horses; most of these losses took place with the two guns of the first regiment that I was with; we were situated part of the time in an orchard. De Ginkle, who was the officer with me, behaved to admiration…it was a miracle that De Ginkle and myself escaped being killed or wounded; the quantities of grapeshot that fell about us would surprise one; we had both several men killed and wounded so close to us that I cannot conceive how we escaped…I have got Lt. Hughes to my guns in place of de Peyster.[73]

Corporal Brown of the Coldstream Guards described how:

The Dutch troops having been driven from the post of Linselles this day, it was deemed necessary to retake it; upon which the three battalions of the guards, under the command of Major General Lake, were ordered immediately on the service; accordingly, we marched about two o'clock p.m. and about six o'clock reached the village of Lincelles, where we found the enemy strongly entrenched, and well prepared for their defence.

General Lake having made the proper disposition, the attack began. The 1st regiment being in front of the column, began the attack, and the 3rd regiment and Coldstream [sic] forming on their left with the utmost celerity, the whole line then rushed in upon the enemy with irresist-ible force, amidst showers of grape shot from their redoubts; and after discharging a volley or two of musketry, made a furious charge, accompa-nied with a loud huzza, mounted their batteries in the face of the enemy, and devoted all they met with to the bayonet.

The French, who had been accustomed to the cold lifeless attacks of the Dutch, were amazed at the spirit and intrepidity of the British, and not much relishing the manner of our salute, immediately gave way, aban-doning all that was in the place, and in their flight threw away both arms and accoutrements.

73   Whinyates, *Wright's Letters*, p.19, Letter 18.

We took one stand of colours, ten pieces of cannon, with two pieces which they had taken from the Dutch, and a number of prisoners. We suppose the number of troops in that place to have amounted to between 5 and 6,000, ours were short of 1,200.[74]

The 'Officer of the Guards' described the action in more detail, although given that Lieutenant and Captain Edwin Hewgill of the Coldstream Guards, the likely author, was the Duke of York's Military Secretary,[75] it is perhaps unlikely that he witnessed the events he described:[76]

The brigade instantly moved forwards to a large bean field in the rear of the village, in which the crop had grown up so high, that it prevented the troops at first perceiving in what direction to proceed. They were, however, very soon relieved from their uncertainty, and saluted by a brisk discharge of grapeshot from some batteries in their front... the men were formed in line, as regularly as circumstances and the nature of the ground would permit, and unappalled by the incessant showers of grape-shot, which descended amongst them, thinning their ranks at every fresh discharge, they rushed on, cheering each other with repeated loud huzza's, and leaping the ditches in front of the very embraisseurs [sic] from whence the pieces of artillery were vomiting forth the dreadful harbingers of death, instantaneously entered the different batteries ere their enemies were able to escape.

At the point of the bayonet, they drove them through the village and thus, in less than half an hour, were in possession of their guns and recovered the different posts which by the Dutch had been so shamefully abandoned. General Lake convinced of the perilous situation of his troops, was extremely apprehensive, that their national spirit would urge them on in the pursuit, further than was prudent; and aware that the Republicans might rally, and perceive before what an inferior force they were by flight escaping, endeavoured to recall them, and at length recalled them assisted by the commanding officers of the separate battalions, Colonels Grinfield, Hulse and Pennington, who severally obtained great credit for their actions. The brigade then forming in a steady line with its centre in an orchard and its flanks in front of the village [on their left] and redoubts [on their right], in which the British artillery-men were posted, sustained for

---

74   Brown, *Impartial Journal*, p.65–66.

75   Stephen George Peregrine Ward, 'The Author of "An accurate and impartial narrative"', *Journal of the Society of Army Historical Research*, vol.LXX, 284, Winter 1992, pp.211–223 (p.216).

76   Burne, *Noble Duke*, p.68. However, Hewgill presumably went to Linselles with the Duke of York, arriving after the attack of the Guards was over.

some time a heavy cannonade, and were annoyed by a discharge of grape and round shot, putting them in a situation at all times irksome to the British, who cannot bear to stand on one spot to be pelted, as they term it, without a chance of returning their enemies the blows they deal them.

The French were then, however, on full march to Lille; and their field pieces were drawn up merely to cover their retreat. At one period their officers certainly intended to lead them back to the attack, as they had faced them round, and their orders issued to march on ('*marchez en avant*') could distinctly and repeatedly be heard. A party actually approached a position where a 6 pounder had fortunately been planted, covered by a detachment of the guards under Colonel Watson, of the Third Regiment, which gun by opening upon them with grapeshot, and when, (as for a moment was the case) its ammunition was expended, the party, by keeping up an incessant street fire,[77] obliged them to sheer off, and join their panic-struck companions.

A serjeant of the First Regiment of Guards, upon entering one of the redoubts, found planted there, a tricoloured Republican banner; and a French officer, who was endeavouring to remove it, instantly delivered up his sword, demanding quarter. The serjeant returned it, attentive only to the colours, which, when he was preparing to secure, the Frenchman aiming a blow at his hand, struck off two fingers, and attempted to escape; and he was punished by the bayonet of a British soldier, who had witnessed the transaction…

When the Guards were forming in the bean field under a tremendous fire of grapeshot, the French had fortunately elevated their guns, and they consequently did less execution than might naturally have been apprehended. In that field, however, most of the men who fell, received their wounds.[78]

These accounts demonstrate the utility of the battalion guns, they clearly provided cover for the battalions as they advanced under fire and then advanced with the battalions to and beyond the redoubts.

The Guards drove the French beyond the village towards Bondues, but this was not the end of the fighting. Jourdan rallied the *demi-brigade* centred on the 1/45e Régiment Infanterie de Ligne, together with the 2e Volontaires de Paris, from Béru's command and led them back towards the village.

In his report to Houchard, the army commander, Jourdan wrote:

---

77   William Duane, *A Military Dictionary* (Philadelphia: Published by the Author, 1810), p.160: 'street fire' refers to defile fire, where the party is formed in depth with enough room on the flanks for the men at the front to file to the rear to reload.

78   Anon., *An Officer of the Guards*, pp.69–72.

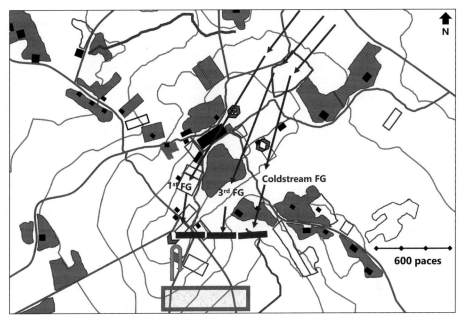

Map Ten: The Guards attack. (© Garry Wills 2022)

Having learned that the posts of Lincelles and Blaton had been forced and that the troops occupying them were retired on Wambrechies. I decided to march with a *demi-brigade* on this last-named post to be better positioned to give the necessary help.

General Béru having warned me that the enemy had abandoned the attacks of Bondues and Mouveaux, we decided to attack Le Blaton and Lincelles. This attack took place at four o'clock in the evening, in three columns, one coming from Le Quesnoi [Quesnoi sur Deûle], the second from Wambrechies and the third from Bondues. Despite the enemy's formidable artillery, these two posts were furiously taken with heroic courage, and we took from the enemy a large amount of artillery and made many prisoners.

At the moment when General Béru entered Lincelles with his column and when he gave orders to occupy all the posts, the enemy reappeared; and I don't know by what chance, a panicked terror took hold of our victorious troops, and in the end they disbanded; It was not a retreat, it was a rout.

I left my *demi-brigade* in line of battle outside the village and I managed to rally it and, while General Béru rallied his troops that had withdrawn on Bondues, I re-attacked Lincelles. I managed to get in, but I could not seize it entirely, so the night necessitated a retreat, which was made in good order to Wambrechies.

We took from the enemy, on this day, which would have been brilliant for the troops and advantageous for the Republic, eleven cannon and a few caissons and made about two hundred men prisoners. The enemy may have lost about five hundred men; but in the rout that took place, we lost seven pieces of cannon; and this had much to do with the limber drivers who, to save themselves more quickly, cut their traces, as the artillery of my *demi-brigade* had not entered the village. I cannot forget the *Représentant du Peuple*, Levasseur, who was present at the affair, and he has infinitely contributed by rallying the troops. Our loss is not as considerable by far as that of the enemy.[79]

Levasseur's bravery was detailed elsewhere:

Représentant Levasseur, whose personal courage was indomitable and who, although a surgeon in his first career, took part in the action and showed rare military skills; too carried away by a desire to save a piece of artillery, he was summoned by three Englishmen to surrender but replied that a deputy never surrendered and had the good fortune to escape them.[80]

Lieutenant Colonel en seconde Pierre Guillaume Gratien[81] earned his promotion to *général de brigade* during the French counterattack when he:

[R]allied the half-battalion [2e Volontaires de Paris] he commanded, had the charge beaten and, despite the cannon and musket fire, retook the redoubts in front of Linselles and advanced almost halfway through the village from where the battalion would have driven the English if they had not been relieved, as he had been fighting the enemy for five hours and did

---

79   SHD B1 17, 136: *Général de Division* Jean Nicolas Houchard, commander in chief of the Armée du Nord, until he was guillotined on 17 November 1793 for alleged 'cowardice' due to his handling of the Battle of Hondschoote.

80   Paul Foucart and Jules Finot, *La Défense National dans le Nord de 1792–1802* (Lille: Lefebvre-Ducrocq, 1893), vol.II, p.26; taken from a letter by *Représentant en Mission* Pierre-Louis Bentabole, dated 21 August, reproduced in *Le Moniteur* on 23 August 1793.

81   Crowdy, *Handbook*, p.12; the rank of *lieutenant colonel* was suppressed in favour of *chef de bataillon* during 1793. He later fought at Sobral and Fuentes de Oñoro in the Peninsular, in Russia in 1812 and in Italy in 1814.

not cease until nightfall, when he made a quiet retreat having received no support.[82]

The Duke of York reported Jourdan's counterattack to the King, 'having received some reinforcements, however, they attempted to attack the village again, but were repulsed with great loss.'[83]

The diary of Lieutenant Thomas Powell of the 14th Foot records the march of the reinforcements sent by the Duke of York and the Prince of Orange:

> Encamped at Menin, Sun. the 18th and march at 7 o'clock the same evening, without having anything to eat, to Lincelles to support the Prince of Orange and the Dutch, who had attacked the place with 10,000 men, but were not able to carry it. In our going we met the Dutch retreating in the greatest confusion, so much so, that we were obliged to make our men make sure of their arms to prevent ourselves from being trod to death. After we passed them, not a single man attempted to return to go with us.
>
> It was about 1 o'clock at night before we could get clear of the Dutch, when we marched on and took the enemy completely by surprise, they not thinking they should be attacked again that night after beating the Dutch.
>
> General Lake commanded and distributed his troops to so much advantage, that with about one third the number to what the enemy were, we stormed and carried their works with about the loss of 200 killed and wounded on our side, and about 700 killed and wounded and taken prisoners on the side of the enemy. After taking their works, we were under arms till 8 o'clock in the morning, when we were allowed to sit down and rest ourselves. As a vast number of the enemy had taken shelter in the houses when we went over their works, I and two or three more of the officers went round the village to see what number had been killed and there was not a house or a room in any of the houses that was not filled with dead bodies, even in the cellars and up in the garrets they were bayonetted by our men.
>
> I got my French dog, Carmagnole [title of song sung by the revolutionaries] in a room where there was a French officer and four men lying dead. The dog was lying by the officer, who I supposed to be his master, it was with great difficulty I could get him away. However, he soon became as much attached to me as ever he was to his late master and proved a very

82 A. Lievyns, Jean-Maurice Verdot, Pierre Bégat, *Fastes de la Légion-d'honneur: biographie de tous les décorés* (Paris: Le Bureau d'Administration, 1845), vol.III, p.252.

83 Burne, *Noble Duke*, p.68.

faithful servant. We took 11 pieces of cannon and returned at 2 o'clock in the evening.[84]

The times in Powell's diary are somewhat inconsistent with other sources; if we accept that the Dutch garrisons of Linselles and Le Blaton were heading back to Menen at or before 3:00 p.m. then it seems unlikely that Powell was still passing them at 1:00 a.m. on the 19th. The march to Menen is only six miles and the Dutch garrisons should have therefore been back in Menen by 7:00 p.m. about the time Powell says he was leaving. Likewise, Powell's arrival in Linselles at 1:00 a.m. suggests that the reinforcements marched at only one mile per hour. However, while Brown has the reinforcements arriving after 10:00 p.m., given that he also recorded that the Guards arrived back at Geluwe at 3:00 a.m., the reinforcements must have arrived at Linselles not later than 11:00 p.m, when the Guards would have departed.[85] Powell also implied that his regiment was part of the force fighting at Linselles, but the French had left the area long before his stated arrival. However, Powell's return to camp at Menen between 8:00 a.m. and 2:00 p.m. on 19 August is consistent with other sources which describe the destruction of the entrenchments by the Hessian troops during that morning.[86]

Casualties

Adjutant General James Murray reported the Guards' casualties as:

> First Regiment: two sergeants, 19 rank and file killed; two captains, three lieutenants, two sergeants and 42 rank and file. A total of 70 men.
> Coldstream Regiment: one captain and eight rank and file killed; one captain, one lieutenant, one ensign, two sergeants and 43 rank and file wounded. A total of 57 men.
> Third Regiment: one drummer and seven rank and file killed; one lieutenant, one ensign, two sergeants and 43 rank and file wounded. A total of 55 men.
> Royal Artillery: one lieutenant and one rank and file killed; three rank and file wounded. A total of five men.

The officers killed and wounded were named as:

84 National Army Museum (NAM), London, Accession: 1976–07–45; diary of Lieutenant (later Captain) Thomas Powell (14th Foot).
85 Brown, *Impartial Journal*, p.67.
86 Hoyer, *Neues Militarische Magazin*, 1801, vol.II, pt.2, pp.39–40.

First Regiment: Colonel [Francis] D'Oyley, Colonel [Kingsmill] Evans (later died of wounds),[87] Captain [William Caulfield] Archer, Captain [George] Bristow, Captain [Arthur] Whetham wounded.

Coldstream Regiment: Lieutenant Colonel [Thomas] Bosville killed; Lieutenant Colonel [Isaac] Gascoyne, Ensign [Henry] Bayley, wounded.

Third Regiment: Captain [David] Cunnynghame wounded.

Royal Artillery: Lieutenant [James] de Peyster killed.[88]

Major William Congreve, who commanded the Duke of York's artillery reported the captured French artillery as two '9-pounders' and seven '6-pounders' plus six 'tumbril waggons' of ammunition, in addition to two recaptured Dutch guns.[89] Congreve was clearly converting the weight of shot to the British measurement. The *Représentant en Mission* René Levasseur confirmed that the French lost two 8-pounders and six 4-pounders.[90] Murray also reported that the French suffered 300 casualties as well as the 11 guns captured.[91] Dupuis has the casualties on both sides, including the Dutch, as 1,000 killed and wounded and 200 prisoners, while the *Neues Militarische Magazin* gave the French casualties for 18 August as 1,200 men.[92]

The Aftermath

The day after the action, 19 August 1793, the Duke of York issued an order:

His Royal Highness the Commander-in-Chief returns his warmest thanks to Major-General Lake, Colonels Hulse, Greenfield, Pennington, Major Wright, and the officers and men belonging to the brigade of Guards and artillery under his command, for the gallantry and intrepidity they so evidently showed in the attack of the French redoubts yesterday afternoon.[93]

---

87   *Saunders's News-Letter*, 1 October 1793.

88   *London Gazette Extraordinary*, 13560, 22 August 1793, p.711; the officers are here named with their rank in the Army. For example, the two captains wounded in the First Guards are Colonels D'Oyley and Evans, while Lieutenant and Captain George Bristow is counted as a lieutenant. First names from 1793 *Army List*.

89   *London Gazette Extraordinary*, 13560, 22 August 1793, pp.711.

90   Levasseur, *Memoires*, vol.II, p.37.

91   *London Gazette Extraordinary*, 13560, 22 August 1793, pp.709–711.

92   Dupuis, *Valenciennes*, p.217; Hoyer, *Neues Militarische Magazin*, 1801, vol.II, pt.2, p.38.

93   Daniel MacKinnon, *Origin and Services of the Coldstream Guards* (London: Richard Bentley, 1833), vol. II, pp.43–44.

The position at Linselles was abandoned on the same day, after the entrenchments had been razed to the ground.[94]

Following the action at Linselles, Béru was promoted to *général de division* by the *Représentants en mission* Levasseur and Bentabole. His new rank was confirmed on 19 September 1793, and he was appointed commander of the division at Lille. At the news of the suspension of noble officers by the Convention, he resigned 1 October 1793 before being suspended 9 October and he was subsequently replaced by *Général de Brigade* Joseph Souham.

In March 1794, the men of Brigade of Guards who had served at Linselles received a reward for their gallantry; 21 shillings for a sergeant, 14 shillings and three pence for a corporal; nine shillings and nine pence for a private.[95]

However, the euphoria around the Guards victory has not been universally accepted. Ditfurth, for one, felt that Lake's direct approach was unsubtle and did not recognise the opportunity offered by the open nature of the rear of the redoubts.[96]

In 1811,[97] the Guards regiments were given the battle honour 'LINCELLES', the earliest such honour of the French Revolutionary and Napoleonic Wars.[98] An affair of posts, which had little effect on the campaign was thus raised to the status of the final battle honour of the Napoleonic Wars 'WATERLOO'.

Conclusions

In terms of the narrative of the battle, the key point to emphasise is that the Guards regiments approached Linselles from the northeast via the direct route from Geluwe across the pontoon bridge near Bousbecque.

The Dutch garrison of Linselles was much maligned by the British, following a pattern of negativity that continued throughout the campaign; however, on this occasion, *Majoor Generaal* van Nostitz's troops faced three times their own numbers attacking from two directions, and they lost 17 percent of their numbers. Nostitz himself was mortally wounded.

The fighting spirit of the Dutch soldiers is perhaps better exemplified by Cadet Wybrand Adriaan De Jongh of the De Schepper Infanterie Regiment Nr.1. He fought at Linselles during the French assault, before becoming separated from his unit in the retreat. Meeting with the British Guards on their way to Linselles, he volunteered to join them in the counterattack. Following the successful assault, he

94   Hoyer, *Neues Militarische Magazin*, 1801, vol.II, pt.2, p.39.
95   Hamilton, *First Guards*, vol.II, p.296.
96   Ditfurth, *Die Hessen*, vol.I, p.79.
97   Ian Sumner, *British Colours & Standards 1747–1881* (Oxford: Osprey, 2001), p.21.
98   Iain Gordon, *Bloodline, the Origins and Development of the Regular Formations of the British Army* (Barnsley: Pen & Sword Military, 2010), p.162; LINCELLES was chronologically the first honour, but not the first to be awarded.

joined the van Welderen Infanterie Regiment, which had been dispatched by the Prince of Orange to reinforce the post.[99]

The spelling of the battle honour LINCELLES most probably reflects that of a contemporary map of the local area, rather than a 'mistake' by the Duke of York.

Acknowledgements

I would particularly like to acknowledge five individuals who have helped and encouraged this project. Paul Demet has both encouraged this project and provided photographs of key sources from the French archives at Vincennes. Geert van Uythoven has also encouraged the project and materially helped by both providing his own research and pointing me to the key Dutch and German sources. Dr Yolande Hodson has significantly helped with the background and interpretation of the Royal Collection map and the mysteries of eighteenth-century map making. I would also like to mention Jan Bruinen whose online work includes extensive information on the Dutch army of the period. Finally, my wife Susan patiently toured the battlefield with me and took some important photographs.

Bibliography

Archival Sources

National Army Museum (NAM), London, Accession: 1976–07–45; diary of Lieutenant (later Captain) Thomas Powell (14th Foot).
Royal Collection Trust, Windsor, RCIN 735016.a, *Attack of Lincelles, 18th Augt. 1793.*
Service Historique de la Défense, Paris, SHD B1 17, *Armée du Nord Correspondence, 16 –31 Août.*
The National Archives, WO1/166 p.755; *Letter dated Menin 19th August 1793.*

Online Resources

Anon., *Biografisch Woordenboek van Nederland: 1780-1830*, accessed 10 May 2020, available at <http://resources.huygens.knaw.nl/bwn1780-1830/lemmata/data/Van%20Merlen>.

---

99 Bruno Indekeu and Marco Bijl, *Mars et Historia, Nederlandse Vereniging voor Militaire Historie*, vol.XLVI, 1, 2012, p.5; Marco Bijl, 'History and Organisation of the Dutch 8th Militia Battalion', *Napoleon Series*, at https://www.napoleon-series.org/military-info/organization/Dutch/8thMilitia/c_dejongh.html, accessed 21 January 2020; both contain a biography of Wybrand Adriaan de Jongh.

Bijl, Marco, 'History and Organisation of the Dutch 8th Militia Battalion', *Napoleon Series*, available at <https://www.napoleon-series.org/military-info/organization/Dutch/8thMilitia/c_dejongh.html.>

Brayard, Laurent and Davin, Didier, *Les troupes Belges et Liégeoises sous la Révolution, 1792–1803* (SEHRI, 2017), available at <http://assosehri.fr/bibliothequemili/les-troupes-belges-de-1792-1803.pdf>.

Carte d' État-major and the Cassini map via Géoportail at <https://www.geoportail.gouv.fr/>.

Le Rouge map, *La chatellenie de Lille et le bailliage de Tournay* at <https://www.flickr.com/photos/britishlibrary/50263216008>.

Marin, Marco, 'The Sacralization of Politics in the Political Catechisms of the French Revolution', 2014, available at <https://www.academia.edu/8547499/The_Sacralization_of_Politics_in_the_Political_Catechisms_of_the_French_Revolution>.

Leuridan, Theodore, *Histoire de Linselles* (Lille: L.Danel, 1883) at <http://www.caue-nord.com/SPASSDATA/ALGEDIM/QOKQWR/D325/D32525.pdf>.

Uythoven, Geert van, 'The Dutch Army of 1793-1794', *Napoleon Series*, at <https://www.napoleon-series.org/military-info/organization/c_dutch.html>.

Books and Periodicals

Anon., *An accurate and impartial narrative of the war by an officer of the Guards in 2 volumes* (London: Cadell and Davies, 1796).

Anon., *Nieuwe Nederlandsche Jaarboeken* (Leiden: P. van der Eyk and D. Vygh; Amsteldam: J. van der Burgh, 1793).

Aa, A.J. van der, *Biographisch woordenboek der Nederlanden*, Deel 2, Eerste en tweede stuk (Haarlen: J.J. van Beederode,1854).

Adye, Ralph Willett, *The Bombardier and Pocket Gunner* (London: T. Egerton, 1813).

Bas, François de, *Prins Frederik der Nederlanden en zijn tijd* (Schiedam: Roelants, 1887).

Brown, Robert, *An impartial journal of a detachment from the brigade of Foot Guards commencing 25th February 1793 and ending 9th May 1795* (Godmanchester: Ken Trotman 2006).

Brown, Steve, *The Duke of York's Flanders Campaign: Fighting the French Revolution 1793-1795* (Barnsley: Frontline, 2018).

Burne, Alfred Higgins, *The Noble Duke of York* (London: Staples Press, 1949).

Chassin, L. and Hennet, L., *Les Volontaires Nationaux pendant la Revolution* (Paris: Cerf, Noblet and Quantin, 1902).

Chuquet, Arthur, *Les Guerres de la Révoluion XI Hondschoote* (Paris: Léon Chailley, 1896).

Crossard, Jean Baptiste Louis, Baron de, *Mémoires militaires et historiques pour servir à l'histoire de la guerre depuis 1792 jusqu'en 1815 inclusivement* (Paris: Migneret, 1829).

Crowdy, Terry, *Napoleon's Infantry Handbook* (Barnsley: Pen and Sword Military, 2015).

Cruyplants, Eugène, *Dumouriez dans les ci-devant Pays Bas Autrichiens* (Bruxelles: A. de Boeck, 1912).

Del Campo, Willem Jacobus, *Het leven en de krijgsbedrijven van David Hendrik Baron Chassé, in leven Generaal der Infanterie, oud lid der Staten-Generaal, Grootkruis der Militaire Willemsorde, Officier van het Legioen van Eer van Frankrijk* ('s Hertogenbosch: Muller, 1849).

Dellard, Jean-Pierre, *Mémoires Militaires du Général Baron Bellard* (Paris: Libraire Illustrée, 1892).

Deyster, Hendrik van der, *Naamregister der heeren militaire officieren* (Leiden: Published by the Author, 1742 and 1746).

Ditfurth, Maximilian Joseph Carl von, *Die Hessen in den Feldzügen von 1793, 1794 und 1795 in Flandern* (Kassel: J.Bohné, 1893).

Duane, William, *A Military Dictionary* (Philadelphia: Published by the Author, 1810).

Dupuis, Victor, *La campagne de 1793 à l'armée du Nord et des Ardennes, De Valenciennes à Hondtschoote* (Paris: R. Chapelot et Cie, 1906).

Foucart, Paul and Finot, Jules, *La Défense National dans le Nord de 1792–1802* (Lille: Lefebvre-Ducrocq, 1893).

Gordon, Iain, *Bloodline, the Origins and Development of the Regular Formations of the British Army* (Barnsley: Pen and Sword, 2010).

Hamilton, Sir Frederick William, *History and Origins of the First Regiment of Foot Guards* (London: J. Murray, 1874).

Harrington, Peter (ed.), *With the Guards in Flanders, the diary of Captain Roger Morris 1793–1795* (Solihull: Helion, 2018).

Haverfield J. and Hofmann H., *Scharnhorst's Military Field Pocket Book*, 1811 (Uckfield: Naval and Military Press, 2009).

Hoyer, Johann Gottfried von, *Neues Militarische Magazin*, (Leipzig: Baumgärtnerischen Buchhandlung, 1801).

Hugo, Abel, *France Militaire. Histoire des Armées de Terre et de Mer, 1792 –1832* (Paris: Delloye, 1835).

Hussey, John, *Waterloo; the Campaign of 1815 from Elba to Ligny and Quatre Bras* (London: Greenhill Books, 2017).

Jomini, Antoine Henri, *Histoire Critique et Militaire des Campagnes de la Révolution*, vol. IV *Campagne de 1793 — Seconde Période* (Paris: Magimel, Anselin et Pochard, 1819).

Levasseur, René, *Mémoires de R. Levasseur* (Paris: Rapilly, 1829).

Lievyns, A. and Verdot, Jean-Maurice and Bégat, Pierre, *Fastes de la Légion-d'honneur: biographie de tous les décorés* (Paris: Le Bureau d'Administration, 1845).

MacKinnon, Daniel, *Origin and Services of the Coldstream Guards* (London: Richard Bentley, 1833).

Maurice, Frederick, *The History of the Scots Guards* (London: Chatto and Windus, 1934).

Pearse, Hugh Wodehouse, *Memoir of the life and military services of Viscount Lake, Baron Lake of Delhi and Laswaree, 1744–1808* (London: William Blackwood, 1908).

Rousset, Camille (ed.), *Recollections of Marshal Macdonald, Duke of Tarentum* (London: Bentley, 1893).

Sumner, Ian, *British Colours and Standards 1747–1881* (Oxford: Osprey, 2001).

Uythoven, Geert van, 'Dutch Generals of the Napoleonic Wars, Herman Willem Daendels, Marshal of Holland', *First Empire*, 39, 1998, pp.4–11.

Uythoven, Geert van, 'Intermezzo 1787–1793: The Dutch during the Revolutionary Wars –5', *First Empire*, 56, 2001, pp.24–30.

Uythoven, Geert van, 'Legion Franche Étrangère', *First Empire*, 76, 2004, pp.21-25.

Verney, Sir Harry (ed.), *The Journals and Correspondence of General Sir Harry Calvert* (London: Hurst and Blackett, 1853).

Ward, Stephen George Peregrine, 'The Author of "An accurate and impartial narrative"', in the *Journal of the Society of Army Historical Research*, vol.LXX, 284, Winter 1992, pp.211–223.

Whinyates, Francis Arthur, *The Wright Letters: being a collection of letters written by Major J. Wright, R.A., and others, during the Duke of York's campaigns in the Low Countries, 1793–4* (London: Eyre, 1902).

Wills, Garry David, *British Battalion Guns*, in Stephen Summerfield (ed.), *Smoothbore Ordnance Journal* (Huntingdon: Ken Trotman, 2013), vol.VI, pp.81–96.

Periodicals

Gazette (London), 22 August 1793.
Saunders's News-Letter, 1 October 1793.

4

'By Beat of Drum, or Otherwise': Assessing Recruitment to the Fencible Regiments, 1793-1802

Rory Butcher

When war came to Britain's shores in 1793 one of the major challenges faced by the British government was the practicality of protecting Britain in the event of French invasion. In England and Wales, the Militia was the well-established method of raising men for military service outside of the regular Army. Militiamen were raised via the compulsion of the ballot system, with counties required to administer and control these regiments for the duration of hostilities.[1] Each regiment's size was relative to the regional population. Because of this, the practical administration of these regiments lay with the county leadership.[2] Ireland utilised a similar Militia system, which was introduced in March 1793.[3] The Yeomanry, and Volunteer Corps, more amateur organisations, also operated in England and Ireland, although they were civilian forces – not military. The Yeomanry was particularly popular with the Irish gentry, who utilised their predominantly Protestant troops of cavalry to protect their own property from

---

1   Paul Langford, *Public Life and the Propertied Englishman, 1689-1798* (Oxford: Clarendon Press, 1991), p.296.

2   J. R. Western, *The English Militia in the Eighteenth Century: The Story of a Political Issue 1660-1802* (London: Routledge and Kegan Paul, 1965); Matthew McCormack, *Embodying the Militia in Georgian England* (Oxford: University Press, 2015) are both crucial to understanding this force.

3   Suggestions for further reading include: Neal Garnham, *The Militia in Eighteenth-Century Ireland: In Defence of the Protestant Interest* (Woodbridge: The Boydell Press, 2012); Henry McAnally, *The Irish Militia, 1793-1816* (Dublin: Clonmore and Reynolds, 1949); Ivan Nelson, *The Irish Militia, 1793-1802: Ireland's Forgotten Army* (Dublin: Four Courts Press, 2007).

unrest.[4] This network of home defence forces was therefore wide reaching, but far from complete. There was also a deep concern about the need for more men to be under arms, which was particularly extensive in Ireland following mixed experiences with the Protestant Volunteer Movement during the American War of Independence.[5]

Scotland had long resisted the ballot as a method of enlisting men into the military.[6] Instead, notable Scottish magnates were asked to raise regiments of men from their spheres of influence – these were the regiments of Fencibles, the name deriving from the word 'defensible'. Unlike the Militia, they were to be exclusively recruited from volunteers. Unlike the regular Army, they were not to be sent abroad.[7] They were to serve full time for the duration of the war, and upon a declaration of peace would be disembodied and the regiments discontinued. The initial cohort of Fencible infantry was Scottish, and, owing to the scheme's regional popularity over the following decade, 44 infantry battalions, from a total of 59, were raised in Scotland.[8] Conversely only 14 of the 34 Fencible cavalry regiments were raised in Scotland, and as a result the Fencibles were present across the whole of Britain in one form or another. What had been created was the beginnings of a territorial defence force – they were to serve locally, but were to wear a regular uniform, be paid like the regulars, and follow the Army's regulations. And, most notably, although they may have been raised by the propertied classes in Scotland, England, or Ireland, they fell under the *de jure* control of the regular military establishment.

However, because they were neither officially part of any established regiment of foot or horse, nor under the designation of the other auxiliary branches of the military, the Fencible regiments have attracted comparatively little attention compared to the aforementioned 'amateur' elements. Historiography of the period is plentiful, with particular recent focus given to the Volunteer Movement post-1803, and a large body of work considering the Irish Militia in the wake of the bicentennial of the 1798 Rising.[9] Yet the Fencibles often find themselves mentioned

4   Allan Blackstock, *An Ascendancy Army: The Irish Yeomanry, 1796-1814* (Dublin: Four Courts Press, 1998), pp.270-271.

5   Blackstock, *An Ascendancy Army*, pp.43-49.

6   John Robertson, *The Scottish Enlightenment and the Militia Issue* (Edinburgh: John Donald Publishers Ltd., 1985), pp.15-16; John Sinclair, *Considerations on Militias and Standing Armies*, Reprint (London: Forgotten Books, 2018), pp.21-23. This latter, written in 1782, gives Fencibles as an alternative to the Militia.

7   National Army Museum Archive (NAMA): 1971-12-22: 'Enlistment Form, 29 Oct 1794; Belonging to John Taylor, Royal Lancashire Volunteers, Formerly a Weaver', 1794.

8   Allan L. Carswell, 'The Scottish Fencible Regiments in Ireland', *The Irish Sword*, 21 (1998), pp.155-159, p.155; Charles J. Esdaile, 'The French and Revolutionary Wars, 1793-1815' in Jeremy A. Crang et al (eds), *A Military History of Scotland* (Edinburgh: Edinburgh University Press, 2012), pp.407-435, at p.414.

9   Suggestions for further reading include: Austin Gee, *The British Volunteer Movement 1794-1814* (Oxford: Clarendon Press, 2003); Thomas Bartlett et al (eds), *1798: A Bicentenary Perspective* (Dublin: Four

only in passing in histories of the home defence apparatus, and normally in relation to their Highland origins.[10] Cookson's *The British Armed Nation* (1997) is the
only recent publication to make a concerted effort to consider them in light of the
larger question of Scotland's relationship with Britain.

This chapter is by way of an introduction to the Fencibles at large. It will first
detail the circumstances in the 1790s which led the government to re-establish the
Fencible corps in Britain, and to explain the principles which entailed their formation. It will then discuss key aspects of the mechanisms by which the Fencibles were
recruited, particularly considering the similarities to the other branches of the
military. This research has focused on the experience of the Fencible infantry, so
as to consider the relevance of the emphasis placed on clanship by Henry Dundas,
first Home Secretary and then Secretary of State for War in Pitt the Younger's
administration. In keeping with this topic, this chapter will conclude by considering the formation and demographics of the 1st, Grant, or Strathspey, Fencibles –
they were a regiment of Fencible infantry, raised in Scotland, and drawn primarily
from one magnate's sphere of influence. Given that not all Fencibles were of Scots
origin, the choice of the Grant Fencibles as a case study enables examination of
the practical effects of Dundas' faith in the Highland Clans to enlist men. The
Fencible corps were not a Highland endeavour in their entirety, but the experience of the Grant Regiment nonetheless offers significant insight into this more
famous aspect of their service. By examining the Fencibles in both the abstract
and the specific, this chapter will explain how several of the key elements of the
Fencible regiments came into being – and why they warrant further investigation.
As an anomaly in the British tradition of amateur soldiery, they were created to
solve a particular issue which confronted the military establishment in 1793. Yet
the Fencible regiments also provide a window into the relationship between the
Scottish nobility and the British government, which the other auxiliary branches
of the military do not.

Introducing the Fencibles

Prior to 1803, the home defence apparatus in Britain was more fragmented than it
later became during the Napoleonic Wars, with a variety of forces serving across
the British Isles. Yet an understanding of its operation is crucial to the context of
the introduction of the Fencibles.

The English Militia had been introduced in 1757, with the commencement of the
Seven Years War, to provide for the protection of England and Wales during the

Courts Press, 2003); Thomas Bartlett and Keith Jeffrey (eds), *A Military History of Ireland* (Cambridge:
Cambridge University Press, 1997).

10   John Fortescue, *A History of the British Army* (London: MacMillan and Co. Limited, 1915), Vol.4, p.83.

period of conflict. This force enlisted the rank and file through the ballot, although the practice of purchasing a substitute to take one's place invariably left the very poorest in the embodied battalions. The officers were required to meet a stringent set of property requirements, or qualifications. These criteria was initially intended to ensure that those with a vested stake in the nation were responsible for its defence, but with a shortage of men willing to fill the roles the qualifications were eased over the following decades. By the 1790s, the social elites who traditionally held these positions were increasingly replaced by the sons of merchants, who had begun to attain the necessary income to meet the qualifications.[11] Those who served in Militia regiments were full-time soldiers during periods of war, but were administered by the county authorities under the guidance of the Lord Lieutenant.[12]

With hostilities unfolding in Europe, the English counties began mobilising their regiments in late 1792, and the Irish parliament in Dublin soon passed the legislation to create its own Militia in 1793. Ireland's version of the Militia was reliant on the English model – but crucially did not require the rank and file to be Protestant. In fact, this appears to have not even been considered until after the Militia Act had begun its passage through Parliament.

These military branches were supplemented from 1794 onwards by the 'amateur' auxiliary branches – the Volunteers and the Yeomanry. They both operated on a part-time basis, with their recruits expected to have an external income to supplement the fact that they were only paid when active and required. [13] The Volunteers were nominally formed to protect Britain from the Revolutionary threat. Although an ideological loyalty to the government was present for many, historian Linda Colley has concluded that English Volunteers may have been more concerned for local protection than national defence.[14] The Yeomanry was predominantly cavalry, to enable it to release the regular cavalry from its garrison duties, and its form varied across Britain.[15] In England, those who formed corps of Yeomanry were of the 'yeoman' class; that is to say that they were men of standing and moderate wealth, and who might previously have enlisted into the Militia before its property qualifications were lowered.[16] In Ireland, the Yeomanry was a largely Protestant force – in some cases little more than private armies to protect the gentry's interests.[17]

---

11   Langford, *Public Life*, pp.296-304.

12   Western, *The English Militia*, pp.130, 304.

13   Kevin Linch, "'A Citizen and Not a Soldier": The British Volunteer Movement and the War against Napoleon', in Alan Forrest, et al (eds), *Soldiers, Citizens and Civilians: Experiences and Perceptions of the Revolutionary and Napoleonic Wars, 1790-1820* (Basingstoke: Palgrave MacMillan, 2009), pp.205-221, at p.212.

14   Linda Colley, *Britons: Forging the Nation 1707-1837*, 4th edn (New Haven and London: Yale University Press, 2019), pp.192-196.

15   Cookson, *The British Armed Nation*, p.27-28.

16   Langford, *Public Life*, pp.302-304.

17   Blackstock, *An Ascendancy Army*, pp.98-99, 138-139.

In the eighteenth century, there was no Militia in Scotland. Events of recent years had proven to Westminster that Scottish loyalty was not to be assumed. Enforced military service was also not popular in Scotland, and involuntary enlistment during the early-period Highland Clearances had further exacerbated this opposition.[18] This opposition was accompanied by a fear of losing large numbers of young men from a society with a strong labour economy – which did eventually happen when the Scottish Militia was introduced in 1797.[19] To resolve this, in 1757, instead of a Militia the suggestion was made to ask nobles who were known to be loyal supporters of the Hanoverian succession to raise their own units.[20] These two Fencible regiments successfully fulfilled their purpose of freeing up regular soldiers for overseas service and, following the success of a further five units raised during the American War of Independence, the concept soon became the *de facto* solution to the fundamental distrust of a Scottish Militia, by both the people and the government.

When war with France came in 1793, the question of Scottish home defence was raised once more. Before being given his posting as Secretary of State for War, a cabinet position created for him, Henry Dundas' tenure as Home Secretary made him key to Pitt the Younger's ministry – but also to the government of Scotland. His network of patronage, through which he gained and sought favours from the Scottish elite, gained him a position as one of the most powerful men in the country.[21] As a political manager, he understood the importance of his chain of influence and regularly worked in the interests of his political allies; the Fencibles offered an opportunity to extend his influence beyond its current boundaries. The Scottish magnates chosen to lead the way in raising their own regiments were therefore either close allies of Dundas, or those who held exclusive power in their domains and were those over whom Dundas sought to gain influence.[22] In the cases of the Argyll, Sutherland, and Manx regiments, their commanders were those asked in previous decades to provide Fencibles.[23]

As a solution to the lack of Militia, there were several key distinctions between the Fencibles and their Militia cousins. The first of these, of course, was that

---

18 Christopher A. Whatley, *Scottish Society 1707-1830: Beyond Jacobitism, towards Industrialisation* (Manchester and New York: Manchester University Press, 2000), p.111.
19 Ian Beckett, *Britain's Part-Time Soldiers: The Amateur Military Tradition 1558-1945* (Barnsley: Pen & Sword Military, 2011), p.79; L.M. Cullen, 'Scotland and Ireland, 1600-1800: Their Role in the Evolution of British Society', in R.A. Houston and I.D. Whyte (eds), *Scottish Society 1500-1800* (Cambridge: Cambridge University Press, 1989), pp.226–244, at pp.238-240.
20 Western, *The English Militia*, p.164.
21 Ronald M. Sunter, *Patronage and Politics in Scotland, 1707-1832* (Edinburgh: John Donald Publishers Ltd., 1986), pp.134-136; Michael Fry, *The Dundas Despotism* (Edinburgh: Edinburgh University Press, 1992), p.129.
22 Cookson, *The British Armed Nation*, p.134.
23 David Stewart, *Sketches of the Character, Manners, and Present State of the Highlanders of Scotland: With Details of the Military Service of the Highland Regiments* (Edinburgh: Constable, 1825), Vol.2, pp.371-375.

the Fencible men were to be exclusively volunteers, so as to appeal to those who opposed the ballot. These volunteers were recruited in much the same way as the regular Army; the enlistment bounty, and proverbial shilling, were key in this effort. Recruitment parties, and posters, were also common. One early recruitment poster for the Argyll Fencibles bears an almost identical resemblance to those used for the regular Army, and uses the same language – promising freedom from 'toiling and sweating' in civilian employment.[24] The rank and file Fencible men therefore appear to have broadly mirrored their regular cousins, although the 1795 cap of the enlistment bounty at 10 guineas per man, compared to the regulars' 15, demonstrates that the establishment did perceive a difference in quality.[25] Instructions issued to officers of the Argyll Fencibles noted that the quality of recruits may be lower than expected, as a result of the country already being 'much drained' of men by the regulars.[26]

Yet this reliance upon volunteers meant that the responsibility for filling the ranks was left with company commanders. With great pressure to complete the regiments as swiftly as possible, these officers were offered their commission, and seniority within their regiment, on the condition that they bring a required quota of men with them. Admittedly, it was then common for subalterns to also be expected to bring a quota. John Harley, later a regular officer, details being offered a lieutenancy in the Loyal Tarbert Fencibles provided he could 'raise or recruit fifteen men'.[27] Further incentives for this to be completed promptly tended to be financial, with a bounty given to each officer for every man he presented fit for service. This varied considerably; although less than five guineas appears to have been the norm, one example boasted of as much as 20 guineas per man.[28]

To improve the chances of returning enough recruits to the regiment, the Scottish Fencible regimental commanders were encouraged to make use of the now-waning clan infrastructure. Henry Dundas was one of those who believed that the clans were still capable of marshalling men behind their banner, and had a deep trust in the motivation for service which a clan leader's command would provide. Michael Fry's biography asserts that Dundas' interest in the Fencibles came from a deeper belief in the power the clans still held in Scotland, and that

24   National Library of Scotland (NLS): APS.4.94.15: 'G. R. Highest Bounty. To All Aspiring Heroes Bold...' 1795.
25   The National Archives (TNA): WO 1/617: 'Duke of York to Henry Dundas', 17 February 1795, f.231.
26   National Records of Scotland (NRS): GD3/9/12/8: 'Recruiting Instructions for Regiment of Fencible Men to Be Raised under the Command of Right Honourable Frederick Campbell as Colonel', n.d.
27   Gareth Glover (ed.), *The Veteran, or 40 Years' Service in the British Army: The Scurrilous Recollections of Paymaster John Harley, 47th Foot – 1798-1838* (Solihull: Helion & Company Limited, 2018), p.30.
28   British Library (BL): Cup.21.g.31/26: 'Sir, His Majesty Having Been Pleased to Appoint Me Colonel of a Corps of Fencibles, to Be Raised in Inverness, and the Neighbouring Counties, for the Internal Protection of North Britain, ...', 1793; NAMA: 1994-04-75: 'Three Letters Relating to the Efforts of Army Agents to Encourage Officers to Raise Fencible Regiments', No. 11 Cleveland Row, 9 December 1794.

they could still provide a ready source of manpower for the regulars in the years to come.[29]

The other key difference to the Militia was that the Fencibles were administered not by the counties, but by the War Office. Their pay and equipment were provided by the Government, and they operated under the King's Regulations.[30] They were operationally controlled by the War Office, such that when Henry Dundas began to centralise their operations around himself, it actually interfered with Army process.[31] Correspondence regarding promotions, over a number of years, includes the comment that 'the Secretary of War has no concern whatever in making Military Appointments', directing enquires to the Commander-in-Chief's office.[32]

However, unlike the regulars, the Fencibles were restricted to serve within specific conditions regarding location and duration. Fencibles were only to serve within designated areas, and only for the duration of the war. For the initial regiments, the men volunteered for service within Scotland alone, with the Manx battalion restricted to the island exclusively. As the scheme broadened in scope (and across the border into England), this widened into the British Isles more generally. As Cookson notes, this seems to have been the plan very soon after the initial surge – John Campbell, the Earl of Breadalbane and Holland, offered a third battalion in his regiment for service across Britain and Ireland as early as November 1794.[33] By the mid-1790s, most regiments appear to have adopted these terms as common practice. Deployment outside of their enlistment terms required the men to consent to the service extension, which severely limited the service of the initial seven regiments. This caused a particular issue when the time came for them to be garrisoned south of the border, in direct contradiction to their enlistments.[34]

Although several regiments of infantry did volunteer for posting overseas – notably the Banffshires spent several years in Gibraltar – Ireland was the base for a large proportion of the Fencibles during their service, outside of their home counties in England, Wales, and Scotland. As a result of this widespread deployment, many Fencible regiments were involved in the suppression of the United Irishmen's uprising and the French invasion. In the following years the establishment relied more heavily upon the Fencibles, as efforts were made to keep the

29   Fry, *The Dundas Despotism*, pp.231-232.

30   BL: 288.a.10.(4.): 'Certain Rules and Orders to Be Observed by the Corps of Fencible Infantry', 1794.

31   The National Archives (TNA): WO 4/1005: 'to John McLeod', 1st May 1795, f.111; WO 1/603: 'Henry Dundas to John Small', 8th December 1795, f.767.

32   TNA: WO 4/1006: 'M. Lewes to Robertson', 3 September 1799, f.300.

33   Cookson, *The British Armed Nation*, p.135; NRS: GD51/6/77/6: 'Lord Breadalbane; Permanent Rank of Lieutenant Colonel for Himself; Also Dealing with Fencible Matters', 1793.

34   John Prebble, *Mutiny: Highland Regiments in Revolt, 1743-1804* (London: Secker & Warburg, 1975), pp.276-277.

regular infantry away from Irish soil.[35] The army in Ireland was therefore largely comprised of Fencibles (at most, in November 1801, 60 percent), with Militia regiments in support.[36]

Yet it was also common for Fencible men to actively volunteer to transfer to the regulars. Lord Breadalbane reported interest from as many as 600 men in his regiment in late 1793, mere months after many had enlisted as Fencibles.[37] This appears to have become far more common throughout the decade, with returns detailing the transfers of men. By 1800 both Fencible and Militia regiments were being frequently used to supply the regulars with men.[38] Their relationship with the military establishment fluctuated during this period, but at its peak in October 1795, the Fencible infantry establishment comprised approximately 15 percent of the British military establishment.[39] Of those in uniform, more than one in 10 were in a Fencible infantry regiment. The Fencibles were therefore a source of manpower through which the regular infantry could be supplemented, either directly by men transferring, or indirectly with Fencible regiments undertaking garrison duties. Although the Fencibles provided an alternative to the Militia in Scotland, their continuation after the introduction of the Scottish Militia in 1797 is testament to the success of the scheme across Britain during the period.[40]

The Mechanisms of Recruitment

Before turning our attention to the particular example of the 1st, Grant, or Strathspey, Fencibles, it is important to further understand the practicalities of how the Fencible regiments were raised. As mentioned, company officers were expected to provide their companies with men; Campbell's recruiting orders even went as far as to suggest that the most successful would be offered seniority when 'their Commissions are made out'.[41] Yet, unlike the Militia, the Fencibles could not rely upon the property qualification to fill the officer corps – and so efforts were made to entice men into Fencible regiments through other means. This section of the chapter will also address the extent to which the historiographical emphasis of the Fencibles as a 'Highland' force has merit.

---

35   TNA: WO 17/1072 – WO 17/1073: Monthly Returns to the Adjutant General, Ireland, 1801-1802.
36   TNA: WO 17/1072 – WO 17/1073: Monthly Returns to the Adjutant General, Ireland, 1801-1802.
37   NRS: GD51/6/77/1-3: 'Lord Breadalbane', 1793.
38   TNA: WO 27/82: Adjutant General and Army Council: Inspection Returns, General, 1799; John Firebrace and Alan Rawlings, *His Majesty's Fraser Fencible Regiment of Foot 1794-1802* (Southsea: John Firebrace and Alan Rawlings; Don Miles, 1993), p.10; J.R. Western, 'The Recruitment of the Land Forces in Great Britain, 1793-99' (unpublished doctoral thesis, University of Edinburgh, 1953), pp.231-232.
39   TNA: WO 17/1159: Monthly Returns to the Adjutant General, General Returns, 1793-1795.
40   Fry, *The Dundas Despotism*, pp.232-233.
41   NRS: GD3/9/12/8: 'Recruiting Instructions for Regiment of Fencible Men…'.

Emulating the regulars, Fencible infantry regiments made use of recruiting parties to fill their rank and file establishment.[42] These were common throughout all regiments, and frequently remained in the regiment's home, even when the regiment was deployed away. Fencible infantry regiments which spent long periods garrisoned in certain locations, namely the Channel Islands and Ireland, would actively recruit from the local population. Inspection Returns from the period display a remarkable variety of nationality in several regiments. Table 1 includes the returns for several regiments which spent significant time garrisoned away from their home regions, with the percentage of men from outside the home region calculated.[43]

Table 1: Origins of the Men of the Banffshire, Loyal Limerick, Loyal Surrey, and Loyal Tarbet Fencibles, 1799-1801, noting the proportion of men recruited outside of the regiment's home region

Year	Regiment	Origin					Non-Home Locations Deployed	% of Non-Natives
		English	Scottish	Irish	Foreign	Total		
1799	Banffshire	124	195	224	0	543	England, Jersey, Gibraltar	64%
1800	Loyal Limerick	195	2	407	6	610	Guernsey	33%
1801	Loyal Surrey	201	39	322	0	562	Ireland, Nova Scotia	64%
	Loyal Tarbert	59	3	490	5	557	Guernsey	12%

This is not to suggest that regiments were inherently wedded to nationality as a focus for recruitment, and early recruitment orders are clear that regiments were to accept any who volunteered. Unlike the Militia, which had a mandate to enforce men into service as required, the Fencibles were reliant upon those willing to serve – which explains the lack of interest in maintaining a geographic recruitment base.

In a number of ways, the process by which Fencible officers gained rank and were promoted was much like the regulars. Officers were appointed and confirmed through the War Office, with regimental commanders given leeway to commission men within their own units.[44] Yet the example of the Militia also appears to have influenced how the Fencibles encouraged service as an officer. When civilians

---

42   TNA: WO 13: General Muster Books and Pay Lists, Fencible Infantry, 1793-1802; NAMA: 1977-03-04: 'Monthly Roll and Pay List of a Recruiting Party of the York Fencible Regiment of Infantry…', 1801.
43   TNA: WO 27/82-3: Adjutant General and Army Council: Inspection Returns, General, 1799-1800.
44   TNA: WO 4/1005: 'M. Lewis to Lieutenant Wynne', 1st April 1795, f.195.

became officers in the Militia, their financial compensation depended on the status of the Militia regiment – when embodied they received pay, and in peacetime they were responsible for the finances of their company. This policy derived from the expectation that these men would be men of property, and therefore able to sustain themselves financially. This caused two issues for Militia regiments: a high turnover in subalterns during peacetime, who were less able to support themselves without a salary; and opposition to the Militia being deployed outside of the county for long periods, as these men often had private affairs they feared neglecting.[45] The Militia also drew from unemployed regular officers on half-pay, through whom it was hoped that the force would be professionalised. Militia service by half-pay officers was encouraged by guaranteeing that, upon the disbanding of the regiment, the officer would resume their half-pay circumstances; they would gain the benefits of full-pay during the war, but would not be any worse off in peace. During the late 1770s a further provision was made that subalterns would receive their Army half-pay in addition to their Militia salary.[46]

Fencible regiments were, as previously stated, originally intended to be raised by a wealthy landowner or influential nobles. The expectation was that these men would use their networks of influence to fill much of the officer corps. With no property qualification, the subaltern ranks were open to men who may have been of no standing, but possessed of a personal connection to the commanding officer. This process was successful, but could leave the regiments without access to military experience. As a result, it became common practice to enlist regular officers from the half-pay list to bolster the core experience of the regiment. Much like the Militia, these men benefitted from the guarantee of returning to half-pay after the conflict. However, where the Militia's officers were of a class expected to be self-sufficient in peacetime, those civilians who enlisted into the Fencibles did not necessarily have the same income stream. The fact that Fencible officers were also not considered to hold permanent Army rank meant that, upon war ending, they would be rendered unemployed. Regular officers could return to half-pay, Fencible officers could not, and this did cause resentment between the two classes of officers. In one instance, officers from eight regiments (of Scots and English origin, and with their colonel's support) petitioned the Prime Minister for an entitlement to half pay in peacetime. This was later adjusted to extend to only the subalterns, and was still rejected.[47]

The Fencibles are commonly referred to in more traditional historiography as 'Highland', and much of the pageantry which is associated with their uniforms and recruiting efforts reflects this – 'Fencible Highlanders' was not an uncommon

45   Western, *The English Militia*, pp.303-316.
46   Western, *The English Militia*, p.321.
47   NRS: GD174/2255: 'Printed circulars by Major Anderson, of the Northumberland Fencibles, to the officers of the Fencible Infantry', 1796.

regimental name, and the Caithness Fencibles issued recruiting cards emphasising this identity.

Even an early nineteenth-century history of the Highland military tradition includes sections on several Fencible regiments.[48] The larger trend towards considering these regiments through this lens is not without some basis in fact. Of the various leaders selected for the first cohort of eight regiments, five were based in the Highlands and only two in the Lowlands. This likely draws its origins from the increasing reliance of the British Army upon Scots to fill the ranks, and the shift in the latter eighteenth century towards capitalising on the cultural icon of the Highland Warrior.[49] As mentioned above, Henry Dundas was confident that clan influence could still prove beneficial to the military establishment.[50] In a 1797 letter to Lord Seaforth, founder of the 78th Regiment of Foot, he wrote that whilst he understood why 'the spirit of clanship' had previously been restrained, it was now his 'opinion that those reasons whatever they were, have ceased and that much good…may on various occasions arise from such a connexion [sic.] among Persons of the same family and name.'[51] Dundas' intention to make use of what he perceived to be the still-influential clan hierarchies is

An Officer of the Caithness Fencibles. 'Recruiting Card' by John Kay. Reproduced in I. H. Mackay Scobie, 'The Caithness Fencibles, and a Recruiting Card of 1799', *Journal of the Society for Army Historical Research*, Vol.6, No.24 (1927), pp.96–106)

---

48   Stewart, *Sketches of the Character, Manners, and Present State of the Highlanders of Scotland*, pp.vi-vii.

49   Esdaile, 'The French and Revolutionary Wars, 1793-1815' pp.414-416.

50   Andrew Mackillop, *'More Fruitful than the Soil': Army, Empire and the Scottish Highlands, 1715-1815* (East Linton, Scotland: Tuckwell Press, 2000). pp.58-64.

51   NRS: GD46/6/35: 'Letter by Henry Dundas to Francis Humberston Mackenzie Forwarding a Plan Put into His Hands by the Duke of York for Arming the Clans as Fencible Corps', 1797.

partially why the initial Scottish Fencible regimental commanders were actively encouraged to raise their regiments from their spheres of influence. This was most pronounced in the officer corps of the infantry, of whom many were taken from the friends and families of the senior regimental staff. Out of the 33 officers and staff of the Glengarry Fencibles in 1797, 13 bore the name Macdonell (the name of the colonel) and a further eight the name Macdonald.[52] The 1796 records of the Argyll Fencibles shows that, of 29 officers and staff, 13 bore the name of the colonel – Campbell.[53] Sir James Grant even wrote of the friends to whom he had promised commissions, in correspondence to the War Office. Clan recruiting did have a prominent role in enlisting the rank and file, with whole regiments comprised of men from the clan or estate of the relevant Colonel. Lord Breadalbane raised the men for two battalions from his holdings in Perthshire in less than six months.[54]

The reality is that, after the failed Jacobite Rebellion of 1745-1746, the British government began a concerted campaign to remove any threat of future distur-bances in Scotland. As a result of the deep association between the clan system and Jacobitism, Highland society was prioritised in the forcible demilitarisation in the years following Culloden. The resulting decay of the traditional clan struc-tures meant that, by the 1790s, very little remained of the 'Highland Clans' as they had been. They still existed, but, with the development of agricultural techniques, there came a desire to maximise income for landowners. The farming groups who had been a mainstay of the northern Scottish society found themselves forced from their homes and way of life; abandoned by those who had historically been their protectors.[55]

What this practically meant for the Fencibles is that, despite emphasis from the government, there is little evidence to suggest that the Highland identity was reflected in their makeup. Of the eleven 'Highland' regiments, Cookson observed that only 50 percent of the rank and file were actually from the Highlands – 36 percent were Lowlanders, and 14 percent were English.[56] The pay records of the Fencible regiments show that English regiments were recruiting in Scotland as regularly as Scottish regiments were recruiting in England.[57] As mentioned above, these regiments also recruited from the populations they were stationed in – and

---

52   TNA: WO 27/80: Adjutant General and Army Council: Inspection Returns, 1797.

53   TNA: WO 27/78: Adjutant General and Army Council: Inspection Returns, 1796.

54   TNA: HO 50/2: 'Sir James Grant to Lord Amherst', 9th April 1793; 'Lord Amherst to Henry Dundas', 11th June 1793.

55   Allan I. Macinnes, 'Landownership, Land Use and Elite Enterprise in Scottish Gaeldom: From Clanship to Clearance in Argyllshire, 1688-1858' in T. M. Devine (ed), *Scottish Elites: Proceedings of the Scottish Historical Studies Seminar University of Strathclyde 1991-1992* (Edinburgh: John Donald Publishers Ltd., 1994), pp.1-42, at pp.2-12, 28.

56   Cookson, *The British Armed Nation*, p.129.

57   TNA: WO 13: General Muster Books and Pay Lists, Fencible Infantry, 'Cheshire, Cornwall and Devon, Elgin, Fraser, Northampton, Reay, Somerset, York' 1793-1802.

as a result it is unlikely that any Fencible regiments had a dominant Highland identity in the way that some of the regular Highland regiments did.

Fencible regiments could also be raised by counties or municipal corporations rather than landowners; this was more common after the embodiment of the initial cohort of Highland Fencible infantry. This varied in practical execution – the Northampton Fencibles were raised by William Kerr, with the support of the corporation and people of the town.[58] In another case concerning the Fencible infantry for Angus, the local MP had delegated the task of raising the regiment to the Lord Lieutenant, who officered it with his personal connections rather than those county gentlemen who had contributed funds. It was described by a contemporary critic as 'more a family than a County regiment', and implies that the practise of using the gentry to form the officer corps was to be expected in these circumstances.[59] This practise, which resulted in regiments dominated by the propertied gentry in similar ways to the Yeomanry, was far more pronounced in the Fencible cavalry than the infantry. Yet because the majority of the cavalry was not Scottish, they lacked the presence of family groups which was so characteristic of many of the Scottish infantry regiments.

The Grant Fencibles

When the first Scottish magnates were asked to raise their Fencible regiments in 1793, the designation of the 'First' Regiment of Fencible Infantry was given to the regiment Sir James Grant of Grant had been permitted to form. In much of the initial paperwork it was referred to as the First Fencible Regiment of Foot, or Sir James Grant's, but another name in use soon after its embodiment was the Strathspey Fencibles – derived from the location of Sir James' landed interests (and historic clan connections).[60] Because it was one of the early regiments, and especially as it was one of those raised from a Highland region, the Grant Fencibles represent, in many ways, the stereotypical Fencible regiment.

As part of the first cohort of Fencible infantry, the regiment was expected to rely upon Sir James' influence to recruit. This would mean that the officers would be men with personal relationships to the colonel, and that the men would originate from the region the regiment was raised in. A regiment raised in this way would therefore expect to have less military experience than one utilising the half-pay list, but still have physical standards for acceptance into the rank and file (as the

---

58   TNA: WO 4/1005: 'W. Windham to Lord Amherst', 24th October 1794, f.14; 'M. Lewis to Dr Kerr', 25th February 1795, f.159.

59   Sunter, *Patronage and Politics in Scotland*, p.137.

60   NRS: GD248/213/2: 'Official Correspondence Sent from the War Office Addressed to Sir James Grant Relative to Raising and Administration of the Strathspey Fencible Regiment and the 97th Regiment of Foot', 3 July 1793.

regulars and Militia did). These criteria were of varying degrees applicable to the Grant Fencibles. Yet the regiment as a whole behaved in a manner which Dundas did not expect: this led to their early demobilisation, and may have affected his perception of the Highlands – the region from which he had initially hoped to draw so much manpower for the conflict.

Sir James Grant's alliance with Henry Dundas was a recent one. In the 1780s Dundas had made it his mission to stretch his web of influence across the bulk of Scotland and, apart from several key areas, he had been largely successful. The northeast was one of the last regions to attract Dundas' attention, as he had few connections with any of the area's leadership. Sir James Grant, as an influential man who formed part of a political union with the Earl of Fife, was one of the men whom Dundas had to bring on board. Through a deal struck in 1787 between Dundas and five regional magnates, Sir James Grant was able to secure a parliamentary seat in Banffshire, and a Moray seat for another Grant.[61] In doing so, Dundas managed to ensure further co-operation with the Duke of Gordon, who later raised his own Fencible regiment, by utilising his personal vendetta with the Earl of Fife. Sir James was therefore in a position where he had already benefitted from his connection with the Home Secretary, and soon after war broke out in 1793 he offered to raise a regiment of 'loyal men to support the Crown'.[62] The following year permission was extended to raise a regiment for general service, which was designated the 97th (Strathspey) Regiment of Foot.

Both regiments were raised with great speed, particularly the Fencibles. The regiment was completed less than two months after the Royal Warrant, issued on 1 March 1793. In fact, on 18 April 1793, Sir James received a communication from the War Office authorising an augmentation of a further 15 men per company, for a total additional 120 privates across the battalion.[63] The regiment was first recorded on the establishment returns from June 1793 with the other six Scottish, and one Manx, battalions; with a strength of 29 officers (plus five staff appointments), 44 non-commissioned officers, and 624 rank and file, making a total 697 men fit for service.[64] This was one of the standard establishments for the Fencible regiments during the period, the other being 1,000 rank and file plus officers.

As will be detailed below, the regiment did not expect that their service would take them out of Scotland. The regiment's early deployment history varied but was consistently away from its home region, yet still within Scotland's borders

61   Fry, *The Dundas Despotism*, pp.147-149.

62   Stewart, *Sketches of the Character, Manners, and Present State of the Highlanders of Scotland*, p.384.

63   NRS: GD248/213/2: 'Official Correspondence Sent from the War Office Addressed to Sir James Grant…', 18 April 1793.

64   NRS: GD248/2013: 'Volume of Weekly States, Monthly Returns and Master Rolls of 1st. Regiment of Fencible Highlanders Commanded by Sir James Grant of Grant', 1793-1799; TNA: WO 27/78: Adjutant General and Army Council: Inspection Returns, 1796.

as Sir James had been promised.[65] Correspondence from Sir James details deployment to Glasgow, and official paperwork records their presence in Dundee and East Lothian.[66] As a Highland regiment, they wore plaid for their entire service. An illustration of the Grants depicts both Sir James and the rank and file in Highland bonnets; but where the rank and file are in kilts, Sir James is in breeches. This was much the same for regular Scottish regiments during the period, and demonstrates how these second line regiments were taking their lead from the regular Army. There also appears to have been an issue with supply, as was often the case with regiments not on foreign service; inspection returns from 1795 and 1796 both recorded that the regiment was lacking its required 600 cartridge boxes.[67] It did

John Kay, 'Sir James Grant, Col. Grant and Strathspey Fencibles. 1798'. (Anne S.K. Brown Military Collection)

not, though, want for men. Recruiting instructions were clear in their expectation that men would be of a standard acceptable to the regulars – but that it was more important to fill the ranks. One circular to the early Fencible colonels noted that they had no demographic restrictions, but that the medical inspectors would reject men who were not fit for service.[68]

65 G. M. Fraser, *The Strathspey Mutineers: A History of the First Highland Fencible Regiment 1793-1799* (East Kilbride: Librario Publishing, 2003), p.17.

66 NRS: GD248/684/5/1: 'Correspondence of Sir James Grant, Mainly on Fencible Affairs', 1793; NRS: GD248/2013: 'Volume of Weekly States, Monthly Returns and Master Rolls of 1st. Regiment of Fencible Highlanders', 1793-1799.

67 TNA: WO 27/76, WO 27/78: Adjutant General and Army Council: Inspection Returns, 1795-6.

68 NRS: GD248/213/2: 'Official Correspondence Sent from the War Office Addressed to Sir James Grant...', 18 March 1793.

As was expected, a considerable proportion of the officer corps which Sir James formed bore the name Grant. Of the 30 officers (other than Sir James) named in the 1794 War Office List, 13 were Grants – by 1795 this had risen to 15.[69] Other names of significance relate to Sir James' ally the 4th Earl of Findlater and to the Duke of Gordon. Yet despite this deep clan connection, the officers were far from inadequate. The subalterns had, of course, little service experience. The mode average (that is to say, the most common value) age of the Ensigns was 20, with two outliers: one aged 60 and another aged 16. The lieutenants ranged widely in experience, with several having been enlisted since they were 18, and three entirely new to the military. However, the captains and majors had all obtained their first commissions in the 1760s and 1770s; of the 10 company commanders, the regimental colonel was the only man with less than 16 years of service experience.[70] In this way, the junior officers tended to be those to whom the Fencibles provided a potential career opportunity, and the senior officers were professional soldiers. It must be noted that all of the officers, with the exception of three lieutenants (two named Grant), were new to their rank in the Grant Fencibles.

The assumption, therefore, that these regiments were raised by a social elite simply bestowing favours is, at best, naïve. In the case of the Grant Fencibles, one third of the officer corps had been regular officers on half-pay; for the Breadalbane Fencibles it was closer to one quarter.[71] The remaining majority, particularly the subalterns, may have been relatives or friends of the colonel, but this was no different to how many gained rank in the regular Army. For many young officers having the necessary personal connections was the best advantage in seeking promotion prospects.[72] When the Grant Fencibles were formed in 1793, the notes Sir James made regarding his officer suggestions included details of previous service in both regular and Fencible regiments.[73] It is clear that his decisions were not defined by family connections, although that is not to say that this was entirely the case. The most prominent indication that Sir James was not exclusively led by clan loyalty was the presence of a company led by the chieftain of the Macdonells of Glengarry, Alexander. These men had enlisted into the Strathspey Fencibles for an opportunity to serve, despite very little association with the Grants. Their presence did cause friction, particularly as a result of the

---

69 War Office, *List of the Officers of the Several Regiments and Corps of Fencible Cavalry and Infantry: Of the Officers of the Militia...* (Charleston: Nabu Press, 2011); TNA: WO 27/78: Adjutant General and Army Council: Inspection Returns, 1796.

70 War Office, *List of the Officers of the Several Regiments and Corps of Fencible Cavalry and Infantry*; TNA: WO 27/78: Adjutant General and Army Council: Inspection Returns, 1796.

71 Mackillop, 'More Fruitful than the Soil', p.72.

72 J. A. Houlding, *Fit for Service: The Training of the British Army, 1715-1795* (Oxford: Clarendon Press, 1981), p.103.

73 Fraser, *The Strathspey Mutineers*, pp.21-22.

religious divide between the Catholic Macdonells and the Presbyterian Sir James. Alexander Macdonell was later allowed to raise his own regiment of Fencibles, seemingly as a way to concentrate the Catholics away from what was perceived to be the more loyal Protestants. He requested permission from Dundas to transfer the Macdonell men into his own regiment; a scheme which the Strathspey's lieutenant colonel especially supported.[74]

The men of the Grant Fencibles were almost exclusively Scottish, as was to be expected. David Stewart's *History* states that, of the rank and file enlisted, 41 were Lowland Scots, three were English, two were Irish, and that the remainder were Highlanders.[75] The official returns gives marginally different information – with six English, three Irish, and the other 660 Scottish – with no distinction made between Scots of different backgrounds.[76] For context, the Argyll and Sutherland Fencible Regiments both recorded the difference between Highland and Lowland later in the period, in their 1799 and 1800 returns respectively. In both instances this division is substantial, and may reflect the desire of both regiments to preserve their Highland identity. The muster rolls for the Grant Fencibles record that in 1797, 151 privates bore the name of Grant. Other names which appear frequently are Gordon, Rose, Macdonald, and Stuart – all names associated with the Grants and adopted to avoid confusion during the decline of clanship.[77] Regimental records note that recruits were taken from the traditional Grant lands in Moray and Strathspey, but also from Edinburgh, Perth, and even from Rosshire.[78] This displays a wide area of recruitment and, although certainly concentrated inside traditional Grant heartlands, in filling the ranks so quickly John Prebble commented that many of the gentry may have 'beat [for recruits] in glens far from their own lands'.[79] The Grant Fencibles do therefore appear to have broadly adhered to the principles of clanship which Dundas had been so keen to exploit. The inclusion of the Glengarry contingent, potentially as many as a whole company, diluted what otherwise would have been Sir James Grant's loyal clansmen.

The question of previous service, with regards to the rank and file, is somewhat simpler to detail, although it does present some queries.

74 Kathleen M. Toomey, *Alexander Macdonell: The Scottish Years, 1762-1804* (Toronto: Canadian Catholic Historical Association, 1985), pp.114-115.

75 Stewart, *Sketches of the Character, Manners, and Present State of the Highlanders of Scotland*, p.384.

76 NRS: GD248/2013: 'Volume of Weekly States, Monthly Returns and Master Rolls of 1st. Regiment of Fencible Highlanders', 1793-1799.

77 NRS: GD248/2013: 'Volume of Weekly States, Monthly Returns and Master Rolls of 1st. Regiment of Fencible Highlanders', 1793-1799. Fraser, *The Strathspey Mutineers*, p.75.

78 NRS: GD248/463/4/4, 19: 'Muster Rolls, Returns and Other Papers Relating to the First Regiment of Fencible Infantry Commanded by Sir James Grant', 1793.

79 Prebble, *Mutiny: Highland Regiments in Revolt*, p.297.

Table 2: Years of Service of the Enlisted Men of the 1st, or Grant, Fencibles, 1793-1798

Year	Years of Service										
	1	2	3	4	5	6	7	8	10	15	20
1793	43	626	0	0	0	0	0	0	0	0	0
1794	140	0	496	0	0	0	0	0	0	0	0
1795	140	0	496	0	0	0	0	0	0	0	0
1796	7	120	427	0	0	0	0	0	0	0	0
1797	20	8	120	406	0	0	0	0	0	0	0
1798	27	9	8	115	395	0	0	0	0	0	0

Source: TNA: WO 27/78: Adjutant General and Army Council: Inspection Returns, 1796; NRS: GD248/2013: 'Volume of Weekly States, Monthly Returns and Master Rolls of 1st. Regiment of Fencible Highlanders', 1793-1799.

For the 1793 return to show 626 men, almost the entire establishment, having between one and two years' service would be impossible if the men were new to military service. This inconsistency is also present in the 1794 and 1795 return – the 1796 records this same initial cohort of recruits, then numbering 427, as having three years' service. Whilst it would be easy to assume that the initial records are correct, the Size Roll for the Grants is more detailed in its record of the ages of recruits. From the data available, the mean average age of the rank and file of the regiment is calculated to be between 22 and 23 years of age.[80] Whilst is it possible for them to have been in service from late 1791, it is unlikely. For these men to have been in service prior to the Fencibles, they would have had to joined the regular Army; there is much evidence of men transferring from a Fencible regiment to a regular regiment,[81] but none for the opposite. The more likely scenario is that the previous service was incorrectly recorded in 1793, and this figure was not questioned until later. This issue does require further examination, but does not prevent this information being relevant in this chapter.

With the entire regiment having served for less than two years, as a certainty, in 1793 these men were new to military service. Regimental records note that common occupations before enlisting included labouring and weaving; both manual trades, particularly common in less agricultural areas of Scotland.[82] However, the age of recruits was one area where the regulations were not as strictly adhered to. The majority of those enlisted in the Grant Fencibles were in their early twenties, with

---

80   WO 27/78: Adjutant General and Army Council: Inspection Returns, 1796; NRS: GD248/2013: 'Volume of Weekly States, Monthly Returns and Master Rolls of 1st. Regiment of Fencible Highlanders', 1793-1799.

81   Examples of this include: NRS: GD40/10/22/14: 'Midlothian Fencible Light Dragoons and the Irish Rebellion: Orderly and other books of the Midlothian Fencible Light Dragoons', 1799; Glover (ed.), *The Veteran*, p.57.

82   NRS: GD248/463/4/2: 'Muster Rolls, Returns and Other Papers Relating to the First Regiment of Fencible Infantry Commanded by Sir James Grant', 1793.

the light company having the youngest average age of the battalion. The regulations were clear that regiments were to accept men aged between 18 and 35; yet the Grant Fencibles recorded men aged 50 and over, and (in 1793) the enlistment of Corporal Robert MacDonald, aged 15. He was recorded as a sergeant by the end of 1794.[83] This is reminiscent of the issues faced by the regulars with meeting the physical standards for recruits, which were relaxed towards the end of the period to reflect the realities of enlistment.[84]

During their first year in service, Sir James Grant commented favourably on his men's appearance, observing that 'they are clean dressed and powdered every day ... their arms ... well-polished as if out of the armourer's hands'.[85] The records show exceptionally low desertion rates for this period, even with companies deployed well away from each other for months at a time.[86] Yet, despite the initial success in recruiting and embodying the regiment, the Grant Fencibles remain infamous for their conduct on several occasions during the 1790s. A persistent theme in these issues was the religious and clan divide created by the commission of Captain Macdonell, and the enlistment of a number of Glengarry men. These men were Catholic, and their clan had longstanding Jacobite sympathies – initial discussions had concluded that it was safer to disperse these men across Protestant regiments than it was to concentrate them in their own.[87]

In early 1794 an invasion scare led to a War Office scheme to deploy 2,000 Fencible men drawn from four Fencible regiments to the south coast of England. Yet it would be an extension of their terms of service to be deployed outside of Scotland without an invasion; the men going had to volunteer.[88] Sir James did not actually inform the regiment of the scheme (being absent on county administration business) until they reached the dockside at Linlithgow, with rumour spreading in the meantime that the men were to be sent to England without their consent.[89] His request for volunteers was therefore met with accusations from the Macdonell company, from Glengarry, that the British government wished to deploy them to the Low Countries. Several days later this request was repeated,

83   NRS: GD248/2013: 'Volume of Weekly States, Monthly Returns and Master Rolls of 1st. Regiment of Fencible Highlanders', 1793-1799; TNA: WO 13/3944: General Muster Books and Pay Lists, Fencible Infantry, Strathspey, 1793-1799.

84   Kevin Linch, *Britain and Wellington's Army: Recruitment, Society and Tradition, 1807-1815* (Basingstoke: Palgrave MacMillan, 2011), pp.87-89, 165.

85   NRS: GD248/684/5/1: 'Correspondence of Sir James Grant, Mainly on Fencible Affairs', 1793-1799.

86   NRS: GD248/2013: 'Volume of Weekly States, Monthly Returns and Master Rolls of 1st. Regiment of Fencible Highlanders', 1793.

87   Prebble, *Mutiny: Highland Regiments in Revolt*, pp.295-297.

88   Fraser, *The Strathspey Mutineers*, p.82.

89   NLS: 5.255: J.M. Bulloch, 'The Scots Fencibles and English Service: An Episode of 1794', 1915, p.4; NRS: GD248/2013: 'Volume of Weekly States, Monthly Returns and Master Rolls of 1st. Regiment of Fencible Highlanders', 1793-1799; Fraser, *The Strathspey Mutineers*, pp.83-88.

and on this occasion men from several companies, but primarily the Macdonells, broke from their ranks and occupied a nearby church.

Eventually the mutiny was quashed, but the experience left a sore reminder for the government that clan loyalties were as much a problem as they were a solution. For those with historic Jacobite loyalties, service to the Crown was far less compelling a motivation for military service than more mundane factors such as pay or adventure.[90] In the rush to recruit to the Grant Fencibles, the traditional clan differences had been forgotten – this caused friction which neither Sir James, nor Dundas, had anticipated.

The Grant Fencible Regiment of Foot was, in many ways, the quintessential Highland Fencible regiment. Its commanding officer was a magnate: a man with significant influence, who saw the outbreak of war as an opportunity to build upon his relationship with Henry Dundas and the British government. Its officer corps was largely formed through the traditional ties of clanship, even going as far as to draw upon other clan allegiances. Its men were enlisted through the same methods – recruiting from historical lands and from those whose livelihoods were under threat from the encroachment of economic shifts. Yet the reality of the Grant Fencibles was far from this initial impression. As was to be expected, the regimental commanding officer had limited military experience; his senior officers, however, had a combined service record of around 200 years between them. In the case of the two majors, both were veterans of the Seven Years War and the American War of Independence.[91] The rank and file of the regiment were, for the most part, those upon whom Henry Dundas hoped to capitalise. They were young men, who were looking to serve their chieftain or their country.

The presence of a not-insignificant number of men outside of the regulation age restriction of 35, and from areas outside traditional Grant lands, does suggest that, in the rush for Sir James to provide his loyalty to Dundas, the regiment drew from men who would otherwise not have been taken. The Fencible and regular regiments near emptied Strathspey of serviceable men; this may explain why Grant so readily accepted the Catholic Glengarry company.[92] Captain Macdonell would later form his own regiment and, in his role as clan chief, took the role of colonel. It is therefore evident that, whilst, the Grant Fencibles may have benefitted in many ways from a clan-led recruitment campaign, this was far from practical in those areas without such ties of kinship. Generalisation of the Fencibles as a 'Highland Corps' negates the reality that even the clan Fencible regiments were not truly what had been envisaged. The poor behaviour exemplified by the initial cohort of Fencible regiments partially originated in a distrust of British interference in Scotland: a legacy of the 1745 Rising. In 1799 the Grant Fencibles, along with the

---

90   Prebble, *Mutiny: Highland Regiments in Revolt*, pp.304-316.
91   Prebble, *Mutiny: Highland Regiments in Revolt*, p.292.
92   Fraser, *The Strathspey Mutineers*, p.77.

rest of the regiments bound to exclusive service in Scotland, were disbanded in favour of battalions who could be deployed across Britain – to avoid any further poor behaviour. Yet the British Army maintained its view of Scottish recruitment until after the Fencible corps at large were disbanded, despite indicators that clanship had not survived the shift towards an economic relationship between landowners and their tenants.[93]

Concluding Remarks

The Fencible regiments of the 1790s were not greatly different from their earlier incarnations. They were a full-time force of volunteers, explicitly enlisted to only serve in the defence of Britain but 'independent' of the politics of the Militia.[94] They owed much of their initial success to the willingness of magnates in Scotland to invest time and energy in the scheme. However, Henry Dundas saw the Fencibles as an opportunity to further cement his dominance in Scottish politics, by utilising them as a tool of patronage. It was for this reason that he became more heavily invested in the corps, and by the mid-1790s had begun to centralise his control over their administration. The Grant Fencibles were one of those initial regiments which were intended to derive support from the 'spirit of [the] clan'.[95] This emphasis in the early years of the Fencibles has influenced the current state of historiography, and has solidified their reputation as part of the late-eighteenth century 'Warrior Highlander' archetype.

Recruitment efforts emphasised the bounty as a reward for service, which explains why the men who enlisted reflected the demographics of those enlisting for general service. Edward Coss' detailed examination of the British Army over the whole period of the French Wars concluded that the most common age for infantry recruits was between 15 and 19.[96] This was similar to the common age for Fencible infantry recruits, potentially reflecting the reality of the shortage of men not already under arms in the Militia, Yeomanry, Volunteer Corps, or regulars across Britain. John Harley's account of his experience inducing men to enlist, in exchange for his commission, notes that he accepted several men who were likely to be unfit for service on account of health and physical description.[97] Many regiments were in desperate need of recruits, and it was not unusual to find men in the Fencibles who would not have qualified for service in the regular Army.

93 Mackillop, 'More Fruitful than the Soil', pp.75-76.
94 Charles Ross (ed.), Correspondence of Charles, First Marquis Cornwallis, second edn (London: John Murray, 1859), Vol.3, p.79.
95 Fraser, The Strathspey Mutineers, p.18.
96 Edward Coss, All for the King's Shilling: The British Soldier under Wellington, 1808-1814 (Norman: University of Oklahoma Press, 2010), p.55.
97 Glover (ed.), The Veteran, pp.30-31.

Yet the ties of clanship were a key motivator for service in the Scottish infantry regiments, and the Highland officers made great use of their local connections to achieve their quota of recruits. The popularity of military service which was to be restricted in location meant that the Army later faced serious manpower shortages, such as in the case of Sir James Grant's regular regiment, the 97th.

In many ways the Fencibles were perceived by the government as an alternative to the Militia, and both these forces were often compared unfavourably with the regulars. The key difference was their contracted deployment location – regiments of Fencibles were only permitted to serve within Britain. To what extent this quantifiably affected recruitment rates will form part of the author's ongoing doctoral research. However, the occurrence of mutinies in the original cohort of Scottish regiments, which had only enlisted for service within Scotland, demonstrates the value that the rank and file placed on the terms of their contract. As the government began to understand how the Fencibles could be utilised across Britain, service locations were gradually expanded to mainland Britain, Ireland, and the Channel Islands. This addressed the issues of fluctuating manpower which the Army faced during the period, and lead to their deployment to Ireland – where many regiments played a major role in suppressing the 1798 Rising.[98]

What is most clear from research into the recruitment to the Fencible regiments is that, whilst an emphasis on their Highland origins is crucial to understanding the principles which underpinned their service, they operated in a largely similar way to the regular Army. Their overall success was partially a result of the political ambitions of Henry Dundas who, in relying upon what he considered to be a dormant martial spirit, turned to this previously established solution to Scotland's protection. In practical terms they recruited in much the same way as the regulars, with a particular emphasis on the gentry to make use of their status as local elites. The Fencibles therefore represent a juncture in political, social, and military history during the 1790s. Their origins, and their reliance upon the relationship between the propertied elites and their social inferiors, meant that their experience, whilst similar, was not identical to any other branch of the military. Yet despite these differences, they were able to induce sufficient men to fulfil their regimental establishments. Their role was to contribute to the protection of the British Isles, and they did so across the nine years in which they operated in the United Kingdom.

---

98 NAMA: 1971-12-22: 'Enlistment Form, 29 Oct 1794; Belonging to John Taylor, Royal Lancashire Volunteers, Formerly a Weaver', 1794; NAMA: 1984-05-173: 'Photocopies of 7 enlistment forms completed on behalf of men joining the Loyal Inverness Regiment of Fencible Infantry', 1795.

Bibliography

Primary Material

British Library (BL)
  BL: 288.a.10.(4.): 'Certain Rules and Orders to Be Observed by the Corps of Fencible Infantry', 1794.
  BL: Cup.21.g.31/26: 'Sir, His Majesty Having Been Pleased to Appoint Me Colonel of a Corps of Fencibles, to Be Raised in Inverness, and the Neighbouring Counties, for the Internal Protection of North Britain, …', 1793.
National Army Museum Archive (NAMA)
  NAMA: 1971-12-22: 'Enlistment Form, 29 Oct 1794; Belonging to John Taylor, Royal Lancashire Volunteers, Formerly a Weaver', 1794.
  NAMA: 1977-03-04: 'Monthly Roll and Pay List of a Recruiting Party of the York Fencible Regiment of Infantry…', 1801.
  NAMA: 1984-05-173: 'Photocopies of 7 enlistment forms completed on behalf of men joining the Loyal Inverness Regiment of Fencible Infantry', 1795
  NAMA: 1994-04-75: 'Three Letters Relating to the Efforts of Army Agents to Encourage Officers to Raise Fencible Regiments', 1794.
National Library of Scotland (NLS):
  NLS: APS.4.94.15: 'G. R. Highest Bounty. To All Aspiring Heroes Bold … ' 1795.
  NLS: 5.255: J. M. Bulloch, 'The Scots Fencibles and English Service: An Episode of 1794', 1915.
National Records of Scotland (NRS)
  NRS: GD3/9/10/3: West Lowland Regiment of Fencible Men: Monthly Returns, 1793-9.
  NRS: GD3/9/12/8: 'Recruiting Instructions for Regiment of Fencible Men to Be Raised under the Command of Right Honourable Frederick Campbell as Colonel', n. d.
  NRS: GD40/10/22: Midlothian Fencible Light Dragoons and the Irish Rebellion: Orderly and other books of the Midlothian Fencible Light Dragoons, 1794-1800.
  NRS: GD46/6/35: 'Letter by Henry Dundas to Francis Humberston Mackenzie Forwarding a Plan Put into His Hands by the Duke of York for Arming the Clans as Fencible Corps', 1797.
  NRS: GD51/6/77/1-7: 'Lord Breadalbane; Permanent Rank of Lieutenant Colonel for Himself; Also Dealing with Fencible Matters', 1793-1794
  NRS: GD174/2255: 'Printed circulars by Major Anderson, of the Northumberland Fencibles, to the officers of the Fencible Infantry…', 1796.

NRS: GD248/213/2: 'Official Correspondence Sent from the War Office Addressed to Sir James Grant Relative to Raising and Administration of the Strathspey Fencible Regiment and the 97th Regiment of Foot', 1793-5.

NRS: GD248/463/4: 'Muster Rolls, Returns and Other Papers Relating to the First Regiment of Fencible Infantry Commanded by Sir James Grant', 1793.

NRS: GD248/684/5/1: 'Correspondence of Sir James Grant, Mainly on Fencible Affairs', 1793.

NRS: GD248/2013: 'Volume of Weekly States, Monthly Returns and Master Rolls of 1st. Regiment of Fencible Highlanders Commanded by Sir James Grant of Grant', 1793-1799.

The National Archives (TNA)

TNA: HO 50/2: Commander-in-Chief Correspondence

TNA: WO 1/603; 617: War Office In-Letters, Guernsey 1793, 1795; Commander-in-Chief, 1794-5.

TNA: WO 4/1005-6: Secretary-at-War Out-Letters, Promotions, October 1794-April 1800.

TNA: WO 13: General Muster Books and Pay Lists, Fencible Infantry, 1793-1802.

TNA: WO 17/1159 – WO 17/1161: Monthly Returns to the Adjutant General, General Returns, 1793-1802.

TNA: WO 27/74 – WO 27/86: Adjutant General and Army Council: Inspection Returns, 1794-1802.

Published Primary Material

Glover, Gareth (ed.), *The Veteran, or 40 Years' Service in the British Army: The Scurrilous Recollections of Paymaster John Harley, 47th Foot – 1798-1838* (Solihull: Helion & Company Limited, 2018).

Ross, Charles, (ed.) *Correspondence of Charles, First Marquis Cornwallis*, second edition (London: John Murray, 1859).

Sinclair, John, *Considerations on Militias and Standing Armies*, Reprint (London: Forgotten Books, 2018).

War Office, *List of the Officers of the Several Regiments and Corps of Fencible Cavalry and Infantry: Of the Officers of the Militia...* (Charleston: Nabu Press, 2011).

Secondary Sources

Bartlett, Thomas and Jeffrey, Keith (eds), *A Military History of Ireland* (Cambridge: Cambridge University Press, 1997).

Bartlett, Thomas, et al (eds), *1798: A Bicentenary Perspective* (Dublin: Four Courts Press, 2003).

Beckett, Ian, *Britain's Part-Time Soldiers: The Amateur Military Tradition 1558-1945* (Barnsley: Pen & Sword Military, 2011).

Blackstock, Allan, *An Ascendancy Army: The Irish Yeomanry, 1796-1814* (Dublin: Four Courts Press, 1998).

Carswell, Allan L., 'The Scottish Fencible Regiments in Ireland', *The Irish Sword*, 21 (1998), pp.155-159.

Colley, Linda, *Britons: Forging the Nation 1707-1837*, fourth edition (New Haven and London: Yale University Press, 2019).

Cookson, J.E., *The British Armed Nation, 1793-1815* (Oxford: Clarendon, 1997).

Coss, Edward, *All for the King's Shilling: The British Soldier under Wellington, 1808-1814* (Norman: University of Oklahoma Press, 2010).

Cullen, L.M., 'Scotland and Ireland, 1600-1800: Their Role in the Evolution of British Society', in R.A. Houston and I.D. Whyte (eds), *Scottish Society 1500-1800* (Cambridge: Cambridge University Press, 1989), pp.226–244.

Esdaile, Charles J., 'The French and Revolutionary Wars, 1793–1815' in Jeremy A Crang et al (eds), *A Military History of Scotland* (Edinburgh: Edinburgh University Press, 2012), pp.407-435.

Firebrace, John and Rawlings, Alan, *His Majesty's Fraser Fencible Regiment of Foot 1794-1802* (Southsea: John Firebrace and Alan Rawlings; Don Miles, 1993).

Fortescue, John, *A History of the British Army* (London: MacMillan and Co. Limited, 1915).

Fraser, G. M., *The Strathspey Mutineers: A History of the First Highland Fencible Regiment 1793-1799* (East Kilbride: Librario Publishing, 2003).

Fry, Michael, *The Dundas Despotism* (Edinburgh: Edinburgh University Press, 1992).

Garnham, Neal, *The Militia in Eighteenth-Century Ireland: In Defence of the Protestant Interest* (Woodbridge: The Boydell Press, 2012).

Gee, Austin, *The British Volunteer Movement 1794-1814* (Oxford: Clarendon Press, 2003).

Houlding, J. A., *Fit for Service: The Training of the British Army, 1715-1795* (Oxford: Clarendon Press, 1981).

Langford, Paul, *Public Life and the Propertied Englishman, 1689-1798* (Oxford: Clarendon Press, 1991).

Linch, Kevin, '"A Citizen and Not a Soldier": The British Volunteer Movement and the War against Napoleon', in Alan Forrest, et al (eds), *Soldiers, Citizens and Civilians: Experiences and Perceptions of the Revolutionary and Napoleonic Wars, 1790-1820* (Basingstoke: Palgrave MacMillan, 2009), pp.205-221.

Linch, Kevin, *Britain and Wellington's Army: Recruitment, Society and Tradition, 1807-1815* (Basingstoke: Palgrave MacMillan, 2011).

McAnally, Henry, *The Irish Militia, 1793-1816* (Dublin: Clonmore and Reynolds, 1949).

McCormack, Matthew, *Embodying the Militia in Georgian England* (Oxford: University Press, 2015).

Macinnes, Allan I., 'Landownership, Land Use and Elite Enterprise in Scottish Gaeldom: From Clanship to Clearance in Argyllshire, 1688-1858' in T.M. Devine (ed), *Scottish Elites: Proceedings of the Scottish Historical Studies Seminar University of Strathclyde 1991-1992* (Edinburgh: John Donald Publishers Ltd., 1994), pp.1-42.

Mackillop, Andrew, *'More Fruitful than the Soil': Army, Empire and the Scottish Highlands, 1715-1815* (East Linton, Scotland: Tuckwell Press, 2000).

Nelson, Ivan, *The Irish Militia, 1793-1802: Ireland's Forgotten Army* (Dublin: Four Courts Press, 2007).

Prebble, John, *Mutiny: Highland Regiments in Revolt, 1743-1804* (London: Secker & Warburg, 1975).

Robertson, John *The Scottish Enlightenment and the Militia Issue* (Edinburgh: John Donald Publishers Ltd., 1985).

Scobie, Ian Hamilton Mackay, *An Old Highland Fencible Corps: the history of the Reay Fencible Highland Regiment of Foot, or Mackay's Highlanders, 1794-1802, with an account of its services in Ireland during the Rebellion of 1798. By Captain I.H. Mackay Scobie...With illustrations and maps.* (Edinburgh; London: W. Blackwood & Sons, 1914).

Stewart, David, *Sketches of the Character, Manners, and Present State of the Highlanders of Scotland: With Details of the Military Service of the Highland Regiments* (Edinburgh: Constable, 1825).

Sunter, Ronald M., *Patronage and Politics in Scotland, 1707-1832* (Edinburgh: John Donald Publishers Ltd., 1986).

Toomey, Kathleen M., *Alexander Macdonell: The Scottish Years, 1762-1804* (Toronto: Canadian Catholic Historical Association, 1985).

Western, J.R., 'The Recruitment of the Land Forces in Great Britain, 1793-99' (unpublished doctoral thesis, University of Edinburgh, 1953).

Western, J.R., *The English Militia in the Eighteenth Century: The Story of a Political Issue 1660-1802* (London: Routledge and Kegan Paul, 1965).

Whatley, Christopher A., *Scottish Society 1707-1830: Beyond Jacobitism, towards Industrialisation* (Manchester and New York: Manchester University Press, 2000).

5

'Nothing So Valuable as the Life and Health of the British Soldier'. The British Army's Medical Services in India 1797–1805: A Study of Wellington's *Dispatches* and *Supplementary Despatches*

Martin R. Howard

Objectives, Methodology and Sources

The primary objective of the study was to understand Arthur Wellesley's attitudes to and interventions in the Indian Army Medical Department between 1797 and 1805. A secondary objective was to further explore the nature of the Indian Army's medical provision during this period.

Wellesley (the future Duke of Wellington) arrived in India in 1796 as a colonel in the 33rd Regiment. His rapid rise to commander in the Deccan campaigns of 1803 was in part due to his aristocratic lineage, his purchase of rank, and having an older brother, Richard, who was Governor-General of India. However, he was already demonstrating the talents that were to permeate his entire military career including common sense and a phenomenal attention to detail. Wellesley later attributed his exceptional stamina to his time in India and his copious Indian dispatches are a testimony to his dynamism and staying power. These key sources were systematically searched for references to the Indian Army Medical Services and also references to Wellesley's own health.[1] All relevant references were identified and sub-classified prior to the selection of excerpts to draw conclusions. Wellesley's own health was

---

1   Colonel Gurwood (ed.), *The Dispatches of Field Marshal the Duke of Wellington during his various campaigns in India, Denmark, Portugal, Spain, The Low Countries and France* (London: Parker, Furnivall

considered separately to other medical themes. A preliminary introduction to the Medical Services of the Indian Army during the period gives essential background information.

An Introduction to the Medical Services of the Indian Army 1797–1805

Each of the East India Company's Presidencies in Calcutta, Madras and Bombay eventually had its own medical service directed by a Medical Board made up of senior army doctors.[2] With the arrival of increasing numbers of regimental medical officers from Britain in the second half of the eighteenth century these surgeons became interchangeable between European and Indian units. The King's infantry regiments had their surgeon and two assistant surgeons, as at home. In the Bengal (East India Company) Army of 1803 most of the Native regiments had the full complement of three British surgeons and also two Native doctors. The same applied in Bombay but army lists show that the Madras Army had less European surgeons.[3] These men ran the regiment's own hospital.

There were also the 'medical staff' who had no regimental affiliation. There was no rank of physician in the Company's service. The staff or superintending surgeons were allocated to divisions and were expected to inspect hospitals and oversee the work of the regimental surgeons, receiving monthly returns of the sick. The large scale of the medical establishment in India – both Company and Crown – gave it a degree of independence from medical opinion in Britain.

The doctors who gave the routine medical care to the armies of Arthur Wellesley in the Deccan and Gerard Lake in Hindustan might be educated men, perhaps schooled at Edinburgh University or a London anatomy institution. Their competence varied widely, a truth reflected in ordinary soldiers' memoirs which refer to surgeons with 'suavity of manners and benevolence of mind' but also to 'cabbage headed West Country Medicine Pounders'. The better Company surgeons were part of a distinct Indian medical culture marked by a tendency to empirical

---

and Parker, 1844), Vols. I and II; 2nd Duke of Wellington(ed.), *Supplementary Despatches and Memoranda of Field Marshal Arthur Duke of Wellington K. G.* (London: John Murray, 1858–1859), Vols. I–IV.

2   For more detail of British army medicine in India at this period see, Martin R. Howard, *Wellington and The British Army's Indian Campaigns 1798–1805* (Barnsley: Pen and Sword, 2020); M. Harrison, 'Disease and Medicine in the Armies of British India 1750–1830', in G.L. Hudson (ed.), *British Military and Naval Medicine 1600–1830* (Amsterdam: Rodopi, 2007); Erica Charters, *Disease, War and the Imperial State: The Welfare of the British Armed Forces during the Seven Years War* (Chicago: The University of Chicago Press, 2014).

3   Anon., *East-India Register and Directory for 1803* (London: Cox, Son and Baylis, 1803), pp.83–87, 206–209, 257–259.

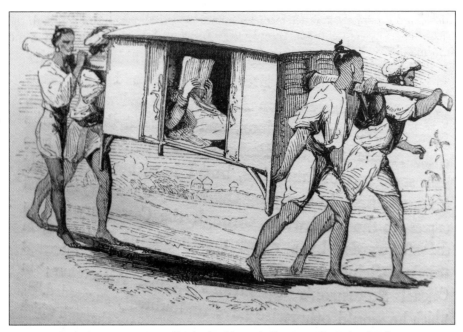

A *doolie*. (From W.H. Maxwell, *Life of Field-Marshal his Grace The Duke of Wellington*
(London: Bohn, 1845))

treatment and innovation. Some were in search of a fortune and status, holding civil and military posts and engaging in trade.[4]

In addition to the regimental hospitals, there were fixed general hospitals to manage the more seriously wounded and to cater for the large numbers of sick. At the outset of campaigns, general hospitals were frequently opened in strategic areas where troop concentrations were likely (for example, at Hurryhur in Mysore in 1803). As in Europe, these hospitals had a poor reputation. Convoys of sick and wounded men moved long distances through difficult terrain. The least infirm might walk. Bullock carts and the local *doolies* (stretchers) were used for the more debilitated.

Medical arrangements for battle were, just as in Europe, improvised and inadequate. Regiments often lacked their full complement of surgeons and the limited provision was overwhelmed by the heavy casualties suffered in the major battles of the Second Anglo-Maratha War (as at Assaye and Delhi in 1803). Some improvised surgery was carried out in dressing stations and temporary field hospitals close to the action, the more serious cases then being moved on to a larger field or general facility. It was common for the wounded to be left on the field untended for several days before they were reached.

4   Lieutenant Colonel D.G. Crawford, *A History of the Indian Medical Service 1600–1913* (London: W. Thacker, 1914), Vol.II, pp.68–84.

Death from disease was a much greater risk to the soldiers of the Indian Army than death in battle. India was not as pestilential as the West Indies but disease rates and mortality were greater than at home. Returns from the King's regiments for 1805 show that of the 9,308 men, 1,947 (21 percent) were sick.[5] In Southern India, the percentage of soldiers dying from their disease varied from only two percent in Nunindroog to 11 percent in Seringapatam.[6] The main afflictions included various types of fever (often malaria), dysentery ('flux'), hepatitis, and venereal disease. Liver disorders were exacerbated by alcohol abuse.

Diseases were related to the season, the rainy months of August and September being the unhealthiest.[7] Climate was clearly important. The medical men of the period were mostly still attached to antiquated views of disease causation, believing that the majority of diseases were caused by 'miasma' or 'miasmata', invisible poisons in the air which were exuded from rotting animal matter, the soil and stagnant water. There was no understanding of the roles of insect vectors and microorganisms. There was, however, a growing comprehension that disease might be suppressed by the enforcement of good discipline and pragmatic measures such as the seasoning of troops, the careful placement of campsites, more spacious accommodation, and strict attention to hygiene, clothing and diet. Doctors relied on good military officers to apply these directives which often appeared in the Indian Army's general orders.

The following pair of tables summarise the extent and nature of Wellesley's references to medical matters in his published correspondence. Of the total of 237 references to the medical services, the greatest number was in 1803, the height of the Second Anglo-Maratha War.

Table 1: Wellesley's References to Medical Services of Indian Army 1797–1805, by Date

Year	Number of references
1797	3
1798	2
1799	7
1800	38
1801	41
1802	29
1803	71
1804	30
1805	16
Total	**237**

---

5   Gurwood (ed.), *Dispatches*, Vol.IV, p.360.

6   G. B. Ballingall, Practical *Observations on Fever, Dysentery and Liver Complaints as they occur amongst the European troops in India* (Edinburgh: Adam Black, 1823), p.306.

7   Harrison, 'Disease and Medicine in the Armies of British India', p.91.

Table 2: Wellesley's References to Medical Services of Indian Army 1797–1805, by Subject

Subject	Number of References
Army Doctors	21
Organisation of Medical Department	13
Hospitals	30
Transport of Sick/Wounded	40
Battlefield Medicine	20
Supply of Medicines	13
Disease General	36
Disease Prevention	26
Miscellaneous Medical	12
Wellesley's Health	26
Total	**237**

In Table 2 medical subject matter is sub-classified into 10 themes. Where a single reference alluded to more than one theme (for example, both hospitals and disease) then it was classified according to the dominant theme. It can be seen that common medical subjects referenced in the *Dispatches* and *Supplementary Despatches* were disease (including the means of prevention), the transport of sick and wounded, and hospitals.

Selected Excerpts from the References

1. Army Doctors

Two references from 1799 and 1800 demonstrate Wellesley's unwavering support for the regimental surgeon of the 33rd, Andrew Trevor.

> Seringapatam, 4 December 1799. To Deputy Adjutant General.
> Being then of an opinion that Dr. Ewart has no right to call for this journal... I have been a witness to the occupations of my surgeon [Andrew Trevor], and can speak with certainty of the fact. He goes into his hospital every morning at 7, and does not quit till 11; he returns to it again at 3, and does not quit till half-past 5. Therefore during the day he has four hours not employed in the hospital... I have seen hospitals in different parts of the world, and since I have been in the army I have not seen any in such good order, or where the sick are taken such good care of...[8]

---

8   Wellington (ed.), *Supplementary Despatches*, Vol.I, pp.406–408.

Seringapatam, 20 February 1800. To Surgeon [Andrew] Trevor, 33rd Regiment

As, however, it appears that the want of my signature to your report has drawn from Mr. Ewart an insinuation that I am not satisfied with your general conduct, I think it but justice to you to state, that you have now been under my command for 7 years, that during this time the regiment has been employed in different parts of the world and various climates, and that upon all occasions your attention to your duty, your humanity, and your skill, have claimed and received my fullest approbation.[9]

John Ewart was a Physician to the Forces and Inspector General of Hospitals with authority over both the Crown's and Company's service. He had demanded that all surgeons in the hospitals keep a casebook of the patient's symptoms and the treatment given. Trevor was not alone in ignoring this order, many medical officers regarding it as an unreasonable demand on their time. Even when the order was followed, Ewart was likely to find fault.[10] It is unclear if Wellesley was aware of the wider issue, but his powerful support of Trevor, a doctor he had high regard for, is noteworthy.

There are other instances of Wellesley using his patronage to further medical careers.

Peepulgaum, 3 July 1803. To Lieutenant Colonel Close.

Mr [James] Gilmour has done all the duty of the staff surgeon greatly to my satisfaction and the general good; and when the subsidiary force was to be established at Poonah, I think that I could not disappoint the expectation which he has a right to form, that he would be its permanent staff surgeon, without doing him great injustice and, in his person, violating a principle which ought always to guide those who have the disposal of military patronage, viz that those who do the duty of the army ought to be promoted, and also ought to enjoy its benefits and advantages.[11]

The closing lines demonstrate Wellesley's determination that in the medical services, as in other parts of the Army, duty in the field should be rewarded with promotion. The general was prepared to heap great praise on those he believed to deserve it. James Anderson, Head Surgeon in Mysore and later the Physician General, was lauded in a letter of December 1801 as being 'the ablest man in his profession in this country'.[12]

---

9   Gurwood (ed.), *Dispatches*, Vol.I, p.69.
10 Harrison, 'Disease and Medicine in the Armies of British India', pp.104–105.
11 Gurwood (ed.), *Dispatches*, Vol.I, p.539.
12 Wellington (ed.), *Supplementary Despatches*, Vol.III, pp.19–20.

It is difficult to find criticism of the Indian Medical Department. There is, however, the following.

> Jaum, 14 November 1803. To Lieutenant Colonel Agnew.
> …as I have found the medical gentlemen not very backward in giving certificates of sickness, I have been obliged to be cautious in giving leave of absence on account of ill health.[13]

Dr James Anderson. Anderson rose from assistant surgeon to the rank of physician general and was highly valued by Wellington. (From Lieutenant Colonel D.G. Crawford, *A History of the Indian Medical Service 1600–1913* (London: W. Thacker, 1914)).

Is this a veiled reference to corrupt practice or a mild admonition for some laxity with sick certificates? Charges of corruption against the Medical Department of the period were rare. Crawford details a number of courts-martial involving Indian medical officers but the only one during the Second Anglo-Maratha War relates to duelling.[14] Most medical courts-martial in the Peninsular War were for drunkenness.[15] In India, some army doctors became fabulously wealthy – John Hume, appointed as an assistant surgeon in 1799, resigned in 1808 worth £40,000 – but these fortunes resulted from trade in drugs and supplies, and also lucrative civilian private practice.[16] There is no overt record of a market in sick certificates for those officers wanting a break from Indian service.

---

13   Wellington (ed.), *Supplementary Despatches*, Vol.IV, pp.287–288.
14   Crawford, *A History of the Indian Medical Service*, Vol.II, p.234.
15   Martin R. Howard, *Wellington's Doctors: The British Army Medical Services in the Napoleonic Wars* (Staplehurst: Spellmount, 2002), p.211.
16   Crawford, *A History of the Indian Medical Service*, Vol.II, p.78.

2. Organisation of the Medical Department

Wellesley wrote to a fellow officer regarding a meeting with Dr James Anderson.

> Seringapatam, 19 November 1802. To Lieutenant General Stuart.
> I have the honour to enclose a letter and certain other papers which I have received from Mr [James] Anderson [First Member of Medical Board], written in consequence of a conversation which I had with him relative to the medical arrangements for the body of troops proposed to be assembled in the field. There are two objects to be provided; one is the field hospitals, and the other the supplies of medicines for regimental hospitals, during the time which it may be expected that the troops will be out of this country…[17]

This reveals Wellesley's close involvement in the medical preparations for the major campaign of 1803 in the Deccan and his readiness to consult with his senior medical staff. At the end of 1803, during the Siege of Gawilghur, he expressed strong views regarding medical manpower.

> Camp before Gawilghur, 13 December 1803. To the Secretary of the Government of Bombay.
> I have had the honour of receiving your letter of the 30th Nov. enclosing one from the Medical Board upon the subject of the surgeons sent to this army. Since that letter was written, this army has fought another battle [Argaum], in which many officers and 300 men were wounded; and one of those surgeons is in charge of the hospital which I have established for them. I am at present engaged in a siege, in which I must expect some loss; and, upon the whole, I do not think that I can allow these surgeons to return to Bombay, with justice to the troops under my command.[18]

Although Wellesley was ready to divert medical resources as demanded by his military operations, he was less inclined to drive fundamental organisational change. This attitude extended to the Army's other support services. In 1803, he informed the Government of Bombay that 'it has been my constant wish to conform to existing rules and establishments, and to introduce no innovations'. This was, he explained, so that at the end of the war, 'every thing might go on in its accustomed channel'.[19]

---

17   Wellington (ed.), *Supplementary Despatches*, Vol.III, pp.408–410.
18   Gurwood (ed.), *Dispatches*, Vol.II, pp.908–909.
19   Gurwood (ed.), *Dispatches*, Vol.II, p.902.

In General Orders issued at the end of 1803, Wellesley supports the anachronistic medical practice of dedicating a scarce surgeon to a sick or wounded senior military officer.

> Surjee Anjengaum, 30 December 1803. General Orders.
> Col. Stevenson, being unable, on account of severe indisposition, to remain longer in the field has permission to return to Hyderabad, and eventually to Fort St. George, for the recovery of his health, without prejudice to his situation as commanding the subsidiary force serving with the Nizam, or his allowances (The head surgeon ordered to attend the Col.)...[20]

Wellesley's sympathy for Colonel James Stevenson is understandable but the order that he be accompanied by the 'head surgeon' makes little sense when the army was in the field and already short of surgeons. The highly preferential treatment of sick and wounded senior officers persisted in the Peninsular War and the Waterloo Campaign. In India, as elsewhere, military conventions of rank outweighed the medical principles of triage and the wellbeing of the majority.

3. Hospitals

Wellesley revealed his views on general hospitals in a letter to Stevenson.

> Poonah, 2 May 1803. To Colonel Stevenson.
> You must immediately establish an hospital and leave in it all the sick of the Scotch Brigade that require carriage. Look for some secure place for this establishment within the Nizam's frontier. If you do not do this, the first action you have will be ruinous to you. I know that the surgeons will carry about the sick men till they die; although I am aware that, generally speaking, it is best to keep the sick with their corps: but in a case of this kind, where there are so many men sick, and the carriage for the sick is so insufficient, and there is every probability that there will more sick, an hospital must be established in which every case not on the mending hand ought to be thrown.[21]

Uncertainty regarding the relative roles of regimental and general hospitals was to fuel the most acrimonious medical debate of the French Revolutionary and Napoleonic Wars. The larger static general hospitals were often opened in unsuitable buildings and were overcrowded. Supporters of the regimental hospitals

---

20 Gurwood (ed.), *Dispatches*, Vol.III, p.935.
21 Gurwood (ed.), *Dispatches*, Vol.I, p.422.

pointed out that they helped to maintain the strength of the Army and limited the spread of infectious diseases. Soldiers often preferred their own regimental facility. From a modern perspective, it is clear that both types of hospital were necessary and were to a degree interdependent.[22] Wellesley acknowledged that it was not always possible to keep the sick with their regiments and that when their numbers increased the creation of a general hospital was inevitable. His tone implies that he judged this to be an evil necessity.

The separation of some medical services for Native troops is evident in a letter of 1799.

> Seringapatam, 27 November 1799. To the Secretary of Government.
> I wish to draw the attention of Government to the situation of the Native sick and wounded ordered into the General Hospital… They have been well attended and taken care of since the capture of Seringapatam, but at a considerable expense to Government. As their numbers are now much diminished, as there will be no inconvenience in taking them into the Native General Hospital, and as it is an object that they should be removed from the mosque in the fort for which the Honourable Company incurs a large expense…[23]

As for the medical services in the field, Wellesley consulted closely with Anderson regarding the location and construction of general hospitals. In a letter of 1801, the general describes awaiting the return of Anderson from the army to ensure that some plans met the doctor's 'notion of a good hospital'. In the event, the engineer was ordered to make a new plan. Wellesley was quick to confirm that this would not be at any greater expense; financial considerations were never far from his mind.[24]

The local Indian population and their leaders did not universally welcome the arrival of British hospitals (see also below regarding battlefield medicine).

> Assaye, 27 September 1803. To Major Kirkpatrick.
> Some time ago, having observed that the city of Aurungabad was by no means in a state fit for defence, and as it was probable that the course of the operations of the war would draw the troops to a distance from it, I desired Col. Stevenson to remove the hospital to Dowlutabad, and to place the sick in the lower fort. Application was accordingly made to the killadar, in my name, by Rajah Mohiput Ram, to admit the hospital into the place proposed for them, and he positively refused to receive them. …the consequence of this refusal to admit the sick and wounded troops into Dowlutabad at

---

22 Howard, *Wellington's Doctors*, pp.91–123.
23 Wellington (ed.), *Supplementary Despatches*, Vol.I, p.401.
24 Wellington (ed.), *Supplementary Despatches*, Vol.II, pp.429–430.

present is, that I must either send them to Ahmednuggur, and thereby delay my operations for a month, or I must leave these brave men exposed in an open place to the violence and ferocity of a barbarous enemy.[25]

Security was always a key consideration in the location of general hospitals in India. Wellesley was faced with the unenviable choice of leaving his sick and wounded in a dangerous place or significantly delaying his military operations to transfer them to relative safety. He faced similar problems in the Peninsula.[26]

There are few references to regimental hospitals in Wellesley's correspondence and orders. They were very much the responsibility of the regimental surgeons. General Orders of 5 June 1803 stipulate that, in view of the expected rainy weather, the 74th Regiment was to obtain tents for the regimental hospital.[27]

4. Transport of Sick and Wounded

Transporting the Indian Army's sick and wounded through an inhospitable country in an extreme climate was a constant challenge to Wellesley and his associates. The following extracts from letters early in the war well demonstrate Wellesley's determination and frustration.

Seringapatam, 24 January 1800. To Lieutenant Colonel Close.
We have had much trouble in procuring dooley boys to send away the [sick of] the 74th regt. ...The inconvenience of all this is, that the corps is delayed. If Purneah's people had said at first, either that they could not get people of the proper kind, or that they would not answer for them, I could have sent off some of our own dooley bearers who are here, and who were to have been employed in emptying our hospitals at Chittledroog, Sera, and Seringapatam. These dooley bearers must now be sent to the 74th; and the hospitals must remain full.[28]

Camp at Oggichully, 10 February 1802. General Orders.
The Colonel is obliged upon this occasion to notice a material defect in the equipments of all the Native corps, viz. an almost entire want of carriage for their sick. He is aware of the difficulty of procuring carriage of the best kind for the sick; but that difficulty, like others, can be surmounted...[29]

25 Gurwood (ed.), *Dispatches*, Vol.I, p.734.
26 Howard, *Wellington's Doctors*, p.106.
27 Gurwood (ed.), *Dispatches*, Vol.I, p.485.
28 Gurwood (ed.), *Dispatches*, Vol.I, p.58.
29 Gurwood (ed.), *Dispatches*, Vol.I, p.282.

There was much reliance on *doolies*. These contraptions, usually constructed of bamboo, are well described by Sergeant Robert Butler.

> The [sick] person is put into what is called a doolie, which is nearly in the form of one of the small houses or boxes used in Scotland for watch-dogs, being about six feet long, and three deep. In the middle of each side there is a door to go out and in by, and upon the top, at each end, there is a strong ring, through which a pole is put, and borne by four natives.[30]

Carrying the *doolies* required skill. In December 1802, Wellesley complains that 'the people are not proper palanquin or dooly-bearers'. They carried the load 'in the same manner they do a stone'.[31] Despite these drawbacks, the *doolie* bearers provided a vital service. After the Battles of Assaye and Argaum, the commander gave them a financial reward for their carriage of the wounded to the hospitals.[32] Other modes of sick transport were used, including elephants.[33]

Wellesley's most explicit guidance regarding the movement of sick and wounded is contained in a memorandum.

> Memorandum to Mr Duncan, Governor of Bombay, on the formation of the subsidiary force at Poonah, 12 July 1804.
>
> In respect to carriage for the sick, I am fully aware of the difficulty under which the governor of Bombay must always labor [sic] in this part of their equipments: I would therefore recommend that the establishment of doolies, with each Native corps, should be only 4; but that waggons should be made at Bombay to carry 20 men of each corps, besides those for whom doolies will be provided. Gen. Bellaris [Major General John Bellaris, commanding the forces at Bombay] will be able to make a pattern wagon: if it could be done with convenience and without great expense, the wagons ought to be upon springs and at all events be covered from the weather. Their wheels and axle-trees ought to be strong, and they ought to have a greater capacity of turning than the waggons which Gen. Bellaris lately sent to Poonah. It is not a matter of much consequence which number of men each wagon is made to contain, although possibly 6 men would be the most convenient number.[34]

---

30   R. Butler, *Narrative of the Life and Travels of Sergeant B------* (Edinburgh: David Brown, 1823), pp.54–55.
31   Wellington (ed.), *Supplementary Despatches*, Vol.III, p.445.
32   Gurwood (ed.), *Dispatches*, Vol.II, p.902.
33   Gurwood (ed.), *Dispatches*, Vol.II, p.896.
34   Gurwood (ed.), *Dispatches*, Vol.II, p.1337.

The French led the way in ambulance design during this period. Most notable was Dominique Jean Larrey's 'flying ambulance', a fully functioning organisation for casualty evacuation.[35] The British arrangements were opportunistic and they fell short of Larrey's humanitarian vision. In this context, Wellesley's suggestions for the design of wagons used solely for the carriage of sick and wounded are of interest. Later, in the Peninsula, he ordered that spring wagons and bullock carts be reserved for the transport of sick and wounded but there is no evidence that these vehicles were adapted for this use.

5. Battlefield Medicine

All the battlefield medical references relate to the bloody Battle of Assaye fought on 23 September 1803. The British emerged victorious over the Maratha forces albeit with approximately 500 killed and more than a thousand wounded. This was between a quarter and a third of the troops involved in the fighting. Many wounds were inflicted by artillery and were severe.[36]

Assaye was a British intelligence failure; it can be argued that both sides blundered in to the battle. There was no time to plan casualty evacuation or to prepare hospitals. The later General Orders reflect efforts to catch up. Four days after the battle:

Camp at Assaye, 27 September 1803. General Orders.
1.   Officers commanding corps will prepare, as soon as circumstances will permit them, returns of their wounded men whom it is desirable to send to a field hospital.
2.   How many of that number require dooley carriage, how many can go in carts, how many upon elephants, how many upon horses or bullocks, and how many can walk.
3.   Numbers of wounded men who might be kept with the army, without detriment to them.

Major General Wellesley wishes to have this return as soon as possible, in order that no time may be lost in making arrangements to send off the wounded men; and he requests that officers commanding Native corps will let Mr. Gilmour (superintending surgeon) have a note of the carriages they have got, so that it may be seen what quantity is available for the service.[37]

---

35   Martin R. Howard, *Napoleon's Doctors: The Medical Services of the Grande Armée* (Stroud: Spellmount, 2006), pp.80–87.
36   Howard, *Wellington and the British Army's Indian Campaigns*, p.104.
37   Gurwood (ed.), *Dispatches*, Vol.I, p.735.

This was mostly information gathering, the commander still uncertain of the number of wounded. A letter of the same date starts to make more definitive arrangements.

> Camp at Assaye, 27 September 1803. To the Governor of Bombay.
> 1. As nearly all the men who were wounded in the action between the British troops and the united arms of Dowlut Rao Scindiah and the Rajah of Berar, on the 23rd inst., were struck by cannon shot, and it is probable that some of them will be disabled entirely, it will be a great convenience if an early opportunity is taken of removing those of this description from the field hospital to Bombay. From hence the Europeans may be sent to England, and the Natives to the coast of Coramandel, as opportunity may offer.
> 2. I cannot at present say the number of cases of this description which there will be, but I think it almost certain that there will be no less than 100; neither can I state the exact place at which I shall establish the hospital, on account of the difficulty of prevailing upon the killa-dars of the forts belonging to the Souhab of the Deccan to receive our wounded soldiers, or the time at which the men will be sufficiently recovered to be moved without injury.
> 3. But I request you to have 100 doolies prepared to be sent off to such place as I may hereafter point out; and to have all the arrangements made for procuring bearers for those doolies, so that no time may be lost in sending them from Bombay, when I may find it necessary to call for them.
> 4. I am greatly in want of medical assistants, and I shall be much obliged to you if you will give orders that 6 assistant surgeons may be sent to Ahmednuggur without loss of time, to place themselves under my orders.[38]

Each regiment had sent out parties to collect the wounded but some lay on the field for several days before being reached. Wellesley made no allusion to dressing stations or temporary field hospitals but these certainly existed. Drummer Roderick Innes recalled visiting a 'hospital' in a tent two miles from the field; 'I counted 12 saws cutting as fast as they could drive'.[39]

In General Orders of 29 September, it was confirmed that the more substantial field hospital was to be at Adjuntee (Ajanta). The first 300 wounded were to be

---

38   Gurwood (ed.), *Dispatches*, Vol.I, pp.735–736.
39   R. Innes, *The Life of Roderick Innes lately of the Seventy-Eighth Regiment* (Stonehaven: Alexander Clark, 1844), pp.132–4.

transferred there by *doolies* on 1 October.[40] Adjuntee was 20 miles north of Assaye and Wellesley was anxious.

> Camp at Assaye, 29 September 1803. To Lieutenant General Stuart.
> I shall have to send 700 men to the hospital which I must estab-lish at Adjuntee, upon the extreme frontier, as the Nizam's killadar of Dowlutabad will not admit one sick or wounded into that place; and I must either put them into Adjuntee, or send them to Ahmednuggur, which will delay my operations for at least a month. At the same time, to place the sick at Adjuntee is very inconvenient. Col. Stevenson, who has gone down the Adjuntee ghaut, says that it is a place of security; but I am much afraid that, if we should move to a distance from it, the wounded may be exposed. But owing to the obstinacy of the killadar of Dowlutabad, I can do nothing better for them without great inconvenience.[41]

Wellesley visited the wounded at Adjuntee on 8 October. His inspection resulted in the following.

> Camp at Assaye, 8 October 1803. General Orders.
> Major Gen. Wellesley requests that officers, excepting those commanding corps, and those whose duty it may be, will not go into the hospital, as the crowds that go there only tend to distress the wounded men. Orders have been given at the gates that no soldiers or sepoys may be admitted in the hospital, excepting those of the latter sent to work, and such men as may have passes from the commanding officer.
> Commanding officers will therefore give passes to such men as may be desirous of seeing their relations, or as they may wish to send into the hospital.
> The wounded men are much distressed by the sun in the buildings which they occupy; and Major Gen. Wellesley will be much obliged to commanding officers of corps if they will order as many shades as possible to be made by the men of their corps, with the boughs of trees, &c. &c.: they should be of a size 12 feet square. Officers commanding Native corps will send into the hospital 1 careful non-commissioned officer, or steady man, and under his command each corps of infantry 12, each corps of cavalry 6, sepoy boys. They are to assist the Native troops in drawing their provisions, &c., and otherwise attend to and take care of them.[42]

40 Gurwood (ed.), *Dispatches*, Vol.I, p.740.
41 Wellington, *Dispatches*, Vol.I, p.741.
42 Wellington, *Dispatches*, Vol.I, p.766.

This reveals a compassionate commander who had a keen interest in the well-being of his wounded men. It was not unusual for General Orders of the period to give instruction as to medical arrangements but Wellesley's attention to detail is striking. Not only did he note that the patients were exposed to the sun but he stipulated the exact size of the manufactured shades. He was determined to leave nothing to chance. He remained concerned regarding the safety of the hospital which was on the high road to Hindustan. In a letter of the same date to Major Shawe, he reflected that, 'I have done the best I can for [the wounded], and have secured them as far as in my power'.[43]

The limitations of the Medical Department, particularly the shortage of surgeons, could compromise military operations. This was the case after Assaye.

> Camp at Phoolmurry, 18 miles north of Aurungabad, 12 October 1803. To the Adjutant-General.
> After the battle at Assye the enemy fled down the Adjuntee Ghaut. They were followed by Colonel Stevenson: but as I was obliged to call his division to my neighbourhood, in order that I might have the assistance of the medical men belonging to the division under his command to dress my wounded soldiers, and of the carriage of his sick to remove them to the hospital, and as it was necessary that I should have repeated conferences with the sirdars in the service of the Soubah of the Deccan before I could fix upon any place to receive the wounded, some days elapsed before Colonel Stevenson descended the Ghaut. The enemy again fled towards Burhampoor…[44]

6. Supply of Medicines

In the earlier eighteenth century, Company doctors often relied on traditional Indian medicines and methods. However, indigenous medicine gradually came to be disparaged and Crown and Company practitioners increasingly turned to European medicine.[45] At the outset of 1803, Wellesley specified the drugs most needed by his medical department.

> Seringapatam, 20 January 1803. To J. Duncan Esq. Governor of Bombay.
> Medical stores: We ought to have 3 months' consumption of these for 3,000 Europeans and 15,000 Native troops, particularly bark, Madeira wine, mercurial ointment, calomel, and not forgetting nitrous acid…The

43   Gurwood (ed.), *Dispatches*, Vol.I, p.765.
44   Wellington (ed.), *Supplementary Despatches*, Vol.IV, p.199.
45   Charters, *Disease, War and The Imperial State*, pp.148–149.

medical and military stores ought each to be under charge of an officer of the departments to which they belong, with the proper number of servants for their care and delivery.[46]

As for other elements of the medical services, Wellesley involved himself in the minutiae of drug supplies. The following letter was written six days before the Battle of Assaye.

> Camp, 17 September 1803. To the Adjutant General.
> The order of the 14th August regarding medical supplies was issued before I found that the corps were likely to be in want of medicines, and I had no reason to believe that any provision had been made at Fort St. George to supply them. The medical supplies are now on the road to Ahmednuggur.
> I have, however, this day seen a letter from the medical store-keeper at Fort St. George, dated the 3rd instant, to the medical staff-surgeon with this division, stating that by order of the Commander-in-Chief he was to despatch medical supplies for the troops under my command to Masulipatam, from whence they would proceed by Hyderabad to join the troops. It is not probable that these supplies will be within reach till the end of November, and in the beginning of January another supply will become due: I therefore propose that the supplies expected from Bombay shall be used in the quarter commencing in October, and that those which the medical storekeeper at Madras will have despatched in the beginning of this month shall be used in the quarter commencing in January. As soon as I find that the latter will approach Hyderabad I will make arrangements for bringing them forward to a situation from which they can be brought in safety to the troops.[47]

There are other communications relating to the labyrinthine nature of drug supply and the means of payment.[48] In October 1803, Colonel Stevenson's Corps alone required 54 bullocks to transport medicines.[49]

---

46 Guwood (ed.), *Dispatches*, Vol.I, pp.326–327.
47 Wellington (ed.), *Supplementary Despatches*, Vol.IV, p.177.
48 Gurwood (ed.), *Dispatches*, Vol.II, p.891.
49 Gurwood (ed.), *Dispatches*, Vol.I, p.813.

7. Disease, General

Two letters from 1800 refer to disease in both the Native and King's troops.

> Camp at Archingherry, 22 May 1800. To Lieutenant Colonel Close.
> I have received a most distressing account of the state of the 1st regt. of cavalry; they had been very sickly; latterly some men have died; the whole regiment are much frightened and out of spirits, and about 20 sepoys, 9 of whom had been many years in the service, have deserted. I have desired Pater to halt them at Hurryhur, to put the sick under cover, and the whole regiment into the fort, if necessary. As Dr. Anderson thinks they will not recover either health or spirits until they reach Arcot, I am afraid that I shall be obliged to send them to the rear entirely, and eventually to the Carnatic.[50]

> Camp at Kalaspoor, 30 September 1800. To Major General Brathwaite.
> I have long wished to write to you about the state of my regiment. They have been exceedingly sickly ever since they went into Seringapatam, and were so much so when I took the field that I could not bring them with me, of which I was very desirous. They have continued so ever since, and latterly their sickness has increased to such a degree as to induce Lieut. Col. Shee to request Col. Saxon to encamp them on the outside of the fort, keeping inside it only the men on duty. I have written to Col. Saxon to desire that he will comply with this request. This, however, will at least be only a temporary relief, and what I have to request is, that you would do me the favour to turn over in your mind whether it will be possible to relieve the 33rd from Seringapatam entirely. It is probable that they would recover if they were to go to the coast, but they certainly never will while they remain at Seringapatam. At the same time I must inform you that it is absolutely necessary that there should be a regiment of Europeans at that place as long as the inhabitants are allowed to remain in the fort.[51]

One potential advantage of recruiting native soldiers (sepoys) to the ranks of the East India Company's army was their greater immunity to the diseases of the country such as malaria. However, the first of these letters makes it explicit that Native regiments were also badly affected by disease. Sick returns from the eighteenth century show surprisingly little difference between sepoys and Europeans.[52]

---

50 Gurwood (ed.), *Dispatches*, Vol.I, p.96.
51 Gurwood (ed.), *Dispatches*, Vol.II, p.1627.
52 Charters, *Disease, War and The Imperial State*, p.170.

The high rate of sickness in the 33rd Regiment raised the question of whether they could be moved to a healthier area without compromising security. This remained a dilemma throughout the War, preservation of the health of the European troops having to be balanced against military necessities. At the end of 1803, Wellesley reported that the European troops in Guzerat were unhealthy:

Camp before Gawilghur, 11 December 1803. To Captain Armstrong.
There are in Guzerat 3 complete regiments of Europeans besides detach-ments which in numbers of companies ought to amount to a fourth; but Col. Murray has been obliged to draw from the garrisons, and from Surat, the troops thought necessary and allotted for their defence, in order to reinforce his corps in the field. The 65th regt., which arrived at Bombay 900 strong in May last, had not now 100 men for duty; and the 75th regt. is nearly in the same state. Under the circumstances, it does not appear to me that it will be practicable to withdraw a regiment of Europeans from Guzerat, without exposing to risk all the British interests in that quarter.[53]

Although Wellesley and the Commander-in-Chief Gerard Lake valued their sepoy soldiers, there was a strongly held view that a core of European troops was vital in battle and to protect wider British interests in the country.

An early letter to his brother, shortly after Wellesley's arrival in India, demon-strates that he already understood the vulnerability of his men to disease and the need for vigilance.

Fort St. George, 23 September 1798. To Hon. Henry Wellesley.
Eight companies of the 33rd are arrived, and nearly every man of them has had the flux [dysentery] upon the passage; among others I have had it. Fifteen men have died of it. It is to be attributed to the neglect of Captain --------------'s office in supplying the water. Instead of sending up to Hooghly for it, it was taken into the casks at Calcutta, and was brackish. It is unpardonable, as I warned him of it, and I am afraid that I must make a public complaint of him.[54]

Wellesley also appreciated the limited efficacy of contemporary medical therapies. He wrote to Colonel Campbell in November 1803, suggesting that he return to England, as '...nothing but that can be a sufficient remedy for the disposition to fevers which you appear to have'.[55] Only a change in climate would lead to a cure. Wellesley further revealed a healthy scepticism of contemporary medical practice

53 Gurwood (ed.), *Dispatches*, Vol.II, p.905.
54 Wellington (ed.), *Supplementary Despatches*, Vol.I, p.96.
55 Gurwood (ed.), *Dispatches*, Vol.II, pp.842–843.

in a letter to James Kirkpatrick, the Resident at Hyderabad, of June 1802. He was happy to send bark to Hyderabad for the use of the Nizam, '…but I acknowledge that I fear the only benefit he will derive from the prescription will be that which a person who has long been affected with sickness, derives from the hope of a cure'.[56] Ironically, Peruvian bark was one of the very few active agents of the period, the quinine it contained having efficacy in malaria. Mercury, the most widely used treatment for fever in India, was both useless and toxic.

8. Disease Prevention

The groundbreaking works of John Pringle, Richard Brocklesby and David Monro in the eighteenth century described practical preventative measures which might be employed to preserve the health of an army in garrison and in the field. These initiatives required the understanding and support of senior military officers.

> Camp at Senboogaum, 21 August 1803. To Colonel Murray.
> Every attention must be paid to economy, but I consider nothing in this country so valuable as the life and health of the British soldier, and nothing so expensive as soldiers in hospital. On this ground, it is worth while to incur almost any expense to preserve their lives and their health.[57]

Wellesley was sustaining a laudable tradition. After the Battle of Plassey in 1757, Robert Clive struggled to protect the health of his soldiers. He informed the Secret Committee that he had garrisoned them in a good location, 'as the lives of men are very precious at this critical juncture'.[58]

Colonel Wellesley's Regimental Orders on board ship in 1797 show the young officer determined to preserve the lives of his men and also his understanding of the necessary pragmatic measures.

> Fort William, July 1797. Regimental Orders for On Board Ship.
> 20. It is almost needless to remind the officers of the necessity of preserving cleanliness in the ship.
> 21. The men should be made to wash their feet and legs every morning and evening, and occasionally water should be thrown over every man; every day if possible.
> 22. The decks must frequently be fumigated…[59]

---

56   Gurwood (ed.), *Dispatches*, Vol.I, p.286.
57   Gurwood (ed.), *Dispatches*, Vol.I, p.648.
58   Charters, *Disease, War and The Imperial State*, pp.162–163.
59   Wellington (ed.), *Supplementary Despatches*, Vol.I, p.21.

The prioritisation of the principles of 'military hygiene' persisted when on land.

> Seringapatam, 1 March 1800. General Orders.
> The commanding officers of corps will be so kind as to give particular orders respecting the preservation of cleanliness in their lines. Every morning all dirt must be removed to a distance in front of the encampment beyond the quarter guards. The privies must be made in one particular place at a distance from the tents. The quarter masters of European corps, and quarter master serjeants of Native corps, are responsible for the cleanliness of the encampment; and the D. Q. M. Gen. will be so kind as to notice and report any neglect in this particular which he may perceive. A captain of the day to mount in camp, to whom all extraordinaries are to be reported, and who will report verbally to Col. Wellesley.[60]

It is noteworthy that Wellesley demanded that he should receive a personal report of any infractions.

We do not know what Wellesley thought of the contemporary views of disease causation. A directive of May 1801 suggests that he may have adhered to the still widely accepted 'miasmatic' theory. In an attempt to reduce disease rates in the 33rd and East India Company regiments he ordered the inner ditch of the Seringapatam fort to be filled in. He was concerned that the open ditch 'is one great cause of disease'.[61] He also believed climatic conditions to have a role in the sickness of his men.

> Seringapatam, 10 December 1802. General Orders.
> The Medical board having stated to the Commander in Chief their opinion that the sickness, particularly when cases with which Native corps stationed in cold damp situations in the vicinity of hills, and surrounded by jungles, are so severely affected, is principally caused by the troops being out at exercise, before the damps and dews are dissipated by the sun, which, from chilling the men, produce fever; and that the most salutary effects might be expected if the time of drill was changed from daybreak to 9 o'clock...[62]

Although Wellesley was reluctant to make profound organisational change, he was open to medical innovation.

60   Gurwood (ed.), *Dispatches*, Vol.I, p.71.
61   Wellington (ed.), *Supplementary Despatches*, Vol.II, p.377.
62   Gurwood (ed.), *Dispatches*, Vol.I, p.316.

Seringapatam, 27 December 1802. To Colonel Montressor.
I shall also be much obliged to you if you will be so kind as to desire Mr.
Gourlay [Assistant Surgeon William Gourlay] to send here two children
inoculated with the cowpox. I want to have my godson inoculated.[63]

The inoculation Wellesley refers to was actually vaccination, introduced by Edward
Jenner four years earlier. Unlike the previous practice of inoculation (the implantation of the *Variola* virus), vaccination using cowpox did not cause an actual case
of smallpox.

Conclusions

Taken in their entirety, the medically themed extracts from the *Dispatches* and
Supplementary Despatches allow us to reach a number of conclusions regarding
Wellesley's attitudes to the Indian Army Medical Department and his associated
actions.

- He valued the contribution of competent army doctors and was very ready to
  praise, defend and support them.
- Regarding the organisation of the Medical Department, he discussed arrangements and staffing with senior army doctors but made no fundamental
  changes to organisation.
- He gave qualified support to the establishment of general hospitals (for
  European and Native troops) and prioritised their security. He faced local
  resistance to general hospitals.
- Made great efforts to provide *doolie* transport for the sick and wounded and
  made explicit suggestions for the design of ambulance wagons.
- Ensured the establishment of a field/general hospital after the Battle of Assaye
  and showed personal concern for the welfare of the wounded. He delayed
  military operations to optimise their treatment.
- He made detailed logistical arrangements for the supply of medicines.
- He comprehended the impact of disease on the viability of military operations
  and took necessary steps (for example, withholding sick regiments from active
  service). He expressed scepticism regarding contemporary medicines.
- He understood the importance of 'military hygiene' in maintaining the health
  and manpower of the Army. He consulted with the Medical Board and took
  practical measures to ensure cleanliness and remove specific causes of infection. He was open to innovations in preventative medicine (for example,
  vaccination).

---

63 Wellington (ed.), *Supplementary Despatches*, Vol.III, p.501.

Wellesley's Health in India 1797–1805

Wellesley had definite views on how to protect his own health in India. He shared them with his brother, Henry:

> I know but one receipt for good health in this country, and that is to live moderately, to drink little or no wine, to use exercise, to keep the mind employed, and, if possible, to keep in good humour with the world. The last is the most difficult, for, as you have often observed, there is scarcely a good tempered man in India.[64]

Despite such precautions and his unusually robust constitution, he had a number of health problems during his service in India. In Madras in 1798, he had an episode of dysentery ('flux'). He rather played this down in his correspondence, but 15 men of his regiment died of the disorder.[65] He was later to be troubled by a skin affliction, possibly fungal in nature, and back pain. The gradual deterioration in his health noted by those around him was due to a remitting and relapsing fever which was almost certainly malaria. In his letters, he made eighteen references to the disorder. In April 1801, he informed Henry that the fever was in remission but that he was feeling weak.[66] His close friend John Malcolm described him suffering from fever and being fretful and anxious.[67]

Wellesley's poor health contributed to his decision to return home in the summer of 1804. He believed that he had served in India as long 'as any man ought who can serve anywhere else'.[68] A year later, on his voyage home, he fully voiced his concerns.

> St. Helena, 3 July 1805. To Colonel Malcolm.
> My health has been much mended by the voyage, and particularly by a short residence upon this island; and I am convinced that if I had not quitted India, I should have had a serious fit of illness. I was wasting away daily, and latterly, when at Madras, I found my strength failed, which had always before held out.[69]

Wellesley had been fortunate to survive his eight years in the Subcontinent. Of 353 officers of the Bengal Army who were promoted to lieutenant colonel by 1820,

64 Wellington (ed.), *Supplementary Despatches*, Vol.II, p.501.
65 Wellington (ed.), *Supplementary Despatches*, Vol.I, p.96.
66 Gurwood (ed.), *Dispatches*, Vol.I, pp.251–252.
67 R. Muir, *Wellington: The Path to Victory 1769–1814* (New Haven: Yale University Press, 2013), p.163.
68 Gurwood (ed.), *Dispatches*, Vol.II, p.1216.
69 Gurwood (ed.), *Dispatches*, Vol.II, p.1456.

42 percent died in India, elsewhere in the East, or in transit. As only three died in action, the overwhelming majority of the deaths can be attributed to disease.[70]

Select Bibliography

Manuscripts

British Library: IOR/F/4/155/2723: Compilation of Medical Regulations (Madras, 1803).
National Army Museum, London: 1963-08-11: Arthur Wellesley's Order Book 1803–1804.

Printed Primary Sources

Anon. *East-India Register and Directory for 1803* (London: Cox, Son and Baylis, 1803).
Anon., *Fifth Report of the Commissioners of Military Enquiry: Army Medical Department* (London, 1808).
Ballingall, G.B., *Practical Observations on Fever, Dysentery and Liver Complaints as they occur amongst the European troops in India* (Edinburgh: Adam Black, 1823).
Moor, Capt. E., *A Compilation of all the Orders and Regulations of the Bombay Army* (Bombay: Courier and Gazette, 1801).
Martin, M. (ed.), *The Dispatches, Minutes, and Correspondence of the Marquess Wellesley during his administration in India* (London: John Murray, 1886–1887).
Wellington, 2nd Duke of, (ed.), *Supplementary Despatches and Memoranda of Field Marshal Arthur Duke of Wellington K.G.* (London: John Murray, 1858–1859).
Gurwood, Colonel (ed.), *The Dispatches of Field Marshal the Duke of Wellington during his various campaigns in India, Denmark, Portugal, Spain, The Low Countries and France* (London: Parker, Furnivall and Parker, 1844).

Secondary Sources

Cantlie, Lt. Gen. Sir N., *A History of the Army Medical Department* (Edinburgh: Churchill Livingstone, 1974).

---

70   B. Collins, 'Effectiveness and the British Officer Corps 1793–1815', in K. Linch and M. McCormack (eds), *Britain's Soldiers: Rethinking War and Society 1715–1815* (Liverpool: Liverpool University Press, 2014), pp.70, 75.

Charters, Erica, *Disease, War and the Imperial State: The Welfare of the British Armed Forces during the Seven Years War* (Chicago: The University of Chicago Press, 2014).

Crawford, Lt Col. D.G., *A History of the Indian Medical Service 1600–1913* (London: W. Thacker, 1914).

Harrison, M., 'Disease and Medicine in the Armies of British India 1750–1830', in Hudson, G.L. (ed.), *British Military and Naval Medicine 1600–1830* (Amsterdam: Rodopi, 2007)

Howard, Martin R., *Napoleon's Doctors: The Medical Services of the Grande Armée* (Stroud: Spellmount, 2006)

Howard, Martin R., *Wellington and The British Army's Indian Campaigns 1798–1805* (Barnsley: Pen and Sword, 2020)

Howard, Martin, *Wellington's Doctors: The British Army Medical Services in the Napoleonic Wars* (Staplehurst: Spellmount, 2002)

Muir, R., *Wellington: The Path to Victory 1769–1814* (New Haven: Yale University Press, 2013).

6

'The Exquisite *Militaire*': The Army Officer, Fashion, and Satire in the aftermath of Waterloo

Luke Reynolds

In 1818, *The Literary Gazette*'s society writer, Felix MacDonogh, visited the wildly popular panorama of the Battle of Waterloo at Henry Aston Barker's Rotunda in Leicester Square. In his detailed report, not just of the panorama itself but of the crowds that flocked to it, MacDonogh identified five military archetypes that could be found at the entertainment. There was the enthusing old general, the silent military spectator, the 'garrulous but worthy' disabled veteran, the helpful officer who acted as a volunteer guide, and finally, the 'Exquisite *militaire*'.[1] This last, according to MacDonogh, was a 'fop',

> …youthful and blooming, affected and vain, lounging with an air of *sans souci*, a toothpick or violet in his mouth, a quizzing-glass either suspended round his neck or fixed in the socket of his eye, seeming to disdain taking an interest in the thing, yet lisping out, 'Upon my *thoul*, it's d----d like, d----d like indeed,- *yeth*, that's just the place where we *lotht tho* many men,- it's quite *ridiculouth*, how *like* it *ith*.' What a contrast! So much valour, yet so much feminine conceit, starch and perfume, whalebone and pasteboard![2]

---

1   Felix MacDonogh, *The Hermit in London, or Sketches of English Manners* (London: Henry Colburn and Co., 1821), Vol.I, p.126.
2   MacDonogh, *Hermit in London*, Vol.I, pp.126–127.

None of this would have been particularly shocking to *The Literary Gazette*'s readers. In the years following Waterloo and the end of the Napoleonic Wars, the military exquisite, fop, beau, or dandy had become a regular character in society pages and satirical works.

There are multiple explanations for the rise in criticism of these fashion forward military men. Dandified officers presented a colourful target for satirists of all stripes, lampooned either to directly criticize their behaviour or used as a vector through which to condemn *du jour* problems in British society. The satirists were aided in their efforts by a general antipathy towards dandies among the public, who viewed excesses in dress and behaviour as at best a misuse of time and resources and at worst as not only the outward expression of social vices and moral failings but also an attempt to violate the natural orders of class and gender.[3] Indeed, British popular culture had a long and proud tradition of ridiculing men who prized appearance above all else, with illustrations, plays, and other forms of entertainments lampooning a succession of coxcombs, fops, macaronis, fribbles, exquisites, beaux, and dandies.[4] While several of these terms originally had specific sartorial connotations, by the period under consideration here many had been folded together.[5] An 1823 dictionary of slang defined the dandy as 'an invention of 1816, and applied to persons whose extravagant dress called forth the sneers of the vulgar' while noting that 'men of fashion all became dandy soon after.'[6] As if to hammer home the point, the same publication defined the 'exquisite' eleven pages later as 'another name for Dandy', while another slang dictionary published the same year used fop to as a catch-all term to describe macaronis, fribbles, and coxcombs.[7] It is

---

3   Thomas Carlyle, *Sartor Resartus: The Life and Opinions of Herr Teufelsdröckh* (London: Saunders and Otley, 1838); Dominic Janes, *Oscar Wilde Prefigured: Queer Fashioning and British Caricature, 1750–1900* (Chicago: University of Chicago Press, 2016); David Kuchta, *The Three-Piece Suit and Modern Masculinity: England 1550–1850* (Berkeley: University of California Press, 2002); Brent Shannon, *The Cut of His Coat: Men, Dress, and Consumer Culture in Britain, 1860–1914* (Athens: Ohio University Press, 2006); Peter McNeil, *Pretty Gentlemen: Macaroni Men and the Eighteenth-Century Fashion World* (New Haven: Yale University Press, 2018); Thomas A. Foster, *Sex and the Eighteenth-Century Man: Massachusetts and the History of Sexuality in America* (Boston: Beacon Press, 2006); Vic Gatrell, *City of Laughter: Sex and Satire in Eighteenth-Century London* (New York: Walker & Company, 2006); David Francis Taylor, *The Politics of Parody: A Literary History of Caricature, 1760–1830* (New Haven: Yale University Press, 2018).

4   See, for example, Colley Cibber, *Love's Last Shift; or, the Fool in Fashion* (London: H. Rhodes, 1702); McNeil, *Pretty Gentlemen*.

5   Ben Townsend has posited that the term 'beau' was superseded in the second decade of the nineteenth century by 'dandy', to the point where the beaux of Wellington's army were retroactively rechristened dandies. Ben Townsend, *Fashioning Regulation, Regulating Fashion: The Uniforms and Dress of the British Army 1800–1815* (Warwick: Helion & Co., 2019–2020), Vol.1, p.263, Vol.2, pp.16–45.

6   Jon Bee, *Slang. A Dictionary of the Turf, the Ring, the Chase, the Pit, of Bon-Ton, and the Varieties of Life* (London: T. Hughes, 1823), p.63.

7   Bee, *Slang*, p.74; Pierce Egan, *Grose's Classical Dictionary of the Vulgar Tongue* (London: Sherwood, Neely, and Jones, 1823), unpaginated, entries for Coxcomb, Fribble, and Macaroni. See also, in the same dictionary, Beau-Nasty and Cully.

also worth reiterating that all of these terms carried negative connotations for the majority of the population.

This chapter will follow the example of the slang dictionaries of the time and treat these epithets as synonymous. This approach is perhaps most controversial when it comes to 'macaroni', which enjoyed a limited and very specific eighteenth-century definition and experienced less generalization of meaning than other terms. However, as we have just seen, the term was still sufficiently in use in the 1820s to be included in dictionaries of slang. Perhaps more significantly, there are notable similarities between the officers under discussion here and the original macaronis: both styles were defined by the specific cut of their clothes, both wore swords, both drew inspiration from the power and politics of royal courts, both, to a certain extent, used money to purchase position, and both favoured styles that extended their height (although the vertically styled wigs of the macaronis had been replaced by overly large military headgear boasting extreme plumes). Perhaps most significant, however, is the role that satire played in establishing these styles in the popular imagination and simultaneously ridiculing them and those that wore them.[8]

Nor were officers or the army itself blameless targets. General Alexander Cavalié Mercer, in a reminiscence of the changes of uniforms he had witnessed in his career, recalled military dandies who sported hair ribbons that 'streamed out to an immense distance in the wind', cravats of such 'immense size, or rather an immense number, one put on over the other' that they hid everything below the mouth, and swords worn so low they required a wheel on the tip of the scabbard.[9] To make matters worse, as the war receded, stories of the poor social behaviour of certain 'elite' regiments became more common in the press. In 1824, for example, the extravagantly dressed but 'ungentleman-like officers' of the 10th (Prince of Wales's Own) Regiment of (Light) Dragoons (Hussars) were banned from 'places of public amusement' by Major General Sir Colquhoun Grant, commander of the Dublin garrison, because of their 'rude and insolent behaviour.'[10] Simultaneously, many officers, both veterans and new recruits, found themselves thrust further into the public eye as they enjoyed the luxuries of peace and life in London. Finally, the tone of the military overall was being set by a Whitehall and Horse Guards establishment who recognized the power of uniforms when it came to preserving order and a Regent – later King – who embraced all forms of pomp and ceremony.[11] The Prince Regent (later George IV) took a direct interest in the sump-

8   For the definitive exploration of both macaronis and their place in satire, see McNeil, *Pretty Gentlemen*.

9   Alexander Cavalié Mercer, 'Military Reminiscences of Latter End of the Eighteenth and Beginning of Nineteenth Centuries', in R.J. MacDonald, *The History of the Dress of the Royal Regiment of Artillery, 1625–1897* (London: Henry Sotheran & Co., 1899), pp.52, 65–67.

10   *The Dublin Evening Mail* quoted in Tenth Hussars, *The Morning Chronicle*, March 23, 1824; see also The Tenth, *The Morning Chronicle*, April 6, 1824.

11   Scott Hughes Myerly, *British Military Spectacle: From the Napoleonic Wars Through the Crimea* (Cambridge: Harvard University Press, 1996); Dominique Gaulme and François Gaulme, *Power & Style:*

tuousness of the armed forces, exerting significant influence on the updates to uniform regulations during his reign. When colonel of the 10th Hussars, he had instituted so many uniform changes that the regiment earned the nickname 'the Prince's Dolls.'[12] Satire of military exquisites became a way to indirectly criticize both militaristic order and the monarchy. The result was that the officers of the British Army, whether they actively participated in the change or not, found their public image shifting from the heroes of the Peninsula and Waterloo to ridiculed dandies in a relatively short period of time.

This chapter seeks to examine a crucial part of that shift in public perception via the depictions of dandified officers in visual and literary satire between the second half of the 1810s and the 1840s. Although spread across four decades and multiple mediums while incorporating a variety of political viewpoints, there are common themes to the criticisms explored here, many of which looked back to the criticisms of coxcombs, fops, and macaronis which emerged in the eighteenth century. Several of the pieces implicitly feminize these officers. For the illustrated works, this meant exaggerating the officers' thighs and buttocks as well as their extreme postures and poses. Literary works, lacking visual clues, instead highlighted the delicate natures and extensive toilettes of their subjects. This feminisation served several purposes. Most obviously it further emphasized the connections with civilian dandies, who were often also depicted in this gendered manner.[13] However, it was arguably meant to be more damaging towards the military, given the explicitly masculine nature of both wartime depictions of soldiers and the abstract idea of a military career. In addition, among certain more conservative artists and audiences, feminization had, since the eighteenth century, been code for excess, providing another vector for criticism that found a new, wider audience in the post-war economic downturn.[14]

Other works seized on another theme of criticism that had been popular since before the Napoleonic Wars – that dandyism was the outward personification of inward moral weakness and failings. Here again we find excess, along with its concomitant sin, pride, condemned. Perhaps less obviously, however, an obsession with outward appearance was also seen as a signifier of lust and idleness. There

---

A World History of Politics and Dress (Paris: Flammarion, 2012); Christine Haynes, *Our Friends the Enemies: The Occupation of France after Napoleon* (Cambridge: Harvard University Press, 2018); Luke Reynolds, '"There John Bull might be seen in all his glory": Cross-Channel Tourism and the British Army of Occupation in France, 1815–1818', *Journal of Tourism History* 12:2 (2020), pp.139–155. For the style and politics of British military uniforms during the Napoleonic Wars themselves, see Townsend, *Fashioning Regulation, Regulating Fashion*, vols.1 & 2.

12 Isaac Robert Cruikshank and S. W. Fores, *The Dandy Tailor, planning a new Hungry Dress*, 1819, London, The British Museum, BM Satires 13237, 1868,0808.8446. See also Townsend, *Fashioning Regulation, Regulating Fashion*, Vol.2, especially pp.172–242; John Mollo, *The Prince's Dolls: Scandals, Skirmishes and Splendours of the First British Hussars: 1793–1815* (London: Leo Cooper, 1997), p.135.

13 Janes, *Oscar Wilde Prefigured*, pp.97–128.

14 Shannon, *The Cut of His Coat*.

are multiple depictions of military fops rising in the late afternoon, overindulging in food and drink, seducing women, and generally living for pleasure alone. Of course, even as satirists condemned these dandies as roués who seduced other men's wives, the traditional portrayal of them in groups combined with their feminization to instil an inevitable undercurrent of homophobia in these depictions. Once again, these were all vices often associated with civilian dandies, but took on an added level of social vice (and potential danger) when associated with men who were, in theory, involved in a disciplined profession tasked with the defence of the realm.

Several of these satirists set out to explicitly exaggerate and puncture the braggadocio of the officers, most notably those who had entered the service after Waterloo, who sought to supplement, or even replace, achievement with frippery. Beyond the general British disdain for those who postured without the skill or experience to back it up, such attempts to purchase respect and position via clothes tied into another long-term criticism laid at the feet of macaronis and fops – that they upset the system of class and societal cues and thus threatened the natural order.[15]

While each artist or author discussed here engaged to one degree or another with these critical themes, they also had their own motivations for burlesquing military exquisites, which influenced which of two groups of officers they targeted. Some almost exclusively targeted officers who had not seem combat, while others made no distinction or deliberately took aim at Peninsular and Waterloo veterans. The creatives who saw a difference between bloodied and unbloodied officers largely targeted officers who had purchased commissions after the Napoleonic Wars. Many of these young men, in an attempt to disguise their lack of proven martial prowess, took advantage of the Army's cost-saving requirement that they purchase their own uniforms and pushed what were already often overly elaborate regulation uniform cuts and designs to extremes.[16] They compensated for the lack of experience with pigeon breasts, padded shoulders, skin-tight breeches and sleeves, and overly large boots and headgear. Satirists, recognizing the inherent absurdity of these military macaronis, exaggerated their accessories and uniform cuts to even more absurd lengths and feigned terror at their false bravado. The political views of these creatives varied. Some were relatively conservative and

15 Janes, *Oscar Wilde Prefigured*; Shannon, *The Cut of His Coat*; Kuchta, *The Three-Piece Suit and Modern Masculinity*. For criticism of male sartorial excess in the eighteenth century, see Foster, *Sex and the Eighteenth-Century Man*; McNeil, *Pretty Gentlemen*; Gatrell, *City of Laughter*.
16 The savings were significant. Captain William Ogilvy, late of the 52nd (Oxfordshire) Regiment of Foot, spent over £150 on his uniforms, boots, and caps in 1816 when he exchanged into the Cape Corps, which was in no way a sartorially elite regiment. William Ogilvy to Walter Ogilvy, February 12, 1816, Edinburgh, National Records of Scotland, GD16/34/383. For a detailed examination of the extremes of uniform regulations and how they interacted with civilian fashion, see Townsend, *Fashioning Regulation, Regulating Fashion*.

viewed these dandies as a blot on an otherwise noble and dignified profession, while others saw the problems in the Army's organization and policies but still chose to concentrate on its youngest officers. Over all, the satire directed at the unbloodied and compensating military dandies, while scathing, is not overly critical of the military as a whole, and often employed veteran officers as unwitting allies, holding them up as laudable figures and a stark contrast to this new generation of preening popinjays.

Those satirists who were either indiscriminate in their targets or specifically attacked combat veterans were much more obviously politically motivated. Made up of those with Radical or at least pro-Reform views, these individuals seized on the expensive and gaudy displays of military fops as a perfect example of poor taste in the economic downturn following Waterloo. While the general population might not have shared their view that the Army, and especially its officer corps, was 'the most enormous Job of all our political institutions', they did support a significant reduction in the peacetime service and many who were struggling financially would have chafed to see such displays of wealth worn openly.[17] Satirizing military fops, therefore, was a socially acceptable way of criticizing the military establishment as a whole. In these more pointed works, we find no exception for officers who fought through the Peninsula and at Waterloo. Instead, several of the works are particularly disdainful of them, implying that they were held to a higher standard and had signally failed to reach it. These more radical and political works direct their sympathy instead to the Army's enlisted men, who are seen as courageous veterans condemned to exist in a deeply unfair system.

In order to examine the differences between these two groups and their styles of satire, this paper is divided into two sections. The first section will explore visual satire, contrasting the works of William Heath, whose prolonged association with the military made him particularly scornful of those young officers who sought to replace experience with frippery, with George Cruikshank, whose more radical views and inherent sense of fairness were deeply offended by military dandies whether they had seen action or not. The second section turns to literary works, first examining two works produced in the immediate post-Waterloo years, and then two published in the 1830s and 1840s in response to the continuing popularity of dandified officers as romantic interests in popular literature. Each pair contains one work that deliberately exempts officers who have seen combat and one that

---

17 William Makepeace Thackeray, *The Book of Snobs* (London: Punch Office, 1848), p.37. On the general demand to reduce the size of the Army, see *The Bury and Norwich Post: Or, Suffolk, Norfolk, Essex, Cambridge, and Ely Advertiser*, January 24, 1816; *The Derby Mercury*, April 11, 1816; Charles Williams, *The British Atlas, or John Bull Supporting the Peace Establishment*, 1816, London, The British Museum, BM Satires 12786, 1868,0808.8321; The Army. Letter to the Editor, *The Morning Chronicle*, December 20, 1817; Rory Muir, 'A Hero's Welcome: Attitudes to Wellington and the Army, 1814–23', in C.M. Woolgar (ed.), *Wellington Studies V* (Southampton: Hartley Institute, University of Southampton, 2013), pp.210–223.

Figure 1: William Heath and S.W. Fores, *Military Dandies or Heroes of 1818*. (Art Institute of Chicago, Gift of Thomas F. Furness in memory of William McCallin McKee, 1928.1227)

specifically targets them. The first pair, both published anonymously, examine dandyism as an outward representation of more damning behaviour. Whereas *Dandymania; Being a Dissertation on Modern Dandies* makes a point to use language that excludes veterans, the title character of the 'Journal of Sir Valentine Sleek, A Colonel in the -------, and Finished Dandy' is unquestionably a veteran. Finally, we turn to the 1830s and 1840s. Here, the role of the more moderate satire directed at unbloodied junior officers will be filled by Charles Dickens and his exploration of 'young military gentlemen' while William Makepeace Thackeray's ruthless condemnation of military snobs provides reinforcements for Cruikshank.

Despite the nickname 'Captain Heath,' it is unlikely that William Heath had a military career alongside his artistic one. Instead, the sobriquet seems to have been inspired by his close links to the Army.[18] Self-described in 1819 as a 'portrait and military painter' his income in the years after Waterloo came not from satirical prints but his work as the illustrator of a number of popular and patriotic military

---

18 Julie Mellby, 'William Heath (1794/5–1840) "The man wots got the whip hand of 'em all"', *The British Art Journal*, 16:3 (Winter 2015/16), pp.3–19; John Brown described him as 'poor Heath, the ex-Captain of Dragoons, facile and profuse, unscrupulous and clever'. John Brown, *John Leech and Other Papers* (Edinburgh: David Douglas, 1882), p.9.

texts, most notably *Historical Military and Naval Anecdotes* (1815), *The Martial Achievements of Great Britain and her Allies* (1815), and *The Wars of Wellington* (1819).[19] Even after he returned to satire his close links to the military remained and are most obvious in his scathing attacks on soldiers behaving in ways that he felt brought dishonour to their profession.[20] While Heath routinely lambasted such classic military vices as drunkenness and idleness, he saved some of his harshest criticism for the excesses of dandyism. Clearly agreeing with Thomas Carlyle that 'a Dandy is a Clothes-wearing Man, a Man whose trade, office, and existence consists in the wearing of Clothes', and thus a man who could not devote the required attention to military duties, Heath produced a number of prints that not only skewered such figures but also made it clear that, in his eyes, this was a problem largely confined to those who joined the service after Waterloo.[21]

The first of Heath's direct assaults on this particular class of officer occurred even as he was glorifying the exploits of those who had served under Wellington. *Military Dandies or Heroes of 1818* (Figure 1) depicts eight officers of different regiments promenading and talking to each other, all in extravagant uniforms with exaggerated details. All have very tight waists and wear incredibly high collars and/or stocks, which in several cases are pushing their heads back at uncomfortable angles. Two of the cavalry officers are in thigh-high riding boots, which widen at the top to an absurd degree, while two of the officers, an infantryman and a lancer, wear an overly large shako and czapka respectively, each with a very high plume. All of the officers boast inflated bulging pigeon breasts, tight sleeves, and overly padded shoulders, all forms of traditional visual shorthand used to connote dandyism, and often particularly associated with military dandies.[22] Notably, only one officer depicted (the Life Guard at the centre of the piece) wears the Waterloo Medal, while the title, *Military Dandies or Heroes of 1818*, invites the viewer to contrast these dandies, the 'Heroes of 1818' with the heroes of the recently ended

19   Lawrence Binyon, *Catalogue of Drawings by British Artists and Artists of Foreign Origin Working in Great Britain, Preserved in the Department of Prints and Drawings in the British Museum* (London: Trustees of the British Museum, 1900), Vol.II, p.301; Anon., *The Martial Achievements of Great Britain and Her Allies From 1799 to 1815* (London: J. Jenkins, 1815); Dr. Syntax, *The Wars of Wellington, a Narrative Poem in Fifteen Cantos* (London: W. T. Gilling, 1821).

20   See William Heath, *15th – the King's Hussars*, 1820, Anne S.K. Brown Military Collection, Brown University Library; William Heath and Thomas McLean, *The Glorious 18th of June*, 1830, Anne S.K. Brown Military Collection, Brown University Library; William Heath and Thomas McLean, *We Sons of Mars – Wot Lives on Brandy and Cigars*, 1830, Anne S.K. Brown Military Collection, Brown University Library; William Heath and Thomas McLean, *That Sentinel's as Drunk as a Beast*, 1830, The British Museum, 1985,0119.287.

21   Carlyle, *Sartor Resartus*, p.283. Nor was the Royal Navy exempt – see William Heath and S. W. Fores, *Things as they were, 1757. Things as they are, 1827*, 1827, Anne S.K. Brown Military Collection, Brown University Library.

22   Janes, *Oscar Wilde Prefigured*; Unknown artist and Thomas Tegg, *Lacing a Dandy*, 1819, Art Institute of Chicago, 1928.1226.

Figure 2: William Heath and S.W. Fores, *Military Parade*, 1820. (Anne S.K. Brown Military Collection, Brown University Library)

war. This comparison is furthered by Heath's tacit feminization of the officers, which deliberately encourages the audience to compare these primped and padded officers with the explicitly masculine-coded representations of soldiers found in his illustrations for *The Wars of Wellington* and similar volumes.

Heath took a broader but equally dismissive approach two years later when he produced *Military Parade* (1820), again for the London publisher S.W. Fores (Figure 2). Expanding his canvas, Heath depicts 18 soldiers strolling either on a beach or in a park, not a single one of whom wears the Waterloo Medal. This wider perspective allowed Heath to ridicule the size of his subjects, turning two heavy cavalrymen into giants while several lancers barely come up to their chests and one diminutive Foot Guards officer does not even reach their waists.[23] Again, the cuts of the uniforms are exaggerated and dandified, with extremely high collars, pigeon breasts, padded shoulders, and headgear that is often several feet tall and, in the case of the Guardsman, the same height as the officer wearing it. While most of the officers are not feminized to the same level as the subjects of *Military Dandies or Heroes of 1818*, the piece does include several soldiers with wasp-waists, one with a remarkably backside-hugging pair of white trousers, and a Highlander in a rather risqué mini-kilt. In addition to highlighting size disparities and providing more subjects, Heath's distance from his subjects allows him to completely anonymize them. By eschewing any facial details beyond the occasional moustache, he not only removes any individuality of person rather than regiment, but also makes

---

23 *Military Parade* was one of a number of wide crowd scenes Heath produced, but the only one where he incorporated such extremes of size. See William Heath and S.W. Fores, *Eccentrics*, 1820, The British Museum, 1935,0522.7.216; William Heath, Joseph Gleadah, and S.W. Fores, *Pinks & Tulips, a Sketch from High-Life*, 1822, The British Museum, 1935,0522.7.215; William Heath, Joseph Gleadah, and S.W. Fores, *Butter Cups & Daisies, a Sketch from Low-Life*, The British Museum, 1935,0522.7.214.

Figure 3: William Heath and Gabriel Shire Tregear, *Military Sketches by William Heath. No. 1. Breakfast. Playing Soldiers at Home!!! (Morning)*, 1834. (Anne S.K. Brown Military Collection, Brown University Library)

the soldiers seem to disappear into their uniforms. This effect is furthered emphasized by the three soldiers that are completely swallowed by their cloaks, with only their headgear and boots visible, while another in the background appears to be nothing but a walking half-cloak. While the effect of a uniform on an individual's psyche and sense of identity is a crucial part of military theory, Heath takes it to such extremes that the result is, at first glance, not an illustration of 18 soldiers, but instead several groups of animated uniforms.[24] The meaning is clear: these are men playing a part – a case where clothes quite literally made the men.

Heath returned to the theme of playing soldiers in 1834 in the first plate of his *Military Sketches*. Entitled *Playing at Soldiers at Home!!! (Morning)* the print depicts a dandified cavalry officer lounging in his rooms (Figure 3). He wears his uniform trousers without boots and a fur-lined robe in place of his uniform jacket and wields, instead of his regulation sword, a hussar pipe. While lacking the

---

24 Sharron J. Lennon, Kim K.P.Johnson, and Nancy Ann Rudd, *Social Psychology of Dress* (New York: Bloomsbury, 2017); Paul Fussell, *Uniforms: Why We Are What We Wear* (Boston: Houghton Mifflin Company, 2002).

exaggerated physical attributes of Heath's previous military dandies, the officer does still sport a narrow waist, carefully coiffed hair, a studied and primped expression, and the hint of a very narrow moustache. The officer is presented in contrast to his batman, who stands at attention in immaculate undress uniform that is drawn in a style more reminiscent of Heath's portrait and narrative work than his satirical prints. Damningly, the paraphernalia of the officer's rank, his swords, sabretache, roman pattern dragoon helmet, undress cap, cloak, breast-plate, and boots adorn his room as decorations rather than being stored or laid out for easy donning. To further highlight the decorative, rather than utilitarian, nature of these items the officer's diminutive coachman stands next to his boots, which are almost as tall as he is. Dressed to perform his duties and holding his driving whip, his very presence emphasizes that the officer's thigh-high riding boots will not be put to their intended purpose but will instead rest comfortably on the floor of the dandy's carriage.

Even as Heath was alternately celebrating military service and lampooning those who regarded it merely as a pastime, George Cruikshank was taking a firm stand against the entirety of what Timothy Alborn has christened 'Britain's military-sartorial complex'.[25] A moderate radical who lambasted anarchy and republicanism as fervently as royal venality and political corruption, Cruikshank had been a fervent supporter of the war effort. He play-drilled at the age of 11 beside his father's volunteer regiment and even briefly considering a career in the Royal Navy before realizing that the most effective (and profitable) weapon he could wield against Bonaparte was his stylus.[26] As the war progressed, however, Cruikshank began to balance his antipathy to Napoleon with an equal disdain for the Prince Regent, 'old corruption', and the excesses of certain portions of Britain's (and especially London's) population.[27]

These feelings came to the fore in the economic downturn that followed peace in 1815, and Cruikshank took particular aim at dandies and all of those who took fashion to an extreme level when others were suffering from severe hardship.[28]

25 Timothy Alborn, *All That Glittered: Britain's Most Precious Metal from Adam Smith to the Gold Rush* (New York: Oxford University Press, 2019), p.104.

26 Robert L. Patten, 'Cruikshank, George (1792–1878), graphic artist.' *Oxford Dictionary of National Biography*. 23 Sep.2004, < https://doi-org.ezproxy.lib.uconn.edu/10.1093/ref:odnb/6843>, Accessed 9 October 2021.

27 There are far too many Cruikshank illustrations that target the Prince Regent/George IV to list them all here, but for a sample see George Cruikshank and M. Jones, *An Excursion to R_____ Hall*, 1812, The British Museum, 1859,0316.33; George Cruikshank and Thomas Tegg, *Gent, No Gent & Re Gent!!*, 1816, The British Museum, 1868,0808.12835; George Cruikshank and John Johnston, *Economy*, 1816, The British Museum, 1865,1111.2089; George Cruikshank and Thomas Tegg, *Royal Hobby's*, 1819, The British Museum, 1868,0808.8431. See also Phillip Harling, *The Waning of Old Corruption: The Politics of Economical Reform in Britain, 1779–1846* (Oxford: Clarendon Press, 1996).

28 George Cruikshank and Thomas Tegg, *An Exquisite*, 1817, The Metropolitan Museum of Art, The Elisha Whittelsey Collection, The Elisha Whittelsey Fund and Harris Brisbane Dick Fund, by Exchange, 1970;

Figure 4: George Cruikshank and Thomas McLean, *Monstrosities of 1819 & 1820*, 1819.
(Rijksmuseum, Amsterdam)

Figure 5: George Cruikshank and Thomas McLean, *Monstrosities of 1821*, 1821. (Anne S.K. Brown
Military Collection, Brown University Library)

From 1816 until 1825 Cruikshank produced an annual or semi-annual print enti-tled *Monstrosities of…* that skewered trends and those who followed them slav-ishly. Nor was the military safe from this particular assault, for Cruikshank shared the radical MP Joseph Hume's feeling that the officers bedecked in 'scarlet and gold… daily parad[ing] about the streets' could have been tailor-made to 'mock the squalid poverty of the lower orders'.[29] Officers appear in all but one of Cruikshank's Monstrosities and are central characters in five of them. *Monstrosities of 1816* and *Monstrosities of 1819 & 1820* both boast cavalry officers (a hussar in a shako and pelisse and a lancer in a czapka) with the regulation moustaches, tight trousers, and gold braid. Their poses are studied, with right hand on hips, pigeon chests thrust forward, and sabres held at the precise angle to be both deeply suggestive and imply a certain lack of functionality. *Monstrosities of 1821* features an officer of the Foot Guards whose scrawny legs and slight build manage to make the still figure appear to totter under the weight of a gigantic bearskin, fully two-thirds the height of its wearer. *Dandies or Monstrosities of 1818* and *Monstrosities of 1783 & 1823* also contain cavalry officers, this time Life Guards sporting roman pattern dragoon helmets with massive plumes. Of particular note here is the officer in *Dandies or Monstrosities of 1818* who proudly wears the Waterloo Medal and, in his padded shoulders and tight trousers, could be the twin of the medal-wearing officer in Heath's *Military Dandies or Heroes of 1818* (Figure 1).

Cruikshank's most direct assault on military dandyism came in February 1819 with the release of his *Ancient Military Dandies of 1450 – Sketch'd by permission from the Originals in the Grand Armory at the Gothic Hall Pall-Mall; Modern Military Dandies – of 1819 – Sketch'd <u>without</u> permission from the Life* (Figure 6). Set up as a deliberate comparison between warriors of the fifteenth century and those of the nineteenth, the piece depicts seven visitors to the exhibition of arms and armour at the Gothic Hall. Two full suits or armour are displayed in more dynamic poses than armour is usually displayed in and boast narrowed waists, full chests, and elaborate plumes on their helmets. The grandest suit stands with one hand on hip and the other holding a sword, and his helmet is open, revealing a lifelike face with a neat van dyke. Despite the outward nods to dandyism that Cruikshank gives them, their poses are more traditionally military – they stand straight and ready and, even accounting for their slightly elevated position, are by far the tallest figures in the room. At the centre of the print, examining the suits of armour arm in arm are two officers, one a Life Guard and one a lancer. Both have wasp waists, pigeon breasts, and padded shoulders, and wear uniforms that cling

---

George Cruikshank and Thomas Tegg, *The Dandies Coat of Arms*, 1819, The Metropolitan Museum of Art, The Elisha Whittelsey Collection, The Elisha Whittelsey Fund and Harris Brisbane Dick Fund, by Exchange, 1970.

29   Henry Brewster Stanton, *Reforms and Reformers* (London: T. Nelson and Sons, 1853), p.247; Alborn, *All That Glittered*, p.104.

Figure 6: George Cruikshank and George Humphrey, Ancient Military Dandies of 1450 – Sketch'd by permission from the Originals in the Grand Armory at the Gothic Hall Pall-Mall. Modern military dandies – of 1819 – Sketch'd <u>without</u> permission from the Life, 1819. (Art Institute of Chicago, Gift of Thomas F. Furness in memory of William McCallin McKee, 1928.1231.33)

tightly to their arms and legs. Their uniforms have high, tight collars that thrust their heads back so far that it seems their helmet chin straps must choke them, and yet each bears a markedly supercilious expression. Finally, each has the toe of one foot extended, in a manner that emphasizes the rehearsed nature of their postures. Behind them stand two more officers in conversation with a lady completely enveloped by her bonnet and pelisse. One is a Foot Guards officer wearing the enormous bearskin that was, by this point, becoming a trope in military prints. He too wears a superior expression, and the bulge both above and below his red officer's sash implies that he has long relied on port and beefsteak rather than padding to fill out his uniform. Finally, behind and somewhat obscured by the lady, stands another officer with a tucked waist, skin-tight sleeves, padded shoulders, and a plumed cap that seems to be in danger of swallowing his head. All wear overly long sashes whose ends flutter around their calves and both cavalry officers sport Waterloo Medals. The Foot Guards officer, in addition to the Waterloo Medal, wears the Army/Peninsula Gold Cross, meaning that he had served as a battalion commander (or higher) in at least four battles between 1808 and 1814. The portion of the fourth officer's chest where a medal would hang is obscured by the lady's bonnet.

Cruikshank was fully aware that his depiction of the officers was unflattering, a point he emphasized by including in the print's title that they were 'Sketch'd without permission from the life'. Nor did it bother him that they were all veterans. In contrast to Heath, his targets were not unbloodied junior officers trying to ape their superiors, but the excesses of the Army as a whole. Lampooning military dandies was a socially acceptable way of criticizing the service in general and the officer corps in particular, and, for Cruikshank, a Waterloo Medal or Peninsular Cross should not shield one from wider responsibilities and criticism when those responsibilities were flouted.

Even as Heath and Cruikshank were burlesquing dandified officers, Britain's satirical authors were also taking aim, albeit anonymously, at the same military macaronis. As with satirical prints, however, literary works varied in their specific targets and thus their aims, with some eschewing veterans while others specifically targeted them. Originally published in 1815 and going through at least seven editions over the next few years, Jacky Dandy's popular *Dandymania; Being a Dissertation on Modern Dandies* sits squarely in the first camp. Although it classifies military dandies as the preeminent form of the professional dandy, the only military dandy it takes specific aim at is the independently wealthy dandy who 'has assumed the military profession by way of an amusement'. That this independent dandy has never seen combat is obvious from the author's reminder that his uniform is 'wholely [sic] and solely a cloak for carrying on all manner of dissipation', and that he should never allow 'courage and patriotism… a place in your bosom'. Instead, said military dandy is a drain on the state and a reprobate of the worst order. Rather than serving his country, he 'rests gloriously contented' as he pockets 'a handsome yearly salary from government' while letting 'vanity, wine, and women, be [his] principal delight'.[30] If that was not damning enough, Jacky Dandy closes his description of the independently wealthy dandy who views the military as a pastime with the advice that he should only seduce 'married women, as you have then no occasion to make provision for your offspring'.[31]

Dandymania, much like Heath's prints, uses dandified military officers to criticize individual behaviour. However, where Heath lambasts unbloodied officers who use outlandish style to distract from a chest naked of campaign medals, *Dandymania* instead targets a strain of dandies that the author clearly viewed as social parasites, who use their wealth and their purchased military

---

30   It is debatable whether the salary of any officer in the British Army could be described as 'handsome' in 1818.

31   Jackey Dandy, *Dandymania; Being a Dissertation on Modern Dandies; Humbly Dedicated to all the Dandies, but more especially to those Exquisites, the Stamford Dandy! The Amateur Dandy! And the Great Dandy-Lion!* 7th Edition (London: Duncombe Book and Music Seller, 1817 or 1818), pp.6, 9.

positions and frippery to disguise their poor behaviour. Other authors seized on these same themes but refused to make a distinction between military amateurs and veterans. Published in 1818, even as *Dandymania* reached its seventh edition, the 'Journal of Sir Valentine Sleek, A Colonel in the -------, and Finished Dandy' deliberately casts an older veteran officer as its protagonist. Included as an appendix in *Replies to the Letters of the Fudge Family in Paris*, an unauthorized sequel to Thomas Moore's verse satire of British tourism in Paris following Waterloo, it takes the form of a poetic day-in-the-life diary that paints Sleek as a man who lives for pleasure (both sartorial and physical) alone.[32] Rising each day at two in the afternoon, Sleek employs a series of 'secret washes' on his hair and face that 'the Ladies' *envy* whilst they praise', before preparing himself 'for lounging – field – and gala days'.

> Pierre drew on my patent boots
> With six inch heels;- looked very tall,-
> Survey'd my regimental suits,
> Not meaning to attend the ball.
> My pigeon breasts, and padded sleeves,
> Made my whole front *en militaire*;
> *Mem.*- By *their* aid a youth receives
> The approbation of the Fair.

Having thus suitably attired himself, he rejects a plea from an old friend – now a politician – to attend a meeting to decide the future of southern Italy and instead, wearied and depressed by his friend's demands, decides to attend the ball after all. This, of course, requires a fresh toilette (complete with cheeks graced by both lily and rose) and an entirely different outfit of 'cork pumps, false calves, high collar,- stays' topped off with a 'fashionable wig – quite new' and Sleek's 'di'mond snuff-box, broche and rings'. Crammed into his outfit and glittering, Sleek ventures out to the ball where he finds his 'ador'd Aspasia', monopolizes her for several dances and escorts her home. There, he 'gr[ows] amorous' and, after her rejection, returns home, weeps, and falls asleep at four in the morning, only to rise again the next day at two to begin the cycle over.[33]

The disdain Sleek's author has for him is palpable. We are reminded multiple times that he is a 'Gentlem[a]n of War', but he is presented as a model of an officer's worst characteristics. It is implied that he chose his regiment based solely on their

---

32   For Moore's disavowal of the sequel, see Jane Moore, 'Introduction to the Fudge Family in Paris' in *British Satire 1785–1840* (London: Routledge, 2016), Vol.5, p.123. For British tourism to Paris after Waterloo, see Haynes, *Our Friends the Enemies*; Reynolds, '"There John Bull might be seen in all his glory"'.

33   T.S., 'Journal of Sir Valentine Sleek, a Colonel in the --------, and Finished Dandy' in *Replies to the Letters of the Fudge Family in Paris* (London: Pinnock and Maunder, 1818), pp.161–165.

uniform, which of course he then pads and stuffs, and at one point a spot on his temple produces such alarm that his batman must aid him further in dressing because his 'nerves were very weak'. It is also implied that he has recently gotten worse, as when Aspasia rejects him, she informs him that he has '*improv'd* in vice'. Even the name of his former lover is a studied insult, encouraging comparison between Sleek and the original Aspasia's most famous lover, Pericles. The most direct damnation, however, comes in the form of the piece's separate Moral which directly contrasts British warriors of previous generations with the fops of the Napoleonic Wars:

> Within their hearts a noble flame
> Our British Ancestors conceal'd
> When sprung their love of honest fame,
> And shew'd them Lions in the field.-
> *Now* call upon that Lion,- see
> A "Dandy"-Lion rears his head!-
> Which Botanists declare to be
> (In vulgar phrase)- *a p-ss-abed!!!*[34]

Sartorial satires in fiction had a longer lifespan than those in art thanks in part to young officers remaining a favourite romantic interest in fiction. Silver Fork novels were especially noted for their fondness for attractive officers. A popular subgenre concerned with fashionable society, Silver Fork novels provided readers with a glimpse into the life of the *ton*, even as they incorporated the middle-class aspirations and ideals of their readers (much as many modern romance novels are influenced by the progressive beliefs of their authors and readers). The subgenre's continued popularity from the 1820s through at least the 1840s, combined with their determination to align with their audience, means that they can safely be seen as representative of the views of their readers when it comes to military fashions.[35] In Benjamin Disraeli's *Henrietta Temple, a Love Story* (1837), the hero, Ferdinand Armine, a captain in the Guards, who receives 'the universal admiration'

---

34 'Journal of Sir Valentine Sleek', pp.162–165.

35 See Edward Copeland, *The Silver Fork Novel: Fashionable Fiction in the Age of Reform* (Cambridge: Cambridge University Press, 2012); Cheryl A. Wilson, *Fashioning the Silver Fork Novel* (London: Pickering and Chatto, 2012); Muireann O'Cinneide, 'The Silver Fork Novel across Romantic and Victorian Views: Class, Gender and Commodity Culture, 1820–1841,' *Literature Compass* 4 (2007), pp.1227–1240; Alison Adburgham, *Silver Fork Society: Fashionable Life and Literature from 1814 to 1840* (London: Constable, 1983); John Sutherland and Veronica Melnyk, *Rouge Publisher: The Prince of 'Puffers' – the Life and Works of the Publisher Henry Colburn* (Brighton: Edward Everett Root Publishers Co., Ltd., 2018). See also Louise Carter, 'Scarlet Fever: Female Enthusiasm for Men in Uniform' in Kevin Linch and Matthew McCormack (eds), *Britain's Soldiers: Rethinking War and Society, 1715–1815* (Liverpool: Liverpool University Press, 2014), pp.155–181.

traditionally lavished on a 'young hero in his regimentals', is forgiven for somewhat scandalous behaviour with women because of his looks and his association
with a 'crack regiment'.[36] 'Captain Armine has been very wild, very wild indeed;
a little of the roué', a lady notes in the second volume, 'but then such a fine young
man, so very handsome, so truly distinguished, as Lady Bellair says, what could
you expect?'[37] In Lady Charlotte Bury's *The History of a Flirt, Related by Herself*,
which appeared three years after *Henrietta Temple*, the narrator compares her
antipathy for two eligible men she spurned to her delight in her near-engagement
to a younger son without prospects, largely because of his uniform:

> ...how had I chafed under my engagement with Mr. Ellis, because my
> heart was not in the matter! How had I turned from Brereton, whom I
> once certainly loved, because my heart rejected him in gaiters and grey
> pantaloons! Here was a man, courted in the world, admired, accom-
> plished, a man of birth, of connexion, and in a dragoon regiment! – how
> very different must my sentiments and feelings be!'[38]

The continued popularity of this trope insured that satire of young officers trying
to disguise inexperience behind swagger was not only not limited to illustrated
works, but also continued to be popular into the 1820s and 1830s, proving a fruitful
subject for certain rising literary stars. In 1838 it was announced in the papers that
Sketches of Young Gentlemen, a companion piece to the popular *Sketches of Young
Ladies*, was being printed by Chapman and Hall.[39] *Sketches of Young Gentlemen*,
although published anonymously, was the work of Charles Dickens, who had only
just abandoned his pseudonym of 'Boz' to place his own name on the first complete
edition of *The Posthumous Papers of the Pickwick Club. Sketches of Young Ladies*
and *Sketches of Young Gentlemen* (followed in 1840 by *Sketches of Young Couples*)
are spiritual successors to Dickens' first success, *Sketches by Boz*, which had been
published as a collection in 1836 after having appeared as individual sketches
in a variety of newspapers and periodicals between 1833 and 1836.[40] *Sketches of
Young Gentlemen* divides up the young male population of the British Isles into
multiple groups, based either on personality traits or profession. It should come
as no surprise that Dickens, well aware of popular literary trends and with a fine

---

36   Benjamin Disraeli, *Henriette Temple, A Love Story* (London: Henry Colburn, 1837), Vol.I, pp.112, 120.
37   Disraeli, *Henriette Temple*, Vol.II, pp.164 –165.
38   Lady Charlotte Campbell Bury, *The History of a Flirt, Related by Herself* (London: Henry Colburn, 1840),
     Vol.II, p.144.
39   Multiple Advertisements, *The Morning Post*, February 3, 1838, p.1.
40   Later 'complete' editions of *Sketches by Boz* include the three further *Sketches* titles. See Charles Dickens,
     *Sketches By Boz: Illustrative of Every-day Life and Every-day People, Sketches of Young Gentlemen, Sketches
     of Young Couples, The Mudfog Papers, and Other Sketches* (London: Chapman & Hall, 1910), Vol.2.

Figure 7: Detail from Hablot Knight Brown's Illustration of The Military Young Gentleman.
(Charles Dickens, *Sketches of Young Gentlemen* (London: Chapman and Hall, 1838))

eye for the ludicrous in British society, dedicated a portion of his new work to 'The Military Young Gentleman.'

Following an illustration by Hablot Knight Brown that echoes the pigeon breasts, tucked waists, and tight sleeves of Heath and Cruikshank's officers, Dickens opened his coverage of the pictured young bloods with a volley directed straight at those novels that insisted upon casting them as romantic heroes. (Figure 7) 'We are rather at a loss to imagine', he confessed, 'how it has come to pass that military young gentlemen have obtained so much favour in the eyes of the young ladies of this kingdom.' It cannot be, he insisted, simply the colour of their coats,

> …because, although the analogy may in some degree hold good in the case of mail coachmen and guards, still general postmen wear red coats and *they* are not to our knowledge better received than other men; nor are firemen either, who wear (or used to wear) not only red coats, but very resplendent and massive badges besides – much larger than epaulettes. Neither do the twopenny post-office boys… find any peculiar favour in woman's eyes, although they wear very bright red jackets, and have the additional advantage of constantly appearing in public on horseback, which last circumstance may be naturally supposed to be greatly in their favour.

Dickens admitted that he can find no reasonable explanation for why 'young ladies … are bewitched by Her Majesty's livery' but consoled himself with the fact that those ladies are not his subject and turned to the young men who occupy the livery instead.[41]

For the young military gentleman, appearance is everything. 'There is nothing', Dickens informs us, 'that he is so learned upon as uniforms.' Even when he deigns to appear in his undress uniform ('somewhat mar[ing] the glory of his outward man') 'how great, how grand he is! What a happy mixture of ease and ferocity in his gait and carriage, and how lightly he carries that dreadful sword under his arm, making no more ado about it than if it were a silk umbrella!' The posturing and posing continues when he encounters

> …three other military young gentlemen, arm-in-arm, who are bearing down towards him clanking their iron heels on the pavement, and clashing their swords with a noise, which should cause all peaceful men to quail at heart … See how the flaxen-haired young gentleman with the weak legs – he who has his pocket-handkerchief thrust into the breast of his coat – glares upon the faint-hearted civilians who linger to look upon his glory; how the next young gentleman elevates his head in the air and majestically places his arms a-kimbo, while the third stands with his legs very wide apart, and clasps his hands behind them. Well may we inquire – not in familiar jest, but in respectful earnest – if you call that nothing.

Dickens' scorn is palpable, but it is, crucially, limited to posturing young men who have not been to war. At a theatrical performance attended by all the officers of the garrison, he recruits those veteran officers who have actually seen combat to help highlight the absurdity of the young military gentlemen. The young officers strut and pose, speaking loudly to ensure that all the ladies in the audience notice them.

---

41 Charles Dickens, *Sketches of Young Gentlemen* (London: Chapman and Hall, 1838), pp.20–22.

What a contrast between them, and that stage-box full of grey-headed officers with tokens of many battles about them, who have nothing at all in common with the military young gentlemen, and who – but for an old-fashioned kind of manly dignity in their looks and bearing – might be common hard-working soldiers for anything they take the pains to announce to the contrary![42]

Of course, literary satires of dandified officers contain the same spectrum of political views and motivation as their visual counterparts. Dickens' focus on young, unbloodied officers and his recruitment of veterans as unwitting allies in his quest to poke fun at untried and immature military gentlemen stands in contrast to more pointed works.

Given William Makepeace Thackeray's reform politics, it unsurprising that he used a dandified veteran officer as the direct target for his much more general criticism of the army and its officer corps in his *Book of Snobs*. Published as a collection in 1848, *The Book of Snobs* was first serialized as 'The Snobs of England, by one of themselves' in *Punch* over a year between February 1846 and February 1847.[43] As with Dickens' *Sketches*, Thackeray divided up the snobs of England into a number of subcategories, largely based either on occupation or location (country snobs and English snobs on the continent, for example). He devotes two chapters to the military, and it is in the first of these that we meet 'Lieutenant-General the Honourable Sir George Granby Tufto, K.C.B., K.T.S., K.H., K.S.W., &c., &c.'[44] Thackeray's Tufto has had an impeccable career; the ideal 'specimen of army-training', he 'has served in crack regiments, or commanded them, all his life … He distinguished himself everywhere: his name is mentioned with praise in a score of Gazettes', and his 'padded old breast twinkles over with a score of stars, clasps, and decorations'. Despite his martial achievements, however, he is 'a greater ass at sixty-eight than he was when he first entered the army at fifteen … he never read a book in his life, and … still writes with a school-boy hand … he is selfish, brutal, passionate, and a glutton.' Tufto's dandyism is clearly an attempt to regain his lost youth, for 'he has reached old age and grey hairs without being the least venerable'. Instead, 'he dresses like an outrageously young man … laces and pads his old carcass as if he were still handsome George Tufto of 1800', and can be found, most afternoons, around Waterloo Place 'tottering in his varnished boots, and leering under the bonnets of the women who pass by'. As with Colonel Sleek, Tufto's dandyism is not only ridiculed in and of itself but is also seen as a sign of other vices. He is

---

42   Dickens, *Sketches of Young Gentlemen*, p.22, pp.25–26.

43   See Gordon N. Ray, 'Thackeray's "Book of Snobs"', *Nineteenth-Century Fiction* 10, no.1 (June, 1955), pp.22 –33. While theoretically anonymous, *Vanity Fair*, which was being serialized at the same time, described him as 'author of … the "Snob Papers" in Punch.' W. M. Thackeray, *Vanity Fair* (London: Punch Office, 1847), cover.

44   KSW appears to be a fictional honour/postnomial.

'incorrigibly idle' and, alongside his military career, 'he has distinguished himself ... privately [by] riding races, drinking port, fighting duels, and seducing women'. 'When he dies of apoplexy', Thackeray concludes, 'the *Times* will have a quarter of a column about his services and battles – four lines of print will be wanted to describe his titles and orders alone – and the earth will cover one of the wickedest and dullest old wretches that ever strutted over it.'[45]

Despite Thackeray's palpable antipathy for officers like Tufto, the unbloodied junior officers who Dickens lampooned are not safe from his wrath either. In his second chapter devoted to the military, he introduces Ensign Robert Famish, the '"larking" or raffish military snob'. Famish's regiment is in India, but he is home on sick leave, and 'recruits his health by being intoxicated every night, and fortifies his lungs, which are weak, by smoking cigars all day.' While his mother, Lady Fanny Famish, is convinced that he consults his physician regularly and 'that he takes gruel every evening, when he puts his feet in hot water', Famish prefers the Union-Jack Club to Harley Street. There, among the other 'beardless young heroes', he 'breakfasts on pale ale and devilled kidneys at three o'clock' in the afternoon while his mother strives 'to have him exchanged into a dragoon regiment, which doesn't have to go to that odious India'.[46]

In 1829, a new satire appeared in London entitled *The Book of Dandies: or Old Friends in a New Shape*. Illustrated by George Cruikshank's older brother Robert, *The Book of Dandies* tells six stories, all in rhyme, and proved popular enough to go through multiple editions over several years. In the fourth vignette included in the work, the dandies of London arm themselves and form an amateur and stylish militia in order to defeat the looming spectre of radicalism. 'The Dandy Corps: Or the Heroes of the City' is, unsurprisingly, largely a chronicle of various gentlemen and dandified tradesmen arming themselves and acquiring uniforms under the dubious supervision of Major Matchlock (who is defeated by his sister's pet monkey) and Captain Lily. Having been suitably outfitted, they gather for a 'grand field-day ... near Primrose Hill' where they are routed by a 'peaceful cow' and flee in all directions, leaving Primrose Hill littered with their carefully accumulated armaments. The message is clear: dandies, even those in the military, are not warriors.[47]

That message, published only 14 years after Waterloo, underscores just how quickly the British Army's officer corps' image was transformed in the minds of the British public from the saviours of Europe to absurd dandies. Satirists, including those discussed here, played a crucial role in that transformation, whether their target was the entire British Army or new officers who tried to make up for their

45 Thackeray, *Book of Snobs*, pp.36, 38.
46 Thackeray, *Book of Snobs*, pp.39–41.
47 'The Dandy Corps: Or the Heroes of the City' in *The Book of Dandies: or Old Friends in a New Shape* (London: D. Carvalho, 1829–1832), unpaginated.

lack of experience with sartorial swagger and braggadocio. While the military could have disarmed this particular weapon by more strictly regulating uniforms and behaviour, many regiments, especially elite cavalry regiments, doubled down. Hussar regiments made moustaches a requirement for all officers, a regulation that was decried in the press as a dangerously foreign 'dandyism' that was 'inevitably incongruous and coxcombish when pasted on an English countenance'.[48] Some efforts were made towards more streamlined uniforms as the century progressed, but even as some of the lace and braid was stripped away, the tailoring became more exact, the luxuries multiplied, and the cost continued to grow. By 1828, *Blackwood's Edinburgh Magazine* estimated the cost of outfitting an officer with regimentals at £500 and dismissed the result of this expense as rendering 'the British soldier [unfit] for anything but a dandy'.[49]

Given the viciousness of the satire and shifting public opinion, it may seem strange that more was not done to curb these excesses. Partially this was the fault of the regimental system: while it provided unquestionably significant group identities and spiritual homes for soldiers, it also simultaneously acted as an echo chamber and encouraged inter-regimental rivalries that superseded civilian opinions. In some cases, it is also clear that the views of certain portions of the officer corps aligned with the satire. General Mercer, whose recollections of dress trends in the Royal Artillery were discussed briefly earlier, was openly critical of some of the 'absurd, horrible, preposterous, [and] tasteless' trends in post-war military fashion and lamented the 'effemina[cy]' of those unbloodied officers targeted by Heath and Dickens.[50] Even Captain Rees Howell Gronow and the anonymous 'Cavalry Officer' author of *The Whole Art of Dress*, both confirmed dandies, were dismissive of the overly vain or those 'possessed of more money than *taste*'.[51] There were also moments in the years following Waterloo when the general population regarding the officer corps as effeminate fops was preferable to the alternative.

---

48   Military Uniforms, *Blackwood's Edinburgh Magazine*, No. CXXXIV, Vol. XXIII (January, 1828), pp.92–93; Myerly, *British Military Spectacle*, p.149. See also John H. Rumsby, '"Of No Small Importance": A Social History of the Cavalry Moustache c. 1790–c. 1860', *Journal of the Society for Army Historical Research* 96:386 (Autumn 2018), pp.152–168.

49   Military Uniforms, *Blackwood's Edinburgh Magazine*, No. CXXXIV, Vol. XXIII (January, 1828), p.93. Britain was not alone in their horror in this case, the French press derided their own military dandies, christened 'Calicots'. See Peggy Davis, 'Montagnes Russes and Calicot: Print Culture and Visual Satire in Restoration Paris', *Historical Reflections/Réflexions Historiques* 44, no. 3 (December 2018), pp.8–28; Christine Haynes, 'The Battle of the Mountains: Repatriating Folly in France in the Aftermath of the Napoleonic Wars', *Historical Reflections/Réflexions Historiques* 44, no. 3 (December 2018), pp.50–70; Haynes, *Our Friends the Enemies*, pp.167–208.

50   Mercer, 'Military Reminiscences', pp.57, 61.

51   Emphasis in original. A Cavalry Officer, *The Whole Art of Dress! Or, the Road to Elegance and Fashion* (London: Effingham Wilson, 1830), p.v; Rees Howell Gronow, *The Reminiscences and Recollections of Captain Gronow: Being Anecdotes of the Camp, Court, Clubs, and Society 1810–1860* (London: John C. Nimmo, 1892), Vol.1, p.161.

Compare, for example, the depictions of soldiers in Heath's *Military Parade* to those in Cruikshank's *Massacre at St. Peter's or 'Britons strike home'!!!*, which was published the year before.[52] While neither is flattering, harmless dandies strolling through a park is infinitely preferable, as a matter of public relations and potentially self-conception, to bloodthirsty butchers massacring civilians. The Army was also partially sheltered from the worst of the criticism by the military/civilian divide, which accelerated throughout the century thanks to increased divides between the professions, political reforms, and even segregated leisure activities. Increasingly separated from civilian life, the opinions of civilian artists and authors may have mattered less to some serving officers.[53] Finally, the officers (and regiments) in question may have simply not cared. It is possible they felt that being lampooned as a dandy (especially by civilians) was a small price to pay for the pleasures of actually being one.

Bibliography

Archival Sources

National Records of Scotland, GD16/34/383

Newspapers

Blackwood's Edinburgh Magazine
The Bury and Norwich Post: Or, Suffolk, Norfolk, Essex, Cambridge, and Ely Advertiser
The Derby Mercury
The Morning Chronicle
The Morning Post

Published Primary Sources

Anon., *The Martial Achievements of Great Britain and Her Allies From 1799 to 1815* (London: J. Jenkins, 1815).

---

52 George Cruikshank and Thomas Tegg, *Massacre at St. Peter's or 'Britons strike home'!!!*, 1819, London, The British Museum, 1876,0510.980.
53 James White, *The Adventures of Sir Frizzle Pumpkin, Nights at Mess, and Other Tales* (Edinburgh: William Blackwood and Sons, 1846); Penelope J. Corfield, *Power and the Professions in Britain 1700–1850* (London: Routledge, 1995); Luke Reynolds, *Who Owned Waterloo? Battle, Memory, and Myth in British History, 1815–1852* (Oxford: Oxford University Press, 2022), pp.74–147.

Anon., *Replies to the Letters of the Fudge Family in Paris* (London: Pinnock and Maunder, 1818).

Anon., *The Book of Dandies: or Old Friends in a New Shape* (London: D. Carvalho, 1829–1832)

Bee, Jon, *A Dictionary of the Turf, the Ring, the Chase, the Pit, of Bon-Ton, and the Varieties of Life* (London: T. Hughes, 1823).

Bury, Lady Charlotte Campbell, *The History of a Flirt, Related by Herself* (London: Henry Colburn, 1840).

Carlyle, Thomas, *Sartor Resartus: The Life and Opinions of Herr Teufelsdröckh* (London: Saunders and Otley, 1838).

Cavalry Officer, A, *The Whole Art of Dress! Or, the Road to Elegance and Fashion* (London: Effingham Wilson, 1830).

Cibber, Colley, *Love's Last Shift; or, the Fool in Fashion* (London: H. Rhodes, 1702).

Dandy, Jackey, *Dandymania; Being a Dissertation on Modern Dandies; Humbly Dedicated to all the Dandies, but more especially to those Exquisites, the Stamford Dandy! The Amateur Dandy! And the Great Dandy-Lion!* 7th Edition (London: Duncombe Book and Music Seller, 1817 or 1818).

Dickens, Charles, *Sketches By Boz: Illustrative of Every-day Life and Every-day People, Sketches of Young Gentlemen, Sketches of Young Couples, The Mudfog Papers, and Other Sketches* (London: Chapman & Hall, 1910).

Dickens, Charles, *Sketches of Young Gentlemen* (London: Chapman and Hall, 1838).

Disraeli, Benjamin, *Henriette Temple, A Love Story* (London: Henry Colburn, 1837).

Egan, Pierce, *Grose's Classical Dictionary of the Vulgar Tongue* (London: Sherwood, Neely, and Jones, 1823).

Gronow, Rees Howell, *The Reminiscences and Recollections of Captain Gronow: Being Anecdotes of the Camp, Court, Clubs, and Society 1810–1860* (London: John C. Nimmo, 1892).

MacDonogh, Felix, *The Hermit in London, or Sketches of English Manners* (London: Henry Colburn and Co., 1821).

Mercer, Alexander Cavalié, 'Military Reminiscences of Latter End of the Eighteenth and Beginning of Nineteenth Centuries', in R.J. MacDonald, *The History of the Dress of the Royal Regiment of Artillery, 1625–1897* (London: Henry Sotheran & Co., 1899), pp.49–72.

Stanton, Henry Brewster, *Reforms and Reformers* (London: T. Nelson and Sons, 1853).

Syntax, Dr, *The Wars of Wellington, a Narrative Poem in Fifteen Cantos* (London: W. T. Gilling, 1821).

Thackeray, William Makepeace, *The Book of Snobs* (London: Punch Office, 1848).

Thackeray, William Makepeace, *Vanity Fair* (London: Punch Office, 1847).

White, James, *The Adventures of Sir Frizzle Pumpkin, Nights at Mess, and Other Tales* (Edinburgh: William Blackwood and Sons, 1846).

Secondary Sources

Adburgham, Alison, *Silver Fork Society: Fashionable Life and Literature from 1814 to 1840* (London: Constable, 1983).

Alborn, Timothy, *All That Glittered: Britain's Most Precious Metal from Adam Smith to the Gold Rush* (New York: Oxford University Press, 2019).

Binyon, Lawrence, *Catalogue of Drawings by British Artists and Artists of Foreign Origin Working in Great Britain, Preserved in the Department of Prints and Drawings in the British Museum* (London: Trustees of the British Museum, 1900).

Brown, John, *John Leech and Other Papers* (Edinburgh: David Douglas, 1882).

Carter, Louise, 'Scarlet Fever: Female Enthusiasm for Men in Uniform' in Kevin Linch and Matthew McCormack (eds), *Britain's Soldiers: Rethinking War and Society, 1715–1815* (Liverpool: Liverpool University Press, 2014), pp.155–181.

Copeland, Edward, *The Silver Fork Novel: Fashionable Fiction in the Age of Reform* (Cambridge: Cambridge University Press, 2012).

Corfield, Penelope J., *Power and the Professions in Britain 1700–1850* (London: Routledge, 1995).

Davis, Peggy, 'Montagnes Russes and Calicot: Print Culture and Visual Satire in Restoration Paris', *Historical Reflections/Réflexions Historiques* 44, no. 3 (December 2018), pp.8–28.

Foster, Thomas A., *Sex and the Eighteenth-Century Man: Massachusetts and the History of Sexuality in America* (Boston: Beacon Press, 2006).

Fussell, Paul, *Uniforms: Why We Are What We Wear* (Boston: Houghton Mifflin Company, 2002).

Gatrell, Vic, *City of Laughter: Sex and Satire in Eighteenth-Century London* (New York: Walker & Company, 2006).

Gaulme, Dominique and François Gaulme, *Power & Style: A World History of Politics and Dress* (Paris: Flammarion, 2012).

Harling, Phillip, *The Waning of Old Corruption: The Politics of Economical Reform in Britain, 1779–1846* (Oxford: Clarendon Press, 1996).

Haynes, Christine, *Our Friends the Enemies: The Occupation of France after Napoleon* (Cambridge: Harvard University Press, 2018).

Haynes, Christine, 'The Battle of the Mountains: Repatriating Folly in France in the Aftermath of the Napoleonic Wars', *Historical Reflections/Réflexions Historiques* 44, no. 3 (December 2018), pp.50–70.

Janes, Dominic, *Oscar Wilde Prefigured: Queer Fashioning and British Caricature, 1750–1900* (Chicago: University of Chicago Press, 2016).

Kuchta, David, *The Three-Piece Suit and Modern Masculinity: England 1550–1850* (Berkeley: University of California Press, 2002).

Lennon, Sharron J., Kim K.P. Johnson, and Nancy Ann Rudd, *Social Psychology of Dress* (New York: Bloomsbury, 2017).

McNeil, Peter, *Pretty Gentlemen: Macaroni Men and the Eighteenth-Century Fashion World* (New Haven: Yale University Press, 2018).

Mellby, Julie, 'William Heath (1794/5–1840) "The man wots got the whip hand of 'em all', *The British Art Journal*, 16:3 (Winter 2015/16), pp.3–19.

Mollo, John, *The Prince's Dolls: Scandals, Skirmishes and Splendours of the First British Hussars: 1793-1815* (London: Leo Cooper, 1997).

Moore, Jane, *British Satire 1785–1840* (London: Routledge, 2016).

Muir, Rory, 'A Hero's Welcome: Attitudes to Wellington and the Army, 1814–23', in C.M. Woolgar (ed.), *Wellington Studies V* (Southampton: Hartley Institute, University of Southampton, 2013), pp.210–223

Myerly, Scott Hughes, *British Military Spectacle: From the Napoleonic Wars Through the Crimea* (Cambridge: Harvard University Press, 1996).

O'Cinneide, Muireann, 'The Silver Fork Novel across Romantic and Victorian Views: Class, Gender and Commodity Culture, 1820–1841,' *Literature Compass* 4 (2007), pp.1227–1240.

Patten, Robert L., 'Cruikshank, George (1792–1878), graphic artist.' *Oxford Dictionary of National Biography*, < https://doi-org.ezproxy.lib.uconn.edu/10.1093/ref:odnb/6843>, Accessed 9 October 2021.

Ray, Gordon N., 'Thackeray's "Book of Snobs"', *Nineteenth-Century Fiction* 10, no. 1 (June, 1955), pp.22 –33.

Reynolds, Luke, '"There John Bull might be seen in all his glory": Cross-Channel Tourism and the British Army of Occupation in France, 1815–1818', *Journal of Tourism History* 12:2 (2020), pp.139–155.

Reynolds, Luke, *Who Owned Waterloo? Battle, Memory, and Myth in British History, 1815–1852* (Oxford: Oxford University Press, 2022).

Rumsby, John H., '"Of No Small Importance": A Social History of the Cavalry Moustache c. 1790–c. 1860', *Journal of the Society for Army Historical Research* 96:386 (Autumn 2018), pp.152–168.

Shannon, Brent, *The Cut of His Coat: Men, Dress, and Consumer Culture in Britain, 1860–1914* (Athens: Ohio University Press, 2006).

Sutherland, John and Veronica Melnyk, *Rouge Publisher: The Prince of 'Puffers' – the Life and Works of the Publisher Henry Colburn* (Brighton: Edward Everett Root Publishers Co, Ltd., 2018).

Taylor, David Francis, *The Politics of Parody: A Literary History of Caricature, 1760–1830* (New Haven: Yale University Press, 2018).

Townsend, Ben, *Fashioning Regulation, Regulating Fashion: The Uniforms and Dress of the British Army 1800–1815* (Warwick: Helion & Co., 2019–2020).

Wilson, Cheryl A., *Fashioning the Silver Fork Novel* (London: Pickering and Chatto, 2012).

7

'The most weird mixture of humanity': British Views of Friends and Foes at the Onset of the Salonika Campaign, October – December 1915

Jake Gasson

Shortly after his arrival at Salonika in December 1915, Private Reginald Bailey wrote to his father to recount his initial impressions of the Salonika campaign. Besides commenting on the mundane irritations of daily life, the diversity of the city of Salonika caught Bailey's attention. Rather than European, the city seemed to him a meeting place between West and East, of the familiar and the "other" in a manner he likened to a 'cross between Petticoat Lane and the Bazaar scene in "Kismet"'. That Salonika reminded him of an idealised Oriental city from a play is unsurprising. With mosques and minarets, it possessed some of the quintessential markers of the East in Western eyes. The human geography of the city seemed no less diverse and impressive, with Salonika populated by the 'most weird mixture of humanity'. Yet what provoked Bailey to make this comment was not the city's indigenous diversity but the presence of British, French, German, and Greek soldiers.[1]

Launching a new campaign in the Balkans led men like Private Bailey to encounter for the first time both the complex indigenous civilian society and the militaries present in the region, comprised of both the Balkan armies and those deployed by the Great Powers. The campaign unfolded in Macedonia, a region ruled by the Ottomans for almost five centuries until annexed by Greece and Serbia following

---

1   The Imperial War Museum (IWM) Documents.2027: Reginald J. Bailey, Typescript Letter, 10 December 1915.

the two Balkan Wars (1912-1913), and home to a religiously and ethnically varied population. Salonika acted as a microcosm for this diversity, being a city where the population was far from homogeneously Greek and, according to the first Greek census in 1913, dominated by Sephardic Jews and Muslims.[2] Because Salonika, already an important port city in the eastern Mediterranean, became a vast military base for the Allied effort, it soon also hosted varied international military encounters. From the city's streets to the bustling cafes and restaurants, British soldiers interacted with armies ranging from their French and Serbian allies to the neutral Greeks and even German, Austrian, and Ottoman officers permitted by Greek neutrality to remain and observe the unloading of men and material. In the Serbian theatre of operations to the north, the British served with French and Serbian soldiers and fought Bulgarians alongside (they believed) Germans and Austrians. This chapter examines these complex international military encounters occurring against the backdrop of the first three months of the Salonika campaign, a tumultuous period and a distinctly challenging one for British soldiers to form their first impressions of different belligerents.

From 5 October 1915, British and French troops began to disembark at the city of Salonika, in then neutral Greece. The opening of a new theatre of war came ostensibly as an attempt to prevent the destruction of their ally Serbia, weakened by its exertions in repelling previous Austro-Hungarian incursions and now threatened once more by invasion. However, the British and French arrived too late and in insufficient strength to prevent Serbia from being overrun by the combined forces of Germany, Austria-Hungary, and Bulgaria. This did not preclude a considerable build-up of troops around Salonika and the advance of three French divisions and Britain's 10th (Irish) Division into southern Serbia. This force retired in early December to Salonika when confronted by numerically superior Bulgarian forces, which inflicted a severe defeat on the British and French at the Battle of Kosturino, 6-12 December 1915. Added to this unfavourable military situation were significant disagreements between the campaign's participants. Most serious were the early stages of the long-running dispute between the Allies and the Greek government that continued until a pro-Allied regime change in 1917. The landing of troops in late 1915 had violated Greek neutrality, fostering an antagonism that at times verged on war and presented significant obstacles for politicians and generals alike. [3] For their part, relations within the *Entente Cordiale* were far from harmonious. The difficulties arising from the lack of unified decision-making and the often-conflicting priorities of the British and French governments have led

2   Misha Glenny, *The Balkans: Nationalism, War, and the Great Powers, 1804-2012* (London: Granta Books, 2012), pp.156-157; Mark Mazower, *Salonica, City of Ghosts: Christians, Muslims, and Jews, 1430-1950* (London: Harper Perennial, 2005), pp.293-304.

3   George B. Leon, *Greece and the Great Powers, 1914-1917* (Thessaloniki: Institute for Balkan Studies, 1974), pp.245-305.

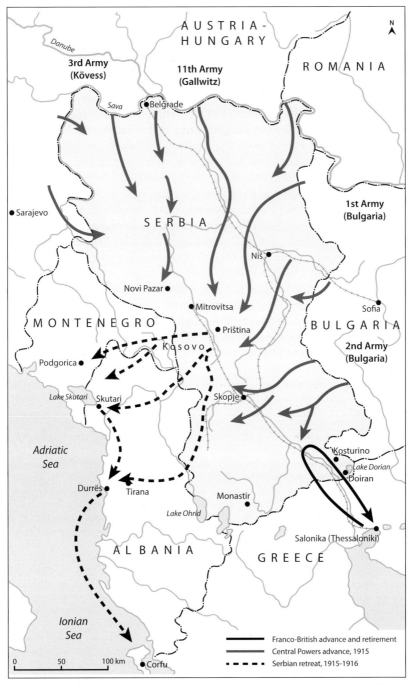

The Salonika Front, 1915. (Map by George Anderson, © Helion and Company 2022)

historian Roy Prete to write of this period that '[s]eldom has a coalition functioned so poorly'.[4]

Given the influence of the fractious international relations between generals and politicians on the conduct and outcome of the Salonika campaign's early stages, it is not surprising that diplomacy and inter-allied relations at the highest levels during this period have been well-studied.[5] Less clear is how British soldiers responded to their own involvement in this arena. Entrusted with the implementation on the ground of the allegiances brokered by Britain's political and military leaders, men like Private Bailey comprised the lowest level of relations with both allies and adversaries. Attitudes towards other combatants took on a character both influenced by and distinct from the relations between their respective nations, with British soldiers also informed by their pre-existing beliefs, wartime realities, and the gulf that often arose between the two.[6] Exploring initial British encounters with the armies of the Salonika campaign sheds light on this neglected but significant level of international relations in a theatre that ultimately became the most diverse front of the entire war.[7] Of the armies encountered by the British between October and December 1915, three stood above the rest in importance: the Greeks, French, and Bulgarians. The French were Britain's ally, the Bulgarians their adversary, and the Greeks, at least officially, were neutral. Examining each of these in turn, this chapter argues that the conditions of this phase of the campaign were not conducive to the creation of certainty in the characteristics or even the allegiances of the different armies, leaving British soldiers not entirely sure of any of the combatants they encountered.

---

4   Roy A. Prete, '*Imbroglio par excellence:* Mounting the Salonika Campaign, September-October 1915', *War and Society*, 19:1 (2001), pp.47-70.

5   In addition to studies by Leon and Prete, also see: David Dutton, *The Politics of Diplomacy: Britain, France and the Balkans in the First World War* (London: I.B. Tauris, 1998), pp.17-78.

6   The main study exploring interallied relations at this level during the First World War is that by Chris Kempshall on British, French, and American soldiers on the Western Front: Chris Kempshall, *British, French and American Relations on the Western Front, 1914-1918* (Cham: Palgrave Macmillan, 2018). For a case study illustrating the complexities of attitudes towards enemy combatants see: Alev Karaduman, 'Recognising the other: Contested identities at Gallipoli', in Metin Gürcan and Robert Johnson (eds), *The Gallipoli Campaign: The Turkish Perspective* (London: Routledge, 2016), pp.163-172.

7   This neglect affects both the Allies and Central Powers. Holger Afflerbach has noted that studies of German-Bulgarian relations have focussed on the highest level and overlooked interactions between ordinary soldiers: Holger Afflerbach, 'Greece and the Balkan Area in German Strategy, 1914-1918', in Daniel Kaplanidou (ed.), *The Salonica Theatre of Operations and the Outcome of the Great War* (Thessaloniki: Institute for Balkan Studies, 2005), p.65. Exceptions to this neglect are: Justin Fantauzzo and Robert L. Nelson, 'Expeditionary Forces in the Shatterzone: German, British and French Soldiers on the Macedonian Front, 1915-1918', in Alan Beyerchen and Emre Sencer (eds), *Expeditionary Forces in the First World War* (Cham: Palgrave Macmillan, 2019), pp.158-162; Rachel Richardson, 'Home away from the home front: the British in the Balkans during the Great War' (PhD thesis, Birbeck, University of London, 2014), pp.49-61.

The Greeks – Neutrals or Enemies?

The series of diplomatic manoeuvres that brought British and Greek soldiers together in late 1915 have been described as an 'Athenian tragi-comedy' by Alan Palmer, one of the leading historians of the Salonika campaign.[8] Greece's pro-Entente Prime Minister Eleftherios Venizelos had invited the British and French to land at Salonika to bring about Greece's entry into the conflict, but his monarch King Constantine remained strongly opposed. Married to the German Kaiser's sister and personally a Germanophile, Constantine sought to maintain a strict neutrality in the expectation of an eventual German triumph. Constantine's unwavering opposition led Venizelos to resign shortly before the first Entente troops arrived off Salonika and too late for the government that succeeded him to stop their disembarkation. On 5 October 1915, the first British soldiers, all drawn from 10th (Irish) Division, arrived to find a neutral nation rather than the allied belligerent expected by those responsible for sending them to Greece. Without active Greek cooperation in support of the Entente's efforts to assist Serbia, from the outset the assumptions that had underpinned the dispatch of troops had dissipated.[9]

Because the Entente had arrived in Greece without the permission of the Greek government and in violation of the country's declared neutrality, the political dimensions of the campaign weighed heavily on ordinary soldiers. Considering that the men of 10th (Irish) Division were the first to land and for almost a month was the lone British formation at Salonika, it is not surprising that many felt considerable anxiety about the perilousness of their position.[10] Principal amongst their concerns was that Greek neutrality would be neither passive nor impartial. In part, this was recognised as a predictable and direct consequence of their own infringement upon it. Turning his thoughts to the prospects of the campaign while onboard a transport anchored off Salonika, Captain Noel Drury admitted that their fate ought to be internment if they disembarked.[11] But it also seemed that the specific circumstances of their arrival made war with the Greeks the probable outcome if Greece were to depart from neutrality. Sergeant James Flanagan felt that hostilities had almost erupted even before their arrival, the Greeks in his eyes having been cajoled to permit the passage of Entente troops by the threat of naval bombardment.[12] These anxieties persisted amongst the men of the four divisions that followed in November and December, even if they joined an established

8   Alan Palmer, *Gardeners of Salonika* (London: Andre Deutsch, 1965), p.35.

9   Leon, *Greece and the Great Powers*, pp.220-247.

10   Cyril Falls, *Military Operations Macedonia* (London: H.M.S.O., 1933; repr. The Naval and Military Press Ltd), Volume I: From the Outbreak of War to the Spring of 1917, pp.50-52.

11   National Army Museum (NAM) 1976-07-69: Noel Edmund Drury, Manuscript Journal, 10 October 1915.

12   IWM: Documents.16012: James Flanagan, Typescript Diary, 15 October 1915.

Greek soldiers at the docks in Salonika. (United States National Archives and Records Administration)

expedition rather than launching it. Lieutenant Albert H. Muggeridge of the 2nd Battalion East Surrey Regiment was one of those men. He arrived in early December to find the attitude of the Greeks towards the Entente was 'still veiled and uncertain' but weighted against the Entente given King Constantine was 'very favourably disposed towards Germany.'[13] Neither had the threat of war lessened over the intervening months. After all, the Entente remained unwelcome intruders on Greek territory. 'Any nonsense from the Allies', reflected one officer in his post-war memoir, 'and straight into the Aegean Sea they would go'.[14]

British soldiers did not possess an awareness of the minutiae of diplomatic relations with the Greeks beyond the rumours that constantly swirled amongst their ranks, but their concerns were a largely correct if imprecise appraisal of the circumstances. Although the neutralist Greek government that succeeded Venizelos had consented to the arrival of Entente troops and promised to assist them short of active participation, there existed serious grounds for concern

---

13   IWM: Documents.8493: Albert H. Muggeridge, Typescript Journal, 6 December 1915.
14   James Hawke, *From Private to Major* (London: Hutchinson & Co., 1938), p.115.

amongst British and French decision-makers.[15] That the Greek government would intern their forces if they retired from Serbia into Greece remained a distinct possibility. Indeed, George Leon has shown that King Constantine considered the threat of internment the means by which Greece could continue to plot a neutral course between the Entente and the Central Powers. In order to remove this danger to their forces, Entente diplomats negotiated with the Greek government throughout November and at the end of the month received the assurances they desired.[16] Around Salonika the British and French expeditionary forces faced more immediate problems arising from the obstructionist attitudes of the Greek authorities. Far from aiding the Entente, the Greeks hindered their use of the city's railways and communications infrastructure, creating issues for the British when they sought to move their forces by rail to the Serbian frontier in late October.[17]

This intransigence was reflected in the welcome afforded to British soldiers by their Greek counterparts. While the Greek government sought to remain uninvolved in the new Balkan theatre of operations, developments related to its opening could not be ignored, and the Greek army had begun to mobilise at the end of September in response to that of Bulgaria.[18] Surrounded by Greek soldiers, the British soon realised that their status as intruders had created an unbridgeable divide between the two armies. Of all those at Salonika, Captain Percy George Mandley noted, 'everyone was quite good humoured, except the Greeks'. Even in the city's cafes, one of the principal locales for international military interactions across the course of the campaign, the Greeks kept to themselves and did not deign to socialise with the British. Barriers created by language and culture could be sufficiently overcome to enable interactions with Frenchmen and Serbians, but not, it seems, those dividing Briton and Greek created by the political circumstances.[19] In an effort to assuage the wounded pride of the Greeks, orders had been issued instructing officers to keep a tight rein on their men's behaviour.[20] However, instructions to salute Greek officers reinforced and deepened the mutual antipathy already in existence. In one encounter, Major Christopher Wyndham Hughes, then a captain in the 7th Battalion Wiltshire Regiment, found himself forced into the gutter by a Greek officer who simply laughed at his salute. As a result, he recalled, he never again made an effort to behave politely towards the Greeks. [21]

The readiness with which men like Hughes discarded their instructions reflected the generally low opinion of the Greeks held by the British. As he went on to explain, 'it was a vast mistake to order us to pretend a respect for the Greek

---

15 Leon, *Greece and the Great Powers*, pp.246-247.
16 Leon, *Greece and the Great Powers*, pp.254, 270-290.
17 Leon, *Greece and the Great Powers*, p.279; Falls, *Military Operations Macedonia*, Vol.I, p.54.
18 Leon, *Greece and the Great Powers*, pp.218-221.
19 IWM: Documents.24945: Percy George Mandley, Manuscript Memoir, p.99
20 The National Archives (TNA) WO 95/4828: 'No.0.466', 10th (Irish) Division War Diary.
21 IWM: Documents.4432: Christopher Wyndham Hughes, Typescript Memoir, p.52.

officers that we did not feel.' 'Nobody in the Balkans, so far as I can make out', he explained, 'has ever shown any respect to the Greek army'.[22] If those belonging to the same region as the Greeks, and therefore familiar with them, were believed to be unimpressed, neither did the British personally find much to support the cultivation of a different opinion during the first months of the campaign. Sight of the Greeks provoked immediate disdain and condescension. Captain Drury dismissed the soldiers as a 'most sloppy-looking lot of cut-throats' and reserved still greater scorn for their officers. Although 'very smartly dressed', they seemed to him 'effeminate and out of condition and…sneaky looking.'[23] This disparagement was consistent with British reactions more broadly towards Greece. Justin Fantauzzo argues British soldiers considered the region of Greek Macedonia to have been in a state of 'perpetual, and perhaps irrevocable, decline', finding much to criticise and little to praise in a region that appeared to lack all the markers of modern civilisation.[24] Greek soldiers fitted into this pervasive disappointment and measured equally poorly against the same standards, most notably in the treatment of animals. The 'wanton cruelty' of Greek soldiers towards their pack animals, and the dead horses left behind by a Greek division, led Major F. Debenham of the 7th Battalion Oxfordshire and Buckinghamshire Light Infantry to conclude 'what we saw of the Greeks at this time was very far removed from our own ideas and traditions.'[25]

First impressions aside, that Greece remained a potential adversary ensured that British soldiers viewed their Greek counterparts with suspicion. Even Captain Drury, so utterly disgusted by what he personally saw of the Greeks, felt that he 'wouldn't trust them an inch'.[26] In fact, as Drury recorded, the possibility that the Greeks would turn on them necessitated a number of precautions, including the wearing of revolvers whenever out and the posting of guards.[27] The precariousness of the Entente's position in the opening months of the campaign even led some to arrive at different conclusions entirely regarding the military abilities of the Greek army. Significant in this respect was the defeat and retirement of the Anglo-French advance into Serbia, a reverse which left them a 'broken army' in the words of Sergeant John McIlwain of the 5th Battalion Connaught Rangers. To McIlwain, retirement in the face of Bulgarian pressure did not ensure their safety as it brought them into contact with the Greek forces around Salonika. Rather

22   IWM: Documents.4432: Christopher Wyndham Hughes, Typescript Memoir, pp.52-53.

23   NAM: 1976-07-69: Drury, Manuscript Journal, 12 October 1915.

24   Justin Fantauzzo, 'Rise Phoenix-Like: British Soldiers, Civilization and the First World War in Greek Macedonia, 1915-1918', in Joseph Clarke and John Horne (eds), *Militarized Cultural Encounters in the Long Nineteenth Century* (Cham: Palgrave Macmillan, 2018), pp.125-147.

25   Cordy Wheeler, *Memorial Record of the Seventh (Service) Battalion, The Oxfordshire and Buckinghamshire Light* (Oxford: Basil Blackwell, 1921), p.46.

26   NAM: 1976-07-69: Drury, Manuscript Journal, 12 October 1915.

27   NAM: 1976-07-69: Drury, Manuscript Journal, 13 October 1915.

than dismissing them as others had previously, he confided in his diary his fears of the threat posed by the large numbers of 'fresh well equipped Greeks'.[28]

The potential for hostilities existed alongside worrying instances of threatening behaviour by Greek soldiers towards the British, who struggled to determine their intent in light of Greek neutrality. This may appear surprising given their conviction that this neutrality was tainted, but because a state of war did not exist between the two it could not be set aside entirely, thus creating an ambiguity that left the British perplexed as to how they should react. Captain Mandley discovered this when a Greek division advanced menacingly on his roadmaking detachment outside of Salonika. Even though it 'really looked as if they meant to attack us', Mandley felt that this was not without doubt. The British 'were not at war with them', he reasoned, and the Greeks 'had every right to carry out what manoeuvres they pleased in what was, after all, their own country.' Bloodshed was ultimately avoided when the Greeks formed into a column and marched past, leaving Mandley to ponder the purpose of such a manoeuvre.[29] This incident reveals with striking clarity the uncertainty afflicting the British during their first encounters with the Greeks. Being able to position other belligerents in relation to oneself is crucial in international military encounters, both to provide certainty in one's mind and to govern interactions, but proved impossible as regards the Greeks. Even if they were clearly not friends of the British, neither could they be definitively classified as foes.

This ambiguity remained a pressing issue until the middle of December, when demands made to the Greek government by *Général* Maurice Sarrail, the commander of French forces at Salonika, served to somewhat alleviate the threat faced by the Entente. Continuing Greek obstructionism had prevented British and French officers from reconnoitring the countryside around Salonika for the purpose of fortifying the city, a task which took on an increased urgency following the onset of the retirement from Serbia. On 11 December, the Greek government acquiesced to most of Sarrail's demands, agreeing to permit the development of fortifications, withdraw their troops encamped east of Salonika, and halve the city's garrison.[30] British soldiers watched as large numbers of Greek troops departed, providing an opportunity for reflection. Describing the scene in a letter to his mother, Second Lieutenant Eric de Normann of the Army Service Corps seemed certain that the Greeks were poor soldiers. 'The officers are great swanks with tin swords', he told her, and 'the men look pretty miserable.' But while he concluded he would not 'like to count on them in a scrap', he could not conceal

---

28 IWM: Documents.5537: John McIlwain, Typescript Journal, 8 December 1915.

29 IWM: Documents.24945: Mandley, Manuscript Memoir, pp.103-107.

30 Alan Wakefield and Simon Moody, *Under the Devil's Eye: The British Military Experience in Macedonia, 1915-1918* (Barnsley: Pen and Sword, 2004), pp.34-35.

his relief at their departure, remarking that they were 'well rid of them'.[31] Even now, the British remained unable to come to a consistent view of the Greeks, torn between their instinctive attitudes towards an unimpressive Balkan "other" and the anxieties arising from their presence.

The French – Imperfect Allies

That the British would not fight alone but as part of a coalition effort was clear from the outset of the campaign. The first units of 10th (Irish) Division arrived off Salonika at the same time as the French 156e Division, this formation being at the vanguard of France's *Armée d'Orient* (Army of the East). The implementation of the *Entente Cordiale* on the ground in this new theatre of war in many ways had solid foundations. Coming over a year after the beginning of the conflict, there was a much-reduced risk of interallied friction arising from unfamiliarity. French soldiers were no longer the entirely unknown entity that they had been to the men of the original British Expeditionary Force on the Western Front in 1914.[32] Because British soldiers at Salonika found themselves in an uncertain and threatening environment, they took a particular strength from the presence of their French ally beside them. Important in this regard was the combined British and French fleet of warships anchored in the Bay of Salonika. As a powerful deterrent against the Greek threat, they were, wrote Captain Arthur Donovan Young, 'the most reassuring sight that could meet the eyes of Britishers in a strange land.' 'We knew that our friend the Greek', he continued, 'would not readily invite a sampling of the quality of those naval guns bristling shoreward.'[33]

The British soon recognised, however, that rather than a partnership of equals, the French were firmly in the driving seat of the campaign. By early November the French force at Salonika had grown to a total of three infantry divisions and three colonial regiments. In the meantime, French troops had promptly pushed into Serbia soon after their arrival. Advancing up the valley of the Vardar River, the French sought to draw off Bulgarian pressure from the hard-pressed Serbians. Despite requests for assistance from general Sarrail, British troops were initially forbidden from advancing from the environs of the city.[34] The men of 10th (Irish) Division endured a frustrating period of *sitzkrieg*, 'watching the French streaming

---

31   IWM: Documents.12712: Eric De Normann Transcript Letter, 12 December 1915.

32   Kempshall, *Relations on the Western Front*, p.67; John Ramsden, '"The French People have a peculiar facility for being misrepresented": British Perceptions of France at War, 1914-1918', in Antoine Capet (ed.), *Britain, France and the Entente Cordiale since 1904* (Basingstoke: Palgrave Macmillan, 2006), p.9.

33   Arthur Donovan Young, *A Subaltern in Serbia And Some Letters from the Struma Valley* (London: Drane's, 1922), p.11.

34   Palmer, *Gardeners of Salonika*, pp.40-41; Falls, *Military Operations Macedonia*, Vol.I, pp.52-54.

French stores of corn and hay at Salonika. (United States National Archives and Records Administration)

up country,-infantry, field guns, mountain artillery and pack transport'.[35] For the moment their role in the campaign appeared to be that of observers while their ally got on with the task at hand.

This was the equivocation and reluctance of British decision-makers towards the campaign manifested for all on the ground to see. Little enthusiasm existed in British political and military circles for the unwelcome distraction of a Balkan expedition. Only a belief in the necessity of participation for the maintenance of the broader Anglo-French alliance compelled the British government to reluctantly dispatch five divisions to Salonika in this period.[36] By contrast, French commitment to the campaign was whole-hearted. The government of René Viviani saw in Salonika an opportunity to address in one swoop a number of immediate and long-term imperatives across domestic politics, wartime strategy, and foreign policy. Most pressing was the need to resolve *l'affaire Sarrail*, a domestic storm created after that officer was removed from his command of the French Third Army around Verdun in July 1915. Politically well-connected and the darling

---

35   Arthur Hamilton Gibbs, *Gun Fodder: The Diary of Four Years of War* (Boston: Little, Brown, and Company, 1927), p.110.

36   See: Dutton, *Politics of Diplomacy*, pp.49-78; Prete, '*Imbroglio par excellence*', pp.47-70.

of the Republican left, his appointment to command French forces at Salonika sought to defuse this political bomb.[37] As David Dutton has argued, this mismatch in motivations left Britain subject to the whims of the French and with little room to carve out their own policy.[38]

Their subservience was not immediately apparent to those on the ground. There was no unified command structure at Salonika until January 1916, when the two governments agreed to place British forces under Sarrail's authority.[39] Instead, it appeared as if 'General confusion' was in charge, as one later wrote in jest, with British and French forces 'getting in each other's way all the time'.[40] It soon became clear, however, that the French were content to act as if they were the only nation engaged at Salonika, relegating the British to a *de facto* position of inferiority. Both sought to acquire the infrastructure necessary to maintain and expand their nascent expeditionary forces, but in the absence of a unified command each pressed ahead unilaterally, with the British decision to temporarily suspend landings after the fall of Venizelos handing the French an advantage.[41] Some found the land on which they assembled their supplies had frustratingly already been assigned to the French.[42] More serious was the rumour that the French had seized control of Salonika's only railway line and had refused the British permission to use it.[43] Regardless of whether this story was true, the French nonetheless appeared to be behaving in a self-interested and high-handed manner, with their failure to cooperate being at odds with unstated British expectations of how their ally should act. That France and Britain were formal allies went without question, but the realities on the ground ensured the desirability of their partnership amongst ordinary soldiers did not.

The decision to permit British forces to advance from Salonika and into Serbia in late October placed new pressures on this already strained alliance. The British commander at Salonika, Lieutenant-General Bryan Mahon, assembled a force drawn from 10th (Irish) Division under the command of Brigadier-General L.L. Nicol, and dispatched it north towards the frontier. Crossing into Serbia, British troops began to relieve the French battalions in reserve at the start of November. The remainder of 10th (Irish) Division followed shortly after, and during the night

---

37   George H. Cassar, *Reluctant Partner: The Complete Story of the French Participation in the Dardanelles Expedition of 1915* (Solihull: Helion, 2019), pp.161-169, 187, 191; Jan Karl Tannenbaum, *General Maurice Sarrail, 1856-1929: The French Army and left-wing politics* (Chapel Hill, North Carolina: University of North Carolina Press, 1974), pp.55-74.

38   Dutton, *Politics of Diplomacy*, p.78.

39   Falls, *Military Operations Macedonia*, Vol.I, p.97.

40   Malcolm Burr, *Slouch Hat* (London: George Allen and Unwin Ltd, 1935), p.105.

41   Falls, *Military Operations Macedonia*, Vol.I, p.42.

42   IWM: Documents.12945: W.J. Mussett, Typescript Journal, 6-12 October 1915.

43   'Cannot discover what is in the air – are we waiting for the Spring', *Fit as Fiddles and as Hard as Nails: Irish Soldiers' Voices from the Great War* <https://www.tcd.ie/library/fitasfiddles/cannot-discover-what-is-in-the-air-are-we-waiting-for-the-spring/>, accessed 29 September 2020.

of 21-22 November it entered the front line, relieving French units entrenched west-east between the town of Kosturino and Lake Doiran.[44] Their proximity to the French during this period provided the British with varied impressions of their ally. Misunderstandings did occur, with Captain Young and two other officers escorted before a French officer when attempting to visit neighbouring French positions. But once straightened out, their apologetic French counterparts proved welcoming hosts, offering wine and regaling tales of their recent operations.[45] Other British soldiers criticised the French given their apparent lack of cleanliness. On taking over a hospital established by the French in the mosque of the village of Tatarli, Private William Knott of the 32nd Field Ambulance recorded with disgust that they had 'left it in a filthy state old dressings, rubbish, and the floors thick with dust'.[46]

Encounters in an active theatre of operations also afforded opportunities for the men of 10th (Irish) Division to size up the French as soldiers. That they were generally impressed indicates that views of the French were not of the overwhelmingly disparaging nature suggested by historian Rachel Richardson to have prevailed throughout the campaign. Fighting in Serbia alongside the French ensured what ultimately mattered most was their capacity for battlefield effectiveness, and assessments of their military capabilities accordingly took on greater importance in informing attitudes than the negative interactions highlighted by Richardson.[47] In his memoir, Lieutenant George William Taylor gushed in his praise: 'I cannot speak too highly of the French who were magnificent in adapting themselves to these novel conditions; and as for their fighting qualities, it is unnecessary for me to laud them, as all the world knows how fine they are.'[48] French weaponry seemed particularly worthy of praise. After observing a battery of France's famed 75mm field guns, Captain Drury felt in awe of their 'extraordinary' rate of fire of up to 20 rounds per minute.[49] Later he had the opportunity to examine a French machine gun up close thanks to the kindness of a French officer. Using the British Vickers machine gun as a yardstick, he compared it favourably, considering it heavier but 'more convenient'.[50]

One rare source of complaint concerned the defensive positions the British inherited from the French. Consisting of stone breastworks built above the

44   Tom Johnstone, *Orange, Green and Khaki: The Story of Irish Regiments in the Great War, 1914-1918* (Dublin: Gill and Macmillan, 1992), pp.166-171.
45   Young, *Subaltern in Serbia*, p.23.
46   IWM: Documents.7987: William Knott, Manuscript Diary, 22 November 1915.
47   Richardson, 'Home away from the home front', p.56. Richardson's neglect of military dynamics can be attributed to her reliance on the accounts of female volunteers to the detriment of the soldiers who served alongside the French in a combat environment.
48   George William Taylor, *The Boy with the Guns* (London: John Lane, 1919), p.130.
49   NAM: 1976-07-69: Drury, Manuscript Journal, 10 November 1915.
50   NAM: 1976-07-69: Drury, Manuscript Journal, 18 November 1915.

ground and known as sangars, these seemed to provide inadequate concealment and protection compared to the trenches dug by the British upon taking over French positions.[51] On the surface, this was a minor tactical quibble borne out of differing appreciations of the defensive requirements of the situation. It is, however, indicative of the self-confidence with which British soldiers approached their assessments of the French. Having fought at Gallipoli, the men of 10th (Irish) Division were sure of their own military worth.[52] These men had shed the inexperience innate to being part of Kitchener's New Armies, and which led those on the Western Front to approach the 'veteran' French eager to learn.[53] Rather than defer to their ally, they were prepared to criticise when French practice did not meet the standards British soldiers felt necessary, even if such criticisms were, in this case, unfair. Indeed, the British themselves relied on sangars, with the rocky ground making the excavation of deep trenches and dugouts an impossibility.[54]

British readiness to highlight perceived French failings extended to the conduct of joint operations. Interallied cooperation at the operational and tactical level brings with it a multitude of challenges, summarised by Elizabeth Greenhalgh as the need for 'harmonisation' between armies differing in doctrine, language, and equipment. Adjoining armies must also liaise to coordinate operations and ensure their effectiveness on the battlefield.[55] In Serbia, tacit expectations of a partnership built on open communication came up against the tendency of the French towards unilateral action. Captain Drury served as his battalion's adjutant during this period and was often exasperated by French conduct. It was, he complained, 'very hard to hear what the French were doing' as they would launch operations without informing the British.[56] More frustrating was French interference in the administration of British units. A French brigade's request for a copy of a battalion move order provoked a furious tirade in his journal towards not only French soldiers but the 'selfishness' of the French nation itself. Not only did the French, at least to Drury, appear poor allies, but he took great satisfaction from the self-reliance of 10th (Irish) Division in holding its sector of the front unassisted.[57] Faced with French domineering comparable to

51 NAM: 1976-07-69: Drury, Manuscript Journal, 8 November 1915.

52 For the experience of 10th (Irish) Division at Gallipoli see: Philip Orr, *Field of Bones: An Irish Division at Gallipoli* (Dublin: Lilliput Press, 2006); Johnstone, *Orange, Green and Khaki*, pp.100-152.

53 Kempshall, *Relations on the Western Front*, pp.151-152.

54 Alan Colquhoun Duff, *65 R.E.: A Short Record of the Service of the 65th Company Royal Engineers* (Cambridge: W. Heffer & Sons, 1920), p.10.

55 See: Elizabeth Greenhalgh, *Victory through Coalition: Britain and France during the First World War* (Cambridge: Cambridge University Press, 2005), pp.4-5; Elizabeth Greenhalgh, 'The Experience of Fighting with Allies: The Case of the Capture of Falfemont Farm during the Battle of the Somme, 1916', *War in History*, 10:2 (2003), pp.157-183.

56 NAM: 1976-07-69: Drury, Manuscript Journal, 16 November 1915.

57 NAM: 1976-07-69: Drury, Manuscript Journal, 17 November 1915.

that displayed around Salonika, some amongst 10th (Irish) Division evidently considered the British would have been perhaps better off waging the campaign in Serbia on their own.

In early December, the context in which the British appraised their ally underwent a drastic change. The position of the French forces engaged astride the Vardar had become ever more precarious and superfluous as the Bulgarians defeated the Serbians and drove them into Kosovo. With Serbia overrun and its defeated armies starting to retire over the Albanian mountains towards the Adriatic, any hope of stemming the invasion evaporated. Sarrail ordered his forces to prepare to withdraw, and on 3 December a general retreat south began. Entrenched to the rear of the advanced French troops, 10th (Irish) Division and the French 156e Division were to remain in situ before withdrawing on 14 December. Their Bulgarian adversary, however, did not conform to this timeline. Pre-empted by days of ranging and searching fire, on 6 December large numbers of Bulgarian infantry attacked the British and French positions, forcing them to steadily withdraw back towards Greece.[58]

Officers searched for an explanation for their defeat at Kosturino as they retired, and several considered the French a suitable scapegoat. Lieutenant-Colonel Henry Francis Newdigate Jourdain commanded the 5th Connaught Rangers, and felt the French bore at least part of the blame for his battalion being driven from their positions. Enemy action had prevented his men from strengthening their defences, he complained, leaving them to 'put up with the inferior and badly sighted' positions constructed by the French and earlier British units, and which were vulnerable to enemy artillery.[59] For Captain Drury the French had contributed to the debacle by delaying the British withdrawal from Kosturino to permit the evacuation of their stores south. Faced by mounting Bulgarian pressure, he felt only the decision to withdraw irrespective of their ally's wishes had saved the British force from disaster.[60]

On the other hand, those engaged at the sharp end of the retreat found little to criticise and saw their alliance with the French as an asset, not a hindrance. Unaware of the decisions taken above them, British soldiers assessed their ally on their assistance rendered in times of need. French artillery validated its earlier praise, clearing the Bulgarian artillery that otherwise threatened the British line of retreat.[61] Some fought in rear-guard actions alongside the French and similarly lauded the contribution of both their infantry and artillery.[62] Minor

58   Richard C. Hall, *Balkan Breakthrough: The Battle of Dobro Pole* (Bloomington: Indiana University Press, 2010), pp.44-49; Falls, *Military Operations Macedonia*, Vol.I, pp.62, 67-68; Johnstone, *Orange, Green and Khaki*, pp.174-184.
59   NAM: 1956-03-11-3: Henry Francis Newdigate Jourdain, Manuscript Diary, 7 December 1915.
60   NAM: 1976-07-69: Drury, Manuscript Journal, 8 December 1915.
61   NAM: 2007-02-46: Nathaniel John Knight, Typescript Memoir, p.11.
62   Young, *Subaltern in Serbia*, pp.52-53.

tactical successes such as these, irrelevant to the outcome of the campaign, took on greater importance in light of its overall failure. Given that Greenhalgh has identified the importance of battlefield 'success' in forming positive impressions of allied combatants, one would naturally assume the retirement from Serbia would have adversely affected views of the French overall.[63] Instead, the effectiveness of the rear-guard actions precluded any criticism of French performance on the battlefield by providing the means by which the British could interpret their experiences positively. Summarising the campaign in his memoir, Captain Young concluded 'no blame' could be assigned to the French, only 'praise and honour'.[64]

Although they did not know it at the time, the importance of their French ally went beyond the instances of tactical cooperation taking place before their eyes. That the British and French forces retreated successfully from Serbia has been attributed by historians to the skilful organisation of Sarrail, who oversaw an orderly withdrawal south of both men and material.[65] Having avoided a rout, the British and French troops converged on the village of Doiran on the Greco-Serbian frontier. A chaotic scene greeted the British. As the 65th Field Company Royal Engineers approached:

> …the traffic thickened. The whole width of the narrow road was crowded. British infantry and transport marched beside and intermingled with French guns and wagons. Here and there a flock of sheep or goats, herded by yelling Frenchmen, surged into any open space they could find. Despatch riders, skidding wildly over the slippery slush, dodged under horses' noses and scraped wagon wheels.[66]

The disorder did not reflect well on the French, but most British soldiers did not care. After all, both had escaped disaster. By 12 December, the entirety of 10th (Irish) Division had safely crossed back across the Greek frontier and continued towards Salonika, where it joined the British and French troops already digging in around the city. Although British attitudes towards the French had fluctuated considerably since both nations had first landed at Salonika, the shared trials of the campaign in Serbia had ensured the Anglo-French alliance ultimately emerged strengthened from its first instance of battlefield cooperation in the Balkans.

---

63   Elizabeth Greenhalgh, '"Parade Ground Soldiers": French Army Assessments of the British on the Somme in 1916', *The Journal of Military History*, 63:2 (1999), pp.283-312.
64   Young, *Subaltern in Serbia*, p.15.
65   Falls, *Military Operations Macedonia*, Vol.I, p.82; Palmer, *Gardeners of Salonika*, p.44.
66   Duff, *65 R.E.*, p.15.

The Bulgarians – Uncertain Foes

Entering the war a week after the first units of 10th (Irish) Division disembarked at Salonika, the Bulgarians were unknown to British soldiers, with their late addition to the list of Britain's enemies resulting from the failure in Allied diplomacy in late 1915. Both the Allies and the Central Powers had attempted to secure Bulgaria's allegiances in recognition of its geographical position at the heart of the Balkans. But because only the Central Powers could promise the return of the Macedonian territory gained from the Ottomans in the First Balkan War (1912-1913) and then lost shortly after to Serbia in the Second Balkan War (1913), Bulgaria signed a military convention with the Central Powers on 6 September 1915. In the meantime, British decisionmakers had hoped the mere presence of an Anglo-French force at Salonika would deter Bulgaria from joining the war on the side of the Central Powers. However, the lack of urgency amongst the British and French governments ensured that the troops arrived a month too late to affect Bulgarian calculations. Accordingly, following the onset of Austro-German operations against the Serbian capital Belgrade on 6 October, Bulgarian forces invaded south-eastern Serbia on 14 October, focusing initially on the defeat of the Serbian army and not the Anglo-French forces advancing north from Salonika.[67]

The prevailing operational conditions experienced by the men of 10th (Irish) Division in Serbia ensured that the Bulgarians remained poorly understood, appearing principally as a distant and often elusive adversary. Before the Battle of Kosturino, both sides were entrenched with several hundred yards of no man's land between them, ensuring that British soldiers could only observe the Bulgarians at a distance when they worked out in the open on their defensive positions.[68] As the Bulgarians limited themselves to sporadic shelling and sniping of British positions, their presence was otherwise far from evident, with the British able to walk along their trench line without coming under fire.[69] The onset of the Battle of Kosturino on 6 December saw British soldiers confront their enemy on the battlefield, but the retreat that followed restored much of the distance between the two sides. The Bulgarians followed up their victory slowly and cautiously, rather than attempting to harry the weakened British and French forces retreating before them, so that only rear-guard actions and isolated incidents created further battlefield encounters.[70]

Because they lacked the substantial personal experience of their enemy necessary to form measured opinions, the British attempted to understand the Bulgarians by

---

67 Hall, *Balkan Breakthrough*, pp.37-49; Palmer, *Gardeners of Salonika*, pp.32-33.
68 IWM: Documents.5537: McIlwain, Typescript Journal, 1 December 1915.
69 Henry Francis Newdigate Jourdain, *Record of the 5th (Service) Battalion the Connaught Rangers from the 19th August, 1914, to 17th January, 1916* (Oxford: Oxford University Press, 1916), p.157.
70 Wakefield and Moody, *Under the Devil's Eye*, pp.18-33.

thinking in stereotypes. Captain Young later wrote that their first impressions had been 'that the Bulgar was little better than an uncivilised savage, who lived for a lust of blood, and would delight in torturing his enemy for the pure joy of seeing him writhe.'[71] On the one hand, this characterisation reflected British awareness of specific acts attributed to the Bulgarians in Serbia. Stories of atrocities committed against French prisoners, whether real or imagined, and the sight of Bulgarians using their rifles and bayonets to butcher the British wounded at Kosturino made a significant impression on the British.[72] One can also recognise the unstated influence of established racial and cultural stereotypes of the Balkan region and its inhabitants in western discourse. Maria Todorova has coined the term 'Balkanism' to denote the 'stereotyping and reductionism' in western imaginings of the Balkans. The result, she shows, is that the region has become a catchword amongst the West for primitivity, barbarism, and violence.[73] Before the First World War, Bulgaria had avoided being tarnished as such, with the British public considering the Bulgarians to be the most modern of all the Balkan races.[74] The presence of such tropes in wartime views indicates that the British resorted to leaning on their general assumptions of the Balkans to delineate the nature of their unknown foe, with the result that rumours and instances of prisoner killing seemed suggestive of the Bulgarians being Balkan savages.

Only meetings with prisoners provided an opportunity to put a human face on this inhuman "other". Lieutenant-Colonel Jourdain, for instance, consid-ered the Bulgarian prisoners that saluted him when entering captivity to be 'fine men'.[75] But although such encounters removed the physical distance separating the two belligerents, they heightened the sense of cultural separation by exposing their differences. British soldiers found their unstated expectations confounded when coming face-to-face for the first time with an enemy that they could not fully understand and that seemed, and indeed did, belong to a very different region to their own. This impression emerges from the account of Private C.E. Jones concerning his capture of three prisoners while returning from collecting water at a village close to his position during the period of trench warfare before Kosturino. To Jones, these captives appeared to be 'strange soldiers', and it was only upon presenting them to his commanding officer that he learnt they were in fact Bulgarian bombers. Confusion ensued when this officer attempted to provide the Bulgarians with new boots, no doubt taking their sandals as a sign of depriva-tion, only to discover they were unused to boots and could not wear them.[76]

71   Young, *Subaltern in Serbia*, p.111.
72   Young, *Subaltern in Serbia*, p.111.; NAM: 1956-03-11-3: Jourdain, Manuscript Diary, 7 December 1915; NAM: 2017-10-3-1-1: Ambrose Keevil, Manuscript Letter, 9 January 1916.
73   Maria Todorova, *Imagining the Balkans* (Oxford: Oxford University Press, 1999), pp.3-20.
74   Eugene Michail, *British and the Balkans: Forming Images of Foreign Lands, 1900-1950* (London: Continuum, 2011), p.135.
75   NAM: 1956-03-11-3: Jourdain, Manuscript Diary, 25 November 1915.
76   IWM: Documents.14938: C.E. Jones, Typescript Memoir, p.12.

The disorientation engendered by such encounters could also be more profound. For British soldiers in this period, perhaps the only absolute point of reference when forming an impression of the Bulgarians was their formal status as a foe. And yet, when the men of 10th (Irish) Division met deserters, even this could be called into question. Facing Lieutenant Taylor's unit at one point before Kosturino was the Bulgarian 28th Regiment, a formation he came to consider 'excellent fellows' because of their pro-Entente sympathies. Being prone to desertion and, according to Taylor, refusing to attack the British on one occasion, it is no wonder he neither considered them a foe nor described them using the stereotyped imagery otherwise reserved for the Bulgarians.[77] That said, the extent to which mental barriers with the enemy broke down should not be overstated. Lieutenant Taylor's account is not only unique, but he himself recognised the exceptionality of the 28th Regiment, contrasting their release of a French officer captured during the retreat with the mistreatment and murder of a captive French Zouave by another unit.[78] Later in the campaign, the British did view the Bulgarians as more friend than foe, but that this occurred following sustained contact during positional warfare indicates that the Bulgarians in Serbia were too novel, and contact too fleeting, for such views to become widespread.[79]

Even if some could feel a degree of camaraderie with the enemy, wartime allegiances ensured the British nevertheless had to treat them as a foe and accordingly assess them on a military basis. While the inactivity of their own front precluded forming an impression from extensive first-hand combat experience, the close proximity of the French provided an opportunity to learn second-hand of the Bulgarians from a force that had already fought them. Recording the assault on a Bulgarian occupied hill by a neighbouring French unit, Captain Drury noted that in pressing the attack with bayonets and grenades, they had 'found the Bulgar a hardy fighter.'[80] The battlefield detritus left from such engagements gave further indications of the attributes of the Bulgarians as soldiers. 'One can easily see the influence of the mountainous country on their equipment and also the experience gained in the recent Balkan Wars', concluded Drury at the sight of well-dressed Bulgarian corpses alongside weapons, ammunition boxes, and pack saddles.[81] Above all, he highlighted the clothing of the Bulgarians, the dead wearing thick shirts, made of sheepskin or quilted cotton stuffed with cotton wool, and boots which some wore with sandals or moccasins over the top.[82] His

77 Taylor, *Boy with the Guns*, p.153.
78 Taylor, *Boy with the Guns*, pp.172-173.
79 Philip Orr, 'The road to Belgrade: the experiences of the 10th (Irish) Division in the Balkans, 1915-17', in Adrian Gregory and Senia Pašeta (eds), *Ireland and the Great War: 'A War to Unite us All'?* (Manchester: Manchester University Press, 2002), pp.177-178.
80 NAM: 1976-07-69: Drury, Manuscript Journal, 7 November 1915.
81 NAM: 1976-07-69: Drury, Manuscript Journal, 14 November 1915.
82 NAM: 1976-07-69: Drury, Manuscript Journal, 14 November 1915, 15 November 1915.

focus on those items suggestive of adaptation to fighting in cold weather conditions is not surprising when one considers the contrasting unpreparedness of 10th (Irish) Division for the Serbian winter, with many men arriving still wearing lightweight khaki drill.[83] Drury's assessment of their weaponry was more mixed, Bulgarian rifles comprising a mix of the latest and older models, but their bayonets seemed much more impressive, being 'short and strong', he explained, 'and in shape very like the one we use with the long territorial pattern Lee Enfield rifle.'[84] In short, all the evidence available to the British pointed to the Bulgarians being a formidable foe both comparable in some areas to the themselves and markedly superior in others.

British soldiers had the opportunity to personally gauge their foe's military abilities first-hand at the Battle of Kosturino. Although weakened physically and numerically by the winter cold, the British put up stout resistance against superior numbers of Bulgarians in bitter fighting, at times conducted at close quarters with bayonets, but ultimately had to withdraw. One would assume that defeat would have added nuance to British views by reinforcing earlier complimentary appraisals of a victorious enemy while highlighting instances of failure. The Bulgarian attack certainly included examples of each: the capture of the forward position known as Rocky Peak by Bulgarian infantry shrouded by the morning mist displayed considerable skill, but the British also inflicted significant casualties on masses of Bulgarian infantry that attempted to rush their positions.[85] Some men belonging to formations uninvolved at Kosturino did suppose that the Bulgarians had outfought the British. W.J. Musset of the 27th Lines of Communication Company, Army Service Corps, believed the entire campaign in Serbia was a 'case of a stranger in a strange land.' 'The Bulgars know the mountains and hills', he posited, 'they outwitted and punished us and the 10th Division retired hastily'.[86]

For their part, the men of 10th (Irish) Division did not consider themselves outfought by the Bulgarians, rationalising their defeat instead in a manner that preserved the superiority of the British soldier over his Bulgarian counterpart. Explanations stressed two points in particular: firstly, that the Bulgarians had had an overwhelming numerical superiority in men and artillery and, secondly, that the British had inflicted heavy losses on the enemy.[87] Many also believed that Bulgaria's German and Austro-Hungarian allies had made a considerable contribution. One such individual was the commander of the 5th Connaught Rangers,

83   Wakefield and Moody, *Under the Devil's Eye*, p.20.

84   NAM: 1976-07-69: Drury, Manuscript Journal, 14 November 1915, 15 November 1915.

85   Johnstone, *Orange, Green and Khaki*, pp.174-180.

86   IWM: Documents.12945: Mussett, Typescript Journal, 3-4 November 1915. The erroneous date is that given in the journal.

87   Young, *Subaltern in Serbia*, pp.45-47; Taylor, *Boy with the Guns*, pp.162, 165; IWM: Documents.7987: Knott, Manuscript Diary, 7 December 1915, 8 December 1915.

Lieutenant-Colonel Jourdain. Reflecting on the causes of his battalion's defeat in several diary entries written during the retreat, he highlighted the enemy's careful artillery preparation and the demoralising effect of their shell fire. But, significantly, he considered this artillery to have been German and Austrian, not Bulgarian.[88] While others did not deny the involvement of Bulgarian artillery, they too presumed the Germans were also involved.[89] In a similar vein, survivors suggested their Bulgarian assailants had comprised a sizeable proportion of German troops, estimated by one officer to have been around one in 10, and generally assumed to have been officers and non-commissioned officers.[90] In essence, the British believed only the Germans, and, to a lesser extent, the Austrians, could have provided the modern firepower and battlefield leadership necessary for victory.

The importance of emphasising the perceived contribution of these European Great Powers can be attributed to the ideas of hierarchy ingrained in British attitudes towards the Balkans. Andrew Hammond has argued that negative conceptions of the region underpin an imagined intra-European cultural hierarchy surmounted by Western Europe and which positions the Balkans at Europe's geographical and civilisational fringe.[91] Suffering defeat at the hands of a Balkan nation like Bulgaria was therefore at odds with presumed British pre-eminence over the region, a fact not lost on Brigadier-General Philip Howell, the British Salonika Force's chief of staff. Having travelled extensively throughout the Balkans before the war, including as a regional correspondent, Howell possessed an insight into Balkan matters rare amongst those at Salonika, and considered the campaign in Serbia to have fundamentally destabilised Britain's position.[92] 'It's humiliating to think', he lamented in a letter to his wife, 'that two years ago an Englishman was a sort of superman amongst these Balkan races: and that they look upon us now as effete!'[93] For ordinary soldiers lacking Howell's expertise but possessing a sense of superiority derived from a universal understanding of modern civilisation based on British (and Western) values, the existence of which has been convincingly argued by Justin Fantauzzo, defeat to the Bulgarians would have been equally problematic.[94] By focusing on the role of fellow Western European powers over that of a Balkan army, the British could attempt to rationalise an otherwise inconceivable defeat in an understandable way and, perhaps, mitigate

88   NAM: 1956-03-11-3: Jourdain, Manuscript Diary, 7 December 1915, 8 December 1915.
89   NAM: 2017-10-3-1-1: Keevil, Manuscript Letter, 14 December 1915.
90   IWM: Documents.10893: J.V. Cope, Manuscript Diary Extract, 7 December 1915; Jourdain, *Record of the 5th Connaught Rangers*, p.191.
91   Andrew Hammond, 'Typologies of the East: On Distinguishing Balkanism and Orientalism', *Nineteenth-Century Contexts*, 29:2-3 (2007), pp.205-206.
92   Rosalind Upcher Buxton Howell, *Philip Howell, a memoir by his wife* (London: George Allen and Unwin Ltd, 1942), pp.16-23, 31-34, 42-43.
93   Howell, *Philip Howell*, p.186.
94   See: Fantauzzo, 'Rise Phoenix-Like', pp.125-144.

the humiliation of losing to a lesser foe. Although engrained views of the Balkans provided an established framework for British soldiers attempting to understand their unfamiliar enemy, such tropes ultimately had to be reconciled with wartime experiences, ensuring that views of the Bulgarians during this initial period of contact were not necessarily immutable.

Conclusion

For British soldiers dispatched to the Balkans at the start of the Salonika campaign, meeting the different armies present in the theatre of war for the first time was a challenging and often confusing experience. The political, military, and cultural circumstances of the campaign's launch provided few stable points of reference when forming their first impressions of the Greek, French, and Bulgarian armies. Even the categories of friend or foe, the fundamental building blocks for attitudes towards other combatants, possessed an absolute nature often ill-suited to applying to those encountered at Salonika. What resulted was that a great deal of uncertainty, fluctuation, and contradiction characterised British views of each throughout this period. Although interacting with different armies and understanding their soldiers as both combatants and representatives of their respective nations was challenging, it remained unavoidable. British soldiers did not serve in isolation at Salonika, and their experiences were shaped and moulded by encounters with 'the most weird mixture of humanity' around them.

Bibliography

Archival Sources

Imperial War Museum, London
    Documents.2027: Reginald J. Bailey, Typescript Letters
    Documents.4432: Christopher Wyndham Hughes, Typescript Memoir
    Documents.5537: John McIlwain, Typescript Journal
    Documents.7987: William Knott, Manuscript Diary
    Documents.8493: Albert H. Muggeridge, Typescript Journal
    Documents.10893: J.V. Cope, Manuscript Diary Extract
    Documents.12712: Eric De Normann, Transcript Letters
    Documents.12945: W.J. Mussett, Typescript Journal
    Documents.14938: C.E. Jones, Typescript Memoir
    Documents.16012: James Flanagan, Typescript Diary
    Documents.24945: Percy George Mandley, Manuscript Memoir
National Army Museum, London
    1956-03-11-3: Henry Francis Newdigate Jourdain, Manuscript Diaries

1976-07-69: Noel Edmund Drury, Manuscript Journal
2007-02-46: Nathaniel John Knight, Typescript Memoir
2017-10-3-1-1: Ambrose Keevil, Manuscript Letters
The National Archives, Kew
    WO 95/4828: 10th (Irish) Division War Diary

Printed Primary Sources

Burr, Malcolm, *Slouch Hat* (London: George Allen and Unwin Ltd., 1935).
Duff, Alan Colquhoun, *65 R.E.: A Short Record of the Service of the 65th Company Royal Engineers* (Cambridge: W. Heffer & Sons, 1920).
Gibbs, Arthur Hamilton, *Gun Fodder – The Diary of Four Years of War* (Boston: Little, Brown, and Company, 1927).
Hawke, James, *From Private to Major* (London: Hutchinson & Co., 1938).
Howell, Rosalind Upcher Buxton, *Philip Howell, a memoir by his wife* (London: George Allen & Unwin Ltd, 1942).
Jourdain, Henry Francis Newdigate, *Record of the 5th (Service) Battalion the Connaught Rangers from the 19th August, 1914, to 17th January, 1916* (Oxford: Oxford University Press, 1916).
Taylor, George William, *The Boy with the Guns* (London: John Lane, 1919).
Wheeler, Cordy, *Memorial Record of the Seventh (Service) Battalion, The Oxfordshire and Buckinghamshire Light* (Oxford: Basil Blackwell, 1921).
Young, Arthur Donovan, *A Subaltern in Serbia And Some Letters from the Struma Valley* (London: Drane's, 1922).

Online Primary Sources

'Cannot discover what is in the air – are we waiting for the Spring', *Fit as Fiddles and as Hard as Nails: Irish Soldiers' Voices from the Great War* <https://www.tcd.ie/library/fitasfiddles/cannot-discover-what-is-in-the-air-are-we-waiting-for-the-spring/>, accessed 29 September 2020.

Secondary Sources

Afflerbach, Holger, 'Greece and the Balkan Area in German Strategy, 1914-1918', in Daniel Kaplanidou (ed.), *The Salonica Theatre of Operations and the Outcome of the Great War* (Thessaloniki: Institute for Balkan Studies, 2005), pp.53-66.
Cassar, George H., *Reluctant Partner: The Complete Story of the French Participation in the Dardanelles Expedition of 1915* (Solihull: Helion, 2019).

Dutton, David, *The Politics of Diplomacy: Britain, France and the Balkans in the First World War* (London: I.B. Taurus, 1998).

Falls, Cyril, *Military Operations Macedonia* (London: H.M.S.O., 1933; repr. The Naval and Military Press Ltd.).

Fantauzzo, Justin, 'Rise Phoenix-Like: British Soldiers, Civilization and the First World War in Greek Macedonia, 1915-1918', in Joseph Clarke and John Horne (eds), *Militarized Cultural Encounters in the Long Nineteenth Century* (Cham: Palgrave Macmillan, 2018), pp.125-147.

Fantauzzo, Justin, and Nelson, Robert L., 'Expeditionary Forces in the Shatterzone: German, British and French Soldiers on the Macedonian Front, 1915-1918', in Alan Beyerchen and Emre Sencer (eds), *Expeditionary Forces in the First World War* (Cham: Palgrave Macmillan, 2019), pp.149-176.

Glenny, Misha, *The Balkans Nationalism, War, and the Great Powers* (London: Granta Books, 2012).

Greenhalgh, Elizabeth, '"Parade Ground Soldiers": French Army Assessments of the British on the Somme in 1916', *The Journal of Military History*, 63:2 (1999), pp.283-312.

Greenhalgh, Elizabeth, 'The Experience of Fighting with Allies: The Case of the Capture of Falfemont Farm during the Battle of the Somme, 1916', *War in History*, 10:2 (2003), pp.157-183.

Greenhalgh, Elizabeth, *Victory through Coalition: Britain and France during the First World War* (Cambridge: Cambridge University Press, 2005).

Hall, R.C., *Balkan Breakthrough: The Battle of Dobro Pole* (Bloomington: Indiana University Press, 2010).

Hammond, Andrew, 'Typologies of the East: On Distinguishing Balkanism and Orientalism', *Nineteenth-Century Contexts*, 29:2-3 (2007), pp.201-218.

Johnstone, Tom, *Orange, Green and Khaki: The Story of Irish Regiments in the Great War, 1914-1918* (Dublin: Gill and Macmillan, 1992).

Karaduman, Alev 'Recognising the other: Contested identities at Gallipoli', in Metin Gürcan and Robert Johnson (eds), *The Gallipoli Campaign: The Turkish Perspective* (London: Routledge, 2016), pp.163-172.

Kempshall, Chris, *British, French and American Relations on the Western Front, 1914-1918* (Cham: Palgrave Macmillan, 2018).

Leon, George B., *Greece and the Great Powers, 1914-1917* (Thessaloniki: Institute for Balkan Studies, 1974).

Mazower, Mark, *Salonica, City of Ghosts: Christians, Muslims, and Jews, 1430-1950* (London: Harper Perennial, 2005).

Michail, Eugene, *British and the Balkans: Forming Images of Foreign Lands, 1900-1950* (London: Continuum, 2011).

Orr, Philip, *Field of Bones: An Irish Division at Gallipoli* (Dublin: Lilliput Press, 2006).

Orr, Philip, 'The road to Belgrade: the experiences of the 10th (Irish) Division in the Balkans, 1915-17', in Adrian Gregory and Senia Pašeta (eds), *Ireland and the Great War: 'A War to Unite us All'?* (Manchester: Manchester University Press, 2002), pp.171-189.

Palmer, Alan, *Gardeners of Salonika* (London: Andre Deutsch, 1965).

Prete, Roy A., *'Imbroglio par excellence*: Mounting the Salonika Campaign, September-October 1915', *War and Society*, 19:1 (2001), pp.47-70.

Ramsden, John, '"French People have a peculiar facility for being misrepresented": British Perceptions of France at War, 1914-1918', in Antoine Capet (ed.), *Britain, France and the Entente Cordiale since 1904* (Basingstoke: Palgrave Macmillan, 2006), pp.8-27

Richardson, Rachel, 'Home away from the home front: the British in the Balkans during the Great War' (PhD thesis, Birbeck, University of London, 2014).

Tannenbaum, Jan Karl, *General Maurice Sarrail, 1856-1929: The French Army and left-wing politics* (Chapel Hill, North Carolina: University of North Carolina Press, 1974).

Todorova, Maria, *Imagining the Balkans* (Oxford: Oxford University Press, 1999).

Wakefield, Alan, and Moody, Simon., *Under the Devil's Eye: The British Military Experience in Macedonia, 1915-1918* (Barnsley: Pen and Sword, 2004).

8

'These Identity Discs Have Gone to Pulp': British Identity Discs used during the Two World Wars

Sarah Ashbridge

Identity discs were introduced to facilitate the identification of fallen soldiers, a role which has made them an iconic piece of military equipment amongst soldiers, the relatives of soldiers, and collectors alike. This is particularly true for the discs of those who fought and died during the First and Second World Wars. The red and green fibre discs introduced between 1914-1916 would influence identification practice for much of the twentieth century, continuing to be issued until around 1960 within the British Army, and for longer within the broader Armed Forces.

Britain was not the first nation to introduce identity discs, with many European nations having introduced their own discs during the nineteenth century as war became increasingly industrialised, resulting in rising numbers of soldiers killed in action. However, the British identification system was not introduced in direct response to the mass loss encountered as a result of continental conflict, as was the case for many of our European neighbours, but was instead implemented in the context of colonial war. Thus, it is important to situate the British developments within the international timeline of identification practice.

This chapter will explore the development of the British identity disc within the international context by reflecting upon the timing of the British policy of individuated identification and the influence of the 1906 Geneva Convention. It will then focus on the discs designed and used during the First World War. Much of the evidence available to inform us about the development of the identity disc system lies within the archives of the Commonwealth War Graves Commission. Given the crucial role of the Commission's founder, Sir Fabian Ware, in the development of the discs, this chapter will allow us to reflect upon how the successes and failures of identity discs have framed the way that we remember fallen soldiers today.

Identification Practice in the Nineteenth Century

Items issued for the purpose of identification within a military structure are not a modern or an explicitly British phenomenon. There are examples amongst the material culture of the Roman period, the Taiping Rebellion (1850-1866), and the American Civil War (12 April 1861–9 April 1865). Many of the items produced during the American Civil War were handmade or sold by sutlers (merchants) who would follow units to sell their wares, as an official system was not introduced at this point.[1] The huge losses incurred during this conflict resulted in the establishment of national memorial cemeteries, within which soldiers of all ranks received an individual marked grave; something which had not been encountered before. This created a new, international precedent which would come to shape the attitude to the dead and their burials across the Western World. Prussia was the first nation to formally introduce an identifying item in 1869 as the *Rekognitionmarke* (later to become the *Erkennungsmarke* in 1878), which was utilised during the Franco-Prussian War (19 July 1870–28 January 1871). This war would also necessitate the creation of identity discs within the French Army, which were introduced in 1881.[2] Discs were also introduced by Belgium in 1891, Italy in 1892, Japan in 1894, and both Austria-Hungary and Russia in 1902, with designs including discs, tags, and lockets.

Despite the popular uptake of identity discs as a means to identify fallen soldiers, Britain decided to take a different approach. Following the Crimean War (5 October 1853–30 March 1856), Britain had fought almost continuously, with historian Hew Strachan noting that only one opponent between 1815-1914 was European.[3] Like France and Germany, Britain was immersed in the 'scramble for Africa' of the 1880's and 1890's, engaging in the Ninth Xhosa War (1877–1879), the Anglo-Zulu War (1879), the Mahdist War (1881–1899), and the Ekumeku Movement against the rising power of the Royal Niger Company of the British Empire (1883-1914), alongside various campaigns in Asia. It was during this period of colonial warfare that the British Army would begin to make use of its own identification system, despite the relatively low number of casualties compared with the experience of intra-continental war within Europe. The British system would provide each soldier with a form which could be filled in with a soldier's personal information, 'Description Card for Active Service' (Army Form B. 2067).

---

1   F. Stansbury Haydon, 'An Identification Disc for the Army, 1862', *The Journal of the American Military Institute*, Vol.3:1 (1939). pp.61-63; Larry B. Maier, *Identification Discs of Union Soldiers in the Civil War: A Complete Classification Guide and Illustrated History* (McFarland & Company: North Carolina, 2010).

2   Sarah I. Ashbridge and Simon Verdegem, 'Identity discs: The recovery and identification of First World War soldiers located during archaeological works on the former Western Front', *Forensic Science International*, Vol.317 (2020), pp.1-14.

3   Hew Strachan, *From Waterloo to Balaclava: Tactics, Technology, and the British Army, 1815-1854* (Cambridge: Cambridge University Press, 1985).

Army Form B. 2067 was printed on glazed calico material and included space for the inclusion of personal information about the soldier, including his name, number, rank, regiment, next of kin, and place of residence. The forms were filled in by hand along with a signature from the Officer Commanding the battery or company. Once mobilised, the form would be sewn into one of the interior pockets of the frock or tunic, with the 'first field dressing' first aid kit held in the opposite pocket.[4] Sewing the form into the pocket reduced the possibility of the form becoming lost, however this did mean that the form had to be cut, or the stitches unpicked, to remove the form in the event of death – something which may not have always been possible in the heat of battle. It is not clear when the form was approved for introduction, though the earliest known reference to the form can be found within the description of the field kit of the Medical Staff Corps in Appendix No. 56 of the 1890 edition of the *Regulations for Army Medical Service* (part I).[5]

The introduction of the Description Card as a form of identification is indicative that Britain was beginning to take seriously the need to identify fallen soldiers of all ranks. In practice, the burial of a soldier on the battlefield remained an operational duty relating to the sanitation of the field and maintenance of hygienic conditions, rather than a response to moral or religious considerations about the dignity or treatment of the deceased. Consequently, burial practices would continue to make use of the historical burial traditions seen during the Napoleonic Wars, the Crimean War, and the South African War (11 October 1899–31 May 1902). Men of the officer class almost exclusively received an individual grave, and, in many instances, these were marked by durable stone grave markers funded by their families, communities, and occasionally units. The ordinary ranks could receive an individual burial, though it was more common for them to be buried within communal graves, particularly where losses were high. Communal or shared graves are also known as mass graves and are a similar practice to the penny or pauper's graves used in British society during the nineteenth century. Communal graves were more likely to be marked by wooden cross markers, which were not particularly durable, and some did not receive a marker at all.

During the South African War, memorials displaying the names of ordinary soldiers appear to feature more prominently than in previous wars. It is possible that this cultural shift to commemorate the graves of ordinary ranked soldiers more prominently was facilitated by the use of Army Form B. 2067; but it is also possible that this represented a shift in socio-cultural values in civilian Britain which had approved a series of Acts of Parliament to improve the sanitation and appearance of

---

4   Edward H. Benton notes that the idea for the first field dressing had been adopted during the Franco-Prussian War, with the British Army introducing the concept in 1884, an example which demonstrates how Britain observed wars and learnt from positive examples of practice. See Edward H. Benton, 'British Surgery in the South African War: The Work of Major Frederick Porter', *Medical History*. Vol.21 (1977), p.280.

5   War Office, *Regulations for Army Medical Services* (Part I) (London: HMSO, 1890), p.412.

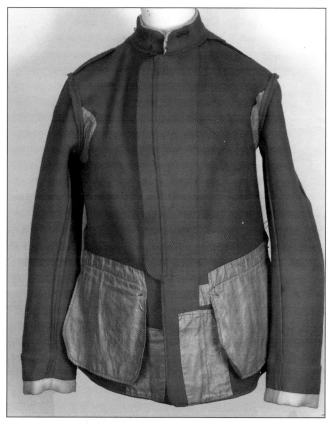

1890s Kersey Frock pictured inside out to show the sewn pockets
design to store the first field dressing and Army Form B 2067.
(Personal collection of Toby Brayley)

burials and graveyards during the long nineteenth century.[6] These acts responded
to societal concerns such as safety from body snatchers, the sanctity of burial, and
how the corpse might act as a vector for disease. The debates which necessitated
the creation of these acts would result in a shift in attitude towards the idea of
what a burial place should look like, the creation of new burial grounds to replace
overflowing cemeteries, and new practices relating to the hygiene of the corpse.
Civilian burial plots in Britain were purchased by those who could afford them
for exclusive use for a fixed period of time only; for example, 15 years. Those who
could not afford a specific grave plot would be interred within a form of communal

6   Such as the Burial Act 1852, Burial Act 1853, Burial Act 1857, Burial Act 1880, and the Anatomy Act
    1832.

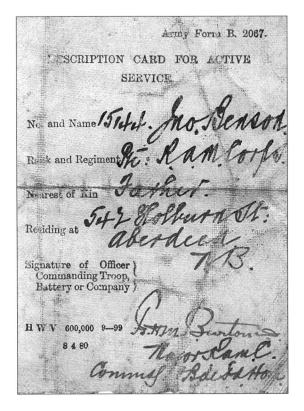

Army Form B. 2067 produced in September 1899 and issued to Private J. Benson RAMC after enlisting at Glasgow on 18th March 1901. (Personal collection of Toby Brayley)

grave, according to their budget. Consequently, there was little to no expectation of a permanent grave whether at home or on service, and the idea of a hygienic, undisturbed burial became tied to moral values and Christian sentiment.

Following the conclusion of the South African War, the British Army had accepted formal responsibility for the dead, assigning the Royal Engineers the task of burying the dead and recording the location of their graves. Military funds were used to pay for the iron crosses which marked graves of this era.[7] Later, in 1905, the British Government would take the responsibility of paying for the markers for graves 'which had not been privately given their memorials', indicating a shift in attitude from policy makers.[8] At this point, there were no laws, treaties or agreements in place which dictated the treatment or burial of the war dead.

---

7   J. P. Garrett, *Tribute to the Fallen: The Evolution of Canadian Battlefield Burials during the First World War* (PhD thesis, University of Western Ontario, 2018), pp.53-54.

8   Philip Longworth, *The Unending Vigil: The History of the Commonwealth War Graves Commission* (Barnsley: Pen and Sword, 2003), p.xxi.

The 1906 Geneva Convention and the Introduction of the British Identity Disc

It was not until the turn of the nineteenth century that the subject of the burial of fallen soldiers was brought to the international table. During the 1899 Hague Conference, within which some of the first laws of war were codified, the need to review the 1864 Geneva Convention was raised. It was necessary to clarify the role of Volunteer Aid Societies on the battlefield, and to consider additional humanitarian issues, such as the treatment of the dead.

Attempts to organise a conference to review the Geneva Convention began in 1901, when a document entitled 'Statement of some of the ideas to be examined for the revision of the Geneva Convention' was circulated, within which Section B, 'Sundry Propositions', proposed the adoption of requirements to a) conduct a careful examination of the dead before inhumation or incineration, b) that every officer and soldier should carry an identifying mark in order to establish his identity, and c) that lists of the dead, wounded and sick who have been taken by the enemy should be sent by the enemy to the relevant army or authority with as little delay as possible.[9]

The conference was delayed because of various wars, including the South African War, and later the Russo-Japanese War (8 February 1904–5 September 1905), and was eventually hosted by the Swiss Federal Council between 11 June and 5 July 1906 in Geneva. Participating nations worked to review the International Convention of 22 August 1864 for the Amelioration of the Condition of Soldiers Wounded in Armies in the Field.[10] Each nation was invited to appoint plenipotentiaries to attend on their behalf, with Great Britain and Ireland electing to send four representatives: Major General Sir John Charles Ardagh, KCMG, KCIE, CB, Professor Thomas Erskine Holland, KC, DCL, Sir John Furley, CB, and Lieutenant-Colonel William Grant Macpherson, CMG, RAMC.[11] During the conference, sessions were held to review specific passages of the Convention having been 'animated by the desire to lessen the inherent evils of warfare as fare as within their power'.[12]

The issue of fallen soldiers on the battlefield was as much a sanitary issue for armies as it was a moral dilemma, if not more so; a perspective which framed the spirit of discussions during the conference. In fact, Brigadier-General George B. Davies, Judge-Advocate-General of the Army of the United States of America,

---

9   Longworth, *The Unending Vigil*, p.2.
10 A. Pearce Higgins (ed.), *The Hague Peace Conferences and other International Conferences Concerning the Laws and Usages of War* (Cambridge: Cambridge University Press, 2014) (Originally published in 1909), p.34.
11 C.S. Sperry, 'The Revision of the Geneva Convention, 1906', *Proceedings of the American Political Science Association*, Vol. 3 (1907), p.49.
12 Sperry, 'The Revision of the Geneva Convention, 1906', p.47.

presented the advances in military sanitation and medicine as a significant motivator for the amendment of the 1864 Convention, describing that:

> In the march of improvements in medicine and surgery, the interval which separates the Italian campaign of 1859 and the Manchurian operations of 1904 is vastly greater than that which separates the medical service of the great Frederick from that of the third Napoleon.[13]

There was an international recognition that the nature of warfare had changed significantly, necessitating updates to the convention to resolve 'much of the inexactness of expression which characterized the old undertaking'.[14] Anxieties over the strength of military forces and large numbers of casualties incurred during the nineteenth century had fuelled the development of shared humanitarian ideals, but this was the first attempt to mitigate those concerns through legislation.

The rapid development of artillery and small arms, and their increased effective range had led to a widening interval between trench lines, often creating an 'impassable' zone littered with wire entanglements, mines, trenches and more.[15] These chaotic landscapes dramatically limited the ability to recover the dead, leaving corpses exposed for days, weeks and even months. In response to this, two new articles were introduced within Chapter One of the Convention. These articles are significant in that they formed the first examples of international law which specifically addressed fallen soldiers. Article 3 instructed that:

> After every engagement the belligerent who remains in possession of the field of battle shall take measures to search for the wounded and to protect the wounded and dead from robbery and ill treatment.
>
> He will see that a careful examination is made of the bodies of the dead prior to their interment or incineration.[16]

This ensured that the victor of the field was responsible for conducting searches for both the dead and wounded, for the protection of their dignity, and for the undertaking of a search of any body for identifying objects, documents and personal effects. Article 4 followed with guidance on what should be done with these possessions, stipulating that:

13 George B. Davis, 'The Geneva Convention of 1906', *The American Journal of International Law*, Vol.1:2 (1907), p.411.
14 Davis, 'The Geneva Convention of 1906', p.411.
15 Sperry, 'The Revision of the Geneva Convention, 1906', p.37.
16 Chapter 1: The sick and wounded – art. 3, Convention for the Amelioration of the Condition of the Wounded and Sick in Armies in the Field. Geneva (1906). 6 July 1906, available at: < https://ihl-databases.icrc.org/applic/ihl/ihl.nsf/ART/180-170004?OpenDocument >, accessed 31 October 2022.

As soon as possible each belligerent shall forward to the authorities of their country or army the marks or military papers of identification found upon the bodies of the dead, together with a list of names of the sick and wounded taken in charge by him.

Belligerents will keep each other mutually advised of internments and transfers, together with admissions to hospitals and deaths which occur among the sick and wounded in their hands. They will collect all objects of personal use, valuables, letters, etc., which are found upon the field of battle, or have been left by the sick or wounded who have died in sanitary formations or other establishments, for transmission to persons in interest through the authorities of their own country.[17]

This section ensured that any identifying or personal items were removed from the body and returned to the nation of the deceased. The first sentence acknowledges the use of both marks (that is, discs) and papers used for the purpose of identification, reflecting the range of systems in use, but neither article explicitly required a combatant nation to provide an identifying item to their soldiers. The question 'is it necessary to state in the Convention that every soldier shall carry a mark of identity?' had been raised during the morning of 16 June when the discussed articles were formulated, however the motion was negated by 14 to seven, with Great Britain voting against the requirement to formally adopt an identity disc.[18] This is interesting given that the British Army had already been using Army Form B. 2067 to facilitate identification for over a decade. However, a 1908 report on the Convention delivered to the Houses of Parliament provides further insight.

The requirement to examine the dead was thought to impose 'rather an onerous duty on the victor', despite having been carried out within recent wars.[19] Additionally, the duty to forward identifying marks was dismissed for fear that 'its performance may require the formation of a very large special staff, and may prove difficult to carry out'.[20] These comments indicate that administrative concerns overrode a driving desire to ensure that all fallen soldiers were treated with equal respect. Regardless, the updated Geneva Convention was ratified on 6 July 1906, formalising the requirements to search and protect the dead. It is important to remember that Britain's perspective was shaped by decades of fighting colonial wars in distant locations where the concept of visiting the grave of a fallen soldier was out of the question for much of society. This was in contrast to the experience of nations such as France and Germany which had experienced mass loss

---

17 Chapter 1: The sick and wounded – art. 3.
18 Parliament. House of Commons & Lords, *Sick and Wounded in War: Papers relating to the Geneva Convention 1906* (Cd. 3933), (London: The Stationery Office, 1908), p.36.
19 Parliament. House of Commons & Lords, *Sick and Wounded in War*, p.27.
20 Parliament. House of Commons & Lords, *Sick and Wounded in War*, p.27.

within close proximity of their home populations in recent decades, as with the Franco-Prussian and Austro-Prussian Wars. These wars had forced socio-cultural changes in both attitudes and practice with regards to the dead that Britain had not yet experienced.[21]

Despite voting against the formal adoption of an identifying mark, Britain would approve a pattern for an identity disc within weeks. Pattern 6444/1906 for 'Disc, identity, aluminium' was approved on 29 August 1906, potentially coinciding with preparations for the publication of *Regulations for Mobilization 1906*. The pattern described a round disc which was produced from 98 percent aluminium and stamped with personal information. Pattern 6453/1906 was later approved on 19 September 1906, introducing the 'cord' which would be strung through the disc allowing it to be worn around the neck. The aluminium disc and its cord were formally introduced for use on active service in Army Order 9, published on 1 January 1907.[22] The disc was categorised as an 'article of kit' and was designed 'to be worn around the neck under the clothing…in lieu of the identity card (Army Form B 2067)', and marked with the soldier's number, rank, name, regiment, and religious denomination. Discs and cords could be ordered from the clothing depot which supplied the district, however the stamps used to mark the discs ('stamps steel, for 1/8 inch') were ordered from the Army Ordnance Department. Once received, the discs were marked and stored along with a 42-inch cord by officers commanding units, issued only upon mobilization.

On 1 May 1907, Army Order 102 removed the requirement to mark the discs with a soldier's rank, presumably to reduce the number of discs issued due to any changes in rank.[23] Italicised letters to describe the abbreviated regiment were prohibited. Details on storage were provided, with additional updates on the storage of discs for soldiers in the Special Reserve provided within Army Order 83 of May 1908.[24] In February 1908, Army Order 38 provided updated details on the marking of the discs, stipulating that during peaceful times the discs would be stamped with the name of the unit, with the regimental number, name, and religious denomination added upon mobilization.[25] These were stored by the officer commanding the unit. None of these Orders describe processes for the removal of a disc from a fallen soldier, nor do they advise where any discs removed should be sent to.

In fact, the first reference to these processes located thus far can be found within *Army Field Service Regulations Part I*, published in 1909. Within Chapter XVI, Section 133 (3) described that 'anyone concerned in burying a solider, or finding

21 Sarah I. Ashbridge and David O'Mara, 'The Erkennungsmarke: The Humanitarian Duty to Identify Fallen Soldiers 1866-1918'. *Journal of Conflict Archaeology*, Vol. 16 (2021), pp.1-32.
22 War Office, *Army Orders, 1908* (London: HMSO, 1909), p.8.
23 Army Order 102. 1907, in War Office, *Army Orders, 1907* (London: HMSO, 1908), pp.14-15.
24 Army Order 83. 1908. In War Office, *Army Orders, 1908* (London: HMSO, 1909).
25 Army Order 38. 1909. In War Office, *Army Orders, 1909* (London: HMSO, 1910).

a body after an action, will remove the identity disc and paybook... and will note the number of the equipment and rifle, or any other means likely to assist identification'.[26] The officer in command would record the soldier's information on Army Form B. 2090a, which was then forwarded along with his pay book, identity disc and any personal items to the Adjutant General's office.[27] Personal items were then returned to the family of the deceased. Whilst *Field Service Regulations* made clear how discs should be used, clearly defining the administrative processes associated with them which embedded the discs into the regulatory framework and administrative procedures of the British Army, the system retained one major flaw. Once an identity disc and identifying papers had been removed from a dead soldier, his body became unidentifiable. If an identified soldier was not swiftly buried within a marked or recorded grave, his identity could become swiftly lost.

The 1907 aluminium disc was in use upon the declaration of war in 1914. However, the British Army was not actively fighting any wars between 1907 and 1914, meaning that the number of losses experienced by the British Army during this period would have been small, and likely irregular, resulting in limited opportunities to demonstrate flaws with the identity disc system or to implement change in response to these flaws. Simply put, the British Army was unable to test the efficiency of the identity disc system before the outbreak of war.

Preparing for Battle: The 1914 Identity Disc

Following declaration of war on 4 August 1914, existing soldiers were mobilised and their partially stamped identity discs brought out of storage for marking, and thousands of new recruits were enlisted to form the 'First New Army'.[28] Perhaps because of the need to supply such huge numbers of incoming soldiers, a pattern for a new identity disc was designed. Pattern 8111/1914 was approved on 21 August, introducing a new disc produced from compressed fibre. The new disc was round, without the protrusion of the aluminium disc, measuring approximately 35mm in diameter and featuring a punctured hole for the cord to be threaded through. The discs were red in colour, though brown examples can be found. It is not clear if brown dye was used as substitute for red when dye was not available, or if the brown colour is the result of the degradation of the red dye over time.

In 2009, historian David O'Mara initially reported that fibre was introduced to replace aluminium when 'it was realised that it would be practically impossible to

---

26 War Office, *Field Service Regulations, Part II, Organization and Administration* (London: HMSO, 1909) [Reprinted with amendments 1913], p.167.
27 War Office, *Field Service Regulations, Part II*, pp.167-168.
28 Richard Holmes, *Tommy: The British Soldier on the Western Front* (London: Harper Perennial, 2005), p.138.

keep up with the demand (and expense of) aluminium discs', presenting a cheaper alternative.[29] However, having checked the costing for both fibre and aluminium within the *Priced Vocabulary of Clothing and Necessaries (including Materials)* of 1913 and 1915 published by HM Stationery Office, O'Mara has since confirmed that this is incorrect, with fibre being the more expensive of the two materials.[30] An explanation for the adoption of a more expensive material for this essential piece of equipment is provided within the minutes from a 1920 meeting of the Imperial War Graves Commission. During the meeting, Chairman and founder Fabian Ware described that the new material was adopted as a result of concerns raised by army doctors, describing how:

> The metal ones were abandoned by the British Army some time in 1915. At the time I drew attention to the fact that these others would not last, but for military reasons and other reasons, it was considered wiser to use the fibre; it inflicts less of a wound. The doctors were altogether against the use of a metal disc, and these fibre discs were introduced.[31]

When questioned by Sir Thomas Mackenzie on whether the wounds were caused when the bullet struck the metal of the disc, Ware responded 'Yes, and the doctors were all against it. I had this fight out at the time. The doctors were very strongly against the use of the metal ones for that reason… They were often struck'.[32] Though it might seem incomprehensible that such a thin metal disc could contribute to a soldier's wounds, examples of this do exist. When Lieutenant Mason of the 3rd Battalion Loyal North Lancashire Regiment was killed during the Battle of the Aisne on 14 September 1914, it was found that the force of the piece of shrapnel which wounded him had driven a portion of his identity disc into his lung'.[33] Mason's college magazine, the *Malvernian* also reported his death, describing that 'the force… had driven the metallic identity disc into his lungs'.[34] This incident took place before the release of pattern 8111/1914 which introduced the new discs,

---

29   David O'Mara, 'Introduction to Identification Discs and Tags of the First World War', Western Front Association (2019) [update of 2009 article], <https://www.westernfrontassociation.com/world-war-i-articles/identifying-the-dead-a-short-study-of-the-identification-tags-of-1914-1918/> accessed 29 November 2021; David O'Mara, personal communication, 2018.

30   O'Mara, 'Introduction to Identification Discs and Tags of the First World War'.

31   CWGC/2//2/1/22: Minutes of the Proceedings of the Meeting of the Imperial War Graves Commission held at The Office of Works, St. James's Park on Tuesday, 20 April 1920, p.40.

32   CWGC/2//2/1/22: Minutes of the Proceedings of the Meeting of the Imperial War Graves Commission held at The Office of Works, St. James's Park on Tuesday, 20 April 1920, p.40.

33   TNA, RG 35/36: General Register Office: Miscellaneous Foreign Death Returns, 'Lieutenant Rowland Charles Mason', *Roll of Honour*, Vol.1, p.258.

34   *Malvernian* (1914), cited in William Bridge, *Malvern College First World War Casualties* (published Independently, 2018). p.359. The section on Mason can be viewed at: <http://www.stanwardine.com/cgi-bin/malvernww1.pl?id=275> accessed 29 November 2021.

which means it is possible that injuries such as this were a factor which necessitated a change of production material for the discs.

Despite the change of material, their practical use remained the same. Discs were to be stamped in accordance with previous Army Orders, and once issued, were to be worn around the neck beneath the uniform. After the approval of the 1914 fibre pattern, the new discs were put into production, but it appears that they were only distributed to new recruits once existing supplies of the aluminium identity disc held in stores had been depleted. Stocks of 1907 pattern aluminium discs were issued to newly enlisted soldiers until supplies ran out, which Ware believed to have been in mid-1915.[35] It is likely that many soldiers who were already in service upon the outbreak of war did not receive a new fibre disc before their discharge or death. Frustratingly, a copy of the Army Order which introduced the new 1914 pattern fibre discs to soldiers has not been located, meaning that it remains unclear what knowledge soldiers were given about how to wear and use their discs.

The lack of preparations to respond to the matter of death and identification upon joining the Great War can be observed in two areas. Firstly, the introduction of the new fibre disc did not respond to the fundamental flaw within the system: the fact that that once the disc and paybook had been removed from a fallen soldier's body, their remains became unidentifiable. This necessitated the creation of a new identification system to improve the potential for identification, particularly for those who could not be buried immediately, or for those placed within temporary graves who would later be concentrated into permanent cemeteries when it was safe to do so. Secondly, the lack of organised structure to record battlefield graves, which would allow Fabian Ware to begin his work as the leader of a mobile unit of the British Red Cross Society – work which would ultimately expand to become the Imperial War Graves Commission (now known as the Commonwealth War Graves Commission) by 1917. Though this chapter will not explore the development of Commission in detail, Fabian Ware would later influence further developments to the identity disc system which would facilitate his work; as such, he is pivotal to the history of identification practice. Indeed, the work of Ware and his mobile unit would transform military burial cultures, graves registration practise, and, ultimately, the British identity disc system, as will be explored in the following section. These developments shaped not only the design of the burial grounds which define the former Western Front today, but they have also shaped the ways in which the First World War and those that fought in it are remembered.

Though the 1914 pattern identity disc did ensure that each soldier was in possession of an identifying object, the requirement to remove the disc was problematic, leaving a body without identification. With rising numbers of unburied

---

35 CWGC/2//2/1/22: Minutes of the Proceedings of the Meeting of the Imperial War Graves Commission, where Fabian Ware states that the metal discs were totally 'abandoned by the British Army some time in 1915'.

dead, and scattered graves on the battlefields, the system did little to ensure that a fallen soldier was identifiable at a secondary point following the confirmation of death, meaning that it was possible to 'lose' the identity of a man reported killed in action if no other identifying object remained with him, or the grave marker used to mark his burial became lost or damaged. It does not appear that the need to inform publics about their dead was considered during the early stages of war, given the lack of sustainable structures in place to respond to informing families about death, or for the burial of mass numbers of dead. In 1914, the 1909 *Field Service Regulations* were republished with amendments, describing the processes for burial of the dead which were to be performed by each unit, and the flow of personal effects through administrative structures. Army Orders were issued to ensure that the new processes were communicated to soldiers, and to describe the role of chaplains in the identification practises.

However, the First World War was a conflict so large that it affected the whole of British society, leaving a huge backlog of casualties within weeks. The intensity of fighting was brutal, and many units did not have the time, manpower, or equipment to bury the dead before moving to their next position, leaving many fallen soldiers on the battlefield. At the same time, civilians were bombarding the Army and the Government with demands for information about their loved ones, and no structures were in place to provide a consistent burial or graves registration service, nor to provide meaningful response to these hopeful requests.[36]

That was, until Fabian Ware took command of a mobile unit of the Red Cross in September 1914. The unit spent the first few months of the war attached to French units with the aim of searching for the wounded, though their work quickly expanded as they recognised the absence of a system to record the many burials performed on the battlefields. Ware noticed the absence of policy and structure to accommodate the marking of graves and the recording of their location *en masse*. Gibson and Ward describe how at the time, 'dead servicemen's graves were marked with wooden crosses after burial by their comrades, but no set official record was kept'.[37] Typically, field burials were only performed as and when the conditions of the field permitted, resulting in scattered graves near the front line, and more organised burials near the field hospitals and casualty clearing stations. To Ware, it was clear that many of the grave markers were at risk of obliteration in the field, meaning that it was essential to record the location of every grave along with the details of the individuals held within the graves.[38]

36   T.A. Edwin Gibson and G. Kingsley Ward, *Courage Remembered: The story behind the construction and maintenance of the Commonwealth's Military Cemeteries and Memorials of the Wars of 1914-18 and 1939-1945* (London: HMSO, 1989), p.44.

37   Gibson and Ward, *Courage Remembered*, p.44.

38   CWGC/1/1/1/25: 'Col. Stewart's Report on his Visit to Major Fabian Ware's Unit on 4th March 1915, Graves Registration Commission' in Copies of Documents Enclosed with Mrs Hutton's Letter Box 2028.

Though Ware's work was not originally performed on behalf of the British Expeditionary Force, his unit would soon become incorporated into the military machine as his unit expanded to become the Graves Registration Commission in March 1915. The Commission was incorporated into the Army under the direct control of Adjutant-General of the British Expeditionary Force, Nevil Macready, and Ware received the status of local major. Ware's work became increasingly important as both the British Armed Forces and the British government 'realised that the conditions of warfare in which the British Empire was involved demanded an attention to the dead less perfunctory and more systemic than could be paid by the existing army organization, strained beyond the limits of its means and powers'.[39]

The issue of identification was not as simple as the removal of the dog tag to confirm death. The identity disc moved through a great number of military structures before it was even given to a soldier in the event of mobilisation as it was purchased, distributed, stamped and stored. The occurrence of death caused the identity disc to move through different kinds of administrative structures, to allow the relevant force to account for the death, to inform the family, and to provide details relating to burial to name but a few processes. As the war progressed, these administrative structures changed, particularly as Fabian Ware's work continued to expand, and became better incorporated into the structures of both the British Army and the British government.

Fabian Ware and the 1916 Double Identity Disc

In February 1916, Ware was promoted to the rank of temporary lieutenant-colonel before the Graves Registration Commission was rebranded as the Directorate of Graves Registration & Enquiries (DGR&E), an organisation which was to act as the 'sole intermediary authority between the British Army in the Field and the French and Military and Civil Authorities' for all matters relating to French and Belgian law.[40] As works continued to grow, Ware decided to relocate his main office to London in May 1916, where he would be closely located to Macready, who had recently been promoted to Adjutant-General to the Forces. The DGR&E office at St James' Square functioned as a department of the Adjutant-General's Branch within the War Office, allowing Ware and Macready to work together within close proximity.[41]

39 Fabian Ware, *The Immortal Heritage: An Account of the Work and Policy of the Imperial War Graves Commission during Twenty Years, 1917-18* (Cambridge: Cambridge University Press, 1937), p.24.

40 Ware, *The Immortal Heritage*, p.17.

41 Anon, 'The Registration and Care of Military Graves During the Present War', *Royal United Services Institution Journal*, Vol. 62 (1917), p.299; *The London Gazette (Supplement)* No. 29658, 7 July 1916, p.6823.

Even before major battles such as the Somme in 1916, Ware's staff were having increasing problems with the identification of soldiers' remains. The absence of information on some bodies caused by the removal of identity discs, paybooks and personal effects was starting to severely affect the progress of the DGR&E, which now had the task of responding to the same problem on multiple fronts, working beyond the initial scope of France and Belgium, with each front presenting its own military and climate-related challenges.

On 16 May, Messer sent a letter to Macready, written on behalf of Ware as director of the DGR&E, to discuss the 'many instances where it is not possible for bodies to be identified at the point of burial through the absence of identity discs'.[42] The letter asked Macready to consider the following points:

(i)   Identity discs are frequently removed at the time of death as evidence of death, and when casualties are heavy, many bodies are not buried for some days; or it may even be weeks as in the case of the Battle of Loos, when burying in some parts of the field of battle was stopped by the Corps General or military reasons.

(ii) When burying parties are eventually able to carry out their work, it is found that numbers of bodies bear no mark of identification, so that the identity of many is never established. The provision of two discs (a system which has been introduced by the French during the present war), one of which is left on the body until the moment of actual burial, would seem to be the only practical means by which in these cases identity at the time of burial could be ensured and the grave marked in the usual way.[43]

The letter also described how previous discussions had taken place to consider whether the British ought to adopt a double identity disc scheme, as had been introduced by the French in 1915, explaining that the scheme had been 'considered inadvisable, as there were serious concerns for doubting if British soldiers would adapt themselves to the system'.[44] However, the system had 'now been found to work satisfactorily in the French Army', and so a request was made to reconsider a system including two discs to respond to the fact that the 'number of graves which are unknown' because of the described issues with the single identity disc system were 'very considerable'.[45]

---

42   CWGC/1/1/1/34/18: 'Letter from Major A.A. Messer to the Adjutant General, 16 May 1916'.
43   CWGC/1/1/1/34/18: 'Letter from Major A.A. Messer to the Adjutant General, 16 May 1916'.
44   CWGC/1/1/1/34/18: 'Letter from Major A.A. Messer to the Adjutant General, 16 May 1916'. For more on the 1915 French System, see Ashbridge and Verdegem, 'Identity discs'.
45   CWGC/1/1/1/34/18: 'Letter from Major A.A. Messer to the Adjutant General, 16 May 1916'.

Ware followed up on this matter on 21 June, writing again to Macready to discuss a potential new system, reiterating that in many cases it had become 'impossible at the time of burial to identify men who have been killed owing to the fact that the identity discs have been removed', meaning that 'a largely increasing number of graves therefore are, and will remain unidentified'. [46] To remedy this issue, Ware proposed a new scheme of a double identity disc which seemed 'in some ways to offer advantages over the French system'. The design included a new octagonal, green disc which would be threaded onto a short piece of cord and attached to the existing red disc. In the event of death, the green disc would be removed, leaving the original red, round disc upon the body. This system acknowledged that 'in the majority of cases these discs would be removed at night' when visibility would be limited, describing that the 'lozenge shape' could be easily felt for in the dark.[47] The scheme was approved on 24 June with instructions given to order four million discs as per the drawing supplied by Ware, with the cords fitted by the contractor.

Though conversations on the issue of the new discs, along with stamps and punches required for adapting existing red discs for the new system, were ongoing for the remainder of June, the particulars of the scheme were questioned in early July.[48] Major A. Courage, Deputy Assistant Adjutant General (DAAG) of 4th Army, wrote to Ware on 10 July describing that three of the four Armies consulted about the disc had been under the impression that the second disc would be worn around the wrist, as in the French system, whilst the fourth Army consulted had not stated where they believed the best location for the disc to be worn. Courage expressed concern that wearing the discs around the neck as per the drawing might 'lead to both discs being cut away', and on that basis, requested that Ware consider a bracelet design, perhaps featuring a chain rather than the string cord worn around the neck.[49]

The matter of unidentified soldiers was clearly taken seriously, as the following day Army Routine Order No. 49 was published, recording that 'it has come to notice that sufficient care is not being taken by Officers and Men to wear their identity discs at all times', with 'all ranks warned that it is their duty to do so on all occasions'.[50] These Routine Orders were intended to complement, rather than overrule existing manuals, acting as an informal opportunity for learning; however they were issued under the assumption that the leaders of each and every unit would have the opportunity to not only read this information, but to share it within their unit, which was not always possible; this may explain varied use of discs across units.

46 CWGC/1/1/1/34/18: 'Letter from Fabian Ware to the Adjutant General, 21 June 1916'.
47 CWGC/1/1/1/34/18: 'Letter from Fabian Ware to the Adjutant General, 21 June 1916'.
48 CWGC/1/1/1/34/18: Letter from B.B. Cubitt to Q.M.G.7, 27 June 1916.
49 CWGC/1/1/1/34/18: Letter from Major A. Courage to F. Ware, 10 July 1916.
50 TNA WO 95/2686: 137 Infantry Brigade: 1/5 Battalion South Staffordshire Regiment, 1915 Feb 1 – 1919 Feb 28.

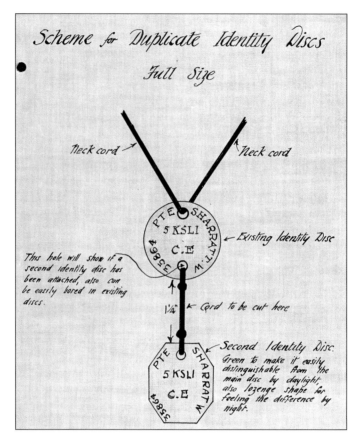

Top: 'Scheme for Duplicate Identity Discs': sketch circulated in June 1916. In Directorate of Graves Registration And Enquiries: File 18 – Scheme for duplicate identity discs' (Commonwealth War Graves Commission Archive, CWGC/1/1/1/34/18)

Below: Identity discs of C. Haywood issued during the First World War. The set includes the 1907 aluminium disc and the two discs used in accordance with the 1916 pattern. (Royal Collection Trust, RCIN 69492)

Ware was also busy responding to Major Courage's feedback, writing to Captain Taylor on 12 July requesting a delay in the manufacture of new discs. He referred to the confusion amongst the four armies reported by Major Courage, highlighting that 'the Ordnance people' had 'remarked that in the original replies from the Armies on the question of the advisability of two discs, three of the Armies had suggested that the additional disc should be worn on the wrist'; information that Ware claimed to have not received at the time of the approval of the new duplicate scheme.[51] The drawing of the new scheme was then shared with all armies, with a request for each to confirm within two to three days whether 'they do not think this system as good as, or better than that of the two separate discs, one of which is worn on the wrist and one round the neck'.[52] Though the feedback from the armies is not held within the CWGC archive, more information can be found within Ware's correspondence.

On 30 July, Major G. H. Stobart (DAAG2), wrote to Ware from the General Headquarters of the 3rd Echelon in France to inform him of 'several complaints received lately regarding the removal of identity discs from the bodies before being brought in for burial', causing him to request more information on whether a decision had been made about the introduction of the duplicate disc system. Five days later, on 4 August, Ware described that many similar complaints had also reached him about this issue, but that the War Office was 'now proceeding with the manufacture of the new discs as speedily as possible', adding that many similar complaints had also reached him.[53] Now that the discs were in manufacture, it was time for the scheme to be formally announced and introduced.

Army Order 287/1916 was published on 24 August 1916 with details about the new identity disc scheme. Interestingly, the location of the discs had changed from the design circulated by Ware. Now the new green disc would take the place of the original red disc, worn on a long cord around the neck, with the original red disc suspended from the green disc on a short cord. Though there are no documents available which confirm the reasons for this decision, it appears that this swap ensured continuity in that the red disc would always be removed. Within the order, the discs were described as 'Disc, identity, No.1, green' and 'Disc, identity, No.2, red'.[54] Though the discs are clearly depicted and described, the order followed the tradition of previous orders in that it did not contain information on how the disc should be used, or why the double disc was being introduced. However, it does appear that this information was shared somewhere, as instructions were published within civilian newspapers, such as the *Daily Mail* which provided

51 CWGC/1/1/1/34/18 L 'Letter from Lt. Col. Fabian Ware to Captain Taylor, 12 July 1916'.
52 CWGC/1/1/1/34/18 L 'Letter from Lt. Col. Fabian Ware to Captain Taylor, 12 July 1916'.
53 CWGC/1/1/1/34/18: 'Letter from G.O.C. for Director of DGR&E to D.A.A.G.2., G.H.Q, 3rd Echelon, France, 4th August'.
54 CWGC/1/1/1/34/18: 'Army Orders, War Office, 24 August 1916'.

guidance within a feature entitled 'Tommy's Necklet' which was published on 25 August 1916. Instructions were later shared within a special Army Order on 24 September which described that:

> In case of the death of an officer or soldier in the field, the lower disc, known as "Disc, identity, No.2, red," will be removed and disposed of in the same manner as heretofore.
>
> The upper disc, known as "Disc, identity, No. 1, green," will not be removed but will be buried with the body.[55]

Leaving the green disc upon the body was described 'as a safeguard against loss of identity', whilst still allowing for the removal of the read discs as a means 'to ensure proper notification of death'.[56] It was made clear that as per Army Order 287/1916, a failure to wear the discs during active service would be regarded as a breach of discipline. Despite this harsh warning, the discs would not begin to arrive in France until November and were not expected to be fully distributed to soldiers within France until the end of December.[57] Information was not provided on distribution to other fronts. It is not clear whether orders were placed for just the green discs, with the expectation that soldiers would rethread these along with their existing red disc, or if orders were placed for both red and green discs and a completely new set issued to each soldier. It seems that the former is most likely given that it is possible to encounter pairings of 1907 pattern aluminium discs suspended from the new green discs.

Shortly after the introduction of the 1916 double disc, the newly established DGR&E was formally incorporated into the British Army with Ware promoted to the rank of Director-General (despite his previous protests over his organisation becoming part of the Army).[58] His duties were extended across all theatres of war, and he was to answer directly to the Adjutant-General to the Forces at the War Office – that is, Nevil Macready. The first duty of the Director-General was to 'meet the demands of relatives', by ensuring provision was made for the care and maintenance of military graves after the war, a requirement which was given increasing consideration as the 'numbers of non-professional soldiers forming the New Armies increased'. The work of the DGR&E more broadly was to 'reflect the spirit of the free co-operation of the Dominions with the United Kingdom during the War', with the costs and responsibilities of works being borne by all partner Governments of the Empire. Working from the new London offices, it

---

55 CWGC/1/1/1/34/18: 'Army Orders, War Office, 24 August 1916'.
56 CWGC/1/1/1/34/18: 'Army Orders, War Office, 24 August 1916'.
57 CWGC/1/1/1/34/18: Copy A.G. telegraphs 06.11.16-26.11.16'.
58 As acknowledged by Macready in an undated typed note to an unknown recipient held within CWGC/1/1/1/1 MU: Narrative Letters and Reports.

was possible for the DGR&E to recruit women as clerks to 'ease the burden on the limited establishment of male workers', a fact which the RUSI journal reported had been 'the chief reason for the decision to remove the directorate to London'.[59] The Directorate struggled to recruit the required number of typists, which created huge administrative backlogs as the Battle of the Somme began on 1 July. As Ware's offices expanded, so did the numbers of fallen soldiers.

The scope of works for the DGR&E would expand so much that by 1917, Ware was able to argue that the required works were far too great for a department which Longworth describes as having 'dealt with so few graves by comparison'.[60] By April 1917, the Directorate had registered 150,000 graves in France and Belgium, 2,500 in Salonika, and over 4,000 in Egypt, with over 12,000 photographs of graves sent to relatives, with thousands more graves still waiting to be registered and photographed.[61] The organisation continued to develop as works expanded, prompting Ware to propose the creation of an 'Imperial Commission for the Care of soldier's Graves'.

The proposal was approved by the King in Council on 10 May 1917 and executed under the Sign Manual on 21 May, formally establishing the Imperial War Graves Commission (IWGC). The Sixth Annual Report of the Imperial War Graves Commission published in 1926 described that 'the Imperial War Conference of 1917 had decided that the permanence of the War Graves should be secured', reflecting that 'perpetuity in sepulchre has in the past been a very rare thing, much rarer than is generally realised' – a public misconception which remains today.[62] And so the idea of a permanent, individually marked war grave for those who died in service became the policy of the Empire, catalysing the transition in British military traditions from mass to individual graves, with appropriate recognition for all ranks, as seen within the national cemeteries of the American Civil War. The IWGC would take on the responsibility of concentrating an estimated 160,000 isolated graves, along with those buried within smaller cemeteries, into larger cemeteries, in addition to their duty to locate and identify the missing, estimated at over half a million. [63] This expansion of works only reinforced the need to locate and record graves whilst also working to identify those recovered, a process which would continue following the Armistice of 11 November 1918.

59 Philip Longworth, *The Unending Vigil: The History of the Commonwealth War Graves Commission* (Barnsley: Pen & Sword, 2003), p.17; Anon, 'The Registration and Care of Military Graves During the Present War'.

60 Longworth, *The Unending Vigil*, p.24.

61 Longworth, *The Unending Vigil*, p.23.

62 CWGC/2/1/ADD 6.2.6: 'Sixth Annual Report of the Imperial War Graves Commission' (London: HMSO, 1926).

63 Peter Hodgkinson, 'Clearing the Dead', *Journal of First World War Studies*. Vol.3:1 (2007) <http://www.vlib.us/wwi/resources/clearingthedead.html> accessed 29 November 2021.

Private Purchase Identity Discs

In addition to the officially issued identity discs, many soldiers chose to buy or make their own identifying objects to wear alongside, or perhaps in some cases, instead of, their issued discs. Today, we tend to call this type of disc 'private purchase', regardless of whether they were bought or handmade. The variety of examples that can be found is extensive, with designs typically being presented as bracelets or metal discs. Those who could afford to do so would purchase their discs directly from a jeweller, who would engrave their personal information onto a bracelet or disc.[64] Soldiers could also purchase identifying objects whilst deployed, choosing items which acted simply as an additional form of identification, sticking to the information presented on their official discs, but they could also purchase discs which we might consider a souvenir today, featuring illustrations of the places where they were presumably made, such as Baghdad or Mesopotamia, along with the soldier's personal information.[65] The most commonly encountered form of private purchase objects are identity bracelets, whether purchased from a jeweller, a private merchant or handmade by soldiers themselves.

Handmade identity discs, tags and objects are a particularly interesting category of items as they often intersect with items that would usually be described as 'trench art'. These items are most commonly found within the hands of private collectors today, with huge levels of variation reflecting their personal nature. It is possible to find examples of handmade discs which were likely mounted to bracelet chains and worn around the wrist, some of which also appeared similar in shape and appearance to the French 1881 design, produced from various metals including the brass from shells;[66] though it is more common to find items adapted to become identity discs or bracelets, for example coins with one side melted and smoothed to allow for the engraving of personal information. Some soldiers chose not to personalise discs or bracelets, but would instead personalise their existing possessions, for example stamping their name and/or number into the back of their spoons, or engraving details into a brass match box cover. The possibilities were only limited by the imagination of a soldier, making it difficult to provide an exhaustive list to reflect all forms of personal identification produced by soldiers whilst in service.

It is difficult to know how common it was for British soldiers to carry additional forms of identification as many of the items produced would have returned to the home front with soldiers who returned home or been delivered to the families of

---

64 For an example of a professionally engraved identity bracelet, see IWM EPH 4728

65 For examples of souvenir style discs see IWM EPH 5091, or the collection of Judy Waugh available at < https://www.trench-art.net/coins/>.

66 For examples of bracelets potentially modelled on the French 1881 design, see NAM.1994-541-1 and IWM EPH 9422.

those who lost their lives during the conflict, meaning it may never be possible to quantify their use. However, the vast levels of variation that can be found can help us to reflect upon the purpose of identifying objects in new ways. Not every identifying object will have been bought in response to a fear of becoming unknown, or out of concern over the official disc system. Many of the discs described will have been bought as a memento of a distant city or country, others may have been purchased as a fashion item, for example copying from another soldier who had a particularly nice bracelet. Many of the items reflect nothing more than the creativity of bored soldiers. Thus, the variety of identity discs is a reminder of the vast range of personalities and beliefs present within the British Army, with each soldier's attitude to death shaped by his life before service and his experience once deployed. Though not all private purchase discs and objects reflect an individual desire to remain identifiable in death, there were many cases where these objects did help to identify or confirm the identity of soldiers who died on the battlefield.

Identity Discs and the Creation of Unknown Soldiers

Following the formal conclusion of the war, the clearance of the dead from the battlefields remained a vital task which would allow civilian landowners to return to their land (with the land appropriately clear to return to its original use) and help to consolidate the large number of missing and deceased soldiers. Rumours were rife in Britain that Germany was still holding Prisoners of War in secret camps, leaving many families holding onto the faint hope that their loved one was still living in one of these camps, rather than within an unknown grave.[67] Any public perception of inaction could generate a negative public reaction, and risked undermining the huge efforts and expenses that had been contributed in efforts to establish the IWGC cemeteries, necessitating the efforts to sustain efforts to clear the battlefields.

For some time, the battlefields remained strewn with the remnants of war, including explosives, fired ammunition, litter associated with food or storage, and more gruesomely, a myriad of isolated graves, accidental inhumations, and the uncleared war dead.[68] The IWGC had to create a systemic approach to search and recovery to ensure that every possible section of the former battlefields had been searched to the best of their ability to facilitate the operation to concentrate burials within the newly established cemeteries, but also to manage the needs of the general public on the home front, a factor which had been proved vital to Ware

---

67   Michael Durey, 'The Search for Answers on the Missing in the Great War: Lt High Henshall Williamson and His Parent's Struggle with officialdom, 1916-2001', *British Journal for Military History*, Vol.2:1 (2015), pp.86-104.

68   Hodgkinson, 'Clearing the Dead'.

in securing political support for his works during the war. Following a conference on the subject of the war dead hosted by Macready at General Headquarters on 18 November 1918, the Army began to recruit volunteers to assist with the clearance of the dead.

The sheer volume of dead soldiers on the battlefields, buried and unburied, meant that the exhumation work required a huge workforce for a sustained period of time, if there was any hope of completing the task. War Zones were divided into areas, with further subdivisions within each area. Each exhumation company featured 32 men, who were provided with 'two pairs of rubber gloves, two shovels, stakes to mark the location of graves found, canvas and rope to tie up remains, stretchers, cresol (a poisonous colourless isomeric phenol) and wire cutters.'[69] A Survey Officer would designate a search area, usually based on DGR&E records, which were not always accurate, and his team would search each area.[70] There were typically four methods of identifying a grave on a former battlefield, as described by Christie:

i.   Rifles or stakes protruding from the ground, bearing helmets or equipment;

ii. Partial remains or equipment on the surface or protruding from the ground;

iii. Rat holes – often small bones or pieces of equipment would be brought to the surface by the rats;

iv. Discolouration of grass, earth or water – grass was often a vivid bluish-green with broader blades where bodies were buried, while earth and water turned a greenish black or grey colour.[71]

It was only during this post-war period that the IWGC was able to collate enough data to begin to reflect on the rates of identification. In the 21st meeting of the IWGC, hosted on 20 April 1920, Ware referred to a 'statement as to exhumations' given to attendees which presented the following figures for works in France and Belgium: There had been 128,577 re-internments in total, with 55,508 of these already known, 6,273 identified for the first time, and 66,796 remaining unknown.[72] This meant that approximately 50 percent of graves could not be identified, a figure which Ware reported reflected his expectations when he first began his work in 1914, if not exceeding them slightly, taking a rather positive approach to the situation at hand.

---

69   Norm Christie, *Canadians on the Somme* (Ottowa: CEF Books, 1999), p.59 cited in Hodgkinson, 'Clearing the Dead'.

70   Christie, *Canadians on the Somme*, pp.57-61, cited in Hodgkinson, 'Clearing the Dead'.

71   Christie, *Canadians on the Somme*, p.59, cited in Hodgkinson, 'Clearing the Dead'.

72   Christie, *Canadians on the Somme*, p.59, cited in Hodgkinson, 'Clearing the Dead'.

Towards the end of the meeting, Ware revisited a query made during the March meeting of the Commission by Mr R.A. Blankenburg, representing the High Commissioner for the Union of South Africa, where he had asked for more information on the role of identity discs within the identification process. [73] Though Mr Blankenburg was not present at the April meeting, Ware reported that that 'identity discs have not proved satisfactory, owing to the way that these identity discs have gone to pulp'.[74] The double disc had been introduced 'so that a man found dead always had a disc on him', but the fibre material had 'proved most unsatisfactory' to the extent that the chief reason of there being such a large number of unidentified, is owing to the unsatisfactory material out of which the discs were made'.[75]

The fibre material was vulnerable to damp and decomposition, making it unsuitable for the majority of burial scenarios, or for circumstances where an individual could not be buried for some time leaving their remains exposed to the elements. The cord or string from which the discs were suspended was also subject to rapid decomposition which could lead to snapping, and the subsequent loss of the identity disc.[76] The Deputy Assistant Adjutant General in charge of Effects had provided statistics on how frequently an identity disc had helped to identify a fallen soldier, or assisted in confirming their identification, reporting that:

20% cases are identified by discs.
25% are confirmed by discs.
30% are identified by other methods.
25% cases are not identified.[77]

This shows that identity discs helped to identify or confirm the identity of only 45 percent of soldiers recovered. The response also acknowledged that the figures did not reflect that they 'only refer to effects received', with many bodies having been recovered with 'no effects whatever', or recovered in scenarios 'where the articles found are in such a condition as to provide no clues as to the identity of the body, and are therefore not sent to the effects branch'.[78] The report which contained these statistics had also provided the conclusion shared by Ware, that

---

73 See CWGC/2/2/1/21: COMMISSION MEETING NO.21 – Mar 1920, for the original enquiry.
74 CWGC/2/2/1/22: Minutes of the Proceedings of the Meeting of the Imperial War Graves Commission held at The Office of Works, St. James's Park on Tuesday, 20 April 1920.
75 CWGC/2/2/1/22: Minutes of the Proceedings of the Meeting of the Imperial War Graves Commission held at The Office of Works, St. James's Park on Tuesday, 20 April 1920.
76 Nina Edwards, *Dressed for War: Uniform, Civilian Clothing and Trappings 1914-18* (London and New York: I.B. Tauris, 2015).
77 CWGC/1/1/7/B/43: 'Unsigned letter dated 1st April 1920 (29/C/7/S)'.
78 CWGC/1/1/7/B/43: 'Unsigned letter dated 1st April 1920 (29/C/7/S)'.

'the ordinary red and green discs were most unsatisfactory, as exposure to the elements and burial even for comparatively short periods rendered them more or less unreadable'.[79] It was also reported that the 'thin metal disc used by the original Expeditionary Force' had been 'more satisfactory', as confirmed by the Australian Forces. The 'thick deeply impressed metal disc' used by the Canadian Forces was described as 'particularly satisfactory'. The French and Portuguese designs were 'equally effective', but the 'German flat metal disc was the most satisfactory of all'.[80] Despite the praise of metal designs, a warning was also given that it must 'be remembered that there are serious objections to the use of metal discs from other points of view besides identification', a statement presumably relating to the 1914 decision to produce discs from fibre to prevent damaged metal discs from affecting or causing injuries.[81]

British Identity Discs Used in the Second World War and Beyond

Though the failures of the fibre discs were acknowledged in 1920, it seems that these lessons were forgotten as fibre discs were used by the British Army and the broader Armed Forces for some decades after the conclusion of the First World War. The British Army, the Royal Navy and the Royal Air Force each continued to use fibre discs during the Second World War, despite the previous recognitions that fibre identity discs were quick to decompose and contributed to an inability to identify huge numbers of soldiers. Soldiers fighting on behalf of Commonwealth Forces, including Australia, and India continued to use the British system of fibre identity discs (though New Zealand, Canada and South Africa would begin to introduce different systems).

The lessons learned about the efficiency and failures of the identity disc system recorded during the First World War appear to have been forgotten, despite the many accounts from the Second World War which described the discovery of decomposing or absent discs. It was common for British, allied and opposition soldiers to remove all identifying objects from a body, leaving behind an unknown soldier whose name could never be recovered. Even within medical structures, instructions to leave one disc upon the body at all times were regularly ignored. In June 1945, Lieutenant Colonel Arthur Owen Stott, of what was then the Graves Registration and Enquiries Office, reported that increasing numbers of hospital burials were later recovered with 'naked

---

79   CWGC/1/1/7/B/43: 'Unsigned letter dated 1st April 1920 (29/C/7/S)'.
80   CWGC/1/1/7/B/43: 'Unsigned letter dated 1st April 1920 (29/C/7/S)'.
81   CWGC/1/1/7/B/43: 'Unsigned letter dated 1st April 1920 (29/C/7/S)'.

bodies wrapped in blankets… without any means of identity being left upon the body'.[82]

The British identity disc system was also used by Commonwealth forces, with the exception of Canada (which introduced its own metal disc scheme), which meant that the low rates of identification facilitated by the fibre discs affected millions of families around the world. The decomposition of discs was a particular problem in humid, tropical climates, such as the South West Pacific area. In 1945, Australian forces located a number of mass graves believed to be from the ongoing war and had the gruesome task of excavating them. The graves contained the remains of 135 Australian and Dutch servicemen who had been executed by the Japanese following their 1942 invasion of Ambon. All that remained of the fibre discs recovered was the cord which they were strung from and 'small deposits of red fibrous material'.[83] Such limited evidence often removed the possibility for an identification, and the unsuitability of the discs for this purpose must have been known amongst soldiers at the time.

Even in cases where a disc was recovered quickly, fibre was easily damaged by water, particularly when submerged for a period of time, but also from prolonged contact with decomposing flesh, causing the stamping of the discs to become illegible.[84] The issue of rotting discs was brought to the attention of the Army Directorate of Graves Registration and Enquiries at the War Office in June 1943, when a report from the General Headquarters of the Middle East Forces described that the discs did not last well, particularly when buried with a corpse, quickly becoming illegible with peeling edges.[85] In November 1943, the Directorate recorded the issue again within their War Diary following the release of a report from the Lethbridge 220 Mission which had also noted the issues with identity discs.[86]

Unlike Britain, Australia was particularly concerned about the long-standing issues with the identity disc system, and informally introduced metal identity discs during the Second World War. In the latter half of March 1943, 16,000 stainless steel identity discs were sent to New Guinea by freight with a further 45,000 sets transported using the 'normal route', which Dianne Rutherford has interpreted as sea routes.[87] The discs had the same shape as the fibre discs, allowing for the same

82 TNA WO 171/3926: 21 Army Group HQ, GR&E, War Diary, January-December 1945, entry for 22 June 1945. Cited in Jennie Gray, 'Nothing can excuse us if we fail': The British and Their Dead Servicemen, North-West Europe, 1944-1951 (PhD thesis, University of Exeter, 2016), p.329.

83 Description of item 030388/05, Australian War Memorial.

84 War Office, A.G.13 (The Army Directorate of Graves Registration and Enquiries), War Diary, January-December 1943, TNA, WO 165/36. Cited in Gray, 'Nothing can excuse us if we fail', p.328n.

85 TNA, WO 165/36. Cited in Gray, 'Nothing can excuse us if we fail', p.328n (entry for June 1943).

86 TNA, WO 165/36. Cited in Gray, 'Nothing can excuse us if we fail', p.328n; TNA WO 202/881: 220 Military Mission Report by Major General J.S. Lethbridge (1944).

87 MP742/1, 52/3/23, National Archives of Australia. Cited in Dianne Rutherford, 'Understanding Australian Identity Discs Part 3: Second World War, Army', Australian War Memorial (2015) < https://www.awm.gov.au/articles/blog/identity-discs-australian-army > accessed 29 November 2021.

information to be stamped into them, and they were worn in the same fashion. It appears that stainless steel proved an effective material, as General Routine Order 87 was issued in March 1944 to inform Australian soldiers that stainless steel discs would be issued to all personnel. This order may represent a cultural shift with regards to identity discs, with Australia adapting the disc system to its own needs, rather than accepting British requirements as had previously been the case. Some historians do report that the British Army introduced stainless steel identity discs strung from a nylon cord for use in 'jungle' climates, though it has not yet been possible to locate British Army Orders which describe the introduction of metal discs for tropical climates if, indeed, they do exist.[88]

It does not appear that there was as broad an appetite within British Forces for privately purchased identity discs during the Second World War, though the Australian War Memorial does hold a small collection of examples. It is possible that this shift in material culture reflects an improved understanding about the lack of efficiency or the general use of identity discs than in the previous war, when they had first been introduced. It may also reflect changing threats on the battlefields, for example, an identity disc which identified a soldier as Jewish might have increased the risk of torture or death if captured by the Nazi regime, causing a soldier to avoid wearing his discs where possible, whether official or privately purchased.[89]

The fibre identity disc system continued to cause problems after the conclusion of the Second World War, with decomposed discs, or a total absence of discs, limiting the potential to identify fallen soldiers. The Graves Registration and Enquiries Service called for a new identity disc in August 1948, describing the current system as 'most unsuitable', condemning the fibre discs as the reason that the 'identification of a large number of casualties' had been lost.[90] These conclusions echo those of the IWGC findings reported in the Commission's meeting held in April 1920, yet the discs were still not replaced. The British Army continued to use fibre identity discs until some time in the 1960s when stainless steel discs were introduced, though examples do exist beyond this point. Worse still, the Royal Air Force and the Royal Navy continued to issue fibre discs until as late as 1988. The British Armed Forces failed to adapt the fibre identity disc system following the First World War, despite the issues having become transparent, and the continued use of the discs during the Second World War ensured that the identification rate for fallen soldiers would remain low.

88   George Forty, *Companion to the British Army 1939-45* (Stroud: The History Press, 2009), p.75.
89   Midge Gillies, *The Barbed-Wire University: The Real Lives of Prisoners of War in the Second World War* (London: Arum Press, 2011), p.18.
90   TNA WO 32/12968: DGR&E, War Office, Brigadier C.S. Vale, Minute 1, 23 August 1948, cited in Gray, *'Nothing can excuse us if we fail'*, p.328.

The failures of the disc system have long been forgotten, and the red and green fibre discs remain an iconic piece of material culture which entice the imaginations of the public and historians alike to this day. These simple items allow us to find a connection to an individual and learn the details of their life during war. However, the discs in personal and public collections are discs that returned home. This chapter has attempted to tell the story of the discs that were never found or had disappeared before they had the opportunity to serve their purpose. Though we often associate identity discs with the hope of a soldier in a known grave, the reality is that they are one of the main reasons that we have so many unknown soldiers lying in our military cemeteries.

Conclusion

The British identity disc was formally introduced to allow for the confirmation of military deaths, but the mass losses of the First World War incurred by every section of society meant that the disc took on a new value. Each soldier had an individual relationship with their disc framed by informal training, personal experience and their individual ideas about recognition after death, though, as demonstrated, not every disc or privately purchased object represented a specific desire to secure a known burial.

The disc played an essential role in the emerging practice of graves registration and facilitated the transformation of military burial traditions for ordinary soldiers from a culture of shared (or mass) graves into an expectation of an individual known grave. Following the First World War, the IWGC graves came to represent the permanence of memory, particularly after the completion of the spectacular cemeteries which paid unprecedented respect to soldiers of all ranks and dominions.

Nevertheless, despite this transformation in identification practices, the long list of names of those who were never recovered are recorded upon the various Monuments to the Missing, such as the Menin Gate in Ypres. Many families never gave up hope that their son or husband might return.[91] The sheer number of soldiers who became 'a soldier of the Great War, known unto God' (to quote the inscription of CWGC headstones) resulted in an elevation of the 'unknown soldier' and the sanctification of this group of fallen combatants.

These successes, but also failures, of identification in the First World War has also shaped public engagement with the archaeology of the two world wars. Archaeologists who work in this field often encounter interested individuals who profess hope that their relative, believed to have been killed in that particular area, might be located, recovered and identified. This, however, is something which

---

91   For a fantastic case study, see Durey, 'The Search for Answers on the Missing in the Great War'.

the majority of archaeologists know is not possible due to the fact that fibre will decompose in all but the most extreme anaerobic environments, which do not typically represent the European battlefields. For the very item that created the expectation that every soldier could be identified in death also created the reverse: the legion of 'unknown soldiers' of the First World War, soldiers who remain unidentifiable today. The failure to respond to the malfunctions of the identity disc system in the interwar period ensured that thousands of unknown soldiers would also be created during the Second World War and beyond, as the discs continued to be issued across the forces well into the late twentieth century. These developments would also facilitate the growth of Fabian Ware's unit into what is now the Commonwealth War Graves Commission, creating an architectural legacy which spans more than 150 counties and allows us to remember the sacrifice of those known or unknown who fell while fighting for King and country.

Acknowledgements

This chapter is dedicated to the late David O'Mara, in memory of seemingly never ending knowledge that he always had time to share, along with the kindness that he showed to all who knew him. Thank you to Toby Brayley, Andrew Fetherston, Michael Greets, and Dianne Rutherford for your support with this research.

Bibliography

Archival Sources

Commonwealth War Graves Commission Archives (CWGC), Maidenhead, UK
    CWGC/1/1/1/1 MU: Narrative Letters and Reports.
    CWGC/1/1/1/25: 'Col. Stewart's Report on his Visit to Major Fabian Ware's Unit on 4th March 1915, Graves Registration Commission' in Copies of Documents Enclosed with Mrs Hutton's Letter Box 2028.
    CWGC/1/1/1/34/18: 'Army Orders, War Office, 24 August 1916'.
    CWGC/1/1/1/34/18: 'Letter from G.O.C. for Director of DGR&E to D.A.A.G.2., G.H.Q, 3rd Echelon, France, 4th August'.
    CWGC/1/1/1/34/18 L 'Letter from Lt. Col. Fabian Ware to Captain Taylor, 12 July 1916'.
    CWGC/1/1/1/34/18: Letter from Major A. Courage to F. Ware, 10 July 1916.
    CWGC/1/1/1/34/18: Letter from B.B. Cubitt to Q.M.G.7, 27 June 1916.
    CWGC/1/1/1/34/18: Copy A.G. telegraphs 06.11.16-26.11.16'.
    CWGC/1/1/1/34/18: 'Letter from Fabian Ware to the Adjutant General, 21 June 1916'.

CWGC/1/1/1/34/18: 'Letter from Major A.A. Messer to the Adjutant General, 16 May 1916'.

CWGC/1/1/7/B/43: 'Unsigned letter dated 1st April 1920 (29/C/7/S)'.

CWGC/2/1/ADD 6.2.6: 'Sixth Annual Report of the Imperial War Graves Commission (London: HMSO, 1926)'.

CWGC/2/2/1/21: COMMISSION MEETING NO.21 – Mar 1920.

CWGC/2//2/1/22: Minutes of the Proceedings of the Meeting of the Imperial War Graves Commission held at The Office of Works, St. James's Park on Tuesday, 20 April 1920.

The National Archives (TNA), Kew

TNA RG 35/36: General Register Office: Miscellaneous Foreign Death Returns, 'Lieutenant Rowland Charles Mason', *Roll of Honour*, Vol.1, p.258.

TNA WO 202/881: 220 Military Mission Report by Major General J.S. Lethbridge (1944).

TNA WO 95/2686: 137 Infantry Brigade: 1/5 Battalion South Staffordshire Regiment, 1915 Feb 1 – 1919 Feb 28.

Published Sources

Anon, 'The Registration and Care of Military Graves During the Present War', *Royal United Services Institution Journal*, Vol.62 (1917), pp. 297-302.

Ashbridge, Sarah I., and O'Mara, David, 'The Erkennungsmarke: The Humanitarian Duty to Identify Fallen Soldiers 1866-1918'. *Journal of Conflict Archaeology*, Vol. 16 (2021), pp.1-32.

Ashbridge, Sarah I., and Verdegem, Simon, 'Identity discs: The recovery and identification of First World War soldiers located during archaeological works on the former Western Front', *Forensic Science International*, Vol.317 (2020), pp.1-14.

Bridge, William, *Malvern College First World War Casualties* (Published Independently, 2018).

Benton, Edward H., 'British Surgery in the South African War: The Work of Major Frederick Porter', *Medical History*. Vol.21 (1977), pp.275-290.

Forty, George, *Companion to the British Army 1939-45* (Stroud: The History Press, 2009).

Davis, George B, 'The Geneva Convention of 1906', *The American Journal of International Law*, Vol.1:2 (1907), pp.409-417.

Durey, Michael, 'The Search for Answers on the Missing in the Great War: Lt High Henshall Williamson and His Parent's Struggle with officialdom, 1916-2001', *British Journal for Military History*, Vol.2:1 (2015), pp.86-104.

Edwards, Nina, *Dressed for War: Uniform, Civilian Clothing and Trappings 1914-18* (London and New York: I.B. Tauris, 2015).

Hodgkinson, Peter, 'Clearing the Dead', *Journal of First World War Studies*, Vol.3:1 (2007). <http://www.vlib.us/wwi/resources/clearingthedead.html>.

Holmes, Richard, *Tommy: The British Soldier on the Western Front* (London: Harper Perennial, 2005).

Gibson, T.A. Edwin and Ward, G. Kingsley, *Courage Remembered: The story behind the construction and maintenance of the Commonwealth's Military Cemeteries and Memorials of the Wars of 1914-18 and 1939-1945* (London: HMSO, 1989).

Gillies, Midge, *The Barbed-Wire University: The Real Lives of Prisoners of War in the Second World War* (London: Arum Press, 2011).

Gray, Jennie, *'Nothing can excuse us if we fail': The British and Their Dead Servicemen, North-West Europe, 1944-1951* (PhD thesis, University of Exeter, 2016).

Longworth, Philip, *The Unending Vigil: The History of the Commonwealth War Graves Commission* (Barnsley: Pen & Sword, 2003).

Maier, Larry B., and Stahl, Joseph W., *Identification Discs of Union Soldiers in the Civil War: A Complete Classification Guide and Illustrated History* (Jefferson: McFarland and Company, 2010).

O'Mara, David, 'Introduction to Identification Discs and Tags of the First World War', Western Front Association (2019) [update of 2009 article], <https://www.westernfrontassociation.com/world-war-i-articles/identifying-the-dead-a-short-study-of-the-identification-tags-of-1914-1918/>.

Parliament. House of Commons & Lords, *Sick and Wounded in War: Papers relating to the Geneva Convention 1906* (Cd. 3933), (London: The Stationery Office, 1908).

Pearce Higgins, A. (ed.), *The Hague Peace Conferences and other International Conferences Concerning the Laws and Usages of War* (Cambridge: Cambridge University Press, 2014) (Originally published in 1909).

Rutherford, Dianne, 'Understanding Australian Identity Discs Part 3: Second World War, Army', Australian War Memorial (2015) <https://www.awm.gov.au/articles/blog/identity-discs-australian-army>.

Sperry, C.S., 'The Revision of the Geneva Convention, 1906', *Proceedings of the American Political Science Association*, Vol. 3 (1907), pp.33-57.

Stansbury Haydon, F., 'An Identification Disc for the Army, 1862', *The Journal of the American Military Institute*, Vol.3:1 (1939), pp.61-63.

Strachan, Hew, *From Waterloo to Balaclava: Tactics, Technology, and the British Army, 1815-1854* (Cambridge: Cambridge University Press, 1985).

War Office, *Regulations for Army Medical Services (Part I)* (London: HMSO, 1890).

War Office, *Army Orders, 1907* (London: HMSO, 1908).

War Office, *Army Orders, 1908* (London: HMSO, 1909).

War Office, *Field Service Regulations, Part II, Organization and Administration* (London: HMSO, 1909; reprinted with amendments 1913).

War Office, *Army Orders, 1909* (London: HMSO, 1910).

Ware, Fabian, *The Immortal Heritage: An Account of the Work and Policy of the Imperial War Graves Commission during Twenty Years, 1917-18* (Cambridge: Cambridge University Press, 1937).

9

Men, Motorcycles and Machine Guns on the North-West Frontier

Paul Macro

Introduction

There is no official history of the Motor Machine Gun Service (MMGS), or even of the Machine Gun Corps (MGC). The MMGS was absorbed into the MGC, as the Machine Gun Corps (Motors) (MGC(M)), when the MGC formed. Yet, in its short existence from 1915 to 1922, over 170,000 officers and men served in the MGC. More than 62,000 (36 percent) became casualties in the course of the Great War, including over 12,000 killed. Not for nothing was the MGC known as 'The Suicide Club'.[1]

Within this huge corps, the men of the MMGS/MGC(M) thought of themselves as a breed apart, something of an elite. They had, initially, all been volunteers and were recruited for their specialist mechanical and/or motorcycle skills. They had to undergo a demanding selection test. This article will tell the story of a tiny part of the MGC, namely the approximately 400 men of the five batteries of the MMGS/ MGC(M) which served in India during the Great War. These were far from being the only MGC troops in India. There were MGC squadrons attached to cavalry divisions and mounted brigades, and Machine Gun Companies supported the infantry formations.[2] All played a distinguished part, both in India and supporting the Indian Army on operations away from India. However, the purpose of this

1   Judith Lapin and Keith Stephenson, 'History', *Machine Gun Corps Old Comrades Association*, at <http://www.machineguncorps.co.uk/history.html>, accessed 16 November 2021.
2   'Motor Machine Guns of the First World War', *The Long Long Trail*, at <http://www.longlongtrail.co.uk/army/regiments-and-corps/machine-gun-corps-in-the-first-world-war/motor-machine-guns-of-the-first-world-war/>, accessed 16 November 2021.

chapter is to examine the selection process and individual and collective training of the MMGS/MGC(M) and the role it played in the Third Afghan War.

To do this, the chapter will look at the formation of the MMGS and its transition to become the MGC(M). It will describe the selection of volunteers and their individual training using the journeys of three typical soldiers as an example. It will also look at how the MMGS was equipped. The chapter will outline the employment of MMGS batteries in France and the decision to send one battery, 22nd Motor Machine Gun (MMG) Battery to India. It will describe life there. The dispatch of further batteries from France to India will be described as will 22nd MMG Battery's role in the Punjab disturbances. The role played by all five batteries during the Third Afghan War will be covered before concluding.

Formation of the MMGS and transition to MGC(M)

Before continuing, it is necessary to delve in the rather muddy origins of the MMGS. The traditional story is that motorcycle despatch riders and armoured cars were used from the earliest days of the war. This is true and the most notable example was the Royal Naval Air Service's Commander Samson who improvised armoured cars and tenders in Flanders in September and October 1914. The cars were used for both the recovery of downed aircrew and for reconnaissance in the face of German cavalry patrols.[3] However, the official formation of the MMGS is rather more prosaic. Army Order 480, dated 12 November 1914 and sanctioned in February 1915, formally approved the addition to each division of the British Expeditionary Force a unit known as an MMG Battery. They were designated to be units of the Royal Field Artillery and were collectively known as the MMGS.[4] Men were found from volunteers or by special enlistment of men known to be actively interested in motorcycles (such as cycle club members). The Coventry office of the enthusiasts' weekly magazine *The Motor Cycle* was listed as a recruiting office for the MMGS. However, when the MGC was created by Royal Warrant on 14 October, followed by an Army Order on 22 October 1915, it incorporated the MMGS.[5] This now became known as the MGC(M). At this time the MGC(M) had around 3,000 men. Furthermore, new evidence is starting to emerge that even before Army Order 480 was issued, MMG Batteries were being formed as 'private ventures', rather like Sir John Willoughby's subsequent armoured car unit. Certainly, in September 1914, according to *The Motor Cycle*, a machine gun equipped motorcycle-sidecar

---

3   'Motor Machine Guns of the First World War'.
4   The National Archives (TNA): WO32/11239 Army Order 480, Other Arms (Code 14(J)): *Formation of the Machine Gun Corps, 1915*, dated 12 November 1914.
5   TNA, WO32/11239 Army Order 480, Other Arms (Code 14(J)): *Formation of the Machine Gun Corps, 1915*, dated 22 October 1915.

outfit had been spotted in London.[6] Then in October the magazine had a small article looking for recruits for 'The First London Machine Gun Battery'. Recruits were required to enlist for 'three years or duration of war, and must provide their own kit, which will cost in each case about £5'.[7] When the MMGS was formed this unit appears to have been taken over and formed the nucleus of 1st MMG Battery. It also appears in a piece in *The Globe* of 13 November 1914 and is referred to as Lord Lyveden's Contingent.[8] In total, 28 batteries of the MMGS/MGC(M) were formed. For the purpose of this chapter, five are of interest, namely 3rd, 14th, 15th, 19th and 22nd.

Selection of Volunteers

In November 1914, Major J.E. Alkin first mentioned the idea of recruiting a Coventry Battery to the MMGS,[9] as Coventry was the centre of the British motor industry. Mr Geoffrey Smith, the editor of *The Motor Cycle* and the Honorary Secretary of the Coventry and Warwickshire Motor Club, also supported the idea, and published an article to that effect.[10] Alkin's Battery eventually became 5th MMG Battery but from here on Geoffrey Smith and *The Motor Cycle* became a focus of recruiting and selection for the MMGS and subsequently the MGC(M). Applicants were invited to *The Motor Cycle*'s office in order to undergo selection interviews and practical tests. Applicants were required to demonstrate that they could ride a motorcycle, show knowledge of how it worked, and have the ability to carry out running repairs. The process attracted motorcycle professionals and mechanical enthusiasts from around the country and from the colonies. Some recruits made long journeys, at their own expense, back to Britain. The process was intense and competitive and often attracted those also applying to the Royal Flying Corps. That a high proportion of MMGS soldiers were either commissioned or decorated is indicative of the quality of the applicants.[11]

6   *The Motor Cycle*, Volume 13, September 1914, available at <https://archive.org/stream/motorcycle17lond_/motorcycle17londpage/n84/mode/1up>, accessed 21 November 2021.

7   *The Motor Cycle*, Volume 13, October 1914, available at <https://archive.org/stream/motorcycle17lond_/motorcycle17londpage/n84/mode/1up> accessed 21 November 2021.

8   *The Globe,* 13 November 1914.

9   *Coventry Evening Telegraph*, 11 November 1914.

10 *The Motor Cycle*, Volume 13, November 1914, available at <https://archive.org/stream/motorcycle17lond_/motorcycle17londpage/n84/mode/1up>, accessed 21 November 2021.

11 Paul Macro, *Action at Badama Post* (Oxford: Casemate, 2019), p.41.

Individual Training

Following selection MMGS training, and subsequently MGC(M) training, took place at Bisley. Selected applicants were given a rail warrant to Bisley where their enlistment paper was approved and they were allocated a service number. At Bisley the heathlands of Surrey provided a major training area which was suitable for both motorcycles and machine guns. Ranges of up to 1,200 yards were available to enable the guns to be fired. The troops were cross trained; they had all established already that they had an element of mechanical ability and riding skills. These skills were developed by riding, both cross country on the heathlands and longer road runs down to places such as Eastbourne on the coast. All were trained to use their primary weapon system, the Vickers Machine Gun. This cross training gave flexibility to each battery in employing its soldiers and resilience in the face of casualties. Accommodation at Bisley was initially rudimentary, but certainly by early 1916 the majority of soldiers undergoing training were housed in 70-man huts. To combat the cold of winter, these were equipped with three stoves, although some recruits report using as many as seven blankets. The standard of food appears to have varied; some letters home record the writers as being well fed. Others, particularly Gunner Frederick Harold Rood,[12] had different memories.[13]

Selection and training into the MMGS inculcated a sense of being special into the recruits. One indicator of this was that many soldiers, instead of adopting the MGC cap badge when this unit formed, continued to wear their original cap badge with crossed guns and the MMG letters.[14] A second indicator is the 22nd MMG Battery War Diary for the Third Afghan War in 1919. Nearly four years after the demise of the MMGS, this was quite clear, on its cover and throughout, that it was the diary of 22nd Motor Machine Gun Battery, rather than the 22nd Battery of the MGC(M).[15] The same naming convention can be seen with the other MMG Batteries.

Briance, Macro and Roberts

Three fairly typical recruits to the MMGS/MGC(M) were 32566 Gunner Claude Henry Briance, 1658 Gunner Ernest William Macro, and 2093 Gunner John Tydwal Roberts.

12   Frederick Harold Rood subsequently served with 1st Armoured Motor Battery in East Africa.
13   Macro, *Action at Badama Post*, pp.39–40.
14   Macro, *Action at Badama Post*, pp.42–43.
15   TNA, WO95/5392, War Diary Kohat-Kurram Force: Force Troops: 22 Motor Machine Gun Battery (May–August 1919).

Claude Henry Briance was born 31 December 1896 in St Pancras, Middlesex. He enlisted as Private 73075 in the 9th Battalion Essex Regiment on 2 September 1914. He transferred to the MMGS on 14 December 1914 and then to MGC(M) 1 December 1915. Briance landed in France 10 March 1915, joining 3rd MMG Battery about a month after they had deployed, presumably as a casualty replacement.[16]

Ernest William Macro was born 5 March 1896 in Stoke Newington, London. From his early days Ernest was known as 'Bill'. He was the third child of William George Macro and his wife Adelaide, nee Broughton. William George Macro worked for the Post Office throughout his adult life. Bill's two elder sisters were Lily and Olive born in 1890 and 1891 respectively. Lily died just after the start of the war, in October 1914, although this was not war related. Shortly after Bill's birth, his parents moved their family to East Finchley, where, in due course, Bill won a scholarship to Finchley County School, his local grammar school. This was a mixed school and it is apparent from the school magazines that Bill was both sporty and intelligent, winning prizes for Mathematics and representing the school in the 1st XI for soccer and the 1st VI for tennis. Attending at the same school, although a couple of years below him, was Bill's wife to be, Avis Mary Prosser.[17]

Bill left school in the summer of either 1913 or 1914 and then went up to University College London. He enlisted in the Army in 1915, aged 19. By this time, he was 'walking out' with Avis, and throughout the war he continued to write to her. His RAF service papers give his enlistment as 1 March 1915, however, if this is the case, he was not formally attested into the MMGS until late June. This is recorded in *The Motor Cycle* and is supported by his service number of 1658; he was signed along with G.F. Bainbridge and W. Letheren (Motor cyclists), H. Colwell and T.C. Pett (Car drivers), and W.R. White and J. Henderson (Artificers).[18] It was not entirely unusual for there to be a period of time between initial signing for the MMGS and actual attestation and being taken on strength, but three to four months is longer than average. However, none of those listed as signing with Bill appear to have served with him in 22nd MMG Battery. It is not known whether Bill knew them and was then separated, nor whether Bill had friends who had enlisted previously and then linked up with them in 22nd MMG Battery.[19]

John Roberts was born in New Tredegar, Monmouthshire in 1895, the son of the Reverend Ellis Maelor Roberts, who was the minister in the town's Welsh Congregational Chapel. John was the eldest of three sons.[20] In 1903 their father

16   TNA, WO363, Service Papers 32556 Gunner Claude Henry Briance.
17   Macro, *Action at Badama Post*, pp.47-48.
18   *The Motor Cycle*, 1 July 1915, p.10.
19   Macro, *Action at Badama Post*, p.48.
20   TNA (PRO), 1901. Census Returns of England and Wales, 1901. Class: RG13; Piece: 5099; Folio: 30; p.4.

died aged only 37.[21] At the time his widow, Anne, was expecting a fourth child, another boy, who was born on 4 June 1903.[22] Life must have been pretty tough for the family. In the first week of August 1915 John travelled to Coventry and enlisted in the MMGS through *The Motor Cycle* magazine. He trained at Bisley during the summer of 1915. On 30 September 1915 John Roberts joined 15th MMG in France as a casualty replacement.[23]

Equipment

So far as the motorcycles are concerned, although the MMGS used a variety including Scotts and particularly Enfields, the primary machines on the North West Frontier were the Triumph Model H for single seat use and the Clyno Combination as a carrier vehicle. The Triumph H was selected for the Army at the start of the war and was Triumph's first true motorcycle, with a belt driven rear wheel and no pedals. Fitted with a Sturmey-Archer three-speed countershaft gearbox operated by a hand gear-change lever, over 30,000 had been produced by the end of the First World War. It became known to the troops as the 'Triumph Trusty' or 'Trusty H'. The Army settled on the Clyno combination, which was produced by Clyno in a partnership with Vickers, in 1915. In the MMGS each section consisted of six combinations, with two carrying guns and the remainder as ammunition and spares carriers. The section commander, and possibly his serjeant, would use a Triumph.[24]

The machine guns were the Vickers Medium Machine Gun. Water-cooled, .303 calibre, it was produced by Vickers Limited, entered service with the British Army in November 1912 and was finally retired in March 1968. It typically weighed 12-15 kilograms and the tripod around 20 kilograms. Generally, a crew was six men; one firing the gun, one feeding the belted ammunition and the remainder as spotters and carriers.[25]

21 General Register Office. *England and Wales Civil Registration Indexes*. FreeBMD. *England & Wales, Civil Registration Death Index, 1837-1915*, accessed via <https://www.ancestry.co.uk/>, 23 November 2021.

22 TNA, Public Record Office (PRO), 1911. Census Returns of England and Wales, 1911. Class: RG14; Piece: 34121; Schedule Number: 207.

23 Army Medal Office (In the Care of the Western Front Association Website); London, England; *WW1 Medal Index Cards*, accessed via <https://www.ancestry.co.uk/>. *UK, British Army World War I Medal Rolls Index Cards, 1914-1920*, accessed via <https://www.ancestry.co.uk/>, 23 November 2021.

24 Macro, *Action at Badama Post*, pp.213-214.

25 Macro, *Action at Badama Post*, p.212.

Gunner Alexander Dowie in India, probably in 1916, mounted on a Triumph 'Trusty H'. (J.P. Jamieson's album)

Gunner James Petrie Jamieson, 22nd Motor Machine Gun Battery, behind the gun while mounted on the Clyno Combination. (J.P. Jamieson's album)

Vickers gun in action near Bannu. Probably a 1916 firepower demonstration for tribesmen. (E.W. Macro's album)

Four Batteries to France

3rd MMG Battery, having formed in the autumn of 1914, sailed for France to join V Corps on 16 February 1915.[26] 14th MMG Battery was formed around May 1915 and attached to 20th Division while still in England. They embarked for France in July 1915 moving with the division to the Western Front. 14th MMG then joined I ANZAC Corps 22 April 1916. The Battery was then attached to 1st Division between 19 July and 17 October 1917. 15th MMG Battery formed on 29 May 1915 before shipping to France on 24 July. Here they served with 18th Division, from August 1915,[27] XV Corps from June 1916, and with First Army from December 1916 to September 1917. 19th MMG Battery was formed over the summer of 1915. It was attached to 33rd Division from 9 November 1915, but moved independently to the Western Front, sailing on 6 February 1916. The Battery joined 30th Division on 10 February 1916, and moved to 18th Division 6 June 1916. 19th MMG Battery then joined Second Army from December 1916 through to August 1917.[28]

However, even as the MMGS batteries were being formed, and subsequently transferred into the MGC(M), the mobile role which they had been recruited to fill was coming to an end. By December 1914 the Western Front was bogged down in trench warfare with few opportunities to exploit tactical mobility. The batteries

14th Motor Machine Gun Battery before proceeding to France. (*The Motor Cycle*, 1915)

26   TNA, WO95/560, War Diary 3rd Battery Motor Machine Gun Service.
27   TNA, WO95/2028, War Diary 15th Battery Motor Machine Gun Service, RFA.
28   TNA, WO95/338, War Diary 19 Motor M.G. Battery.

found themselves acting as conventional machine gun sections in the line. Their motorcycle sidecar combinations were used for transport rather than in action. However, their work was appreciated; following the March 1915 battle at Neuve Chapelle the MMGS received an official acknowledgement from BEF headquarters of the invaluable work it had rendered in the fighting line.[29] At the time of Neuve Chapelle seven MMGS batteries had been deployed on the Western Front. By October 1915 there were 18 MMGS batteries serving with the BEF.[30] As trench warfare continued and the air threat developed, the batteries also found themselves being employed on anti-aircraft duties behind the front lines.[31]

Throughout this service in France there is relatively little known of the individual soldiers, as they are rarely mentioned in the War Diaries. However, from his service papers, it is known that Gunner Briance was wounded by a gunshot wound to the face on 1 March 1916. He was also awarded the Military Medal 23 November 1916 although the reason for this has not been established.[32]

22nd MMG Battery to India

22nd MMG Battery also formed in the United Kingdom during the summer and early autumn of 1915. However, this battery was not destined to follow its predecessors to the Western Front. Instead, transport records show that 22nd MMG Battery shipped out of Devonport on 26 February 1916 onboard the SS *Beltana*.[33] Sailing via the Mediterranean and Suez, this battery arrived in Bombay 20 March 1916 and was then moved north by train to join 2nd (Rawalpindi) Division.[34] They were to remain in India until they were disbanded in late 1919/early 1920.

Quite why 22nd MMG Battery were selected for service in India remains a mystery. Of the other batteries in the number range 20 to 28, 24th MMG Battery shipped to France in February 1916 and was disbanded in November that year.[35] The remainder, less 20th MMG Battery, never left the United Kingdom and were disbanded in spring 1916. 20th MMG Battery converted to armoured cars and became 13th Light Armoured Motor Battery in June 1916.

---

29   *The Motor Cycle*, 29 April 1915.
30   Michael Carragher, *San Fairy Ann? Motorcycles and British Victory 1914–1918* (Brighton: FireStep Press, 2013), pp.163-164.
31   TNA, WO95/2028, War Diary 15th Battery Motor Machine Gun Service, RFA.
32   TNA, WO363, Service Papers 32556 Gunner Claude Henry Briance.
33   TNA, WO25/3544, Embarkation Returns.
34   Macro, *Action at Badama Post*, pp.50-56.
35   'Motor Machine Guns of the First World War'.

Life in India – Familiarisation Training

Having arrived in Rawalpindi, in late March 1916 22nd MMG Battery moved into their new quarters of Cambridge Lines. This was a barracks, which doubtless seemed relatively luxurious after tents and huts of accommodation in Bisley, or the confines of the troop deck onboard the *Beltana*. At Rawalpindi, 22nd MMG Battery formed an element of the Divisional Troops (that is to say that they belonged to, and were under the orders of, the divisional headquarters, not one of its subordinate brigades) of the 2nd (Rawalpindi) Division. As such, their role was to form part of the response force should trouble break out on the North-West Frontier; they could be sent quickly to the point of greatest need as a quick reaction force. In this role it was important that they were familiar with the whole of the frontier, as in time of crisis, they could find themselves being rushed to pretty much any point of it.

The men of the battery had little time to settle into their new accommodation.[36] Almost as soon as they had arrived in Rawalpindi, they were deployed on a month-long familiarisation tour around the North-West Frontier. Afterwards, Sergeant Fielder, the battery sergeant mechanic, wrote to *The Motor Cycle*. A large section of his letter was reproduced in the issue of 13 July 1916, and is worth quoting here:

> We are very comfortable here, and, although rather hot, are getting used to it. We have just returned from a thousand mile patrol duty, and a brief description might interest you. We started from Pindi on April 5th for Nowshera, a distance of eighty miles, passing Fort Attock, near Hindus [sic], and Kabul [the junction of the rivers Indus and Kabul was at Attock] on the way and had a decent journey, except for the dust, which was awful. We stopped at Nowshera on the 6th. On the 7th we left for Chakdara Fort, up on the frontier, passing Mardan Malakan Forts, etc.; distance sixty miles. As this is up on the Himalaya Mountains, it was a fairly stiff climb. On the 8th we went field firing. The object of this was to put the fear of God into the native chief and tribesmen, which we fairly succeeded in doing, returning afterwards to Mardan; distance fifty miles. In the evening we went to see an Indian war dance, which is a very impressive affair.
>
> The 9th, being Sunday, we spent tuning up our cycles. On the 10th we left for Peshawar in the pouring rain, and arrived covered with mud, etc.; distance forty five miles. On the 11th we went to Landikotal [sic] Fort, through the Khyber Pass, returning to Peshawar the same day; distance seventy-five miles. The road was very dangerous, being twisty and right at the edge of the cliffs. On the 12th we were inspected by the Chief Commissioner, who was very satisfied with our work. On the

---

36   Macro, *Action at Badama Post*, p.59.

The North West Frontier – Theatres of Operation. Rectangles indicate areas covered in more detail below. (Map by George Anderson, © Helion and Company 2022)

Sergeant Alfred Fielder ASC, almost certainly in Rawalpindi. (J.P. Jamieson's album)

13th we went to Chubcudda [location not identified] for field firing (this was where a big "scrap" took place last August), returning afterwards to Peshawar; distance fifty miles. The 14th (day of rest) was spent overhauling the machines. On the 15th we were inspected by the General in Command before leaving for Kohat; distance forty miles. On the 17th we left Kohat for Thal, a nice journey; distance sixty-one miles. On the 18th we left for Parachinar, right up on the hills, where it was very cold at night, snow being on the hills just above; distance fifty-nine miles. On the 19th we went field firing on the Afghan frontier, afterwards returning to Thal; distance eighty miles. Here the natives held sports in our honour, and some of the performances were very good, especially their horsemanship.

On the 20th we left for Kohat, where we were inspected by the General in Command, afterwards going field firing; distance seventy miles. On the 22nd we left for Banu [sic], a good journey, crossing several fords two feet deep; distance seventy-nine miles. On the 24th we left for Mirenshaw, over most awful roads; distance forty miles. One of the biggest frontier "scraps" have occurred here. Quite a pleasant place to spend Bank Holiday in. On the 25th we left for Banu, a distance of forty miles, tuned up machines, etc. On the 26th we went field firing, and afterwards had a lecture by General Fane. On the 27th we returned to Kohat, a good journey; distance seventy-nine miles. On the 29th we returned to Peshawar, the hardest climb in the whole journey. On May 1st we left Peshawar for Pindi, a distance of 117 miles, in the pouring rain, and so ended a month's hard travelling.

Being the sergeant mechanic, in charge, I had a fairly busy time of it.[37]

Continuation Training

Once the Christmas season was past 22nd MMG Battery returned to training. In another letter home Bill Macro described one of the exercises in which he was placed in charge of the Battery.

> On Friday last we were with all the machine guns in Pindi with quite a good show on. We did the same on Saturday morning but after we had finished the Major arranged a little stunt presumably for my benefit. He sent a message which was handed to me saying that all Officers and NCOs, with the exception of myself, were out of action and that I was to take command of the Battery. He also stated that the enemy (imaginary of course) were in possession of a place some 3 miles distance and that I was to take the Battery and take up positions to engage the enemy and prevent their advance. Imagine my position. I had this dropped on me without the slightest warning. The Officers and NCOs who had also been informed by a message simple [sic] got into one of the cars and vanished away to the scene of action. I had no map of the district and only a faint notion where the place where the enemy were existed and I had no body to take charge of the sections and guns or the machines men left behind when the guns went into action. Anyhow something had to be done so I went round to the sections, appointed section commanders, and rearranged things a bit to suit the new arrangement. Then I got the Battery moving and managed to recognize the roads sufficiently well to get to my destination. There I called the section commanders and told them where to put their guns and their targets and left them to get on with it. After a bit the Major appeared and questioned me a bit and would you believe told me that he was very pleased with the show and that he only had one thing to criticize and that was that I had the cycles and men who were not in action too much exposed to the enemies [sic] view and if I had left them 50 yds further back they would have been entirely out of sight. Of course I told him I hadn't a map and didn't know the locality very well and so had [not] recognised the position until I actually arrived there. So he told me I should have gone on ahead to observe. Personally of course I think that was rather rough as I'd no one to leave in charge of the Battery and to bring it along and I hadn't got a solo cycle to go ahead on and I couldn't

---

37   *The Motor Cycle*, Volume 17, 13 July 1916 p.35, at <https://archive.org/stream/motorcycle17lond_/ motorcycle17londpage/n84/mode/1up> accessed 7 November 2018.

very well have taken a gun carriage. Anyway I was told to retire the guns and form up in column of route. This I managed by the judicious use of scouts and then the Major took command again. Since then nothing has been said about it so I suppose my Section Commander either thought it so rotten that he let it drop or else he could [not] find anything to criticize and so said nothing. Anyway I don't think I did too badly considering the circumstance although what I think doesn't count for anything.[38]

Such exercises, to test the alternate command chain, were probably conducted fairly frequently, both for that reason and also to highlight natural leaders and identify potential candidates for commissioning. The Machine Gun Corps, having attracted and been selective over their applicants, always had a high percentage of soldiers who later took commissions. 22nd MMG Battery was no exception, and a number of its soldiers applied for commissions in 1917 and 1918, as the war dragged on. Amongst these were Alexander Dowie,[39] and William Welsh.[40] Both commissioned into the Highland Light Infantry, although this appears to be something of a wartime convenience as no Highland Light Infantry battalions were serving in India at the time. Others, with the technical background which had brought them into the Motors in the first place, got involved with the light armoured car batteries as experiments were made in India in the early forms of armoured cars.

Life in India – Routines

When 22 MMG Battery returned to Rawalpindi in May 1916, following their familiarization tour, the hot season would have been coming on fast. However, there was still plenty to keep them occupied. Bill Macro wrote home on 4 May:

> We arrived back at Pindi last Monday and although we are supposed to be resting after the tour we've found very little time to ourselves. I've had to take the sidecar off my cycle and take it to the arsenal to have a cracked bar replaced. We've had to check all our ammunition and stores as they are very particular out here. The hill tribesmen pay a lot for any army stores they can get and so there are a lot of thieves (we call them loose wallahs) knocking about. In the hills you can get 1 rupee (1/4) for one round of ammunition and 1000 rupees for a rifle.[41]

---

38   Macro family papers. Letter Ernest Macro to Avis Prosser dated 29 January 1917.
39   TNA, WO374/20520, Officers Services 2/Lieutenant Alexander Morrison DOWIE, Machine Gun Corps.
40   TNA, WO374/73106, Officers Services Lieutenant William WELSH, The Highland Light Infantry.
41   Macro family papers. Letter Ernest Macro to Avis Prosser dated 4 May 1916.

British troops would routinely leave their normal barracks on the plains during the hot season and move to what were referred to as summer stations or hill stations in the foothills of the Himalayas, in order to escape the worst of the heat and associated disease. 22nd MMG Battery was no exception and the Battery was split into two halves in order to do so. In early June the first half of the Battery moved to a tented/hutted camp at Kuldana in the Muree Hills, for six weeks. Muree remains a popular summer retreat in modern day Pakistan. Bill Macro was in the second half of the battery and moved to Kuldana in mid-July, returning to Rawalpindi in late August.[42]

Soccer, swimming and fishing appear to have been popular diversions, both at Rawalpindi and while up in the hills. There was a unit soccer league and within the battery there was an inter-section competition. Life for 22nd MMG Battery settled into a routine of training and showing the flag, in order to impress, or intimidate, the natives. However, it is clear that there was a strong feeling amongst the men of the battery that they would rather be in France. One of Bill Macro's 1916 letters home expresses pity at the rumour that another MMG battery was about to be sent to India. In fact this battery never arrived; until early 1918 22nd MMG remained the only MMG battery in India. Those batteries that were still raising in the United Kingdom were either transferred as tank crews, formed Light Armoured Motor Batteries, or were transferred into the remainder of the MGC. The raising of 25th Calcutta MMG Battery also caused considerably disquiet amongst 22nd MMG Battery, as Bill Macro wrote home again in late September 1916:

> A very rotten thing is happening out here just now, all the papers are advertising for recruits for a Calcutta Machine Gun battery which is to be trained at Rawalpindi and promise that 2 months after the Battery is complete that it will be sent to France. You can understand how we feel about it and the Major is awfully wild and swore that he would [not] assist them in the least degree. He says that if they do send them away in two months he'll complain and risk a court martial because they cannot be properly trained in two months.[43]

However, the chance to take leave appears to have been available and appreciated. From his letters to *The Motor Cycle* it is known that Sergeant Fielder spent his Christmas leave of 1916 in Calcutta, although he also reported that troops were not well respected by civilians. The Taj Mahal was also a popular destination.[44]

---

42   Macro family papers. Letters Ernest Macro to Avis Prosser June-September 1916.
43   Macro family papers. Letter Ernest Macro to Avis Prosser dated 29 September 1916.
44   *The Motor Cycle*, Volume 18, May 1917, available at <https://archive.org/stream/motorcycle17lond_/motorcycle17londpage/n84/mode/1up>, accessed 7 November 2018.

Photos in Bill Macro's album, and his letters home, confirm that 22nd MMG Battery spent the summer from late May 1917 through to late September 1917 in a tented camp at Topa. Topa is situated in the Murree Hills, close to both Murree town and Kuldana, about 50 miles (80 kilometres) northeast of Rawalpindi. This year it appears that the complete Battery relocated for the season. Bill wrote home again on 17 May 1917:

> We're going up to the hills tomorrow leaving here at 6.30 am so I'm pretty busy today packing up the four months we expect to spend up there and handing stuff in to store. If the mail doesn't arrive till tomorrow morning we shan't get it for several days.
>
> It's deucedly hot here now so I'm glad we're going up to Topa although I wish we were going in to Bungalows instead of tents. I expect we shall get pretty wet during the monsoon season.[45]

Bill's next letter was from Upper Topa, and although he complained about the hour long walk into Murree, he also said there was nothing much to go there for. The tent situation, however, was perhaps not as bad as he had feared:

> As you'll see by the address we are now up in the hills under canvas and I am not too badly off as I happen to be in the best tent on the best site in the camp. In fact the Major told us this morning that he'd sooner be in our tent than in his own, I very nearly told him that he didn't know how to work things.
>
> We had a pretty bad time when we first got up here rushing up enough tents to sleep in and getting beds etc and since then we've been busy making paths and lining them with whitewashed stones, so as to be able to see our way to our tents. Still the worst is over, although I suppose we shall be continuing this game for sometime to come.[46]

The raising of the 25th Calcutta MMG Battery continued to impact amongst 22nd MMG, although on this occasion the result was more fortuitous for Bill Macro:

> By the way last Saturday Acting/L/Cpl Macro was promoted Cpl. This occurred because our Section Sgt got transferred to the 25th Bty and is on his way to Egypt with them now. So the section Cpl and myself got a step up. It was just about 18 months before that I got my first stripe.[47]

---

45   Macro family papers. Letter Ernest Macro to Avis Prosser dated 17 May 1917.
46   Macro family papers. Letter Ernest Macro to Avis Prosser dated 23 May 1917.
47   Macro family papers. Letter Ernest Macro to Avis Prosser dated 17 June 1917.

Gunner John Travell Maton Gough, with Barr & Stroud Rangefinder and tripod. (Walter Patrick's album, courtesy of Alex Bowell)

The Battery returned to Rawalpindi at the end of September 1917 and Bill's letters at this point contain details of the refurbishment of rooms for the mess and also the Badminton club. It continued to be possible to take leave.[48] However, the troops were not always appreciated, as 1068 Gunner John Travell Maton Gough recorded:

> We have now been in country for almost two years, and our views [about being sent to India rather than France] have undergone a considerable change. Being accustomed to receiving the best treatment in Blighty, it felt very strange to be stationed in a country where the 'duration man' is not understood. No one realises that practically every man in Kitchener's Army has sacrificed an excellent civilian position in order to serve his country. We have heard of a park not a hundred miles from Calcutta where a notice once appeared to the effect that 'Dogs and soldiers are not allowed in here.' It is to the credit of the Territorials and 'duration' men that they are living down this prejudice.[49]

Four Batteries to India

In January 1918 the solitary status of 22nd MMG Battery in India came to a close when 3rd, 14th, 15th and 19th MMGs were sent out from France. For the majority of the previous two years the batteries in France had been acting in either the

48   Macro family papers, various Letters Ernest Macro to Avis Prosser of September and October 1917.

49   'The Momagu', *The Motor Cycle*, Volume 20, 28 March 1918, available at <https://archive.org/details/ motorcycle20lond_/page/n393/mode/2up?q=Momagu&view=theater>, accessed May 2017.

infantry or anti-aircraft roles, with the sidecar combinations being used as transport. The timing also coincided with the increasing rise to prominence of the tank, after the Battle of Cambrai, and the need to raise additional manpower for tank battalions for use in 1918. Some MMG batteries were disbanded and had the majority of their manpower transferred to the newly formed Tank Corps. Other batteries were used to man new armoured car units which were proving successful in Africa, the Middle East and, indeed, in India itself. There was also increasing concern in India about the threat from Russian and German agents agitating trouble in Afghanistan and amongst the population of India. So MMG batteries would have been considered ideal for policing duties as they could cover a large area with a small number of men but with plenty of firepower.

During October and November 1917 the four batteries were transported across France to Marseilles. Certainly in the case of 15th MMG Battery this was by cattle truck and there was no opportunity for leave.[50] All four batteries then sailed on 28 November 1917 from Marseilles on SS *Manitou*. Each battery was recorded as being at a strength of four officers and 56 other ranks, less 15th MMG which had 54 other ranks. Each battery shipped a motor lorry, four box cars, eight solo motorcycles, 19 motorcycle combinations and six Vickers machine guns.[51] According to Gunner Briance's record, SS *Manitou* docked in Bombay to allow disembarkation 9 January 1918.[52]

3rd MMG Battery, on arrival in India, was stationed in Ambala, just to the east of Punjab state. Throughout their time in India the Battery commanding officer appears to have been Captain Nevill Rupert Farmer. The only other 3rd MMG officer traced from the time in India is Lieutenant (acting Captain) Keith Alfred Knight.

On arrival in India 14th MMG served with 5th (Mhow) Division at Jubbulpore.[53] The names of the battery officers have not yet been established, however, a few names of battery members are known. Gunners 625 James Lomas Barratt, 660 Rhydwon Jones, 668 Fred Mowbray, 721 Herbert Hulm, 952 Alexander Kellas and 1138 Albion William Osgood were all part of a group of 23 MMGS men who were deployed to France on 17 July 1915 as reinforcements. These six all ended up deploying to India with 14th MMG Battery.[54] 14th MMG Battery, in common with the others, suffered a number of casualties during their time in India. James Barratt, mentioned above, was one of these, drowned on 11 August 1919. Earlier 14th MMG casualties buried in Jubbulpore include 1156 George Galloway who died from appendicitis 29 October 1918 and 80593 Gunner Horace Dodworth who

---

50   With regards Gunner Phillip Henry Hampton, see account by grandson David Henshall on the *Great War (1914-1918) Forum*, post dated 27 March 2022, at <https://www.greatwarforum.org/topic/280902-15th-motor-machine-gun-battery-india-1918-and-1919/page/2/>.

51   TNA, WO95/4038-3, War Diary of the Marseilles Base Commandant.

52   TNA, WO363, Service Papers 32556 Gunner Claude Henry Briance.

53   'Motor Machine Guns of the First World War'.

54   Correspondence Macro-Murdoch via the *Great War (1914-1918) Forum*, 16–17 April 2020.

died 5 November 1918. 2208 Gunner Thomas Cardigan Went was not an original member of 14th MMG but enlisted in August 1915, appearing in *The Motor Cycle* 19 August 1915. He was also drowned in a bathing accident 14 April 1919, aged 25, in Sewri (Bombay).[55]

15th MMG Battery were stationed in Peshawar, as part of 1st Indian Division.[56] The commanding officer was Captain Claude Outram Dalgairns Anderson, who appears to have commanded from 1917 through to the end of 1919. Anderson was gazetted temporary 2nd Lieutenant, Motor Machine Gun Corps, on 3 June 1916. He was awarded the Military Cross in the Birthday Honours of 1916. The only other officer known to have served with 15th MMG during their time in India was Lieutenant Philip Jeffries. Philip was from Birmingham and originally served in the Honourable Artillery Company. He was commissioned into the MMGS during the war but died of appendicitis at Peshawar Station Hospital 3 December 1918. His age at the time is not known.[57]

On arrival in India 19th MMG served with 4th (Quetta) Division.[58] For much of the time the battery spent in France the commanding officer was Major Archibald Gray;[59] however, his second in command was Captain Ernest Henry Carnochan, and, by the time the battery deployed to India, Carnochan had assumed command.[60]

In India, through the course of 1918, it seems that the 19th MMG section officers were Lieutenant Charles M. Frank, attached from the Gloucestershire Regiment, Lieutenant F.G. Squire and Lieutenant Woodland Bernard Erlebach. As the war in Europe came to an end there were further officer movements. Lieutenant Frank spent the Third Afghan War attached to 263 MGC Company and Lieutenant Squire also disappears from 19th MMG Battery records. In the place of these two section commanders the Battery received Lieutenant G. Turner of the MGC (Cavalry) and Lieutenant A.M. Ketley. Turner, formerly of the Royal East Kent Yeomanry, was later commissioned in the MGC (Cavalry) and was Mentioned in Despatches in Mesopotamia. He served with 19th MMG Battery during the Third Afghan War and returned to the United Kingdom in September 1919. Ketley also served in Mesopotamia. He was originally a Petty Officer Mechanic in the Royal Naval Air Service before commissioning into MMGS. He too served with the battery during the Afghan War, as probably did Lieutenant Erlebach. It appears that Erlebach took on the role of battery second-in-command, and, possibly after the war, took over as the commanding officer.[61]

---

55 Research conducted by Mr David Murdoch and the author through various genealogy sites.

56 'Motor Machine Guns of the First World War'.

57 Principal Probate Registry. *Calendar of the Grants of Probate and Letters of Administration made in the Probate Registries of the High Court of Justice in England*, accessed via <https://www.ancestry.co.uk/>, September 2020.

58 'Motor Machine Guns of the First World War'.

59 TNA, WO95/2028, War Diary 15th Battery Motor Machine Gun Service, RFA.

60 TNA, WO95/2028, War Diary 15th Battery Motor Machine Gun Service, RFA.

61 Discussion between Mr David Murdoch, Martin Cassell and the author via the *Great War (1914-1918) Forum*, thread '19th Motor Machine Gun Battery in India 1918 and 1919' at <https://www.greatwarforum.

25th Calcutta MMG Battery, consisting of volunteers, was raised in India in October 1916. The battery was shipped from India to Egypt on 2 July 1917 to take part in the Middle East campaign. However, it was disbanded in January 1918 without, it is thought, having seen any action.[62]

Marri Punitive Expedition of 1918

Of the new arrivals, 19th MMG Battery was in action pretty much as soon as it had arrived in India. In eastern Baluchistan the Marri tribes rose against the British authorities around 18 February 1918. They were encouraged by rumours that the British were short of manpower. British attempts at conciliation were repulsed and, on 20 February, a major attack was made by 1,000–3,000 Marri upon Gumbaz Fort. This was repulsed by the British, who inflicted heavy losses upon the Marri. A subsequent withdrawal of British forces from Kohlu and its occupation by the Marri led the Khetrans to join the rising. The town of Barkhan was also occupied by Marri-Khetran forces and raids were made upon villages and railways in the area.

The British assembled the Marri Field Force under Major-General Richard Wapshare to combat the rising. Two columns under Brigadier-Generals T.H. Hardy and Philip Miles went on the offensive into territory occupied by the tribes. Miles inflicted a heavy defeat upon a Marri-Khetran force at Fort Munro on 15 March and then captured Barkhan, ending Khetran involvement in the rising. Hardy defeated a large Marri force at Hadb on 3 April and, afterwards, assisted by bombing by the Royal Flying Corps, captured the Marri capital of Kahan. The Marri Sardar Khair Bux Mari surrendered to the British on 8 April.[63]

19th MMG Battery formed part of the Duki column under Brigadier-General Hardy. However, it is recorded that owing to a lack of roads beyond Duki, it was decided to convert the machine gun sections to pack-animal transport with the ammunition belts carried in packing cases by mules and camels. The 'former motor cyclist riders had worn the soles off their boots cornering on their bikes, and being in no condition to march a long distance,' passed Gumbaz Fort 18 March. They persevered to Kohlu, about 100 kilometres from Duki, which was reached 23 March, remaining there as a garrison.[64] However, by July 1918 the battery was back at its major station, Quetta.

org/topic/280998-19th-motor-machine-gun-battery-in-india-1918-and-1919/>.

62   '25th Motor Machine Gun Battery (Calcutta Volunteers)', *Families In British India Society (FIBIS) Wiki*, at <https://wiki.fibis.org/index.php/25th_Motor_Machine_Gun_Battery_(Calcutta_Volunteers)>, accessed 25 November 2021.

63   *London Gazette*, Supplement Number 31235, 17 March 1919, p.3586.

64   'The British Raj: Fighting The Marris And The Khetrans, *Balochi Linguist*, at <https://balochilinguist. wordpress.com/2015/12/10/the-british-raj-fighting-the-marris-and-the-khetrans/>, accessed 23 March

Elements of 19th Motor Machine Gun Battery at Gumbaz Fort in 1918. The officers in the centre are believed to be Lieutenant W.B. Erlebach (left) and Lieutenant C.M. Frank (right). (Lieutenant F.G. Squire's album, courtesy of Martin Cassell)

15th Motor Machine Gun Battery Armistice Day Parade Peshawar, 11 November 1918. (Collection of G.Walker)

22nd MMG Battery and the Punjab Disturbances – April to early May 1919

It is known, through personal letters and the Hunter Commission reports, that 22nd MMG Battery were involved in the Punjab Disturbances, although they were not at Amritsar at the time of the massacre. However, no evidence has been uncovered of any of the other batteries being involved. Given both the slowness of communication between London and Delhi, and the onset of the war with Afghanistan, there was no immediate follow up to the massacre and the wider disturbances. However, in October 1919, the Secretary of State for India, Edwin Montagu, issued instructions for the government of India to conduct an inquiry into the events in Punjab. Formally entitled the Disorders Inquiry Committee, it was later more widely known as the Hunter Commission. The purpose of the commission was to investigate the causes of the disturbances in Bombay, Delhi and Punjab, and the measures taken to deal with them. The evidence taken by this enquiry includes a statement made by a Captain J.A.S. Ewing of the 19th Lancers (Fane's Horse). This makes it clear that 22nd MMG Battery was involved in the policing operations in Punjab after Amritsar, as Captain Ewing mentions the battery commanding officer, Major Molony. Ewing's statement describes how half squadrons from the 18th (King George's Own) and 19th Lancers were operating in the Sialkot and Wazirabad area of Punjab on policing and patrol duties from 13 April. 22nd MMG Battery was certainly involved from 19 April as Ewing's report states 'Mobile column composed of half squadron 19th Lancers, two sections Motor Machine Gun Battery, under command of Major Maloney [sic], left Wazirabad for Lyallpur.' The patrols appear to have been effective because the following day Ewing reported 'Motor Machine Gun Battery proceeded to Jaranwala to make arrests there, and arrested 12 men.'[65]

Up until the end of April, the focus of operations was on policing and making arrests. The method used was to 'march to the village by night and surround it before dawn, then have out the *Lambardars* [landowners] and make them produce offenders, then hold a "*jirga*" [tribal gathering] and get as much information as possible regarding other miscreants in surrounding villages.'[66] But the greater range of 22nd MMG Battery, when compared to the cavalry, meant they were often employed on these strike and arrest operations while the cavalry undertook more local patrols. Ewing recorded on 29 April, 'Motor Machine Gun Battery went to a village 57 miles away to make two arrests, returning same evening, distance 114

2022.

65   Report of Captain J.A.S. Ewing, 19th Lancers, on operations with mobile column in Sialkot area during the Punjab disturbances. Disorders Inquiry Committee, *Evidence taken before the Disorders Inquiry Committee* (Calcutta: Superintendent Government Printing, 1920), Vol.V, p.200.

66   Ewing Report, Disorders Inquiry Committee, *Evidence*, Vol.V, p.200.

Left: Major A.W. Molony, officer commanding 22nd Motor Machine Gun Battery, near Thal, 1916. (E.W. Macro's album)

Below: Near Parachinar, demonstrating the guns to tribesmen, probably in 1916. Lance Corporal Macro bending forward to clear the gun. (E.W. Macro's album)

miles.'[67] From May the focus appears to switch to 'showing the flag' rather than arrests; more *jirgas* were held at the villages and demonstrations were given of the machine guns firing.[68]

On 1 May 1919, Captain Ewing's report states; 'Mobile Column went to Sukeke where it picked up one troop of 18th Lancers having left one troop, 19th Lancers, at Lyallpur. Motor Machine Gun Battery had to go on to Hafizabad to detrain and come back by road. Camped Sukeke for the night.'[69] The following day the combined column 'Commenced a march "showing the flag". I marched to Chuharkana, interviewed Deputy Commissioner, visiting *en route* village of Khanga Dogran where a small durbar was held, distance 21 miles. Road good, passable for motor transport.'[70] The next day, 3 May 1919, the Afghans initiated the Third Afghan War via the Khyber; they crossed the frontier at the western end of the pass to capture the town of Bagh. The British initially considered this a minor border infraction, but it was actually part of the wider invasion plan, which had been launched ahead of schedule. Amanullah Khan, the Emir of Afghanistan, had intended for it to coincide with an uprising that was being planned in Peshawar later in May.[71]

On 5 May 1919, Captain Ewing's mobile column marched in two parties to Harpoki on the Chenab Canal. The cavalry party moved across country. The other party, 22nd MMG, 'went along banks of canal, visiting village of Chiohoki Mallian. Camped at Harpoki the night. Distance 29 miles.'[72] The following day the column marched to Gujranwala, a distance of another 21 miles, and camped for the night. They then received orders to return to Wazirabad the following day.[73] This, 6 May 1919, was also the day the British declared war on Afghanistan and ordered a general mobilisation of the British and Indian forces.[74]

Ewing's column returned to Wazirabad on 7 May. Ewing's evidence records that the 19th Lancers' horses had covered about 300 miles in the preceding three weeks of policing operations and that 'every horse finished as sound he started and accomplished the whole trip.'[75] The motorcycles of 22nd MMG Battery must have covered considerably more than 300 miles; whether they finished in the same sound condition as the horses is not recorded. The elements of 22nd MMG Battery then returned to Rawalpindi.

67   Ewing Report, Disorders Inquiry Committee, *Evidence*, Vol.V, p.200.
68   Ewing Report, Disorders Inquiry Committee, *Evidence*, Vol.V, p.200.
69   Ewing Report, Disorders Inquiry Committee, *Evidence*, Vol.V, p.200.
70   Ewing Report, Disorders Inquiry Committee, *Evidence*, Vol.V, p.200.
71   Brian Robson, *Crisis on the Frontier, The Third Afghan War and the Crisis in Waziristan 1919-20* (Staplehurst: Spellmount, 2007), pp.43–48.
72   Ewing Report, Disorders Inquiry Committee, *Evidence*, Vol.V, p.201.
73   Ewing Report, Disorders Inquiry Committee, *Evidence*, Vol.V, p.201.
74   Robson, *Crisis on the Frontier*, p.17.
75   Ewing Report, Disorders Inquiry Committee, *Evidence*, Vol.V, p.201.

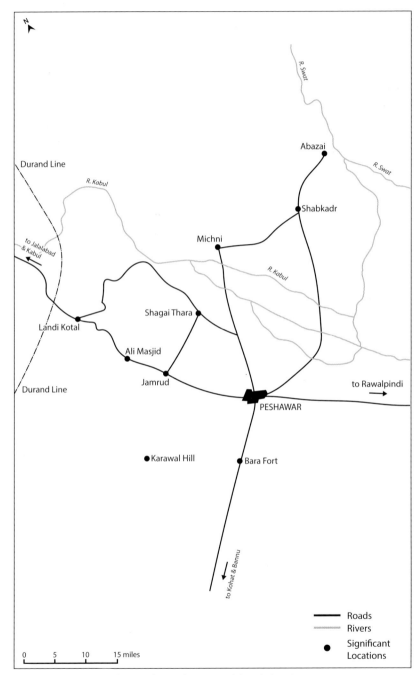

The Northern Theatre and the Khyber Pass.
(Map by George Anderson, © Helion and Company 2022)

Throughout this period Bill Macro acted as Major Molony's driver, although what had happened to Sergeant Fielder is not known. Bill's two letters home from this deployment confirm the contents of Captain Ewing's report. He also states; 'I am O.C.'s driver but besides that one does a lot of running about for the Deputy Commissioner but it has its compensations in that I'm living in the Dak Bungalow with the officers and getting the same food they are and a bed to sleep in.'[76]

Third Afghan War and After

During the Third Afghan War 3rd MMG Battery were sent to Kohat and remained there from 25 May to 29 June 1919. It does not appear that they were in action as a battery at any stage. Gunner Claude Briance was with them throughout, thereby qualifying for the India General Service Medal, but had three days in hospital in Kohat 18 June to 21 June 1919. After the war he returned to the United Kingdom via Deolali and Bombay to demobilise 21 November 1919.[77] Briance married Grace Lillian Murrell on 22 August 1925 but they do not appear to have had any children.[78] On the 1939 register he is shown as being an ambulance driver.[79] He died 12 October 1948 in Romford, Essex.[80] Less fortunate than Gunner Briance was 757 Gunner Albert Alfred Lloyd who died on 23 June 1919. He is listed on the Karachi Memorial but is actually buried at Lahore Cantonment North Cemetery. Lloyd is the only MGC(M) man listed in Pakistan by CWGC and offers a further example of the elite attitude of the MMGS. His mates obviously thought highly of Albert; his headstone must have been erected after the war and may have been paid for from battery funds. It has the MMG badge and 'Motor Machine Gun Service' engraved on it. In contrast, on the official graves report, Alfred is shown as MGC (Motors).[81]

14th MMG Battery also appear to have had no role in the Third Afghan War. According to the official account, the battery was temporarily in Bombay,[82] possibly as a prelude to disbanding back to the United Kingdom, and away from Jubbulpore. Although the battery played no part in the conflict, it is possible

76   Macro family papers. Letter Ernest Macro to Avis Prosser dated 25 April 1919.
77   TNA/WO363, Service Papers 32556 Gunner Claude Henry Briance.
78   Essex Record Office; Chelmsford, Essex, England; *Essex Church of England Parish Registers*, accessed via <https://www.ancestry.co.uk/>, February 2021.
79   TNA, RG 101/1535E.
80   Principal Probate Registry. *Calendar of the Grants of Probate and Letters of Administration made in the Probate Registries of the High Court of Justice in England.*
81   Research conducted by Mr David Murdoch and the author through various genealogy sites.
82   General Staff Branch, Army Headquarters India, *Third Afghan War 1919 Official Account* (Uckfield: Naval & Military Press, 2004 reprint of original 1926 edition), p.164.

Gunner Albert Lloyd's gravestone in Lahore, post Third Afghan War, with a former comrade, believed to be Walter Emery. (David Murdoch)

members had been detached to make up numbers in the armoured motor batteries, or other units.

Stationed at Peshawar, 15th MMG Battery played an active role in the war. In mid-May 1919, the Mohmands were again threatening to attack Peshawar out of their lands to the east of the Khyber. On 21/22 May two columns were dispatched to block them. The first column, under the commander of 44th Infantry Brigade, was sent to Shabkadr, in the centre of the Mohmand Blockade Line, to where it was believed the Afghans were headed. This column contained 15th MMG Battery and an armoured car battery of 1st Armoured Motor Brigade. The second column went to Michni, at the southern end of the Line. Beyond burning some empty towers on the Line, the tribesmen showed little activity and soon dispersed when their food ran out. The Afghan regulars then retired to their original bases on the Kunar River, 60 miles from Peshawar. Both British columns were withdrawn on 25 May and were back in Peshawar by the 30th.[83] The battery then lost John Tydwal Roberts, now a corporal, killed in action 1 June 1919 aged 23. According to his Indian burial record, he was buried in Peshawar the following day.[84] He was another of over a thousand British and Indian casualties of the Third Afghan War. After this, 15th MMG Battery was also part of the operations on 19 July, which located a party of Afridi tribesman on Karawal Hill. They do not, however, appear to have taken part in the subsequent clearance.

83   General Staff Branch, *Third Afghan War 1919 Official Account*, p.96.
84   UK, Soldiers Died in the Great War, 1914-1919, accessed via <https://www.ancestry.co.uk/>, 23 February 2021.

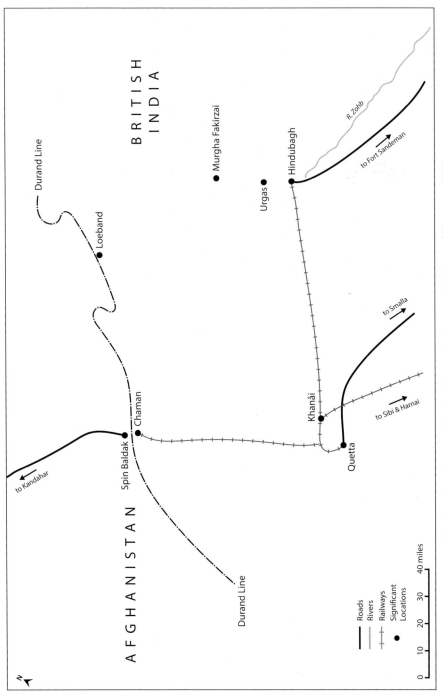

The Southern Theatre. (Map by George Anderson, © Helion and Company 2022)

Switching to the south-western theatre, 19th MMG Battery was still stationed at Quetta as part of the Baluchistan force when war broke out. They had two sections almost permanently employed in patrolling the vital Quetta-Hindubagh-Peshin road to support the East Persia Cordon. The official history specifically records 19th MMG Battery as being in action, with two sections, north of Hindubagh and Karezgi Fort, approximately 50 miles north east of Quetta, in late July (26-30) 1919, but there are no further details. However, it appears that the armoured cars of 11th Armoured Motor Battery were also involved.[85]

The major player of the MMGs during the Third Afghan War was 22nd MMG Battery, which, as the crisis broke with the men freshly returned from policing in the Punjab, was rushed from Rawalpindi to Kohat to reinforce Major General Eustace's Central Front. On arrival at Kohat an infantry battalion and 22nd MMG Battery were immediately sent forward to reinforce the Kurram Militia at Parachinar.[86] Here, in late May as Nadir Khan invested Thal, the skirmishes on the frontiers increased in intensity, particularly around Peiwar Kotal, Kharlachi and Lakka Tiga. The Kurram Militia had picquets out at these border locations, and, as various Afghan forces gathered, machine guns, cavalry, guns and infantry were rushed forward from Parachinar to push them back and relieve the picquets. Once the Afghans had been driven back, the reinforcements would be withdrawn to their reserve location in Parachinar. 22nd MMG Battery was heavily involved at this stage; the mobility provided by the motorcycle sidecar combinations was highly prized.

Thal was relieved by 3 June 1919 and the Kurram Militia, with a section of 22nd MMG Battery took the battle back across the Durand Line and invaded Afghanistan. The attack had been planned on 1 June and at 6:00 p.m. on 2 June Major Percy Dodd, Commandant of the Kurram Militia, led a column out of Parachinar and up to Kharlachi, arriving after dark. The MMG section and the Guides company then occupied a ridge overlooking the Afghan fort at Amir Thana. At dawn on 3 June the guns opened fire and under their cover the Kurram Militia assaulted the fort which surrendered. The advance continued and the Afghans abandoned their headquarters at Mir Kalai. In total two Afghan forts and six villages were burnt.[87] Bill Macro was still driving the commanding officer and commented in a letter home; 'We're the only white troops here & we have at least a section on every scrap & as the O.C. goes out on nearly every occasion I see a good deal of the fun.'[88]

85 General Staff Branch, *Third Afghan War 1919 Official Account*, p.84.

86 TNA, WO95/5392, War Diary Kohat-Kurram Force: Force Troops: 22 Motor Machine Gun Battery (May–August 1919), 14-20 May 1919.

87 TNA, WO95/5392, War Diary Kohat-Kurram Force: Force Troops: 22 Motor Machine Gun Battery (May–August 1919), 2-3 June 1919.

88 Macro family papers. Letter Ernest Macro to Avis Prosser dated 5 June 1919.

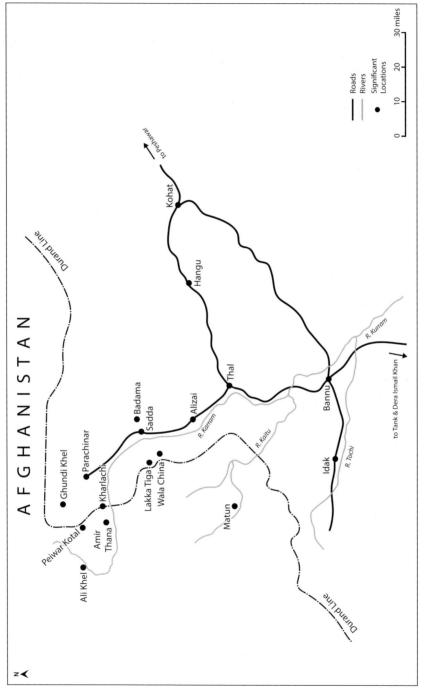

The Central Theatre and the Kurram Valley. (Map by George Anderson, © Helion and Company 2022)

Although the armistice had now been signed, confused fighting continued in this area for about a week before the regular troops were able to withdraw and hand picquet duties back to the Kurram Militia. And tensions with the tribes in the area continued to run high right through until August, particularly when a gathering of tribesmen threatened the posts at Badama and Sadda. This resulted in a patrol of the Kurram Militia and Number 3 Section of 22nd MMG Battery moving rapidly to reinforce the garrisons of the posts. The section of 22nd MMG Battery was now under command of Bill Macro, 'promoted acting Sgt in charge of No 3 Sect while their Sgt is sick down the line.'[89] Then a 20 Squadron aircraft was brought down near Sadda on 30 July. Fortunately the Kurram Militia and Number 3 Section 22nd MMG Battery were able to recover the downed aircrew and the bombs, machine guns and ammunition from the aircraft before the onset of darkness drove them back into the shelter of the posts. The overnight arrival of a relief column of 3rd Guides Infantry from Parachinar then enabled the recovery of the aircraft's engine the following day. The full story of this incident is told in the author's published work, *Action at Badama Post*.[90]

Bill Macro was discharged on 8 December 1919. He briefly resumed his engineering studies at University College, London, but then transferred to teacher training at the London Institute of Education. He married Avis Prosser on 23 July 1921 at the East Finchley Congregational Church and the couple had one child, a son, John Anthony Macro, who was born in Barnet in July 1931. During the Second World War Bill and Avis were evacuated with their school to the Peterborough area. Here Bill Macro served in the Home Guard. He retired from teaching in 1959 and died on 5 May 1974.

Conclusions

The MMG Batteries on the North West Frontier were largely a volunteer force. This was particularly the case for 22nd MMG Battery, which spent the war in India although its members had expected to deploy to France. The other batteries' ranks were thinned by casualties on the Western Front, although many of the replacements, certainly initially, were also volunteers. All these men, however, had key specialist skills which were enhanced by thorough training. This all engendered a distinct esprit de corps which was invaluable to these small units whether they were in the thick of the action on the Western Front or feeling isolated in India. Despite forming just a small part of the British forces in India this esprit de corps enabled the MMG Batteries to play a significant role in the Third Afghan War, the only occasion on which the Afghan Army invaded British India. The British public

---

89   Macro family papers. Letter Ernest Macro to Avis Prosser dated 6 August 1919.
90   Macro, *Action at Badama* Post, Chapters 8-10, pp.129-177.

may have largely forgotten the men who garrisoned India and held the North-West Frontier during the First World War. They may have little interest in the stories of those who fought in the Third Afghan War, overshadowed as it was by terrible tragedy of the Western Front. Yet the stories of these men deserve telling. Doing so opens a window into the MMGS which, small and short-lived though it was, played its full part in both the First World War and the Third Afghan War.

Bibliography

Unpublished Sources

Macro Family Papers
    Letters Ernest William Macro to Avis Prosser and other personal papers.
Army Personnel Centre, Support Division, Glasgow
    Service Papers of Alexander Weldon Molony, R Dub Fus and MGC (M), P/42817 including Army Form B199A.
    Local Defence Volunteers Service Papers of Ernest William Macro.
National Archives, Kew (TNA)
    WO32/11239, Army Order 480, Other Arms (Code 14 (J)): Formation of Machine Gun Corps, 1915.
    WO33/3026 Report of the Advisory Committee on Motorcyclists (Technical Reserve), 1911.
    WO25/3544, Embarkation Returns.
    WO100; Piece: 400, UK, Military Campaign Medal and Award Rolls, 1793–1949.
    WO95/338, War Diary 19th Motor M.G. Battery.
    WO95/560, War Diary 3rd Battery Motor Machine Gun Service.
    WO95/2028, War Diary 15th Battery Motor Machine Gun Service, RFA.
    WO95/4038-3, War Diary of the Marseilles Base Commandant.
    WO95/5392, War Diary Kohat-Kurram Force: Force Troops: 22 Motor Machine Gun Battery (1919 May–Aug).
    WO95/5392, War Diary Kohat-Kurram Force: Force Troops: Commandant KURRAM Militia (1919 Apr–July).
    WO329 WWI Service Medal and Award Rolls.
    WO363, Service Papers 32556 Gunner Claude Henry Briance.
    WO374/20520, Officers Services 2/Lieutenant Alexander Morrison DOWIE, Machine Gun Corps.
    WO 374/73106, Officers Services Lieutenant William WELSH. The Highland Light Infantry.
    WO364, British Army WWI Pension Records 1914–1920, Piece: 2046.

Published Sources

Army Headquarters India, *Indian Army List January 1919* (Uckfield: Naval & Military Press, reprinted 2001).

Army Headquarters India, General Staff Branch, *Third Afghan War 1919 Official Account* (Uckfield: Naval & Military Press, 2004 reprint of original 1926 edition).

Carragher, Michael, *San Fairy Ann? Motorcycles and British Victory 1914–1918* (Brighton: FireStep Press, 2013).

Chenevix Trench, Charles, *The Frontier Scouts* (London: Jonathan Cape, 1986).

Crutchley, C. E., *Machine Gunner 1914–1918, Personal Experiences of the Machine Gun Corps* (Barnsley: Pen & Sword Books, reprinted 2013).

Disorders Inquiry Committee, *Evidence taken before the Disorders Inquiry Committee* (Calcutta: Superintendent Government Printing, 1920).

Fletcher, David, *War Cars* (London: HMSO, 1987).

Gregg, Martin, *War Bike: British Military Motorcycling 1899–1919* (Lulu, 2015).

Macro, Paul, *Action at Badama Post* (Oxford: Casemate, 2019).

Molesworth, Lieut-Gen G.N., *Afghanistan 1919* (London: Asia Publishing House, 1962).

Moreman, T.M., *The Army in India and the Development of Frontier Warfare, 1849–1947* (Basingstoke: Palgrave Macmillan, 1998).

Popplewell, Richard J., *Intelligence and Imperial Defence: British Intelligence and the Defence of the Indian Empire 1904–1924* (Oxford: Routledge, 1995).

Robson, Brian, *Crisis on the Frontier, The Third Afghan War and the Campaign in Waziristan 1919–20* (Staplehurst: Spellmount, 2007).

Online Resources

Ancestry, at <https://www.ancestry.co.uk/>.

Families in British India Society (FIBIS) Wiki, at <https://wiki.fibis.org>.

Machine Gun Corps Old Comrades Association, at <http://www.machinegun-corps.co.uk./>.

The Balochi Linguist, at <https://balochilinguist.wordpress.com/>.

The Great War (1914-1918) Forum, at <https://www.greatwarforum.org/>.

The Long, Long Trail, at <https://www.longlongtrail.co.uk/>.

Newspapers and Magazines

The Gazette, London.
The Motor Cycle, London.
The Globe, London.
Coventry Evening Telegraph, Coventry.

10

Invasion, Liberation and Occupation: British Soldiers' Wartime Encounters in Sicily

Fabio Simonetti

Introduction

In 1940, when Britain faced possible defeat and the *Wehrmacht* had started to subdue much of Europe, an Italian anti-British comic radio programme written by Michele Galdieri and entitled *Radiopanzane* ('Radiononsense') broadcast a parody of Radio Londra – the BBC's Italian-language broadcasts – and its war bulletins. In a letter to his nanny posted from Italy, a fictitious British war correspondent described an imaginary landing in Sicily:

> I write you, my dear nanny, / from the shores of Italy / where our ships / are landing at any moment. / When we landed in Sicily / every head of the family / from its deserted coasts / was waiting for us open-armed. / As soon as we got down / they took us arm in arm / and to us they have been / so good, so grateful![1]

At that time, the show was meant to be a hilarious send-up of the British propaganda appeal to the Italian people to rebel against the fascist government that had dragged the country into the war. In one of his speeches, on 23 February 1941, Mussolini also gave his own verdict on the likelihood of a successful British invasion:

---

1 Aurelio Lepre, *L'occhio del Duce. Gli italiani e la censura di guerra, 1940-1943* (Milan: Mondadori, 1997), p.175. All quotations from Italian language sources have been translated by the author.

> In order to defeat the Axis, the armies of Great Britain should land in the continent, invade Germany and Italy, defeat their armies; and no Englishman, however mad and delirious from the use and abuse of drugs and alcohol, can even dream of this.[2]

On 10 July 1943, memories of these instances must have rung hollow when the paradoxical situations imagined at the beginning of the war became a reality. On that day, following their victory in North Africa, aided by the United States and the other Allied nations, the British successfully landed in Sicily. The fascist parody, in fact, unintentionally foreshadowed by three years both the Italian soldiers' defection on the shores of Sicily and the largely welcoming attitude of the civilians towards the arrival of the Allied soldiers. Some of the best-known photographs of the encounter between the Allies and the Italian civilians in Sicily reproduce almost exactly the grateful and benevolent attitude of the locals imagined by Galdieri. On many occasions the Allied photographers captured overjoyed Sicilians kissing and hugging soldiers, while the symbol of the successful campaign soon became Robert Capa's photograph of an elderly Sicilian who indicates the way with his stick to a young American soldier who listens carefully. The evident intention of these photos, which were probably staged, is to represent the first phase of the invasion of Italy – at that time an enemy country and a key component of the Axis alliance with Nazi Germany – as a 'liberation' and a 'co-operative venture' between the Allies and the Italians.[3]

The ambiguous use of the term 'liberation' in the context of the invasion of Sicily was first introduced by the Allies themselves. The vast Allied propaganda campaign towards Italy aimed to prepare for the landing of the soldiers on Sicilian shores by inducing the Italians to consider them as 'liberators'.[4] Under the circum-

---

2   Edoardo and Duilio Susmel, *Opera Omnia di Benito Mussolini. Dall'intervento dell'Italia nella Seconda guerra mondiale al discorso al Direttorio Nazionale del P.N.F. del 3 gennaio 1942 (11 giugno 1940-3 gennaio 1942)*, vol.XXX (Florence: La Fenice, 1960), p.57.

3   See Robert S.C. Gordon, 'Adano: Sicily, Occupation Literature, and the American Century', in *ISLG Bulletin: The Annual Newsletter of the Italian Studies Library Group*, 17 (2018), pp.3-23 (pp.12-13); Tommaso Baris, 'La memoria della Seconda guerra mondiale nel Mezzogiorno d'Italia' in *Italia e le sue regioni. L'età repubblicana. Culture* (Rome: Istituto della Enciclopedia italiana, 2015), pp.331-350.

4   On the British propaganda towards Italy see, among the works available, Maura Piccialuti Caprioli, *Radio Londra (1940-1945). Inventario delle trasmissioni per l'Italia* (Rome: Ministero per i Beni Culturali e Ambientali, 1976); Ester Lo Biundo, *London Calling Italy: La propaganda di Radio Londra nel 1943* (Milan: Unicopli, 2014); Ester Lo Biundo, 'Voices of Occupiers/Liberators: The BBC's Radio Propaganda in Italy between 1942 and 1945', in *Journal of War and Culture Studies*, 9 (2016), pp.60-73; Ilaria Favretto and Oliviero Bergamini, '"Temperamentally Unwarlike": The Image of Italy in the Allies' War Propaganda, 1943-1945', in Mark Connelly and David Welch (eds.), *War and the Media: Reportage and Propaganda* (London-New York: I.B. Tauris, 2005), pp.112-126; and Mario Bussoni, *Radio Londra. Voci dalla libertá* (Fidenza: Mattioli, 2017). Large collections of British propaganda leaflets disseminated in Italy are available at the Library Department of the Imperial War Museum (IWM) and at The National Archives (TNA), Kew.

stances, the war-wary Sicilians grew more receptive to such rhetoric and viewed the 'liberation' as an emancipation from the suffering inflicted by the war and the dictatorship.[5] Significantly, in the Allied plan the landings represented the moment when their propaganda switched from – in the words of a British Foreign Office directive – a 'hard' to a 'soft line'. With this transformation, the Allies set aside their threats towards Italy in favour of promises aiming at 'holding out some ray of hope to the Italians about their future'.[6] The most important aspect of the 'switch' was the representation of the Allied armies 'in the guise *not* of conquerors but liberators'.[7] On the morning of 10 July 1943, the landings were accompanied by the distribution of millions of leaflets announcing to the Italian population that 'The Allied armies have landed on Italian soil ... AS LIBERATORS'.[8]

Undoubtedly, despite the authorities' concerns over the reception that the first Anglo-American soldiers would receive from the civilians of an enemy country, the Allies met with little or no resistance on the day of the invasion and during the Sicilian Campaign a significant section of the population showed a benevolent attitude towards them.[9] Yet, in December 1943, less than five months after the first encounter between soldiers and civilians, an Allied poll on the condition of the local population depicted a very different situation. Between November and December 1943, 70 trained Italian interviewers entered one house in every five in selected areas of Palermo, Messina, Catania and Caltanissetta and asked the population about their most pressing needs. Their questions ranged from the quality – and often the availability – of food, shelter, and clothing, to the trustworthiness of public officials and the safety of Sicilian towns.

> The overwhelming majority of people affirmed by 98% that public security had seriously deteriorated since one year ago. Rumours of crimes

5   See, among the many works available: Rosario Mangiameli, 'La regione in guerra (1943-1950)', in Maurice Aymard and Giuseppe Giarrizzo (eds.), *Storia d'Italia. Le regioni: la Sicilia* (Turin: Einaudi, 1987), pp.485-600; Marco Fincardi, 'Lo sbarco in Sicilia', in Mario Isnenghi (ed.), *Gli italiani in guerra. Conflitti, identità, memorie dal Risorgimento ai nostri giorni*, vol. IV: *Il Ventennio fascista: la Seconda guerra mondiale* (Torino: Utet, 2008), pp.234-241; Salvatore Lupo and Rosario Mangiameli (eds.), *Sicilia 1943* (Rome: Viella, 2015).

6   TNA, FO 371/37303: 'Operation HUSKY: propaganda'. Document dated 10 May 1943. At the beginning of May 1943, Anglo-American strategists agreed to use their 'propaganda weapon' – the 'switch' from a hard to a soft line – immediately before, rather than after, the landings, to aid military operation. FO 371/37303: 'Propaganda plan for Italy', 6 May 1943. See also: FO 898/349 and CAB 121/587.

7   TNA, FO 371/37303: 'Operation HUSKY: propaganda'. Document dated 10 May 1943. Highlighted in text.

8   IWM, LBY K. 84/2580-3: 'Soldati d'Italia!'. Highlighted in text. A few days after the landing, the concept of the 'liberation' was used again by Eisenhower in an official message to the Italian people after the fall of Mussolini, on 26 July 1943: 'We are coming to you as liberators'. TNA, FO 371/37263B.

9   See Tommaso Baris, 'Lo sbarco alleato tra storia e memoria', in Lupo and Mangiameli (eds.), *Sicilia 1943*, pp.59-83.

circulated freely … This caused much nervousness and sharpened the traditional reluctance of Sicilians to wander freely from their hearts, so that nearly everyone is now afraid to go out at night, and many by day. … [T]he belief that danger lurks for whoever wanders abroad is endemic in Sicily.[10]

The escalation of bombing raids in the summer of 1943, the collapse of the food supply chain, the passage of the war throughout the island, and the establishment of the Allied occupation had left indelible marks on the Sicilian population. The poll also highlighted a further significant element in the quick deterioration of the relationship between the Italians and the Allies: the disillusionment caused by the behaviour of the soldiers. For the Sicilians, after years of propaganda promises, the arrival of the Allies had initiated a loathed foreign occupation, and their forced cohabitation with the soldiers had rapidly become a burden. How could the idyllic relationship between soldiers and civilians portrayed by war correspondents at the time of their first encounter transform so swiftly? What were the main factors behind this change? Was the narrative of the 'liberation' telling the whole story of this wartime encounter?[11]

In the public narrative of the events, the arrival of the Allies in Sicily is generally represented as a 'non-battle', a bloodless landing culminating in towns and villages filled with civilians happily welcoming their enemies in their own home country.[12] Within this stereotypical representation, memories of invasion merge with and disappear into liberation accounts: while the Allied soldiers were depicted in the act of giving out chocolate and cigarettes to overjoyed civilians, people living in the areas just captured by the Allies were celebrating the end of a long struggle. Despite the absence of an existing military occupation in Sicily at the time of the invasion, the representation of the arrival of the Allies appears similar to other conventional Second World War liberation narratives from other parts of Italy and Europe.[13]

10   TNA, FO 898/172: 'Survey of Public Opinion Held in Sicily', November 1943-January 1944.

11   Nowadays, the terminology used to commemorate the landing in Sicily often comprises the word 'libera-tion' and refers to the event as to the 'beginning of the liberation of Italy' from Nazi-fascism. See, for example: 'Sicilia 10 luglio: 77° Anniversario dell'inizio della Liberazione in Italia', <https://anpisicilia. wordpress.com/2020/07/09/sicilia-10-luglio-77-anniversario-dellinizio-della-liberazione-in-italia/>, accessed 18 February 2022.

12   See Nicola Gallerano, 'L'arrivo degli Alleati', in Mario Isnenghi (ed.), I luoghi della memoria. Strutture ed eventi dell'Italia unita (Rome-Bari: Laterza, 1997), pp.455-464 (p.459); Baris, 'Lo sbarco alleato', pp.61-62; and Rosario Mangiameli, 'Sicilia 1943: Immagini e rappresentazioni di una sconfitta tra politica, storio-grafia e mercato', in Lupo and Mangiameli (eds.), Sicilia 1943, pp.85-108.

13   See, for example, Hilary Footitt, War and Liberation: Living with the Liberators (Basingstoke: Palgrave Macmillan, 2004), p.11; and Peter Schrijvers, The Crash of Ruin: American Combat Soldiers in Europe during World War II (Basingstoke: Macmillan, 1998), p.265.

In recent decades, the emergence of an extensive number of memories by both soldiers and civilians has challenged the pre-established Liberation 'script'. As the focus of the historians has moved to a more realistic and complex appraisal of the war, a conflict made by real people, with and without uniforms, and understood as individuals, a new, multifaceted appraisal of war events led historian David Ellwood to write about the overlooked 'trauma of liberation'.[14] In line with the biographical turn that in the last decades has involved not only history but social sciences in general, multidisciplinary studies of wartime encounters aim to analyse how war shapes the sphere of human relations. By shifting the focus away from the battlefields, the centre of the discourse becomes the transnational clash of cultures that takes place in war zones, when people thrown together by the circumstances of war come face to face.

While historians have so far dedicated more attention to the experience of American – and Italian-American – soldiers in Italy, this chapter aims to focus on the often marginalised evolution of the British soldiers' perception of their encounter with Italian civilians in Sicily during the Second World War Allied occupation of the island.[15] By using autobiographical sources such as diaries, letters, memoirs and oral history interviews, I intend to demonstrate that while the indisputable but simplistic version of events depicting the idyllic encounter between soldiers and civilians certainly contains elements of truth, a deeper examination of individual recollections and official documentation reveals that mistrust, resentment and hatred also shaped truthful experiences. Yet, to reconstruct the evolution of the soldier-civilian relationship in the perceived contexts of invasion, liberation, and occupation it is necessary to go back to the first encounter. On the early morning of 10 July 1943, off the coast of Sicily.

Invasion: The Beachhead Clash

Mount Etna, 'a muntagna for the Sicilians, is the highest volcano in Europe and was the first part of the island visible to British soldiers on the invasion ships. On the evening of 9 July 1943, the Allied armies were about to invade Italy in an attempt to gain the initiative in the war against the Axis powers and bring the

---

14   See David Ellwood, 'The Trauma of Liberation: Rape, Love and Violence in Wartime Italy', in Patrizia Sambuco (ed.), *Transmissions of Memory: Echoes, Traumas, and Nostalgia in Post-World War II Italian Culture* (Vancouver: Farleigh Dickinson University Press, 2018), pp.125-142. See also Manoela Patti, *La Sicilia e gli Alleati. Tra occupazione e Liberazione* (Rome: Donzelli, 2013), p.64.

15   The subjects discussed in this article formed part of the author's AHRC CDP PhD research at the University of Reading and the IWM. This project was based on the study of a large corpus of autobiographical sources relating to the experience of British soldiers and Italian civilians during the Second World War. Fabio Simonetti, 'Encounters in Wartime Italy: British Soldiers and Italian Civilians, 1943-1944' (doctoral dissertation, University of Reading, 2021).

conflict to their home countries. Operation HUSKY would be the largest amphibious attack of the Second World War in terms of divisions involved; it mustered some 3,000 ships and landing crafts, and around 160,000 troops.[16]

The plan for Operation HUSKY involved troops of the American Seventh Army and the British Eighth Army, which also comprised Canadian, South African, Indian, New Zealand and Polish soldiers. The so-called 'Desert Army' had been formed in 1941 and had already captured attention thanks to the victorious outcome against Italian and German forces in the North African Campaign. On 10 July 1943, its soldiers were scheduled to land on 26 beaches along 105 miles of coast in south-east Sicily. Eighth Army landing beaches spread from Cape Passero up to just south of Syracuse, through Avola and the Gulf of Noto. According to the plan, once onshore each division had to push 10 to 30 miles inland to reduce the risk of artillery fire on newly captured coastal airfields.[17] The attack on Sicily, though, started before the landing crafts set sail for the Sicilian coast. On the night of 9 July, thousands of paratroopers were dropped over several vital road junctions and bridges all over south-east Sicily. The purpose of what would be the first ever large night airborne attack was to obstruct Axis counterattacks and give the soldiers time to move inland.[18]

War Office predictions of the outcome of the operation anticipated that the Italians would fight 'with much more determination' in defence of their homeland than they had done in North Africa.[19] However, when the landing happened, British soldiers often met with little or no resistance on the shores. In his memoir, David Fenner, of the 6th Battalion Durham Light Infantry, described how his landing craft landed on the wrong beach north of Avola under 'continuous but not very accurate' enemy fire.[20] In his account, Arthur Bastone, of the Corps of Military Police, recorded his uneventful landing on the Cape Passero peninsula:

> Running down the steep ramps ... we found that the water only came up to our knees, the ship had run aground on one of the many sand-bars in the bay. Then we realised that there was no gunfire, and our only problem was to wade ashore. We soon stepped off the edge of the sand-bar and the water was up to our shoulders but soon shallowed again as we struggled to

---

16   Rick Atkinson, *The Day of the Battle: The War in Sicily and Italy, 1943-1944* (London: Abacus, 2013), pp.52-55; Robin Neillands, *Eighth Army: From the Western Desert to the Alps, 1939-1945* (London: John Murray, 2004), p.253. The Allies landed seven divisions in Sicily, two more than the five involved in the Normandy landings, on 6 June 1944. On the planning of Operation HUSKY, see Ian Gooderson, *A Hard Way to Make a War: The Allied Campaign in Italy in the Second World War* (London: Conway, 2008), pp.39-79.

17   Atkinson, *The Day of the Battle*, p.69.

18   See Mike Peters, *Glider Pilots in Sicily* (Barnsley: Pen & Sword Military, 2012).

19   TNA, WO 220/260: 'Sicily invasion propaganda communiques'. Document dated 27 April 1943.

20   IWM, Documents.3854: Private papers of Colonel D.J. Fenner, p.2.

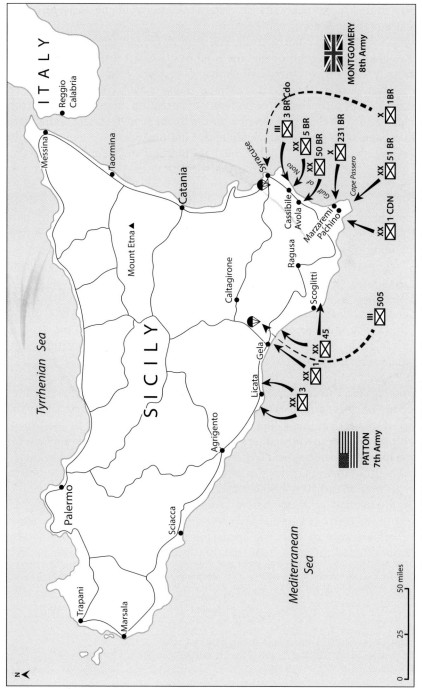

Operation HUSKY. Sicily, 10 July 1943. (Map by George Anderson, © Helion and Company 2022)

the shore. … The biggest danger was to fall and not be able to get up again without first shedding some gear.[21]

In that sector, British engineers on the beachhead quickly realised that most Italian potentially dangerous landmines were old and defective. War correspondent Christopher Buckley thought it 'a miracle' that an Allied landing in an obvious location such as Sicily 'would be so feebly opposed' by the enemy.[22] According to William Eves, an NCO who served with the Royal Army Medical Corps, 'it was a piece of cake, there was no attack, there was nothing'.[23]

However, in other sectors of the coast, the landing proved more hazardous, and the spirit of the soldiers appeared very different. Twenty-two-year-old seaman Kenneth Oakley landed under machine gun and sniper fire near Marina di Avola:

Suddenly a flare burst above us and surprise was lost, when we still had about a mile to go. The formation split up and began to make for their own landing places with fire from enemy machine guns passing over them.

Tat-Tat-Tat-Tat, Bren guns began to speak and then 'Crunch', 'Down Door' and we were there. A sapper began to cry, plead and cling to the floor-boards, swearing he would not move. We left him (his nerve was gone) and dived into about three feet of water to wade fifty yards to the shore. The shrill whine of bullets speeded us on and at last we went to earth at the water's edge. Bren guns engaged the enemy machine-guns and we began to take our bearings.[24]

Advancing British commandos soon silenced the Italian machine-gun fire and made the beach secure. Oakley, though, remained behind to help the following waves of soldiers coming ashore. An hour after the landing of the first men, the beach came under enemy artillery fire and when a landing craft was hit, killing many on board, panic spread. After having helped some wounded soldiers who were about to drown, Oakley, in considerable distress, fainted on the beach and was sent back to the ships off the coast to be looked after.

The dissolution of many Italian coastal divisions facilitated the capture of seaside towns such as Avola and Syracuse within the first 24 hours of the landings. The coastal defence of Sicily had been assigned to *Regio Esercito* battalions made of demoralised locals in the hope that they would defend their homes better than soldiers from other parts of the country. Such resolution did not prove effective. On the contrary, almost at the first sight of danger many local soldiers rushed

---

21   IWM, Documents.8601: Private papers of A.L. Bastone, pp.24-25 (1943).
22   Christopher Buckley, *Road to Rome* (London: Hodder and Stoughton, 1945), pp.33-34.
23   IWM, Sound 18676/11: William Eves.
24   IWM, Documents.6652: Private papers of K.G. Oakley, p.2.

home to protect their nearby families from the enemy. During the first hours of the battle for Sicily, one of the most unexpected sights for the invading troops was that of the masses of surrendering Italian soldiers. For Canadian war correspondent Lionel Shapiro, the Italian soldier's unwillingness 'to raise a rifle in defence of his homeland' after having 'fought hard and sometimes most effectively' in North Africa was 'the most fabulous circumstance in the tragedy of Italy' as well as a complete surprise to the troops.[25] Only in the Gulf of Gela, in the American sector, did troops meet with stiff Italian-German resistance.[26]

In the early morning of invasion day, the British moved inland and found themselves face to face with Italian civilians on Italian soil for the first time. The weapons in their hands inevitably shaped the nature of the first encounter with isolated civilians around the beachheads and immediately set the rules and hierarchies of this new, unbalanced, relationship. The helplessness and subjugation of the locals before the approaching soldiers were particularly evident when the encounter took place in the proximity of a battlefield. As soldiers found themselves advancing into unknown enemy territory, fear and diffidence embittered them. Their hostility had been moulded by three years of war against Italy and fuelled yet further during the tense lead-up to the invasion. During the planning for Operation HUSKY, the Allies codenamed Sicily 'Horrified', while the soldiers' password exchange on the field was 'Desert Rats – Kill the Italians'.[27] On 10 July 1943, the first encounter was not that between the cheering crowds and the triumphant soldiers perched on their vehicles, but the violent beachhead clash between terrified civilians and suspicious armed soldiers.

In the Avola sector, Fenner's platoon met an old Sicilian hunter who was cycling with his shotgun near the coast. He was the first civilian they had encountered, and the man appeared to be 'very shocked' by the sight of unknown foreign soldiers. Carrying on his path, after the sight of an abandoned glider in a field, Fenner entered a village. He noticed that the peasant population was mostly made of 'old or very young, who were terrified by us, pleading for mercy'.[28] In a later interview, Derek Thomlinson, another officer of the 6th Battalion Durham Light Infantry, recalled a similar experience with frightened civilians near Marina di Avola: 'I do remember people occupying a farm and what they did was... a very nice house but they took frightened and disappeared, ran off. So much so that they left all their food on the table and didn't do any action of clearing the place at all, they

25 Lionel Shapiro, *They Left the Back Door Open: A Chronicle of the Allied Campaign in Sicily and Italy* (London: Jarrolds, 1944), p.73.

26 For an analysis of the military events of 10 July on both British and US landing sectors, see: Carlo D'Este, *Bitter Victory: The Battle for Sicily, July-August 1943* (London: HarperCollins, 1988), pp.254-289, and James Holland, *Sicily '43: The First Assault on Fortress Europe* (London: Bantam Press, 2020).

27 Sandro Attanasio, *Gli anni della rabbia: Sicilia 1943-1947* (Milan: Mursia, 1984), p.26; Buckley, *Road to Rome*, p.33.

28 IWM, Documents.3854: Private papers of Colonel D.J. Fenner, p.3.

just ran'.[29] Early in the morning, Dunkirk veteran Private William Knowles was trying to link up with paratroopers who should have previously taken Avola's main square. However, the only people he saw during his wait in the middle of the night were some frightened, silent civilians: 'There was an Italian family standing at the door, watching us. It was like an ordinary street. Never said a word. I never said a word to them and they never said a word to me. Just looking, in the dark'.[30]

The encounter on and around the landing beaches happened 'on the run'.[31] Soldiers and locals initially met in the moving, transitory context of the troops' quick passage through towns and villages. In the recollections relating to the first hours of the invasion, the Italians' part was predominantly static, as they passively watched the activity and movement of the terrifying invading forces through the curtains of their windows. Conversely, the soldiers' perception was inevitably affected by their constant movement and advance, with no possibility to pay attention to the locals. Upon entering Sicilian towns for the first time, the feelings of the Eighth Army soldiers were well represented by the silent but triumphant parade described by Peter John Lovett, of the Royal Tank Regiment, who recorded that 'We passed through several rather bare stone towns, usually built on top of a hill, the people staring in mixed awe and intrigue at the novelty, while we drove down the streets standing up in the front truck, feeling like Caesar himself!'[32]

After spending a year on the North African front, war artist Edward Ardizzone managed to find a place among Eighth Army troops landing in Avola on 10 July 1943. Ardizzone would paint some of his finest works in Italy. In his wartime diary, the artist wrote that soldiers soon learnt to move around Sicilian ruined towns that smelled of dead bodies, 'a smell that haunts one everywhere'.[33] In a later interview, he also recorded the surreal atmosphere characterising newly captured towns, with the contrast between the deserted streets and the crowded interior of the houses. Soldiers walked among the ruins under the eyes of terrified women and among poor, barefoot children begging for food: 'you went up through these villages and could see all the women watching you, it was fascinating. You went through these quiet villages, you were being watched all the way. ... Behind the curtains. Whispering, you could hear the voices'.[34]

29   IWM, Sound 13360/8: Derek Edward Ingram Thomlinson.
30   IWM, Sound 16725/36: William Knowles.
31   I borrow the expression from Footitt, *War and Liberation*, pp.39, 48-49.
32   IWM, Documents.3060: Private papers of P.J. Lovett, p.164.
33   Edward Ardizzone, *Diary of a War Artist* (London: The Bodley Head, 1974), p.13.
34   IWM, Sound 4525/4: Edward Jeffrey Irving Ardizzone.

Liberation: Welcoming the Enemy?

As the front moved inland, the relationship between British soldiers and Italian civilians in the areas already under the control of the Allies eased with each passing hour, giving way to some of the most famous images of the Sicilians' welcoming reception of the Allies. With hindsight, referring to the initial frictions, Derek Thomlinson argued: 'that wasn't the general picture, … farming people were generally pleased to see us'.[35] Only when soldiers started to ease the tension of the attack did they focus on their surroundings for the first time. As servicemen put it in their private letters, after the long months spent in the desert the varied Sicilian landscape appeared to veterans of the North African campaign 'a pleasant place'.[36] George Iceton commented on the peculiarities of this part of Sicily:

> It was quite a lovely countryside, really, it was the first time I saw toma-
> toes growing flat on the ground. … You could just lay on the ground and
> pick anything you wanted. There's tomatoes, potatoes, vegetables, fruit,
> flowers. … And coming out of the hills there was quite a stream of very
> pretty young ladies [who were returning to Avola], but we didn't have
> much time to speak with them, unfortunately.[37]

Others focused on the war-weary local population. Sergeant Blyth wrote in his memoir: 'We passed through the ruins of towns and villages which had been heavily shelled: people, homeless, pathetically trudging the roads aimlessly with their reality of war – the terrible affliction to these misled people'.[38] Soldiers appeared horrified by the shortages suffered by the Sicilians: 'The poverty here is simply appalling and the starving kiddies terrible to see, we never really knew what the horrors of war can do'.[39] When an old Sicilian woman stretched her hands to David Cole and whispered 'Viva Inglesi', he 'thought uncomfortably of the Eighth Army challenge – "Desert Rats" for which the password was "Killing Italians"'.[40]

Personal letters intercepted by the British censorship in the days after the invasion offer an invaluable window over the soldiers' perception of Sicily and the Sicilians. Significantly, the invasion and the civilian population was the most discussed subject.[41] The curiosity shown by the British towards the 'otherness'

---

35   IWM, Sound 13360/8.
36   TNA, WO 204/10381: 'British North African Force. Appreciation & Censorship Report' (BNAF, A&CR) no. 27, 1-15 August 43.
37   IWM, Sound 11938/50: George Edward Iceton.
38   IWM, Documents.14772: Private papers of W.F.H. Blyth, p.2.
39   TNA, WO 204/10381: 'BNAF, A&CR' no. 27, 1-15 August 43.
40   David Cole, *Rough Road to Rome: A Foot-Soldier in Sicily and Italy, 1943-1944* (London: William Kimber, 1983), p.23.
41   TNA, WO 204/10381: 'BNAF, A&CR' no. 27, 1-15 August 43.

of the Italians demonstrates the importance many posed towards intercultural encounters. Soldiers dwelled on the surprising welcome the locals reserved them as well as on the impressive generosity and hospitality they experienced at their arrival – a subject that characterised some of the main *topoi* of the Allied presence in Italy:

> The streets were lined with cheering crowds giving us the V sign and, as we reached the outskirt of town, we met a bunch of prisoners who were cheering us harder than the civvies were – just shows how pleased the Itis are to get finished with the war.

> Can say I have had my washing done by a Sicilian woman, wouldnt [sic] take anything for it, but loaded us with figs fresh from the trees.

> The civilians are very friendly and as we pass through the villages most of them give us the V sign. … The soldiers have been very good to the locals; as they pass through they give them biscuits and bully. You feel sorry for them, especially the old folks, but such is the war, and it is very pleasant travelling here, a change from the desert when it was nothing but sand.[42]

Before the end of the first day of the invasion, Christopher Buckley depicted an idyllic picture of the relationship established between the British soldiers – who showed their 'prosaic gentleness which is so characteristic of them where civilians are concerned' – and the people of Marzamemi: 'I saw them drawing water at the well of a little cottage …. I saw them paying out [occupation] *lire* for tomatoes and eggs at exactly the rate demanded by the cottager. They had not been onshore above twelve hours yet'. On the following day, he wrote of how pleased he was to see 'for the first time, our men being received as liberators by the population of an allegedly hostile country'; a 'stimulating and profoundly stirring' sight for him.[43]

However, the same sources provide several hints able to tell a completely different story to the historian willing to embrace a more complex, multifaceted, and realistic depiction of the encounter. Despite the largely positive reception they had received, some soldiers still distrusted the Sicilians and noticed worrying signs of hostility: 'The natives… seem to be very friendly, clapping their hands and giving the V sign, but I suppose they would just as leave put a knife in your back as not'.[44] Others noticed resentment in specific sections of the population:

---

42   TNA, WO 204/10381: 'BNAF, A&CR' no. 27, 1-15 August 43.
43   Buckley, *Road to Rome*, pp.39, 41.
44   TNA, WO 204/10381: 'BNAF, A&CR' no. 27, 1-15 August 43.

In nearly all the towns we were greeted heartidly [sic] and if it wasnt [sic] sincere, then it was damned good acting. The young folks and the men were all cheers for us, but I could notice a look of constraint and hatred in the faces of the old women, I could imagine and guess how that was though – they had sons and husbands whom we were killing and taking prisoners – could you blame them.[45]

Major General Francis Rodd, 2nd Baron Rennell, was considered an expert in Italian affairs and, although he and other members of his family were suspected of having been somewhat favourable to the rise of Mussolini and his fascist regime, he was appointed Chief Civil Affairs Officer (CCAO) of Sicily. Rodd reached Sicily on 22 July and established his headquarters in Syracuse before to move to Palermo.[46] In the summer of 1943, he wrote two detailed reports on the evolution of the situation in Sicily providing precious information on the Sicilians' changing attitude towards the Allies. The first document, written on 3 August, offers a very positive judgment of the impact of the arrival of the Allied soldiers on the locals. Rodd argued that from 'the very outset the attitude of the population generally has been friendly. In certain areas and on particular occasions the population has been definitely enthusiastic'. He had been particularly impressed 'by the absence of expressed resentment or bitterness about bombing or civilian casualties' and considered 'genuine' the widespread anti-fascist feeling demonstrated by the people at the perspective of the party's dismantling. Yet, on the same occasion, Rodd expressed some concerns regarding the behaviour of the Allied soldiers in Sicily and suggested that 'general directions to all ranks regarding their behaviour on occupying a country should be issued before any operation'.[47]

Less than a month later, Francis Rodd submitted a new report that was also judged as 'very satisfactory on the whole'. Alongside the rise of the Sicilian separatist movement and the resurgence of Mafia activity, however, Rodd highlighted a new important issue, arguing that 'there has been a considerable change in public feeling'. On the one hand, he confirmed some of the judgments made in his first report: 'The Sicilian has remained friendly and generally has accepted the consequence of invasion with fair grace'. On the other, he warned that the population 'is already complaining that food is not available, that railways and telecommunications do not work, and that a new administration has not replaced the old one'. The

45   TNA, WO 204/10381: 'BNAF, A&CR' no. 27, 1-15 August 43.
46   Philip Boobbyer, *The Life and World of Francis Rodd, Lord Rennell (1895-1978): Geography, Money and War* (London: Anthem Press, 2021), pp.89, 95-96, 164, 167, 181. On Francis Rodd's experience in Italy, see also: Francis Rodd, 'Allied Military Government in Occupied Territory', *International Affairs*, 20.3, July (1944), pp.307-16; Francis Rodd, 'Foreword', in Robert Gayre, *Italy in Transition: Extracts from the Private Journal of G.R. Gayre* (London: Faber and Faber Limited, 1946), pp.7-16.
47   TNA, FO 371/37326: 'Situation – Sicily', first report by Francis Rodd, pp.2-4.

increasing antagonism developing between soldiers and civilians emerges in the unexpected tone Rodd used to open his second report:

> Since my arrival in Sicily, I have to report a substantial change in public sentiment. From being, and adopting the attitude of, whipped dogs or fawning puppies immediately after the landing of the Allied troops, the Sicilians, of all classes, have reacted. They seem to me again to be becoming thinking, emotional and definite human beings.
>
> As a whole they accepted the Allies as liberators. They have not ceased to do. As a whole they are still friendly and anti-Fascist. They have been perhaps somewhat disillusioned by the behaviour of the Allied troops, ... but they have not as yet displayed resentment. Superficially they are no doubt aware that the advent of the Allied troops has not meant a reign of plenty ... They have been disappointed and impatient at the delay in completing the conquest of the island. ... The 'Liberation' propaganda and the innate Anti-fascism of the Sicilian has led him to regard himself almost as quasi Ally. The consequences of not so being treated may be more serious. From an attitude of fawning the Sicilian has begun to ask, and in the larger centres to demand.[48]

Occupation: The Impossible Cohabitation

The Sicilians had been the first people in Europe to experience the ephemeral joy provided by the arrival of the Allied armies. Disillusionment at the beginning of their military occupation, in fact, spread rapidly among the people living under the authority of the Allied Military Government of Occupied Territories (AMGOT, later shortened to AMG).[49] Locals did not take long to understand that the touted 'reign of plenty' the pre-invasion Allied propaganda had induced them to hope for would not materialise in the short term. With time, the impossibility of the new authorities to carry out rapid improvements to the island's precarious food supply situation hampered their efforts to win the trust of the locals. The Sicilians' frustration towards the Allies' decision to maintain the loathed system of the *ammassi* – the bread-grain and olive oil collection and storage system used by the fascist regime – and the unsuccessful handling of the task of de-fascistising the local administration added to the widespread problems of reconstruction,

---

48   TNA, FO 371/37326: 'Situation – Sicily', second report by Francis Rodd, p.1. Undated document written before 20 August 1943.

49   See Charles R.S. Harris, *Allied Military Administration of Italy, 1943-1945* (London: HMSO, 1957).

unemployment, inflation, strict rationing, and the persistent lack of housing and clothing.[50] As for the epuration process, war correspondent Alan Moorehead put it simply: 'If we sacked the existing Fascist bosses [the CAO] found he had no one capable of taking their place'. This issue affected essential services such as the clearance of debris from the streets or the re-opening of hospitals, schools, and banks. As Moorehead concluded, most of the times if the Allied authorities wanted 'to get this job done', the only choice was to re-hire the former 'fascist official' who knew how to do it. Inevitably, solutions of this kind always left Italians doubtful 'since they had believed we were fighting on their side'.[51]

Leslie Mewis, of the Royal Army Service Corps, witnessed the deterioration of the civilians' feelings towards the Allies and blamed the failures of the AMG:

> The political set up in Allied occupied Italy has steadily deteriorated since the first landings. The Allies came after many propaganda promises of the virtue of the Freedom that was to come. Fascism, said the Allies, would be utterly eradicated … . The first shock came with the recognition of the Badoglio government, which was quite alien to the interests and aspirations of the Italian workers and peasants. The removal of Fascist officials […] was strangely ineffective since people were able to recognise Fascist officials in their original positions in various towns. […] Food prices rose alarmingly, and the workers who remained at their pre-invasion posts did not receive any increase of salary to compensate for the rapid rise in the cost of living. The price of defeat was indeed heavy – falling almost entirely upon the workers and peasants.[52]

However, according to the Survey of Public Opinion carried out by the Allies in December 1943 and quoted at beginning of this article, in many cases it was the behaviour of the soldiers themselves that had greatly contributed to making the local communities feel like an occupied mass at the mercy of their conquerors. According to historian Mirco Dondi, who studied post-war violence and criminality in Italy, soldiers who practised illicit activities in contexts of war zones, or

---

50 In the first years of the war, the increasingly precarious condition of the population had led the Sicilians to devise sophisticated ways of dodging the *ammassi* system, then simply re-named *granai del popolo* ['people's granaries'] by the Allies. When the new authorities realised that the system had already 'broken down' before the invasion it was already too late. In September 1943, they estimated that in the previous year the Italian government had failed to collect six-sevenths of the estimated crop. TNA, WO 204/2589: 'Sicily: political and economic'. Report by Henry T. Rowell dated 17 September 1943. See Cinzia Spingola, 'Crisi alimentare e problemi di ordine pubblico in Sicilia nel secondo dopoguerra', in Nicola Gallerano (ed.), *L'altro dopoguerra. Roma e il Sud, 1943-1945* (Milan: Franco Angeli, 1985), pp.341-54 (p.348); and Isobel Williams, *Allies and Italians under Occupation: Sicily and Southern Italy, 1943-45* (Basingstoke: Palgrave Macmillan, 2013), pp.118-121.

51 Alan Moorehead, *Eclipse* (London: Hamish Hamilton, 1946), p.46.

52 IWM, Documents.23386: Private papers of L.H. Mewis, p.155.

who did not respect basic civil rules of pacific coexistence, were predominantly animated by 'the victors' presumption of the impunity'.[53] Combined with the unbalanced power relationship and the loosening of moral and ethical refrains characteristic of the environment created by occupation, some soldiers developed that 'predatory' behaviour that was typical of some servicemen in Italy. After all, violence was an integral component of the soldier's trade.

Criminal behaviour was also fuelled by the recrudescence of local common violence and delinquency typical of the aftermath of conflict and transitional periods between war and peace. Both in parallel and response to the attitude of the soldiers, in fact, Italian micro and macro-criminality also grew, enhanced by factors such as the political and institutional vacuum, the economic and unemployment crisis, the widespread availability of weapons, the violent mentality endorsed by the war and – finally – the frustration about the defeat and the occupation. These circumstances created the atmosphere of lawlessness and chronic insecurity glimpsed by the Allied survey and confirmed by the impressive volume of files held at Italian and British archives concerning the soldiers' and locals' war against each other in Italian cities.

At the beginning of August 1943, CCAO Francis Rodd suggested leaving troops to stand guard with the appointed CAOs in Sicilian towns 'to restrain troops from looting, of which' – he wrote – 'there is an inordinate amount prevalent here'.[54] As the Battle for Sicily reached its end, with the capture of Messina on 17 August 1943, the gravity of the issue escalated until, at the end of the month, the War Office warned about unruly soldiers and the 'seriousness of the crimes of looting, stealing, and causing wilful damage to lives and property'.[55] Most episodes of looting involving Eighth Army troops had taken place when soldiers first entered war-torn Sicilian towns. The diary written by Educational Adviser Robert Gayre proves that the situation was growing out of control: in 'Messina our 8th Army which has borne itself so magnificently in the fighting and saved us [in] Egypt, has behaved disgracefully, looting and raping'. Gayre mentioned in his charge 'Canadians, Scots, Irish as well as English' soldiers'. According to the officer, in these circumstances 'democracy is in danger of becoming a laughing stock'. Soon after soldiers entered Palermo, Gayre recalled that people were already making up verses: 'When we said *Buon Giorno* we had bread, now that we say "Good-bye" we starve'.[56]

---

53   Mirco Dondi, *La lunga liberazione. Giustizia e violenza nel dopoguerra italiano* (Rome: Editori Riuniti, 2004), p.82. On British soldiers' wartime criminal activity, see the works by Clive Emsley, *Exporting British Policing during the Second World War: Policing Soldiers and Civilians* (London: Bloomsbury, 2017), and *Soldier, Sailor, Beggarman, Thief: Crime and the British Armed Services since 1914* (Oxford: Oxford University Press, 2013).

54   TNA, FO 371/37326: 'Extracts from a letter from Lord Rennell to Col. French dated 3 August, 1943', p.1.

55   TNA, WO 204/6712: 'Wilful Damage and Looting', 30 August 1943.

56   Gayre, *Italy in Transition*, pp.41, 98.

The landings in Sicily set in motion a chain of crucial events that further complicated the Italians' position within the network of war alliances. On 19 July 1943,
only nine days after the invasion, Rome, the capital city that had been so far spared
by most war devastation, was hit for the first time by a heavy bombing that deeply
shook its population. Less than a week later, on 25 July, at a meeting of the *Gran
Consiglio del Fascismo* some of the main fascist personalities turned their backs on
Mussolini with a motion calling King Vittorio Emanuele III to resume full military powers.[57] The *duce* was arrested the following day and replaced by Marshal
Pietro Badoglio, the general who led Mussolini's armies to victory in Ethiopia. Yet,
while the population throughout the country celebrated the long-awaited fall of the
regime and hoped for the end of the conflict, in an attempt to reassure the feared
German ally of Italy's loyalty the new government promptly announced that the
war would continue on the Axis' side. At the same time, Badoglio secretly began
peace negotiations with the Allies that concluded at the beginning of September.[58]

On that occasion, the southeast coast of Sicily was again the setting for the
unfolding of crucial events for the future of Italy. On 3 September 1943, in the
temporary headquarters set up by the Allies in the countryside near Cassibile,
representatives of the Italian government secretly signed an armistice between
Italy and the Allied forces. While American General Walter Bedell Smith and
Italian General Giuseppe Castellano were signing the armistice, the British were
crossing the Straits of Messina, bringing the war back to continental Europe.

In the weeks that followed, the nature of the encounter became even more
complex and developed according to the rapid evolution of the war and the diplomatic choices made by both the Allied and the new Italian government. On 8
September 1943, the Allies publicly broadcast the news of the armistice; soon after,
on 13 October, Italy declared war on Germany. Following these crucial events, the
British and the Italians officially ceased to be enemies; furthermore, the unprecedented and ambiguous status of 'co-belligerent' abruptly promoted the Italians to
quasi-ally status. After the armistice, Christopher Buckley wrote that the country
was then 'in spirit' an ally of the British.[59] But how did soldiers in the field take the
evolution of diplomatic relations between the two countries?

The apparent haste with which the Italian authorities had rejected their war
alliance with Germany once the situation had become hopeless had made it more
difficult for the British to believe in the Italians' candour. A strong change in the
British soldiers' behaviour was noted especially after the October 1943 controversial announcement of Italy's new co-belligerent status in the war against Germany.
The ambiguity of this compromise solution was soon discredited even by the

---

57   On the fall of Mussolini, see: Emilio Gentile, *25 luglio 1943* (Rome-Bari: Laterza, 2018).

58   Elena Aga Rossi, *Una nazione allo sbando. 8 settembre 1943* (Bologna: Il Mulino, 2003), pp.9, 25; David
     Ellwood, *Italy 1943-1945* (Leicester: Leicester University Press, 1985), pp.37-42.

59   Buckley, *Road to Rome*, p.164.

Foreign Office, which described it as 'trying to treat the Italians as friends and foes at the same time'.[60] The repercussions of this decision on the soldiers' attitude were clearly visible in their letters. According to the censor, the news – 'definitely unwelcome to the great majority of British troops who seem to despise the Italians more and more as they get to know them better'[61] – led to 'a marked anti-Italian reaction' based on the contempt for their 'about-face policy' in the war.[62]

Private Helm, a British veteran of the Sicily landings, reported in his memoir an anecdote that offers a significant example of how the relationship between soldiers and civilians had suddenly changed as soon as the news of the armistice had spread: 'an Italian army officer approached me and said "We are friends now aren't we? Will you give me a cigarette?" I told him to go away'.[63] At that point, British soldiers started wondering whom the Italians were siding with and looked at them with contempt: 'I don't know which side the Italians were supposed to be on' – a soldier wrote in a letter – 'They don't have anything to do with the Jerries (or rather vice versa) and some of them were shouting, "Berlin, 6 months, Tommy!". They were quite peeved when we replied, "Rome, 3 months!"'.[64]

The short-sighted choices of the Allied governments and the irresponsibility shown by the Italian political and military classes in managing the war, the surrender, and what many saw as an opportunistic declaration of war against Germany, deeply altered the nature of the encounter.[65] As long as soldiers perceived the Italians as enemies and victims of the reckless acts of Mussolini they seemed able to empathise with their troubles. However, when they found them standing on their side, the initially positive impression gathered from their letters gave way to hostile remarks contaminated by strong racist connotations:

> What do you think of Italy throwing in the towel – yellow rats, they can't even defend their own country the Jerry at least puts up a fight – candidly I am sorry he packed in first of all we can't loot any more [sic] and secondly they think they are our pals.[66]

> So the Italians have changed their line now and joined us! They are all smiles and cheer you when you ride along but I have nothing but contempt for them. What a people, to join with Germany and stab France in the

---

60   Ellwood, *Italy 1943-1945*, p.71.
61   TNA, WO 204/10381: 'A&CR' no. 33, 1-15 Nov 43. Part I – Troops in Italy.
62   TNA, WO 204/10381: 'A&CR' no. 32, 16-31 Oct 43. Part I – Troops in Sicily & Italy.
63   IWM, Documents.543: Private papers of D.O. Helm, p.64.
64   TNA, WO 204/10381: 'A&CR' no. 25, 1-15 July 43.
65   For a documented analysis of the secret negotiations between the Badoglio government and the Allies as well as the events that preceded and followed the signing of the armistice, see Aga Rossi, *Una nazione allo sbando*, pp.84-186.
66   TNA, WO 204/10381: 'A&CR' no. 30, 16-30 Sep 43. Part I – Troops in Sicily and Italy.

back and then put up a poor fight against us, and when they are licked turn round and fight for us against their old ally – I figure they are a detriment and not an asset to anybody.[67]

For all their sociability I cannot say I particularly care for or respect the Ities, for the men are a dirty scrounging yellow set of bastards and I can prove all these epithets, not to mention that they are robbing thieving blighters, by incidents [sic]. You will guess that I don't particularly care for them, even if they have some lovely women, many of whom will oblige you with a dose.[68]

The civilians' cheerfulness that had impressed the soldiers on their first encounter was now perceived as deceiving, selfish and inappropriate. Soldiers paradoxically portrayed themselves as exploited as they believed they were fighting to liberate Italy from Nazi-fascism while the Italians expected to be fed and seemed not to care about the ongoing conflict:

The people here seem to be rather enjoying the occupation. I think they regard it as a great free gift scheme for asking food and hitch-hikes in fact, Social Reform over-night.[69]

These Italians have sure surprised us with the simple attitude and manner they have accepted their defeat. I expected to find a very sullen and dis-spirited nation, but on the contrary they are quite happy, rather confident of themselves and determined that now Musso cant [sic] look after them we must![70]

Further analysis of the rapid deterioration of the relationship between the British and the Italians revealed that soldiers newly arrived in Italy did not seem to carry with them any anti-Italian prejudice. On the contrary, they focused almost unanimously on the favourable impression given by the friendliness of the locals, still considered 'people suffering for the sins of their Fascist rulers'. The inevitable conclusion was that it was after 'further acquaintance' with the Italians that a considerable deterioration of the favourable first impression would become visible. In their letters home, soldiers started to describe locals as 'dirty, lazy, treacherous and avaricious'. According to the war censor, the phrase 'little better than Wogs' often recurred in British correspondence.[71]

---

67   TNA, WO 204/10381: 'A&CR' no. 32, 16-31 Oct 43. Part I – Troops in Sicily & Italy.
68   TNA, WO 204/10381: 'A&CR' no. 35, 16-31 Dec 43. Part A – British Troops in Italy.
69   TNA, WO 204/10381: 'A&CR' no. 29, 1-15 Sep 43. Part I – Troops in Sicily.
70   TNA, WO 204/10381: 'A&CR' no. 32, 16-31 Oct 43. Part I – Troops in Sicily & Italy.
71   TNA, WO 204/10381: 'A&CR' no. 38, 1-15 Feb 44. Part A – British Troops in Italy.

A noticeable feature in the soldiers' considerations is the demarcation line they seemed to have drawn between their relationship with the inhabitants of large cities and the peasants of the countryside. One of the most recurrent accusations they directed against locals, in fact, regarded 'high prices charged to the British troops' in shops and facilities. The image of the Italian citizen as an unscrupulous profiteer was juxtaposed to that of the honest and generous countryside farmer:

> It's really disgusting the way we have to behave toward those d – d [sic] Italians. And they never think of thanking us for freeing them from the Germans. Instead they are charging us ten times more for everything we have to buy. If I had my way I'd treat em [sic] the same way as Jerry, take everything away from them and if they complained shoot the lot.[72]

Autobiographical accounts suggest that the main factor behind the deterioration of the relationship between British soldiers and Italian civilians was time. The longer the soldiers remained in a town, taking over larger portions of the locals' space, the quicker their presence – initially perceived as a liberation – transformed into a loathed military occupation. In February 1944, censorship officers noted that most of the positive comments towards the Italians were written by soldiers engaged in front-line areas. They, in fact, were the protagonists of Liberation: those who passed through the cheering crowds before restarting their march, chasing the Axis troops retreating northwards. In contrast, those who were stationed in the rear lines experienced the entirely different environment of occupation. Less than eight months after their first encounter, the soldiers' relationship with the Sicilians seemed to have already reached its lowest as the war censor sorely reported:

> The utter laziness, slovenliness, spinelessness, avariciousness, treach-erousness and insolence of the [Italian] men – their unsuitability for soldiering – the loose morals of the [Italian] women – the squalor, poverty and lack of hygiene and sanitation in the country, have all been freely remarked upon, coupled with questioning as to why a state of co-belliger-ency with Italy was ever created and, if this had to be done, why we were so weak and submitted to the high price rackets and general exploitation of the troops?[73]

72   TNA, WO 204/10381: 'A&CR' no. 32, 16-31 Oct 43. Part I – Troops in Sicily & Italy.
73   TNA, WO 204/10381: 'A&CR no. 39, 16-29 Feb 44. Part A – British Troops in Italy.

The Many Facets of Wartime Encounters

At the end of 1943, statistics compiled by the British censorship service reported that about a quarter of the soldiers who mentioned their encounters with Italian civilians 'loathed' them, while half of them expressed a 'rather contemptuous indifference'. The remaining quarter were 'sympathetic [with the population] on account of the poverty observed, or kindness met with from individual[s]'.[74] In mainland Italy, one year after the invasion statistics recorded a predominance of positive remarks towards the presence of Allied soldiers, with 60 percent of comments expressing a positive opinion about the co-habitation. Sicily, however, the region that had experienced the Allied occupation for longer, reported a meagre 16 percent of positive remarks.[75]

At the end of 1944, the unwelcome call-up – or re-call – aiming at swelling the ranks of the new Italian co-belligerent army with southern Italians fuelled the Sicilians' discontent caused by the deterioration of their conditions after the arrival of the Allies. A series of local demonstrations soon turned into generalised riots contesting the authority of both the Allies and the new Italian government, which violently suppressed the rebellion in the south.[76] By involving the Allies in their protests, locals manifested their conflicted relationship with the former 'liberator', now largely perceived as an occupier and a stranger. An anonymous writer from Southern Italy, considering the problems affecting the country at that difficult time, summarised the feelings of many by posing a momentous question in a letter intercepted by the censorship: 'how are we going to liberate ourselves from… the liberators?'[77]

While the behaviour of the soldiers predominantly changed after the armistice, the attitude of the civilians towards the Allies transformed at the very moment they ceased to see them as their propaganda had depicted them: as willing bene-factors. As historian David Ellwood has pointed out: 'All armed liberations quickly turn into occupations by a foreign army, no matter how friendly or high-minded the intentions'.[78] What needs to be stressed when discussing the concepts of 'occu-pation' and 'liberation' is that while the former has a 'legal formulation', the latter

---

74   TNA, WO 204/10381: 'A&CR' no. 34, 16 Nov-15 Dec 43. Part A – British Troops in Italy.

75   Archivio Centrale dello Stato (ACS, Rome), PCM, 1944-47, b. 1-2-2, f. 14884, 3284: 'Relazione mensile (gennaio 1945)', p.36.

76   On the *nonspiparte* ['we shall not leave'] uprising and its bloody repression in Sicily, see Patti, *La Sicilia e gli Alleati*, pp.192-211.

77   ACS, MI, Gab., 1944-46, b. 15, f. 1119: Salerno, 24 September 1944.

78   David Ellwood, 'The American Challenge in Uniform: The Arrival of America's Armies in World War II and European Women', *European Journal of American Studies. Special Issue: Wars and New Beginnings in American History*, 7:2 (2012), pp.1-13 (p.8).

is not officially recognised by the law.[79] For both the British soldiers and the Italian civilians, time, in fact, was the defining factor in determining the conversion from 'liberation' to 'occupation'. Thus, while the concept of 'liberation' is useful to the occupier as a political and propaganda tool to prepare for the occupation of enemy territory, from the point of view of the occupied the term appears more ephemeral and, depending on individual experiences, can be likened to a feeling or a mindset.[80]

The use of a variety of autobiographical sources for the exploration of the British soldiers' evolving perception of their wartime encounters with Italian civilians in Sicily reveals a complex, multifaceted reality. This chapter demonstrates that the first encounter, as opposed to the dominant narratives of the event, saw no jubilant crowds and triumphant marches. It was rather a series of scattered, violent clashes taking place on the beachhead between terrified civilians and suspicious soldiers whose weapons immediately dictated the rules of their new, unbalanced relationship. The first, therefore, was an encounter 'on the run' as soldiers focused on winning the ongoing battle, and civilians on avoiding any contact. It was only after the front had moved inland, in the hours and days following the invasion, that the situation eased, giving way to the iconic images of the Sicilians' welcoming reception of the Allies.

Such popular snapshots, however, do not tell the whole story. The unbalanced distribution of power between soldiers and civilians and the rapid evolution of the military and political situation deeply affected the attitudes and feelings of everyone involved. Following the largely favourable impressions initially expressed by the British, a major turning point in their relationship with the locals came with the news of the armistice and the announcement of the co-belligerence. At that point, most of the feelings of goodwill gave way to widespread hostility, as in their eyes locals seemed to shift from gratitude to expectancy. Once defeated and turned into semi-allies, in fact, for the soldiers the Italians were no more the oppressed people in need of saving, but rather a 'difficult' presence whose problems now passed from the Germans to the Allies to contend with. Since then, the civilians' affable behaviour was perceived as opportunistic and double-crossing. Eventually, in addition to the growing British soldiers' war-weariness, the establishment of occupation, which had already exacerbated the feelings of the Italians, caused the loosening of the occupiers' moral and ethical refrains resulting in that predatory behaviour that made the Italians feel growingly unsafe.

In line with the biographical turn that in the last decades has involved not only history but social sciences in general, the intent of this chapter is to restore

79   David Ellwood, 'Liberazione/Occupazione', in Eric Gobetti (ed.), *1943-1945. La lunga liberazione* (Milan: Franco Angeli, 2007), pp.13-26 (p.15).

80   See also reflections in Marisa Escolar, *Allied Encounters: The Gendered Redemption of World War II Italy* (New York: Fordham University Press, 2019), pp.1-2.

the centrality and plurality of the individuals' experiences and perceptions in an attempt to go beyond dominant, simplistic narratives of events. By re-tracing the experience of British soldiers in Sicily, it was possible to uncover several different responses to their encounters with the Sicilians that went beyond the stereotyped image of the idyllic co-habitation. The use of life histories as evidence for historical research allows for an exploration of views often contradictory to each other but closer to the complex reality of wartime encounters. When individuals are put at the forefront of the historical analysis, it becomes evident how marginalised experiences acquire their place in a more realistic larger frame where the idea of a cheerful first encounter does not exclude different perceptions, but rather cohabits alongside them as an important, more accurate counterpoint to the predominant narrative and more embedded view.

Bibliography

Archival Sources

Archivio Centrale dello Stato (ACS), Rome
    MI, Gab., 1944-46, b. 15, f. 1119: Censura postale.
    PCM, 1944-47, b. 1-2-2, f. 14884, 3284: Censura postale.
The National Archives (TNA), Kew
    CAB 121/587: Propaganda policy in the Allied invasion of Italy.
    FO 371/37263B: Situation in Italy. Code 22 file 242 (papers 6940-7406).
    FO 371/37303: Operation HUSKY: propaganda. Code 22 file 6050 (papers 6231-6262).
    FO 371/37326: Sicily: situation in. Code 22 file 6712 (papers 8139-9094).
    FO 898/172: Opinion Survey Section (P.W.B.).
    FO 898/349: 'HUSKY': invasion of Italy (Maj.-Gen. Brooks' file): Correspondence, directives and policy papers.
    WO 220/260: Sicily invasion propaganda communiques.
    WO 204/2589: Sicily: political and economic.
    WO 204/6712: Discipline: policy.
    WO 204/10381: Appreciation and censorship reports: Nos 1-52.
Imperial War Museums (IWM), London
    Documents.543: Private papers of D.O. Helm.
    Documents.3060: Private papers of P.J. Lovett.
    Documents.3854: Private papers of Colonel D.J. Fenner.
    Documents.6652: Private papers of K.G. Oakley.
    Documents.8601: Private papers of A.L. Bastone.
    Documents.14772: Private papers of W.F.H. Blyth.
    Documents.23386: Private papers of L.H. Mewis.
    LBY K. 84/2580-3: 'Soldati d'Italia!'.

Sound 4525/4: Edward Jeffrey Irving Ardizzone.
Sound 11938/50: George Edward Iceton.
Sound 13360/8: Derek Edward Ingram Thomlinson.
Sound 16725/36: William Knowles.
Sound 18676/11: William Eves.

Published Sources

Aga Rossi, Elena, *Una nazione allo sbando. 8 settembre 1943* (Bologna: Il Mulino, 2003).

Ardizzone, Edward, *Diary of a War Artist* (London: The Bodley Head, 1974).

Atkinson, Rick, *The Day of the Battle: The War in Sicily and Italy, 1943-1944* (London: Abacus, 2013).

Attanasio, Sandro, *Gli anni della rabbia: Sicilia 1943-1947* (Milan: Mursia, 1984).

Avagliano, Mario and Palmieri, Marco, *Paisá, sciusciá e segnorine. Il Sud e Roma dallo sbarco in Sicilia al 25 aprile* (Bologna: Il Mulino, 2021).

Baris, Tommaso, 'La memoria della Seconda guerra mondiale nel Mezzogiorno d'Italia' in *Italia e le sue regioni. L'età repubblicana. Culture* (Rome: Istituto della Enciclopedia italiana, 2015).

Baris, Tommaso, 'Lo sbarco alleato tra storia e memoria', in Salvatore Lupo and Rosario Mangiameli (eds.), *Sicilia 1943* (Rome: Viella, 2015).

Boobbyer, Philip, *The Life and World of Francis Rodd, Lord Rennell (1895-1978): Geography, Money and War* (London: Anthem Press, 2021).

Buckley, Christopher, *Road to Rome* (London: Hodder and Stoughton, 1945).

Bussoni, Mario, *Radio Londra. Voci dalla libertá* (Fidenza: Mattioli, 2017).

Cole, David, *Rough Road to Rome: A Foot-Soldier in Sicily and Italy, 1943-1944* (London: William Kimber, 1983).

D'Este, Carlo, *Bitter Victory: The Battle for Sicily, July-August 1943* (London: HarperCollins, 1988).

Dondi, Mirco, *La lunga liberazione. Giustizia e violenza nel dopoguerra italiano* (Rome: Editori Riuniti, 2004).

Ellwood, David, *Italy 1943-1945* (Leicester: Leicester University Press, 1985).

Ellwood, David, 'Liberazione/Occupazione', in Eric Gobetti (ed.), *1943-1945. La lunga liberazione* (Milan: Franco Angeli, 2007), pp.13-26.

Ellwood, David, 'The American Challenge in Uniform: The Arrival of America's Armies in World War II and European Women', *European Journal of American Studies. Special Issue: Wars and New Beginnings in American History*, 7:2 (2012), pp.1-13.

Ellwood, David, 'The Trauma of Liberation: Rape, Love and Violence in Wartime Italy', in Patrizia Sambuco (ed.), *Transmissions of Memory: Echoes, Traumas, and Nostalgia in Post-World War II Italian Culture* (Vancouver: Farleigh Dickinson University Press, 2018), pp.125-142.

Emsley, Clive, *Exporting British Policing during the Second World War: Policing Soldiers and Civilians* (London: Bloomsbury, 2017).

Emsley, Clive, *Soldier, Sailor, Beggarman, Thief: Crime and the British Armed Services since 1914* (Oxford: Oxford University Press, 2013).

Escolar, Marisa, *Allied Encounters: The Gendered Redemption of World War II Italy* (New York: Fordham University Press, 2019).

Favretto, Ilaria and Bergamini, Oliviero, '"Temperamentally Unwarlike": The Image of Italy in the Allies' War Propaganda, 1943-1945', in Mark Connelly and David Welch (eds.), *War and the Media: Reportage and Propaganda* (London-New York: I.B. Tauris, 2005), pp.112-126.

Fincardi, Marco, 'Lo sbarco in Sicilia', in Mario Isnenghi (ed.), *Gli italiani in guerra. Conflitti, identità, memorie dal Risorgimento ai nostri giorni*, vol. IV: *Il Ventennio fascista: la Seconda guerra mondiale* (Torino: Utet, 2008), pp.234-241.

Footitt, Hilary, *War and Liberation: Living with the Liberators* (Basingstoke: Palgrave Macmillan, 2004).

Gallerano, Nicola, 'L'arrivo degli Alleati', in Mario Isnenghi (ed.), *I luoghi della memoria. Strutture ed eventi dell'Italia unita* (Rome-Bari: Laterza, 1997), pp.455-464.

Gayre, Robert, *Italy in Transition: Extracts from the Private Journal of G.R. Gayre* (London: Faber and Faber Limited, 1946).

Gentile, Emilio, *25 luglio 1943* (Rome-Bari: Laterza, 2018).

Gooderson, Ian, *A Hard Way to Make a War: The Allied Campaign in Italy in the Second World War* (London: Conway, 2008).

Gordon, Robert SC, 'Adano: Sicily, Occupation Literature, and the American Century', in *ISLG Bulletin: The Annual Newsletter of the Italian Studies Library Group*, 17 (2018), pp.3-23.

Harris, Charles R.S., *Allied Military Administration of Italy, 1943-1945* (London: HMSO, 1957).

Holland, James, *Sicily '43: The First Assault on Fortress Europe* (London: Bantam Press, 2020).

Lepre, Aurelio, *L'occhio del Duce. Gli italiani e la censura di guerra, 1940-1943* (Milan: Mondadori, 1997).

Lo Biundo, Ester, *London Calling Italy: La propaganda di Radio Londra nel 1943* (Milan: Unicopli, 2014).

Lo Biundo, Ester, 'Voices of Occupiers/Liberators: The BBC's Radio Propaganda in Italy between 1942 and 1945', in *Journal of War and Culture Studies*, 9 (2016), pp.60-73.

Mangiameli, Rosario, 'La regione in guerra (1943-1950)', in Maurice Aymard and Giuseppe Giarrizzo (eds.), *Storia d'Italia. Le regioni: la Sicilia* (Turin: Einaudi, 1987), pp.485-600.

Mangiameli, Rosario, 'Sicilia 1943: Immagini e rappresentazioni di una sconfitta tra politica, storiografia e mercato', in Salvatore Lupo and Rosario Mangiameli (eds.), *Sicilia 1943* (Rome: Viella, 2015), pp.85-108.

Moorehead, Alan, *Eclipse* (London: Hamish Hamilton, 1946).

Neillands, Robin, *Eighth Army: From the Western Desert to the Alps, 1939-1945* (London: John Murray, 2004).

Patti, Manoela, *La Sicilia e gli Alleati. Tra occupazione e Liberazione* (Rome: Donzelli, 2013).

Peters, Mike, *Glider Pilots in Sicily* (Barnsley: Pen & Sword Military, 2012).

Piccialuti Caprioli, Maura, *Radio Londra (1940-1945). Inventario delle trasmissioni per l'Italia* (Rome: Ministero per i Beni Culturali e Ambientali, 1976).

Rodd, Francis, 'Allied Military Government in Occupied Territory', *International Affairs*, 20.3, July (1944), pp.307-316.

Rodd, Francis, 'Foreword', in Robert Gayre, *Italy in Transition: Extracts from the Private Journal of G.R. Gayre* (London: Faber and Faber Limited, 1946).

Schrijvers, Peter, *The Crash of Ruin: American Combat Soldiers in Europe during World War II* (Basingstoke: Macmillan, 1998).

Shapiro, Lionel, *They Left the Back Door Open: A Chronicle of the Allied Campaign in Sicily and Italy* (London: Jarrolds, 1944).

Simonetti, Fabio, 'Encounters in Wartime Italy: British Soldiers and Italian Civilians, 1943-1944' (doctoral dissertation, University of Reading, 2021).

Spingola, Cinzia, 'Crisi alimentare e problemi di ordine pubblico in Sicilia nel secondo dopoguerra', in Nicola Gallerano (ed.), *L'altro dopoguerra. Roma e il Sud, 1943-1945* (Milan: Franco Angeli, 1985), pp.341-354.

Susmel, Edoardo and Duilio, *Opera Omnia di Benito Mussolini. Dall'intervento dell'Italia nella Seconda guerra mondiale al discorso al Direttorio Nazionale del P.N.F. del 3 gennaio 1942 (11 giugno 1940- 3 gennaio 1942)*, vol. XXX (Florence: La Fenice, 1960).

Williams, Isobel, *Allies and Italians under Occupation: Sicily and Southern Italy, 1943-45* (Basingstoke: Palgrave Macmillan, 2013).

11

Sappers and the Scheldt: Anglo-Canadian Combat Engineers in the Scheldt Estuary Campaign and Reconstruction Phase, Autumn 1944[1]

Philip Brazier

Introduction

The Dutch island of Walcheren lies at the mouth of the Scheldt estuary. Its position makes it the 'key' to any attempt to seize the Belgian port of Antwerp. A British campaign on the island in 1809 suffered from poor planning, disorganisation and disease, leading to the loss of almost half the landed force of 40,000 troops – with relatively few killed in action. In 1944, British forces returned to Walcheren as part of the Anglo-Canadian 21st Army Group.

This chapter explores the performance of British and Canadian combat engineers during operations to clear the Scheldt estuary in late 1944. Firstly, it sets the topic in context by explaining the importance of the campaign to clear the Scheldt. Recent studies of 21st Army Group's doctrine have concentrated on the use of armour, infantry and artillery, rather than how it applied to combat engineers.[2] For the British Royal Engineers (RE), the use of 79th Armoured Division's amphibious

---

1   The author gratefully acknowledges the assistance of Tineke van Liesdonk, of Van Hall Larenstein University, Leeuwarden, Netherlands with the translation of Dutch text and explanation of terms that could not be directly translated to English.
2   W. Murray, 'British Military Effectiveness in the Second World War', in A.R. Millett & W. Murray (eds), *Military Effectiveness: Volume 3. The Second World War* (Cambridge: Cambridge University Press, 2012 [1988]), p.107; D. French, *Raising Churchill's Army: The British Army and the War Against Germany 1919-1945* (Oxford: Oxford University Press, 2010 [2000]), p.284.

and other specialist vehicles was lauded after the operation, while 'standard' RE and Royal Canadian Engineers (RCE) field companies were not so well praised.[3] Additionally, Canadian forces have been criticised for poor performances during the campaign.[4] An also under-reported aspect has been the amount of support given by either corps to the task of post-conflict reconstruction. By examining training undertaken prior to the operations, investigating examples of combat engineer support as well as post-liberation reconstruction tasks, this work seeks to improve understanding of the use of combat engineers in the 1944-1945 North West Europe campaign.

Most battlefield studies to Normandy will include coverage of specialised engineer tanks including the Armoured Vehicle Royal Engineers (AVRE) or Sherman Flail of 79th Armoured Division. Indeed, the Royal Engineer corps history states that the value of 'Hobart's Funnies' was soon proved on D-Day.[5] However, operations in the Scheldt estuary and during the landing on Walcheren in October-November 1944 do not receive the same praise, despite the fact that 79th Armoured Division was there. A problem for researchers is that the Scheldt operations came after the more well-known and researched D-Day and Arnhem operations and before the Ardennes offensive and Rhine crossing. Why were the specialised vehicles not praised as much during the Scheldt campaign? Did they fail? What of the work of the 'standard' RE/RCE field companies and other roles performed under the umbrella of 'Military Engineering'? Indeed, the use of the term 'Zoo' when describing Major-General P.C.S. Hobart's 'Funnies' has been cited as an indication of flippancy by British High Command by at least one author.[6] However, the 'Zoo' was effective and utilised a level of specialist planning and engineering beyond German capability in 1944. Rather than study 79th Armoured Division in isolation, it is important to consider how it and the other British and Canadian sappers fitted with what has been termed as 'Monty's Functional Doctrine' of a master plan, concentration of force, firepower-based attrition, and caution.[7] Or, more simply 'Metal before Flesh'.[8]

Map One shows the Area of Operations around Antwerp. This was captured in early September 1944, intact. Resources were then diverted to Operation MARKET

3   H. St George Saunders, *The Green Beret: The Story of the Commandos 1940-1945* (London: Michael Joseph, 1949), pp.303-304; Anon, *The Story of 79 Armoured Division* (Hamburg: The British Army On the Rhine, 1945), pp.174-177.

4   M. Hastings, *Armageddon: The Battle for Germany 1944-45* (London: Macmillan, 2004), p.156.

5   The Institution of Royal Engineers, *A Short History of the Corps of Royal Engineers* (Chatham, UK: InstRE, 2006), p.50.

6   A. Beevor, *D-Day: The Battle for Normandy* (New York: Penguin, 2009), p.15.

7   S.A. Hart, *Colossal Cracks: Montgomery's 21st Army Group in Northwest Europe, 1944-45* (Mechanicsburg: Stackpole Books, 2007), pp.48-49.

8   T. Van Gent, 'The Allied Assault on Walcheren' in C. Steenan-Marcusee and A. van Herk (eds.), *Building Liberty: Canada and World Peace, 1945-2005* (Groningen: Barkhuis, 2005), p.27.

GARDEN and the Belgian/Dutch territory either side of the Scheldt estuary was not cleared.[9] Operating a functioning port of this size would save having a logistics trail going all the way back to the beaches and Mulberry harbour at Normandy. With winter coming, the Allies needed a large port. However, the situation was akin to capturing the old docklands of London, but not clearing the Kent/Essex banks of the Thames.

The operations launched were:

- SWITCHBACK to clear the Breskens Pocket, cross the Leopold Canal and Braakman inlet.
- VITALITY I to clear South Beveland.
- VITALITY II crossing the Scheldt.
- INFATUATE I assault Vlissingen/Flushing.
- INFATUATE II Royal Marine and Army Commando assault on guns at Westkappelle, once dykes had been bombed by RAF Bomber Command to flood the island and isolate German bunkers.

Within these operations, doctrine was a factor. As far as the Armoured Corps was concerned, tanks should not support infantry.[10] However, Montgomery was adamant that tanks should do infantry support as well as tank-versus-tank engagements.[11] Additionally, Lieutenant-General Norrie, then the Armoured Corps advisor to 21st Army Group, had in 1943 sent a directive to 79th Armoured Division that Flails should maintain their gunnery skills in the event of a tank-versus-tank action.[12] However, Hobart was equally determined that AVRE/Flail should not be seen as a 'Jack of All Trades' and not be used as 'normal' tanks,[13] and also that AVRE/Flail crews should not be cross-trained.[14] Despite the utility of armoured engineers, it is important to remember that there was still a role for standard RE field companies. For example, while infantry could be tasked to assist

9   J. Buckley, *Monty's Men: The British Army and the Liberation of Europe* (London: Yale University Press, 2014), pp.208-219; T. Copp, *Cinderella Army: The Canadians in Northwest Europe 1944-45* (Toronto: University of Toronto Press, 2006), pp.41-44.

10   John Buckley, *British Armour in the Normandy Campaign* (New York: Routledge, 2004), pp.77-81.

11   Harrison Place, *Military Training in the British Army: From Dunkirk to D-Day* (Abingdon: Routledge, 2000), p.153.

12   The National Archives (TNA), WO205/420, 79th Armoured Division: Mechanical Minesweeping, Appendix 51A, Norrie to BGS (Training), 23 November 1943, para. 1-2.

13   Hobart Papers (HP), Liddell Hart Centre for Military Archives, King's College London (LHCMA), *79th Armoured Division Operational Bulletin No. 2*, June 1944, Pt. IV: Assault RE, Section A: General Employment, para. 19. 15/11/13.

14   TNA WO205/420, *79th Armoured Division: Mechanical Minesweeping*, Appendix 5A: Extract from Notes on Meeting to Discuss ARE and Flails, 17 August 1943.

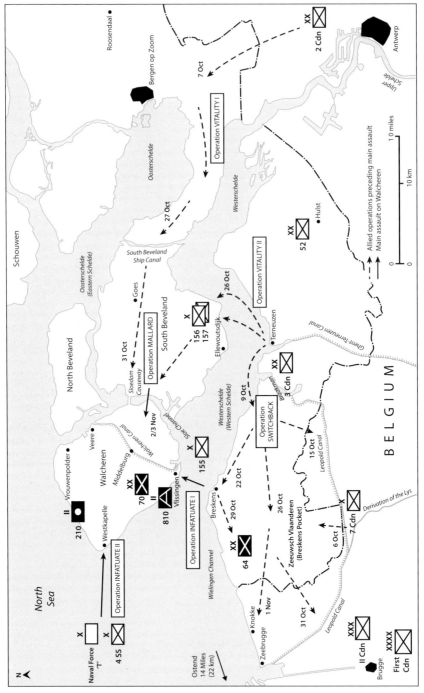

Map One: Area of Operations around Antwerp. (Map by George Anderson, © Helion and Company 2022)

in searching for mines, reports from Normandy indicated that they were very reluctant to do so – especially if a Flail had been seen in the local area.[15]

Operation SWITCHBACK

The primary obstacle in the opening phase of this operation was the Leopold Canal. The RCE had been 'in theatre' since Normandy so training for SWITCHBACK was undertaken 'in the field'. To improve the capability of infantry units, RCE sappers were used as subject matter experts to train the infantry in mine clearance, booby trap removal and mine detection.[16] In order to keep up with armour, 2 Field Company RCE improvised a prefabricated, transportable bridge by obtaining trailers from Antwerp. It also 'borrowed' half-tracks to enable it to support tanks.[17] Prior to the assault, other RCE units conducted Exercise HOTSHOT with flamethrowers and experimented with D-7 bulldozers to pull artillery out of mud and dig them into embankments – which were generally the only firm ground in the area of operations as much of the rest of the ground had been flooded, restricting mobility.[18]

After the campaign, Canadian 3rd Infantry Division conducted a study period about the Scheldt operations. It concluded that, in line with doctrine, armour would have been 'invaluable' against German positions in dykes.[19] However, narrow roads on top of dykes being the only means of traversing the landscape 'precluded the use of tanks'.[20] Where there was space to deploy armour, the likelihood of turning the ground to mud meant tanks could only be used in 'penny packets'.[21] Having identified the importance of armour and the loss of mobility caused by soft ground, it was then logical that the German defenders laid mines on the only available roads. In addition to the narrow roads not being suited to tanks like the Flail, this equipment would not be as effective on a roadway hardened with concrete, bitumen or cobbles as opposed to a field or even a trackway constructed from aggregate. The chains that were spun in front of the tank could not penetrate

---

15 HP, LHCMA, 15/11/13, *79th Armoured Division Operational Bulletin No. 1*, June 1944, Pt 3, Section B: Technical, para. 3: Mechanical Mine Clearing Devices.

16 Library and Archives Canada (LAC) RG24-C-3, Vol. 14708, File 173, War Diary, 7 Field Company RCE, 20 October 1944; LAC RG 24-C-3, Vol. 14766, Reel T-18598, 8 Field Company RCE, War Diary, 8 October 1944.

17 LAC RG 24-C-3, Vol. 14776, File 172, War Diary, 2 Field Company RCE, 19-23 October 1944.

18 LAC RG 24-C-3, Vol. 14766, Reel T-18598, War Diary 8 Field Company RCE, 8 October 1944; LAC RG 24-C-3, Vol. 14766, Reel T-18612 to 18613, War Diary 1st Field Park Company RCE, November 1944, Appendix: Unit History, Chapter IV, para. 2.

19 LAC RG24, Vol. 10912, File 235C3.033(D2) Training, 3 Canadian Infantry Division: Study Period for Dyke and Polder Fighting, 20 November 1944, para. 24, b.

20 A.J. Kerry and W.A. McDill, *The History of the Corps of Royal Canadian Engineers* (Ottawa: The Military Engineers Association of Canada, 1966), p.344.

21 LAC RG24, Vol. 0912, File 235C3 Dyke and Polder Fighting, para24, b & c.

Oosthoekbrug over the Leopold Canal at St Laurens, Belgium. The Bailey Bridge was constructed post-war on the site of a crossing in boats by 1st Battalion Canadian Scottish Regiment on 6 and 7 October 1944, as part of Operation SWITCHBACK. (Author's Collection)

such surfaces adequately to 'clear' them. While the Flail could have been used as a 'normal' tank it suffered, in the opinion of the Study, 'extreme awkwardness' on the poor roads in the area and would have become a road block if disabled.[22] Not only that but, as pointed out by Catsburg in *Polder Fighting*, when Flails worked on unpaved dyke roads, the tank's periscopes became covered in mud inside a few minutes.[23]

With mechanical means not particularly effective in such conditions, it fell back to field company sappers being required to clear routes by hand. In this, the Polish mine detector was found to be more effective than the alternative No. 4 Light Mine Detector. Due to its robustness and ability to operate in damp and muddy conditions having been proved, it was specifically requested for use in the Walcheren landings. Despite being robust, it was also sensitive enough to detect the low metal content of wooden 'Schu' anti-personnel mines.[24] However, even with equipment like mine detectors, clearing such obstacles using the correct drill was a slow task and difficult to achieve under fire – especially as all minefields could be expected to be covered by observation and weapon systems.

Bridging in the SWITCHBACK area of operations was problematic. As would be expected of a competent enemy, most existing crossing sites had been destroyed and sown with mines. The soft ground made constructing bridges '...an engineer nightmare'.[25] While the AVRE could carry a Small Box-Girder Bridge (SBG), it experienced the same problems as for the Flail. Again, much use was made of D-7 bulldozers to open up routes over dykes by lessening the gradients of the banks.[26]

If a wet gap could not be bridged, Folding Bridge Equipment (FBE) was an alternative. It was light and shoulder-portable by teams of sappers across ground that vehicles would sink into. However, it was proved to be obsolete in combat, lacking durability and the ability to carry heavy equipment or armour.[27] While assault bridges could be carried to site, they could not bear the weight of stores required to sustain a unit in action. Additionally, the more robust – but much heavier – Bailey bridging equipment could not be constructed without unacceptable losses close to a bridgehead.[28] So, despite having specialist machinery, it did not greatly favour the Allies in the performance of close support tasks in this area of operations.

22   LAC RG24, Vol. 0912, File 235C3 Dyke and Polder Fighting, 24, d.

23   R. Catsburg (trans I. Hardy), *Polder Fighting: The Battles for the Liberation of Oostburg. 29-30 oktober 1944* (privately published, 2020) p.49.

24   TNA WO199/88, RE Reports From Theatres of War. No. 11, p.4.

25   Kerry and McDill, *The History of the Corps of Royal Canadian Engineers* p.336; LAC RG24-C-3, Vol. 14708, File 173, War Diary, 7 Field Company RCE, 9 October 1944.

26   LAC RG 24, Vol. 912 File 235C3, Dyke and Polder Fighting, para.25 c-d.

27   TNA WO205/1178, Summary of the Major Engineer Lessons of the Campaign in NW Europe 1944/45, Annex 1: 1st Army, Part iii) Equipment, 1.For River Crossings, c) i and ii.

28   Maj.-Gen. R.P. Pakenham-Walsh, *The History of the Corps of Royal Engineers* (Chatham: Institute of Royal Engineers, 1958), Vol.IX, p.413.

RCE sappers prepare to sweep for mines with a No.4 Light Mine Detector on the Belgium/ Netherlands border, October 1944. Note the cobbled/pavé road raised above the surrounding flooded polder. Each posed problems for mobility. (Lieut H. Gordon Aikman. LAC, PA-116738)

Operations VITALITY I & II

2nd Canadian Division advanced into the South Beveland area of operations in late October, but here too the crossing of the South Beveland Ship Canal was delayed due to the slow pace at which boats could be brought up. It was recorded that the commitments required of sappers in the area of operations were much more than under the terrain and route conditions that were considered 'normal' since Normandy.[29]Attempts were used to clear mines kinetically and this operation saw the last use of the Conger device: an antecedent of Giant Viper and Python, which saw service during the Cold War and as recently as Afghanistan. Mounted on a Bren carrier and towed behind an AVRE, a converted fire hose would be launched into a minefield, pumped full of stabilised nitro-glycerine and detonated. On 20 October, in the harbour area of 284 Armoured Assault Squadron, 6 Assault Regiment RE, there was an explosion killing 41 and wounding 43, the cause of which has never

29   LAC RG 24, Vol. 912 File 235C3, Dyke and Polder Fighting, para.25, b.

Operation SWITCHBACK: LVTs taking Canadian troops across the River Scheldt to Hooftplaat, 13 October 1944. (LAC image PA-136754)

been completely explained. The Conger device was withdrawn from service soon after this incident as it was far too dangerous to operate.[30] Such events put extra responsibility onto infantry battalion pioneers to clear mines and IEDs, and to open transport routes to bring fighting echelons into battle. While the infantry could cross fire-swept ground, the doctrine of heavy fire and armour required increased engineering assets. The CRE of 2nd Army made it clear that this vital task was not prioritised, leaving field companies to do the best that they could.[31]

Even the Landing Vehicle Tracked (LVT) required sapper support. To enable them to negotiate steep dyke banks and enter canals or the sea, bulldozers had to lessen the gradient. Two RCE field companies were required to constantly maintain and repair the ramps out of the waterways, without which the LVTs would have

---

30   J. Q. Killip, 'Take a Bull's Horn, a Snake, a Conger, a Goat and a Crab… Assault Engineer Equipment: Witchcraft for the Battlefield' in *Royal Engineers Journal*, Vol. 131, No.2, (August 2017), p.87.

31   TNA WO205/1178,Summary of Major Engineering Lessons of the Campaign in NW Europe by CE 21 Army Group, Annex 2: Part II, Road Construction and Repair, pp.14-15, paras. 83-85.

floundered at the water's edge.[32] What these events make clear is the importance of maintaining mobility. Indeed, the CRE of 1st Army wanted future sappers to be more 'road conscious' – aware of the need to keep routes open.[33] His final point was that infantry units would have to work on the principle that there would 'never be sufficient Sprs and equipment to go around – especially on wide and divergent frontages.'[34]

Operation INFATUATE I

Unlike planning for OVERLORD, there was no specialised command structure of staff for the INFATUATE operations and the plans were produced in a series of ad hoc meetings beginning on 22 September, five weeks before the landings.[35] During these meetings, the importance of armoured RE support to this operation soon became apparent. The Specialised Armour Commander (Brigadier Duncan) was quizzed on such matters as: how well could the armour work with the marines? Could a representative from 79th Armoured Division live with and advise each unit during training? How well could AVRE and Flail remove obstacles? Could the untried LVT traverse dunes and concrete-covered dykes?[36] While Duncan could answer all of these questions, and demonstrated an understanding of the value of firepower in combined-arms doctrine, he also agreed to the ruling from the acting commander of II Canadian Corps that weather conditions precluded armoured support to the landings.[37] However, the commanding officer of 4 Special Service (SS) Brigade and the commander of naval forces then produced an outline plan that would use AVRE and Flail instead of amphibious Duplex Drive tanks – without the agreement of II Canadian Corps.[38] Duncan was (in)conveniently unable to attend the next meeting, having been summoned to a conference at 79th Armoured Division headquarters.[39] However, prior to

---

32   Kerry and McDill, *The History of the Corps of Royal Canadian Engineers*, p.338.
33   TNA WO205/1178, Summary of Major Engineering Lessons, pp.1-2 para. 10; LAC RG 24-C-3, Vol. 14766, Reel T-18598, War Diary 8 Field Company RCE, November 1944, Appendix 11, Letter: CRE 2 Cdn Corps to All Unit Commanders RCE, dated 26 July 1944.
34   LAC RG 24, Vol. 912 File 235C3, Dyke and Polder Fighting, para. 25, d. iv.
35   N. de Lee, 'Command, Control, Co-ordination and Communication at Westkappelle in November 1944 ⊠ Operation Infatuate II' in J. Buckley & P. Preston-Hough (eds), *Operation Market Garden: The Campaign for the Low Countries, Autumn 1944: Seventy Years On* (Solihull: Helion, 2016), pp.244-245.
36   Royal Marines Museum Archive (RMMA), Operation INFATUATE: Minutes of Conference, 4 October 1944, paras. 3-4 & 22. File 7/19/3.
37   TNA ADM 202/405, 4 Special Service Brigade Orders and Miscellaneous Reports, Minutes of Meeting at HQ 4 SS Bde 7 October 1944, paras. 1-3 & 12.
38   TNA ADM 202/405, 4 Special Service Brigade Orders and Miscellaneous Reports, Captain Pugsley to Admiral Ramsey, 10 October 1944, ref: 0030/0/NCFT.
39   TNA WO171/629, War Diary 30 Armoured Brigade, 13-16 October 1944.

departing, Duncan issued a Training Directive ordering Flail units to learn how to provide direct fire support to the marines.[40] At the next INFATUATE meeting, 'Contentious Points were brought to the notice of the GOC II Canadian Corps' and the landing of AVRE and Flail alongside the marines was agreed.[41] Duncan must have been aware of Hobart's dislike of a 'Jack of all Trades' role for 79th Armoured Division. It is, therefore, unfortunate that Duncan made no record of whether or not Hobart agreed with the change of role for the Assault Teams for this operation.

Training for the landings happened in dunes near Ostend. 5 Assault Regiment RE lost its AVREs after Normandy and was given the LVT and Terrapin wheeled amphibian in September. Despite receiving the new equipment, there were no instructors and the regiment was also sent unqualified drivers.[42] 6 Assault Regiment had retained its AVREs and was sent to Ostend to clear the beaches before training could be conducted.[43] The CRE of 59 Divisional Troops RE recorded feelings that not enough detail was extracted from planning meetings about what the marines would do, which in turn prevented a 'Spr plan' being produced.[44] He also observed a demonstration at Ostend which showed that the Petard was not so effective against bunkers and dragon's teeth.[45] While marines and REs got on with training, there was no time for a landing rehearsal, recorded as being 'Inadequate'.[46] 155 Brigade of 52nd (Lowland) Division had spent four years training for mountain warfare following an invasion of Norway and were now deployed at or below sea level. They arrived at Ostend one week before the assault, their attached RE unit – 241 Field Company – began training by lifting mines, first by NCOs and then other ranks.[47]

Operation INFATUATE I was launched to capture the town and harbour of Vlissingen and provide a bridgehead for an assault on Middelburg, the main town on Walcheren. Landings took place in darkness on a relatively undefended beach close to the Oranje mill at Vlissingen and were supported by massed artillery from South of the Scheldt. After initial landings by 4 (Army) Commando between 5:45 and 6:30 a.m, infantry landed two hours later and entered the town. Here sappers used charges to 'mousehole' a way through buildings and avoid the arcs of fire of pre-sited heavy weapons.

40   TNA ADM 202/405, 30 Armoured Brigade Training Directive No. 11, 12 October 1944, 03/82.
41   TNA ADM 202/405, Minutes of Conference held at HQ 4 British SS Bde., 14 October 1944.
42   TNA WO171/1800, War Diary 5th Assault Regiment RE, 7-9 September 1944.
43   TNA WA 171/1801, War Diary 6th Assault Regiment RE, 6 October 1944.
44   TNA WO171/1494, War Diary, 59 General Headquarters (GHQ) Troops RE, 4October 1944.
45   TNA WO171/1494, War Diary, 59 General Headquarters (GHQ) Troops RE, 18 October 1944.
46   Anon, *The Alternative to Arnhem* (Portsmouth, UK: Naval Historical Branch, 1994), p.20.
47   TNA WO171/1601, War Diary 241 Field Company RE, 22-26 October 1944.

Operation INFATUATE II

To enable the Scheldt to be opened, landings had to be made near Westkapelle at the western end of the island to neutralise a number of large-calibre guns housed in concrete emplacements. To isolate these emplacements and other positions on the island, RAF Bomber Command breached the sea dyke here and at three other sites on Walcheren. Although this achieved the initial aim, it created a gap at Westkapelle through which the sea flowed at a traversable six knots at low tide, but which became a 300-foot impassable gap at high tide.

Vertical photograph taken after a daylight bombing raid on the sea wall at Westkapelle. The breach in the sea wall was widened by the incoming tide and inundated the village. (Imperial War Museum Photography Archive © C 4668)

Oblique photograph looking east showing the breach in the sea wall at Westkapelle on Walcheren. The village is in the centre foreground between the two areas of flooding behind the sea wall. (Imperial War Museum Photography Archive © C 4677)

INFATUATE II was also launched on 1 November with fire support from RAF Typhoons and heavy-gun monitors from the Royal Navy. At 9:45 a.m. Flails and AVREs were landed directly onto the beach alongside No. 4 Commando, while converted Royal Navy landing craft engaged shore defences. There then followed 'The Great Sapper Tragedy', where nine AVREs and Flails 'drowned'.[48] This was caused by vehicles being landed in to undiscovered patches of clay on the beach through which the armour could not move. Those which avoided the clay then did not have the power to overcome the basalt rocks which had been the hardened face of the sea dyke and now lay as a wide 'barrier' near the dyke gap.[49] Bulldozers were used in an attempt to extract them, but these too were lost. Although LVTs could swim ashore, they were a slow-moving target and a number were lost. As the receding tide exposed more mud, getting equipment ashore became more difficult.

48 Royal Engineers Museum, Library and Archive (REMLA) MO283, Notes on Operation INFATUATE, pp.5-6, para. 12.
49 P.M. Crucq, *Turning the Key: The Capture and Liberation of Walcheren Island, October 30 – November 8, 1944* (Vlissingen: ADZ, 2009), pp.246-250.

Sherman Flail of the Lothian and Border Horse, landing at Westkapelle. Note the mud that would claim most of the Armoured Engineer vehicles during 'The Great Sapper Tragedy.' (Imperial War Museum Photography Archive © B11632)

Most of the underpowered Weasel amphibious vehicles were either 'drowned' or hit by mortar fire.[50] As they carried liaison teams and radios, this added to the difficulty in coordinating spotter aircraft and fire support.

The landing area was effectively cut in two. While south of the gap, artillery fire could be called upon, the only artillery powerful enough to support 41 Commando were 155mm pieces to the south of the Scheldt and they required a safety margin of 1,000 yards. When called upon, artillery fire generally fell 200 yards short. Concrete bunkers had to be taken out by rocket-firing Typhoons as the Petard was not strong enough. While 84 Group RAF were meant to have a 'cab rank' of Typhoons and Spitfires on call, in reality this was often found to be patchy due to weather and other demands on the Group.[51]

The CRE of 59 Divisional Troops RE stated that practically nothing went as arranged from an RE perspective. While a platoon of 59 Divisional Engineers was attached to each Commando, they generally fought as infantry. The remainder were severely stretched covering for the loss of Flails. Fortunately, the probability of this had been impressed on all sappers during training beforehand.[52] Being

50   de Lee, 'Command, Control, Co-ordination and Communication', pp.254-255.
51   de Lee, 'Command, Control, Co-ordination and Communication', pp.251-254.
52   REMLA, MO283, Notes on Operation INFATUATE, p.8, para 19, i.

adaptable enabled the marines to take objectives and reflected well on the efforts of the sappers involved. Such flexibility of thought and action is often only attributed to German forces.

Flexibility is also relevant when considering the work of the AVREs and Flails that managed to get ashore. German prisoners of war stated they were prepared to stand behind their machine guns while there were only marines in front of them. The presence of armour made a difference in their willingness to fight, and raised the morale of the commandos who relied upon the close support they provided.[53] The AVRE's wider tracks could carve a path through the dunes for the less squat Sherman. 79th Armoured Division's post-operational report emphasised the use of LVTs and the value of fire support from Flails and AVREs during 3-8 November Two Flails fired 1,400 rounds of 75mm and 30 boxes of Browning ammunition between them, while the AVREs fired 46 boxes of Besa machine gun rounds.[54] The surviving Flails and AVREs were 'worth their weight in gold' – a point emphasised to a civilian post-war audience. However, this was also the case with the single D-7 bulldozer (out of 10 landed) that was left to keep lines of communication open, construct the beach logistics area, and assist in the removal of beach obstacles. Additionally, maintaining the mobility of the armour and bulldozer was only possible due to sappers hand-clearing mines from the shifting sands of the dunes.[55] Had 79th Armoured Division become a 'Jack of All Trades' as Hobart feared? Why did Hobart agree to the publishing of a report and later works that emphasised the number of rounds fired? Possibly, it was because the utility of the concept of armoured engineers had to be recorded, with an eye towards post-conflict reduction of the Army.

Operation MALLARD

Having cleared the Breskens pocket, advanced over South Beveland and landed at Westkappelle and Vlissingen, it was then necessary to link-up the forces and advance over the Sloedam Causeway onto Walcheren island and seize Middleburg. Here was proved the importance of reconnaissance. At Westkapelle, beach reconnaissance by TARBRUSH RE teams in the weeks prior to the landings had not been able to get close enough to the defences to survey the damage to the sea dyke or find the mud and clay that swallowed the 79th Armoured Division teams.[56] For the crossing of the Sloe channel, intelligence reports stated that it was 14 feet deep

53 TNA CAB 106/1090, Army Operational Research Group (AORG) Report 299: The Westkapelle Assault on Walcheren, pp.49-50, para. 25.7.
54 TNA CAB 106/998, Final Report of 79th Armoured Division, p.72, paras. 12-13.
55 Packenham-Walsh, *The History of the Corps of Royal Engineers*, Vol. IX, p.420.
56 TNA ADM 202/230, War Diary, 1 Engineer Commando (RM) December 1944, Appendix 'Diary of Events Affecting Engineer Personnel in 'KEEP' Force, 15 October, 17 October and 22 October 1944.

and the issued maps indicated navigable water. Therefore, it was planned to paddle the channel. Unfortunately, the 'ground truth' was that this was not possible, due to mud banks and marsh.

However, it was imperative to maintain the initiative and keep the enemy 'off balance', so Canadian infantry were tasked to assault along the 40-metres-wide, 1,600-metres-long causeway, which has been recorded as being 'a perfectly engineered killing ground'.[57] Between 31 October and 2 November, three successive battalions attempted to establish a bridgehead. The minor gains were taken over by the Glasgow Highlanders of 156 Infantry Brigade, 52nd (Lowland) Division. Faced with the sack for refusing to launch another frontal assault, the divisional commander requested a 48-hour pause. This enabled a more detailed reconnaissance by an officer and NCO from 241 Field Company RE who found a boat and foot route over the channel, mud flats and salt marsh.[58] Two battalions were then put across by this route and supplied at high tide via Folding Bridge Equipment, which was adequate in this situation.

Surrender and Reconstruction

Advancing from Vlissingen to Middleburg, the headquarters of German defences, LVTs were used to intimidate the commander of German defences (*Generalleutnant* Daser) to surrender. Large, noisy, and the nearest armoured fighting vehicle that the commandos had to a tank, LVTs were a 'Force Multiplier' that enabled advance parties to by-pass blocking positions on the road from Vlissingen to Middelburg by negotiating flooded ground. However, as the LVTs were often heavily loaded, high losses were incurred when they hit landmines. A particular case in point was the loss of an LVT from 79 Armoured Assault Squadron RE at Serooskerke on 8 November, along with marines from 48 Commando, when 19 were killed and eight wounded from a total loading of 37.[59]

The flooding of Walcheren affected sanitation systems and brought a real prospect of typhoid outbreaks.[60] A lack of training and spare parts often reduced the ability of the RE to provide water during the campaign.[61] After Liberation, field companies were involved with improving roads, docks, canals and clearing mines,

---

57 M. Zuehlke, 'A Perfectly Engineered Killing Ground: The Calgary Highlanders and the Walcheren Causeway Battle', *Journal of Military History*, 16 (3) (2015), p.63.

58 TNA WO171/544, War Diary, HQ RE 52 Division, 31 October–4 November 1944.

59 Cruq, *Turning the Key*, pp.312-213.

60 TNA WO171/1494, War Diary HQ 59 GHQ Troops RE, November 1944, Appendix G1, Memo. To all Coys, CRE/OPS/129, 18 November 1944, p.1, i-ii.

61 TNA WO205/1178, Summary of Major Engineering Lessons of the Campaign in NW Europe by CE 21 Army Group, Annex 2: Part II, Water Supply, p.13, para. 37.

as well as managing the supply of water to communities on the island.[62] RE and Royal Tank Regiment (RTR) LVT units were then essential to keeping the British forces on Walcheren mobile. A company of DUKW and Terrapin vehicles also assisted the local population by ferrying civilians around the island. One such vehicle, carrying then Minister of State Clement Attlee on a tour of the island, was involved in the rescue of a farmer and his bogged-in horse and cart.[63] During the reconstruction works mines continued to be a 'perpetual curse' as they could still function after immersion in sea water and float some distance from where they had been originally laid.[64]

Ridding the island of the nuisance of daily flooding, with the associated hazards of disease and loss of agricultural productivity, was the natural priority for the local population. Responsibility for reclaiming Walcheren from the sea lay with DDW (Dienst Droogmaking Walcheren – Reclamation Service of Walcheren). Given the destruction brought upon Walcheren, it may have been some comfort to the DDW that official British support for the task came from Sir Anthony Eden, the Foreign Secretary. Eden demanded that the required materials – and the means to transport them – be provided to enable 21st Army Group to assist the islanders.[65] Works to reconstruct the docks at Flushing began soon after Eden's intervention. However, Royal Engineers were only tasked in May 1945 to work alongside the Rijkswaterstaat (the State Department responsible for road and canal projects) and Delft University – which created a physical laboratory to study the possible effects that progress at the four gaps would have on Walcheren's water levels during construction. The challenge for the RE was to assist the local population in reclaiming the island, without being perceived as acting like a 'saviour'.

Local tradition and experience existed to repair the sea dykes. A gap could be repaired by constructing and floating large reed and brushwood mattresses (15-100 metres square) in place between tides, usually a three-to-six-hour timeframe. These mattresses would then be enhanced with brushwood fascines and covered with a bund of clay advanced from each end of the gap. The bund would then be reinforced with layers of German basalt rock, 60 centimetres of clay and sand on the seaward-facing wall and sand pumped in by dredgers on the landward-facing side. However, the breaches in the dykes varied from 400 to 800 metres wide with the shallowest at Westkappelle (four metres) and the deepest at Rammekens (27 metres). All four breaches allowed seawater into/onto Walcheren, often at in excess of 10 knots, although most flowed out again through the breach at Veere.[66]

62   TNA WO171/1601, War Diary 241 Field Company RE, 8-13 November 1944; TNA WO171/1494, War Diary HQ 59 GHQ Troops RE, November 1944, Appendix D1 section 1, i-v.
63   Major I.H. Johnson, 'The Dykes of Walcheren', *The Royal Engineers Journal*, Vol. 100 (2) (1986), p.108.
64   Brigadier E.E. Reed, *The Saving of Walcheren* (Chatham: The Institute of Royal Engineers, 1947), p.2.
65   TNA FO 371-49408, Letter from Anthony Eden, 3 January 1945. p.1.
66   Reed, *The Saving of Walcheren*, p.13.

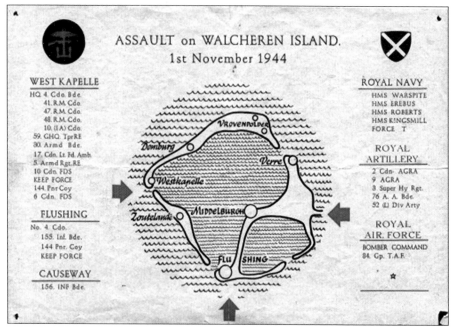

Commemorative certificate for Operations INFATUATE I & II. The arrows indicate the attacks at Westkappelle, Flushing/Vlissingen and across the Sloedam Causeway. Also shown are the four breaches of the sea dykes. (Author's Collection)

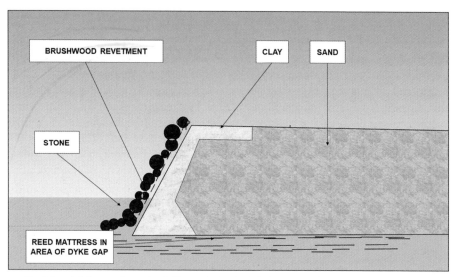

Traditional dyke repair method. (Drawn by WO2 (CSM) D. Waterfield, 101 (City of London) Engineer Regiment (EOD&S)), attached EMUOTC between the two closing brackets.

The effects of five years' occupation had deprived the local workforce of the means by which they could complete the task. In addition, the diet available during occupation had not provided the energy levels required to sustain arduous work in winter conditions. Supporting the local population to 'help themselves' was therefore considered the best way forward.

Here, the role for REs was to provide supporting technology namely: surplus elements of Mulberry harbour; kite anchors which could hold up to 26 tons firmly in place; D-8 tractors, which could pull a 23-ton object better than tugs could push it; Bailey equipment to allow for dredger equipment to be placed on islands in the gaps; filled sandbags; explosives and hand tools. It was considered necessary to have a 100 percent reserve of all of the items just mentioned. Having designed both the flexible roadway for Mulberry and the kite anchors that held them in place, Captain A.H. Beckett RE was a natural choice to be tasked as liaison officer and advisor to the Walcheren dykes repair force. That being said, he recalled that it was clear that the RE did not hold all of the answers, given that the Dutch were considered to be the world's foremost maritime engineers and mostly wanted to know how sections of Mulberry could be adapted to their plans.[67] Considering the size of the task, numbers of RE at the sites were relatively small:

- Chief Engineer Netherlands
- One to two mechanical equipment platoons
- Field company detachments for sinking Mulberry sections
- An anchoring officer
- Works company for bridging or preparing demolitions
- Stores officers to supervise movement of stores, equipment and plant to Walcheren

Other military support came from German divisional engineers, re-roled from minefield clearance, a company of Dutch pioneers, a company of Royal Army Service Corps (RASC) amphibian drivers, and Civil Affairs staff. Despite small numbers, the quantity of equipment and stores was great and vital to the completion of the task ahead of winter storms.

It was decided to prioritise the sites as follows: Westkappelle, Nolle, Veere and Rammekens. Facing directly southwest into the prevailing winds and exposed to the North Sea, Westkappelle would receive the worst of winter storms and provided no shelter for craft involved in repairing the dykes. Although also facing the North Sea, Nolle benefitted from being a short distance up the coast from Vlissingen, meaning that craft could seek shelter in that harbour if necessary. The widest gap was at Veere, but fortunately it was on the leeward side of the island and sheltered from the worst of wind and tide. Last in the planning table came Rammekens, east of Vlissingen. Although the deepest gap, it was decided to give this a lower priority

---

67   Johnson, 'The Dykes of Walcheren', p.111.

as the area flooded by it was much smaller than the others. Equipment was only sent to this location if not needed at the other three.

As mentioned above, time was critical when attempting to avoid a battle with the tide. As work progressed to close a gap, the speed of inrushing water would increase the scour rate on the seabed, with the possibility of undoing the vital work. Beckett tried to convince the Dutch engineers that sinking sections of Mulberry and securing them in place with kite anchors would close the gaps rapidly and securely. However, he was then asked to provide evidence of his previous experience and success rate with this method, of which he had none. The tried and tested method over centuries was to use stone, but each gap could need up to 60,000 tons.[68] Unfortunately, in 1945 this natural resource was in very short supply. To gain their trust, Beckett conducted a demonstration that showed a winch-equipped D-8 bulldozer at maximum power could be held in place by with a kite anchor, whilst the bulldozer could plough a furrow with a ship's anchor. Kite anchor-secured concrete 'Beetles' were successfully tested at the Nolle gap by senior Rijkswaterstaat engineers.[69]

When six 'Beetles' were sunk straight afterwards, they were swept away by the next high tide.[70] However, it was found that the cause was inadequate securing, rather than a poor concept, and the situation was soon made good.[71] This strained the working relationship in the short term and was not helped when a high side and sea gale in September reopened the Nolle gap. The British liaison officer's apparent prevention of the use of stone was to blame, according to the Dutch engineers. Despite these grumblings, the Nolle gap was closed on the 2 October and the Westkappelle gap shortly afterwards on 12 October. To find a more 'failsafe' solution, Beckett searched Vlissingen harbour and found a lengthy concrete pontoon as well as the first sections of 1,200 tons of German torpedo netting which could be used to reinforce clay and fill gaps under the keels of sunken craft, as well as being used as extra ballast. Initial reluctance by the Dutch to this idea led to Beckett issuing an ultimatum that he would quit the task and recommend the withdrawal of British assistance.[72] Sinking the netting was quicker than constructing reed matting, but performed much the same task and helped to ease 'moments of great stress' and later evolved as a means to create a block between ships scuttled to close a gap.[73] Beckett would probably have been relieved to know that a later Dutch study proved that the traditional methods would not have closed the dyke gaps ahead of the main 1945/1946 winter storms.[74]

68   Reed, *The Saving of Walcheren*, p.15.
69   Johnson, 'The Dykes of Walcheren', p.111.
70   Reed, *The Saving of Walcheren*, p.15.
71   Johnson, 'The Dykes of Walcheren', p.111.
72   J ohnson, 'The Dykes of Walcheren', p.111.
73   Reed, *The Saving of Walcheren*, p.6.
74   K.E. Zuiderbann, *Luctor et Emergo: Het Sluiten van de Dijksgaten van Walcheren* (Delft: Technische Universiteit Delft), p.60.

Mulberry Harbour Phoenix caisson sections with abandoned AVREs and Flails at Westkapelle in 1946. (Planbureuen Bibliotheek van Zeeland, Foto39838)

The Corps' official publication includes much praise and understandably emphasised successes rather than the trials and tribulations. Beckett, on the other hand, was humble enough to admit that the overall credit for the success at the dyke gap came from liaison with the real experts – the Dutch engineers and work-force. Such an undertaking was 'resource-heavy', beyond that provided by the British. Specialised equipment included three barge suction dredgers, a stationary pump unit and two floating stone-transporter cranes as well as 182,000 tons of limestone quarried near Liege in Belgium and shipped by barge from Terneuzen; 221,000 tons of clay was dredged and transported from the Hollandse Diep near Moerdijk, about 80 miles from Walcheren;[75] 250,000 trees were sourced from Belgium, in part replaced by a British programme of reforestation from 1945–1948.[76] The Belgian limestone was for the facing of the dykes. Traditionally, the facing stone was a naturally hexagonal-shaped basalt rock quarried from near Bonn in Germany, which could be packed relatively easily to form an interlocking structure. However, this could not be sourced and greater quantities of the lighter limestone were used instead, up to 10,000 tons a week. The process stretched the

75   Reed, *The Saving of Walcheren*, pp.7-8.

76   K.W. Goodlet, 'Reduced to the Banks of Mud From Which They Were Reclaimed: The Province of Zeeland, War and Reconstruction, 1940-1945', *Canadian Journal of Netherlandic Studies*. Vol. 34 (2) (2013), p.46.

capability of RE lines of communication from: the German prisoners of war quarrying it under American control, via Belgian and Dutch civil authorities, through to the exposed coastal dykes where the works were always on the verge of a 'stone famine'.[77] All in all this was not cheap: £2,775,000 in 1945.[78]Allowing for inflation, this would equate to just over £133,000,000 in 2022.[79]

It was not just the Allies' work that had to be made good. As well as the dykes, RAF Bomber Command had targeted heavy gun emplacements around Flushing's port.[80] The effects of the bombing were enhanced by German pioneers, who had cratered much of the dock area not hit by bombs and demolished many of the lock gates leading into the port. A consequence of this was that the level in the Walcheren Canal could not be maintained, which denied coolant water to the Vlissingen power station. Power could therefore only be generated twice a day, at high tide. In the De Schelde shipyard in Vlissingen was the unfinished ship No. 214 – later the *Willem Ruys* and then *Achille Lauro*, the subject of a terrorist hijack in 1985 – which contained the only desalination plant on the island. This had been prepared for reserved demolition as the occupying forces wished to have access to potable water until they withdrew. Fortunately, the Dutch Resistance managed to negotiate a 24-hour reprieve to the demolition during which time they removed the charges from the ship and enabled a supply of fresh water to be provided.

21st Army Group agreed to the temporary repair of the locks on 14 January 1945. Advance Parties of RE arrived on site over the following week to carry out recce tasks and plan the works, followed by 931 Port Construction and Repair Company RE, 977 Port Repair Ship RE and 238 Company Pioneer Corps from No. 6 Port Construction and Repair Group RE.[81] Bad weather delayed the arrival of the balance of personnel until 27 January, after which accommodation and access roads were constructed to enable works to begin.[82]

Advice was provided by a Royal Navy salvage officer, supported by the Admiralty Salvage Vessels *Kingarth* and *Swin*. In all, about 300 British personnel were posted to the town to support 200 Dutch in restoring the shipyard and docks to full operating capacity.[83] The NV KoninklijkeMaatshappij 'de Schelde' (Royal Society of the Scheldt), the ship and dock company in Vlissingen, repaired and rebuilt the 35-metre lock gates in their dry dock. Their workshops also provided the fabrications and alterations required to bring the 20-metre gates back to working standard.

77   Reed, *The Saving of Walcheren*, p.8.
78   Reed, *The Saving of Walcheren*, p.23.
79   £133,121,089.90 according to Inflation Calculator at <https://www.officialdata.org/UK-inflation>, accessed 13 October 2022.
80   P.M. Crucq, *Aiming Point Walcheren* (Vlissingen: ADZ, 2003), pp.35-40.
81   D.P Bertlin, 'Temporary Repairs to the Locks at Flushing' in *The Civil Engineer in War: A Symposium of Papers on War-Time Engineering Problems* (London: Institute of Civil Engineers, 1948), p.183.
82   Bertlin, 'Temporary Repairs to the Locks at Flushing', Appendix III, Fig. 20, p.190.
83   Johnson, 'The Dykes of Walcheren', p.110.

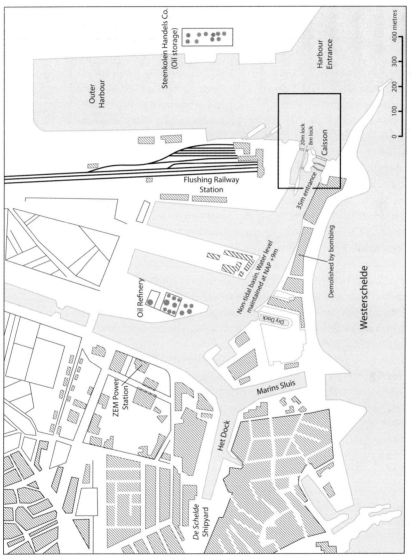

Map Two: Diagram of Vlissingen/Flushing Docks. The highlighted section shows the location of the 35-metre, 8-metre, and 20-metre locks. After D.P. Bertlin, 'Temporary Repairs to the Locks at Flushing' in *The Civil Engineer In War: A Symposium of Papers on War-Time Engineering Problems* (London: Institute of Civil Engineers, 1948), Appendix III, Fig. 1. (Map by George Anderson, © Helion and Company 2022)

Both Inner and Outer Harbours at Flushing had been damaged by the RAF during targeted attacks on the shipyards between 1940 and 1944, the raids that preceded the invasion, and deliberate demolitions to structures and cutting charges on steel performed by German forces to deny the facilities to the Allies. All the gates to the 8-metre, 20-metre and 35-metre docks had been damaged, mostly by German action. The gates to the larger locks had been blasted into the bottom of the harbour and a ship caisson, 148 feet by 16 feet by 40 feet, vital for future repair work to submerged structures, had been badly damaged by a direct bomb hit.[84] South of the 35-metre lock, damage was so severe that, during a spring tide, water from the Scheldt poured via craters through to the inner harbour.[85] Therefore, work similar to that undertaken by Beckett and the dyke builders had to be completed to ensure that any repairs were not by-passed every two weeks.

As mentioned above, with five gates lying on the floor of the locks the harbour basin had become tidal, with a current of nine knots flowing through the 20-metre gap where the outer lock gates had been. In turn, this caused scouring and silting inside the docks. If the wet and dry docks could be made navigable, then Flushing's shipyards could return to use. Not only would this be a valuable 'In Theatre' resource, but also a means to bring the local economy back into operation, as the water supply to the power station could be maintained via the Walcheren Canal. Although desired, a complete repair and return to an 'as new' standard was not a practicable solution. This meant that the task undertaken was to repair the outer lockheads, 35-metre gates, and the gates to the Walcheren Canal, in order to retain water in both harbours and allow ships to enter the basin at high tide.

To repair the 35-metre lock, the damaged gates of the 20-metre lock's inner lockhead had to be pulled clear, which enabled shallow-draft vessels to enter the port at half tide. One of the 35-metre lock gates was raised through the combined efforts of the Admiralty Salvage Vessels *Kingsgarth* and *Swin*. A reserve 35-metre gate sited at Veere and was floated to Flushing along the Walcheren Canal, before being hoisted and lowered into place by a 60-ton capacity set of sheerlegs. Repairs to the gates were completed in mid-May 1945 and debris cleared from the site by 16 June 1945.[86]

The caisson had been badly damaged by a direct hit and pierced several times by bomb fragments. As it sat directly on the granite base of the lock, cables and ropes could not be passed underneath it to facilitate lifting. To create watertight compartments in the vessel, a concrete bulkhead was cast in-situ between tides. It was then lifted via Admiralty pontoons and bolting saddles onto the sides of a damaged compartment to distribute forces throughout the structure whilst being lifted. Lifting and dry-docking was completed on 11 May 1945.

---

84 Bertlin, 'Temporary Repairs to the Locks at Flushing', pp.174-175.
85 Bertlin, 'Temporary Repairs to the Locks at Flushing', p.182.
86 Bertlin, 'Temporary Repairs to the Locks at Flushing', Appendix III, Fig. 20, p.190.

All four gates for the 20-metre lock had to be raised from the floor of the lock chamber, with divers attaching lifting tackle in the 15-minute period of slack water between tides. Once lifted, a salvage vessel could carry and remove the gate, which allowed brick and masonry debris to be cleared from the gate recesses. Gate anchorage points had been blown out of position by bombing and all top anchorages had been destroyed by steel cutting charges. Damage to the salvaged lock gates was such that it was decided to re-use older gates which had been removed in 1924 and placed into storage at Veere. Transport to site was again by launching and floating and then lifting them into place with ship-mounted 60-ton sheerlegs.

The wall around the 8-metre lock had been displaced by 20 inches (50 centimetres) and sheared at the top, causing the door-style gates to overlap. Rather than replace them like-with-like, the option of using a lifting gate was chosen instead, with a 20-ton concrete sill constructed at the gate to maintain water levels at low tide. This task had to take place at low water, with RE divers sandbagging the joints between the shuttering and lock walls, as well as examining the base of the shuttering to ensure that it was seated correctly on the lock bed. A means of pouring concrete into the framework was improvised by constructing a winch-controlled telescopic tube fed by a hopper made from half of a conical buoy. The new gate's framework was constructed from welded structural steel framework which lifted shutters constructed from timber sheets with the aid of a petrol winch.[87]

Before the war, water levels inside the basin had been maintained by timber lock gates where it fed the Walcheren Canal. Although the preferred means, such a system could not be reverted to immediately due to the flooding of Walcheren west of the canal. Middleburg was also flooded and required draining, which entailed maintenance of the canal level at – or below – NAP for a period each day.[88] One pair of the original timber lock gates had been wrenched from their hinges and floated downstream and those that remained in place were badly damaged. It was decided to adapt and re-use the salvaged curved steel 20-metre lock gates by fitting a shelf at their base to enable them to fit the straight sill that remained in place. Similar adaptations were necessary to fenders, anchorages and gate stoppers. The complicated nature of this work was not aided by slack water only existing for around five minutes at each tide, with a current of 10 knots at half-tide. Officially, this was recorded as 'awkward and tantalizing' work which the use of a salvage vessel could do little to assist.[89] Emplacing the gates required four attempts at slack water with the support of barge-mounted 60-ton sheer-legs, an 8-ton crane and the winch power of two D-8 caterpillar bulldozers. Once complete, the new gates

---

87 Bertlin, 'Temporary Repairs to the Locks at Flushing', pp.178-181.

88 NormaalAmsterdaamsPeil (NAP; Normal Amsterdam Level). The average high watermark of the Zuiderzee (now Ijsselmeer), which is taken as the zero reference level for elevation across the Netherlands and now the European Union.

89 Bertlin, 'Temporary Repairs to the Locks at Flushing', p.182.

had negligible leakage and enabled water to be retained in the canal at low-tide. They also reduced the current at half-tide from 10 to three knots.

While British and Canadian Royal Engineers may take pride in the tasks completed in arduous conditions, there is the question of how this was seen by Zeelanders and the inhabitants of Walcheren in particular. An anonymous resident of Westkappelle stated in a post-war interview that there was little animosity towards the RAF crews for the destruction and death brought to their town, although this was different for those who lost family members.[90] *Luitenant* C.J.G Spolstra of the Netherlands Army, writing under the pen name of A. Den Doolaard, later lamented that Walcheren 'drowned' for the liberation of Europe.[91] Historian K.W. Goodlet adds to this by pointing out that the enduring theme at Westkappelle's Polderhuis museum is that of reconstruction, rather than liberation.[92] Spolstra's influence while working at the task sites led to Beckett's need to demonstrate the anchoring of 'Beetles' in the gaps. which would then reduce the amount of stone needed to reinforce the dykes.[93] Beckett was somewhat coy when writing later about Spolstra/Den Doolaard's liaison work.[94] However, it is doubtful whether he would have appreciated being portrayed as the clichéd English officer, 'Major Young' – the Joker with the plan – in Doolaard's *Roll Back the Sea*.[95]

Conclusion

Both the RE and RCE demonstrated imagination and flexibility in their conduct of operations, as shown by training conducted in theatre or becoming competent in the handling of new equipment and working with other units inside a month. This is especially so given that both RE and RCE units were under-resourced. That 79th Armoured Division's presence was demanded by 4 Special Service Brigade shows the importance that armour could have in support of infantry.

Operations around the Scheldt were conducted over ground that often negated the advantages that mechanisation sought to provide. Parallel to all-arms counter-IED training during recent operations, the cascading of mines and booby-trap training to infantry and pioneers demonstrated the importance even then of maintaining an army's mobility and morale.

90 P.M. Crucq, *We Never Blamed the Crews: The Flooding of Walcheren Island, October 1944* (Vlissingen, Netherlands: ADZ, 2000), p.106.

91 A. den Doolaard (trans. Barrows Massey), *Roll Back the Sea* (London: Heinemann, 1948), p.32.

92 Goodlet 'Reduced to the Banks of Mud From Which They Were Reclaimed' pp.50-51.

93 Johnson, 'The Dykes of Walcheren', p.111.

94 A. Beckett, *Record of Army Service Including Experience of Design and Construction of Mulberry Harbour* (N.P., 1991), p.11.

95 den Doolaard, *Roll Back the Sea*, p.314.

The 'Great Sapper Tragedy' at Westkappelle illustrated the value of a thorough reconnaissance. Strong tides and alert German defences prevented it in that case, but how much more could the Flails and AVREs have achieved if they had been able to get ashore? For Operation MALLARD, exhausted infantry were consigned to a difficult frontal assault. Luckily, a delay of 48 hours was possible which enabled another route to be found.

Post-Liberation, it was demonstrated that front-line sappers could make a vital contribution to the health of a civilian population. Providing fresh water, sanitation and improving lines of communication saved lives and supported 'Hearts and Minds' programmes. It was imperative that the liberators not leave the local population to enjoy the 'freedom' of a shattered land, devoid of utilities and infested with disease, sending Walcheren back to the conditions of 1809. The modern example of the 2010 typhoid outbreak in Haiti being found to be due to the poor sanitation of UN troops stationed there is a case in point.[96]

Although the 'Funnies' of 79th Armoured Division were the most obvious manifestation of the Allied 'Metal before Flesh' doctrine it was not the defining aspect of RE/RCE involvement in the Scheldt operations, but neither was this involvement faultless. While the 'Funnies' have entered the psyche for their work in Normandy, the flexibility, adaptability, and improvisation of RE and RCE units enabled 21st Army Group doctrine to be applied in the most unfavourable conditions. The acknowledgement that there would 'never be sufficient Sappers' suggests that Higher Command knew that too.

While it is relatively easy to concentrate on the efforts of British and Canadian sappers and reflect that much was achieved in trying circumstances, it is worth considering how it is remembered in the area today. Goodlet acknowledges that Allied aid was considerable, but as living memory of the joys of liberation fades away, the efforts of the locals during reconstruction – rather than Allied military assistance – are remembered more today. Indeed, this had been recognised by Beckett, who wrote about the need for liaison between the RE and Dutch *Rijkswaterstaat* engineers. At times the relations may have been strained almost to a level that might cause a kite anchor to fail, but Beckett was gracious enough to recognise that most credit should go to the Dutch. While the sappers enabled a successful conclusion to the Scheldt campaign and brought considerable technical and technological expertise to the reconstruction process, their efforts assisted, rather than led, the true experts in that phase.

---

96 Transnational Development Clinic, Yale Law School, Global Health Justice Dept. and School of Public Health, Yale University, Association Haitienne de Droit de L'Environment, *Peacekeeping Without Accountability: The UN's Responsibility for the Haitian Cholera Epidemic*, 2013, p.49, available online at <https://www.law.yale.edu/system/files/documents/pdf/Clinics/Haiti_TDC_Final_Report.pdf>, accessed 28 August 2016.

Bibliography

Archival Sources – Canada

Department of National Defence and the Canadian Forces, Directorate of History and Heritage (DHH), Canadian Military Headquarters (CMHQ).
 Report No. 83: Preliminary Report on Operation 'JUBILEE' (The raid on Dieppe), 19 Aug 42.
 Report No. 89: The Operation at Dieppe, 19 Aug 42. Personal stories of participants.
 Report No. 108: Operation 'JUBILEE': The raid on Dieppe, 19 Aug 42. PART II: The Execution of the Operation.
Library and Archives Canada (LAC), Ottawa
 Record Group (RG) 24-C-3 (War Diaries)
  Vol. 14708: File 173, War Diary, 7 Field Company RCE.
  Vol. 14766: Reel T-18598, War Diary, 8 Field Company RCE.
  Vol. 14766: Reel T-18612 to 18613, War Diary, 1st Field Park Company RCE.
  Vol. 14776: File 172, War Diary, 2 Field Company RCE.
 RG24, File 235C3.033
  Vol. 10912: (D2) Training, 3 Canadian Infantry Division: Study Period for Dyke and Polder Fighting, 20 November 1944 (from Historical Officer 3 Canadian Infantry Division).

Archival Sources – United Kingdom

Liddell Hart Centre for Military Archives (LHCMA), King's College London, Hobart Papers
 79th Armoured Division Operational Bulletin No. 1, June 1944.
 79th Armoured Division Operational Bulletin No. 2, June 1944.
Royal Engineers Museum, Library and Archive (REMLA)
 MO283: Notes on Operation INFATUATE, to Open Antwerp Port by Silencing the Guns on Walcheren Island, October 1944.
Royal Marines Museum Archive (RMMA)
 File 7/19/3: Papers relating to Operations VITALITY, SWITCHBACK and INFATUATE.
The National Archives (TNA)
 ADM 202/230: War Diary, 1 Engineer Commando (RM), December 1944.
 ADM 202/405: 4 Special Service Brigade: Orders and Miscellaneous Reports.
 CAB 106/998: The Final Report of 79th Armoured Division.

CAB 106/1090: Army Operational Research Group (AORG) Report 299: The Westkapelle Assault on Walcheren.

FO 371-49408: Letter from Anthony Eden, 3 January 1945.

WO 171/629: War Diary, 30 Armoured Brigade.

WO 171/1800: War Diary, 5th Assault Regiment, RE, June-December 1944.

WO 171/1801: War Diary, 6th Assault Regiment, RE, May-December 1944.

WO 171/1601: War Diary 241 Field Company RE, October-November 1944.

WO 171/1494: War Diary, 59 General Headquarters (GHQ) Troops RE, October-November 1944.

WO 171/544: War Diary, HQ RE 52nd Division, October – November 1944.

WO 199/88: RE Reports from Theatres of War.

WO 205/420: 79th Armoured Division: Mechanical Minesweeping.

WO205/1178: Summary of the Major Engineering Lessons of the Campaign in NW Europe 1944/45.

Secondary Sources

Anon., *The Alternative to Arnhem*, Operation Infatuate, *The Capture of Walcheren, 1 November 1944 and the Opening of Antwerp* (Portsmouth, UK: Naval Historical Branch, 1994).

Anon., *The Story of 79th Armoured Division* (Ukfield; UK: Naval and Military Press (reprint), n.d. [1945]).

Beckett, Alan, *Record of Army Service Including Experience of Design and Construction of Mulberry Harbour* (N.P., 1991).

Beevor, Anthony, *D-Day: The Battle for Normandy* (New York: Penguin, 2009).

Bertlin, Dennis, P., 'Temporary Repairs to the Locks at Flushing' in *The Civil Engineer in War: A Symposium of Papers on War-Time Engineering Problems* (London: Institute of Civil Engineers, 1948), pp.173-190.

Buckley, John D., *British Armour in the Normandy Campaign 1944* (New York: Routledge, 2004).

Buckley, John D., *Monty's Men: The British Army and the Liberation of Europe* (London: Yale University Press, 2014).

Catsburg, Robert (trans. I. Hardy), *Polder Fighting: The Battles for the Liberation of Oostburg 29-30 oktober 1944* (Privately Published, 2020)

Copp, Terry., *Cinderella Army: The Canadians in Northwest Europe 1944-1945* (Toronto: University of Toronto Press, 2012).

Crucq, Paul M., *We Never Blamed the Crews: The Flooding of Walcheren Island, October 1944* (Vlissingen: ADZ, 2000).

Crucq, Paul M., *Aiming Point Walcheren* (Vlissingen: ADZ, 2003).

Crucq, Paul M., *Turning the Key: The Capture and Liberation of Walcheren, October30-November 8 1944* (Vlissingen: ADZ, 2009).

Doolaard, A. den, (trans. Barrows Massey), *Roll Back the Sea* (London: Heinemann, 1948).

French, David, *Raising Churchill's Army: The British Army and the War Against Germany 1919-45* (Oxford: Oxford University Press, 2010 [2000]).

Goodlet, Kirk W., 'Reduced to the Banks of Mud From Which They Were Reclaimed: The Province of Zeeland, War and Reconstruction, 1940-1945', *Canadian Journal of Netherlandic Studies*, Vol. 34 (2) (2013), pp. 29-56.

Harrison Place, Tim., *Military Training in the British Army, 1940-1944: From Dunkirk to D-Day* (London: Routledge, 2000).

Hart, Stephen. A., *Colossal Cracks: Montgomery's 21st Army Group in Northwest Europe, 1944-45* (Mechanicsburg: Stackpole Books, 2007).

Hastings, Max, *Armageddon: The Battle for Germany 1944-45* (London: Macmillan, 2004).

Institution of Royal Engineers, *A Short History of the Corps of Royal Engineers* (Chatham, UK: InstRE, 2006).

Johnson, Maj I.H., 'The Dykes of Walcheren', *The Royal Engineers Journal*, Vol. 100 (2) (1986), pp.106-115.

Kerry, Col. A.J. & McDill, Maj W.A., *The History of the Corps of Royal Canadian Engineers*, Vol II: 1936-1946 (Ottawa: The Military Association of Canada, 1966).

Lee, Nigel de, 'Command, Control, Co-ordination and Communication at Westkappelle in November 1944 – Operation Infatuate II' in J. Buckley & P. Preston-Hough (eds), *Operation Market Garden: The Campaign for the Low Countries, Autumn 1944: Seventy Years On* (Solihull: Helion, 2016), pp. 241-257.

Murray, Williamson, 'British Military Effectiveness in the Second World War' in A.R. Millar & W. Murray (eds), *Military Effectiveness Vol.III The Second World War* (Cambridge University Press, 2010 [1988]), pp.90-135.

Pakenham-Walsh Maj.-Gen. R.P., *The History of the Corps of Royal Engineers*, Vol. IX, 1938-1948 (Chatham, UK: Institution of Royal Engineers, 1958).

Read, Brig. E.E., *The Saving of Walcheren* (Chatham: The Institution of Royal Engineers, 1947).

St George Saunders, Hilary, *The Green Beret: The Story of the Commandos 1940-1945* (London: Michael Joseph, 1949).

Transnational Development Clinic, Yale Law School, Global Health Justice Dept. and School of Public Health, Yale University, Association Haitienne de Droit de L'Environment, *Peacekeeping Without Accountability: The UN's Responsibility for the Haitian Cholera Epidemic*, 2013, p.49, available online at <https://www.law.yale.edu/system/files/documents/pdf/Clinics/Haiti_TDC_Final_Report.pdf>.

Zuiderbann, K.E., *Luctor et Emergo: Het Sluiten van de Dijksgaten van Walcheren* (Delft: Technische Universiteit Delft, 1999).

12

Thank you, Padre. Change and Continuity in the Royal Army Chaplains' Department, 1914 to 2021

Linda Parker

In February 1919 the Army Chaplains' Department won the accolade of becoming the Royal Army Chaplains' Department, acknowledging the way that it had adapted in the First World War to perform multifunctional roles on the battlefield, supporting the wounded spiritually and materially and by bringing in wounded to aid posts. Behind the lines they conducted services and funerals, ministered pastorally to the troops, and organised social and material comforts. Many were decorated for bravery and three, the Rev. Theodore Bayley Hardy, the Rev. William Addison, and the Rev. Noel Mellish, were awarded the Victoria Cross. Anglican chaplains were awarded 37 Distinguished Service Orders and 205 Military Crosses.[1] Chaplains such as G.A. Studdert Kennedy became well known in the war and for their post war careers.

A service to commemorate the centenary of the department as the RAChD was held on 22 February 2019. The British Army website commented:

> The Centenary Service will reflect upon the sacrifice and service of those chaplains who rose to the challenges of the great conflicts that have beset our nation, those who made the ultimate sacrifice, those that continue to

---

1   M.F Snape, *The Royal Army Chaplains' Department, 1796-1953: Clergy under Fire (Studies in Modern British Religious History)* (Woodbridge: Boydell Press, 2007), p.224.

support soldiers on operations today but also, those who have simply been there when a soldier has asked "Padre have you got a minute…?"[2]

The service was held in the Guards' Chapel and a new book of remembrance containing the names of the 315 Army chaplains who had died in the wars of the twentieth and twenty-first centuries was dedicated.

This chapter will examine both the role of the Army chaplain in the twentieth and twenty-first centuries, assessing its changes and continuities, looking at the historiography of the changing attitudes to chaplaincy in the army during this time, and considering the challenges that the department faces in the present century. The British Army has been involved in many conflicts in the last 100 years – too numerous to mention, but including two World Wars, the Falklands conflict, Bosnia, Northern Ireland, Afghanistan, and Iraq, to name but a few – and during this time has been affected by defence cuts and reviews, changes of policies, and changes to in the role expected of it by the British Government. The department has seen many changes in the national churches and in British society, including the rise of secularism, the growth of numbers of men and women of world faiths in the Army, and changes in the role of women in the Army not least the arrival of women chaplains. It is impossible to cover the changes and continuities chronologically in the space available, but by concentrating on some key issues and drawing on examples from different eras, is possible to draw out main developments and continuities of the chaplain's role over this period of time.

The main aspects to be considered are the chaplain's role in battle, the extent to which the chaplain's presence condones violence and killing, the effects of chaplains on morale, the cooperation with the medical services including issues of mental health and moral injury, and the provision of religious services and the challenges of ministering to servicemen and women from a British society which has become virtually unchurched compared with that of the early twentieth century. A final consideration is the role of the Royal Army Chaplains' Department in the Army of the future.

Chronological Overview

The chaplains of the First World War, particularly the Temporary Chaplains to the Forces, had worked hard to establish a role in the novel conditions of trench warfare and total war. They had to contend with the attitudes of commanding officers that

---

2   'Royal Army Chaplains' Department Centenary' at <https://web.archive.org/web/20211217154522/https://www.army.mod.uk/news-and-events/events/2019/royal-army-chaplains-department-centenary/>, accessed 28 October 2022.

chaplains were only for taking funerals,[3] and for organising what became known as 'Holy Grocery' – that is to say, the provision of material comforts and social activities. The chaplains heartily refuted these claims and emphasised that a chaplain had a multiplicity of tasks, foremost of which was the spiritual support of the men.[4]

When the Rev. E.C. Crosse, an Anglican padre, arrived in France in September 1915 he was told in no uncertain terms that he was 'absolutely forbidden' by his senior chaplain from venturing into the front line.[5] It was thought that chaplains would be in the way and serve no useful purpose. These orders were often disregarded, especially by Roman Catholic chaplains who had the theological imperative of administering the sacraments of Holy Communion or the last rites to soldiers.

When General Sir Douglas Haig became commander of the British Forces on the Western Front in September 1915 the situation was made easier for chaplains as Haig encouraged their fuller participation. Although chaplains were not encouraged to actually 'go over the top' – albeit that some did – many chaplains won decorations, including three Victoria Crosses for courage at the front line, staying with wounded in shell holes, and repeatedly going out to bring in injured. By the beginning of 1918 the chaplains had gained confidence and experience and felt they had the support of both men and officers. During 1918, 51 chaplains were killed – 26, in the last 100 days – possibly due to their increasing eagerness to be close to the action and increasing confidence that they could be of use in the front line. The most highly decorated chaplain, the Rev. Theodore Bayley Hardy, VC, DSO, MC died in October 1918. He was awarded his Victoria Cross for remaining in no man's land under fire for many hours to tend to and comfort a badly wounded soldier.

At the beginning of the war the majority of chaplains had been Anglican. In July 1915 Bishop Gwynne became the Deputy Chaplain General in charge of Anglican chaplains on the Western Front while nonconformist chaplains were led by Principal Chaplain, Presbyterian Rev. J. Simms. The enlargement and diversification of the department continued throughout the war. The Baptist, Congregationalist, United and Primitive Methodists became members of a United Navy and Army Board which oversaw appointments and quotas for chaplains in these denominations. By November 1918 there were 215 United Board Chaplains.[6] The Wesleyan Methodists had been well represented in the department pre-war but also saw a growth in their numbers to 256 by the end of the war. In 1920

3   D. Winnifrith, *The Church in the Fighting Line* (London: Hodder and Stoughton, 1915), p.19.
4   See discussion in Linda Parker, *The Whole Armour of God: Anglican Chaplains in the Great War* (Warwick: Helion, 2009), Chapter 6, pp.56-62.
5   Imperial War Museum (IWM) 8/20/1, Papers of the Rev. E.C. Crosse.
6   Snape, *Clergy under Fire*, p.199.

the Army Chaplain's Department was reorganised, consisting of an Anglican Chaplain General, a deputy of another denomination, and a Principal Roman Catholic Chaplain.[7] The only provision for soldiers of a non-Christian religion was for soldiers of the Jewish faith. The first Jewish chaplain to serve on the Western Front was Dr Michael Adler, and the rapid expansion of numbers of Jewish soldiers resulted in 16 Jewish Chaplains serving by November 1918.[8]

At the beginning of the Second World War, therefore, the department was assured of a role which would be regarded as helpful and, in many minds, essential. A total of 3,629 chaplains served in the Second World War.[9] They were expected and encouraged to be with their men at every stage of their combat experience. The Rev. Freddie Hughes managed to achieve a high profile for army chaplaincy in the 8th Army. Field Marshal Montgomery famously said:

> I would soon think of going into action without my artillery as without my chaplains… The most important people in the army are the nursing sisters and the padres – the sisters because they tell the men they matter to us – and the padres because they tell the men they matter to God. And it is the men who matter.[10]

By 1944, the realisation that chaplains were often in the heat of battle resulted in more practical battle courses being provided at Church Stowe which dealt with vehicle maintenance, radio communication, mines, booby traps, camouflage and security, first aid, and mapping skills. It was decided that all chaplains taking part in the D-Day landings should attend this course.

However, 100 commissioned chaplains died in the war, mainly killed in action or died of wounds. Significantly, overall losses were proportionate to the number of fatalities suffered by the British Army in the war.[11] Chaplains were in action in all theatres of war offering their 'ministry of presence' in many different front-line situations. At Dunkirk they were described as 'the last off the beach' and several were captured. Airborne padres in particular, operating in a completely new operational context, were similarly at risk throughout the conflict as they parachuted or landed with gliders into situations where there was often no possibility of retreat, as at Arnhem. Fifteen British chaplains landed at Arnhem, of whom nine became prisoners of war, one was sheltered by the Dutch until

7   'Roman Catholic Bishopric of the Forces', at <https://www.rcbishopricforces.org.uk/royal-navy>, accessed 28 January 2022.

8   Snape, *Clergy Under Fire*, p.202.

9   Snape, *Clergy Under Fire*, p.202.

10 M.F. Snape, *God and the British Soldier: Religion and the British Army in the First and Second World Wars* (Oxford: Routledge, 2005), pp.124-126. Snape, *Clergy under Fire*, p.306.

11 Snape, *Clergy under Fire*, p.336.

liberation, two died of wounds, and three escaped during the evacuation of the remnants of 1st Airborne Division.[12]

The padres in the Second World War had acted as a bridge between the role of chaplains at the beginning of the twentieth century and the beginning of the twenty-first century. It was in this war that it was accepted that as imperative that chaplains should be in the front line of battle and accompany their troops at all times.

Chaplains in Post-War Germany

From the end of the Second World War, the rebuilding of religious life in Germany was a fraught and complicated issue, overseen by the Religious Affairs Section of the Allied Control Commission. Army chaplains who had been taking services in a variety of temporary venues and buildings since D-Day were encouraged to make use of Protestant churches as garrison churches, pending the provision of permanent garrisons and garrison churches. Peter Howson has pointed out that the role of the chaplains was more sensitive than for many others in in the Army:

> Whilst members of the army, serving the religious needs of their fellows…
> In most cases they were also members of churches which had views and policies of their own… In most cases the chaplains could be certain that their sending churches would have an interest in the religious side of the German people and the life of the churches.[13]

Chaplains gradually expanded their remit to include humanitarian work in aid of the German population with some, for example Chaplain Douglas Lister in 1947 made a national appeal for clothing parcels for the help German civilians in the coming winter.[14] Chaplains were also involved in the screening of German pastors and priests in prisoner of war camps to ensure their suitability to be released and continue their ministry.

An inspiring chaplain caught up in the post-Second World War conflicts was the Rev. Sam Davies who was chaplain to the 1st Battalion Gloucester Regiment when it was overrun at the Imjin River in Korea on 22 April 1951. During the battle he ministered to the dying and wounded. He decided to stay with the severely wounded and later explained his reasoning: 'Whatever happens it was my duty

---

12 'The Chaplains at Arnhem', at <https://www.paradata.org.uk/article/chaplains-arnhem>, accessed 28 October 2022.
13 Peter Howson, *Britain and the German Churches, 1945-1950: The Role of the Religious Affairs Branch in the British Zone* (Martlesham: Boydell and Brewer: 2021), p.32.
14 Snape, *Clergy under Fire*, p.345.

as a chaplain, really to stay with these few men who cannot move... My duty to them was to remain with them as chaplain to give what solace I could'. [15] Davies was then marched 600 miles to an prisoner of war camp where he spent two and a half years.

The British Army was involved in the troubles in Northern Ireland from the late 1960s to 1998. The incident known as 'Bloody Sunday' in January 1972 swelled the IRA's ranks. Civil unrest continued and violence against the security forces increased. In February 1972 Aldershot barracks was bombed in retaliation. Six civilians and a British army chaplain, Fr Gerard Weston, were killed. He had recently returned from Northern Ireland where he had taken part in peace nego-tiations in dangerous situations and been awarded the MBE for gallantry.[16]

The complicated mix of nationalism and religion was difficult for army chap-lains, particularly Roman Catholic Priests. Fr David Smith considered that 'As Roman Catholic priests we "got it" from both sides: the Nationalists were suspi-cious of us since we were identified with the occupying force. The army was suspi-cious of us since we were identified with the enemy.'[17] In his work on 'Terrorism and Interrogation, as an Issue for Chaplains on Operations' Peter Sedgwick quoted a telling caption on the chaplains in Northern Ireland in a display in the Museum of Army Chaplaincy when it was based at the British Armed Forces Chaplaincy, then at Amport. The caption described the chaplains in the insurgency as being 'exhausted, emotionally physically and spiritually' and continued with the opinion that this caption is probably appropriate.[18]

Fifteen Army Chaplains accompanied the Falklands Task Force in 1982. One, the Rev. David Cooper, was mentioned in despatches. In an interview in 2005 he commented: 'As chaplain, you're often the one who breaks the news of losses to the blokes'. He explained:

> I couldn't say anything I didn't believe. I couldn't tell them what happens after death, I had no idea, but I could tell them that I believe in a God who has the power to care beyond death. That they mattered and whatever happened they would still matter to God. But I didn't believe in a God who would divert the path of a bullet, so they had to accept what was coming and remember their training. [19]

---

15   Snape, *Clergy under Fire*, p.6.

16   'Padre Gerry E. Weston MBE', at <https://www.paradata.org.uk/people/gerry-e-weston>, accessed 28 October 2022.

17   Peter Sedgwick, 'Terrorism and Interrogation as an Issue for Chaplains on Operations' in Andrew Todd, (ed.) *Military Chaplaincy in Contention: Chaplains, Churches and the morality of Conflict* (Farnham: Ashgate 2013), p.71.

18   Sedgwick, 'Terrorism and Interrogation as an Issue for Chaplains on Operations' p.71.

19   Rev. David Cooper quoted in Stephen Armstrong, 'The Good Fight' in *The Guardian*, 15 October 2005, avail-able online at <https://www.theguardian.com/world/2005/oct/15/iraq.comment>, accessed 14 October 2022.

Padre Cooper was with 2 Para as it advanced to Goose Green, talking to the wounded and dying as the medics attended to them. The first soldier killed was one whose marriage he had performed only two years before. The boy had been shot through the eye, so he could not actually recognise him.

BBC reporter Robert Fox praised the unit padres who 'had been quite outstanding in their service …. they do a lot of good for the health, care and welfare of the troops'. He also praised their handling of funerals of Argentinian dead in a 'correct and proper way'.[20]

In the ships going south to the Falklands, army chaplains accompanied troops. There were four chaplains on the *Canberra* and three on the *Queen Elizabeth II*, both of which had been 'taken up from trade'. Interdenominational services were held in the ships, some for large groups, such as those held in the theatres, followed by smaller Holy Communion services. Daily services were held and smaller groups prayed regularly, such as the group led by the Rev. Peter Brooke of the Welsh Guards who recalled that: 'Significant for me was a small group of six or seven of us who met for prayer each morning between breakfast sittings. One who prayed with us did not return. How can we measure the spiritual importance of these sacred moments for him?'[21]

Once ashore chaplains took services as and when possible. The Rev. Derek Heaver remembered the second Sunday that he was on the islands, when he took a service at San Carlos that was attended by civilians from the settlement as well as the few soldiers who were not under orders to move. On Sunday 13 June, he was with 3 Para in the thick of the fighting on Mount Longdon where they lost 23 men:

> That was a full day of shelling; we were so busy with the wounded and the dead. I found myself looking after the dead, caring for them, making than decent, putting them to one side, preparing them, taking personal possessions from them, documenting than. I thought of taking a service, but with the constant shelling, it didn't arise on that Sunday. But one thing that I did do that day was to get back by helicopter to Teal Inlet. In the late afternoon we buried eighteen Paras, sharing the service with the Marines and in the end there were 24 buried at that service.[22]

The United Nations peacekeeping mission to Bosnia began in early 1992, when efforts by the Bosnian Serbs to achieve independence from Bosnia-Herzegovina and unite with Serbia resulted in conflicts involving ethnic cleansing and mass

20   *Church Times*, 11 June 1982.
21   Editorial, 'Falklands Recollections: Interviews with Revs David Cooper and Derek Heaver', *R.A.Ch.D. Journal*, Vol.27 No.2, December 1982, p.6.
22   Editorial, 'Falklands Recollections', p.9.

destruction of lives and property. Although the United Nations force was crucial in distributing humanitarian aid to the impoverished population of Bosnia, it was unable to stop the fighting. The tensions and frustrations of the limitations of being a peace keeping army along with witnessing brutality of the conflict took its toll on British soldiers who served there. They felt that they were 'stuck in the middle of someone else's battlefield to do what they could'.[23]

The Rev. Tyrone Hillary was chaplain of the Cheshire Regiment in 1993 attached to an ambulance unit that was tasked with clearing bodies after the massacre at Ahnici. One April day near Vitez they recovered the bodies of 96 Muslim men women and children. Hillary organised the regimental aid parcels sent from the soldiers' families for the victims of the war. The *Church Times* reported: 'Through his contacts with local clergy, Catholic, Muslim and Orthodox, he heard of remote villages in need and wrote off six vehicles in reaching them'. He told the *Church Times*: 'One of the biggest problems they faced was the conflict between political considerations and what they considered to be their moral obligations'. His report on the six-month tour of duty ended: 'I don't know what the politically correct solution might be. But I do know that we, as a force, were able to stand as caring human beings in the midst of a horrible situation, helping where it was possible and sharing the tears when it wasn't.'[24]

In 1996 Nick Cook was the chaplain of the Second Battalion, The Light Infantry, one of the two British infantry units to implement the Dayton Accord. He described the tensions the army. He felt: 'We were not there to remonstrate, nor to arrest and detain: we were there to ensure compliance, militarily, with the Dayton Agreement. Nor were the Bosnians allies whom we might have admonished, or disciplined. So we were caught in a cleft stick.' He was particularly troubled by the fact that he could discern no remorse or regret from the situation from either side. At one stage he recounted: 'I shut down. Like some overloaded computer, I developed a general protection fault, and turned off my ability to see any purpose or good in any of the population to protect myself from burnout.'[25]

The conflicts of the twenty-first century in Afghanistan and Iraq have seen ample opportunity for the chaplain's role in the front line to be developed in response to the nature of those conflicts, both in the TELIC and HERRICK operations. Chaplains, although unarmed, faced the dangers that the troops faced, being present at Forward Operating Bases, going put on patrol, joining supply convoys and coming under fire at base camps. Michael Snape has commented that during the HERRICK operations relatively inexperienced chaplains were facing difficult

23   *Church Times*, 15 August 1993.
24   *Church Times*, 15 August 1993.
25   *Church Times*, 19 April 1996.

and new operational and pastoral challenges in a similar manner to the temporary chaplains to the forces in the First World War.[26]

Chaplains receive the same training as officers (except firearms training) and it is their job to be alongside their men and women. Major Nigel Jordan-Barber in Afghanistan in 2009 had soldiers of varying denominations under him and stated that padres offer a 'ministry of all soul' that is respected by all, going on to say that he had 'been assisted in my role as a commander by a great number of padres conducting their ministry in arduous and extreme environments. Their presence alongside us is as valuable as their role.'[27] At the service of Prayer and Remembrance for the armed forces held by the Defence Christian Network in November 2021, the congregation heard recorded reports from chaplains with the United Nations peacekeeping operations in Mali, the Royal Tank Regiment in Estonia, and in Qatar who had been helping in Operation PITTING and the evacuation of Kabul earlier in 2021.

Services and Liturgy

The taking of services has obviously been a given during the history of the Chaplains' Department since its inception. Services in the First and Second World Wars took place in all kinds of informal settings on the battlefield and more formally and leisurely at base camps. The First World War Anglican chaplains found the formal liturgy used by the church, particularly for funerals, archaic. Chaplain Eric Milner White in his contribution to *The Church in the Furnace* summed it up: 'Liturgy vanished with peace and rubrics paled in a redder world'.[28] He also described the Book of Common Prayer as 'semi-usable and semi-used.'[29]

Airborne chaplains in the Second World War took services in the field hospitals on the frontline at Arnhem and in the shelter of mines in the North African desert.[30] An SAS chaplain, Fraser McCluskey, took service behind the lines in the forests of the Morvan where the volume of singing that was allowed depended on the proximity of German patrols.[31] In the retreat from Burma in 1942, the Rev. N.S. Metcalfe remembered the long trek through the jungle with the 7th Queen's Own Hussars, arriving exhausted at Imphal in time for a Whit Sunday service. His

26 M. Snape and V. Henshaw, 'Flanders to Helmand: Chaplaincy, Faith and Religious Change in the British Army 1914-2014', *Journal of Beliefs and Values*, Vol 38. (2), p.12.

27 *The Guardian*, 5 October 2011.

28 E. Milner-White, 'Worship and Services', in F.B. Macnutt, (ed.) *The Church in the Furnace* (London: McMillan, 1918), p.175.

29 Milner-White, 'Worship and Services', p.177.

30 L. Parker, *Nearer My God to Thee: Airborne Chaplains in the Second World War* (Warwick: Helion, 2019), p.35.

31 Fraser McLuskey, *Parachute Padre* (London: SCM Press, 1951), p.79.

altar was a packing case; a sports cup took the place of a chalice, Army biscuits for wafers and local whisky for wine. However, the service 'went with a swing'. [32] In the Far East in the Second World War and in Korea, chaplains continued to take services in appalling conditions in prisoner of war camps. The Rev. Sam Davies, chaplain to the Glosters in Korea, managed to conduct services, battling against the opposition of his communist warders. He was only given an allowance of bread and wine for Holy Communion five times during this time. [33]

The peacekeeping role of the British Army in Bosnia saw the early development of the repatriation ceremonies which were to be a prominent part of the army chaplains' duties in the late twentieth and early twenty-first centuries. On 1 February 1996 a repatriation service took place at the Divulje Barracks in Croatia for three members of The Light Dragoons killed by an anti-tank mine in central Bosnia. During the ceremony the Rev. Lesley Bryan offered the prayer: 'We ask God's help that in all the ways of our lives we may walk worthy of their sacrifice.' [34]

At Camp Bastion the tri-service chaplains worked closely together and maintained a chapel in a tent and space for prayer and reflection. Lieutenant-Colonel David Vassalo recalled some of the medical staff pausing in the chapel for prayer and reflection on the way to work. [35]

The First and Second World Wars saw the necessity of burying soldiers in situ, and then perhaps concentrating them in larger cemeteries at a later date. The chaplains in the First World War at first were the only people noting where people had died and were buried and their work was invaluable to the Imperial (later Commonwealth) War Graves Commission in their work after the First World War. From the Falklands conflict onward, bodies could be repatriated though many remain in the islands. From the author's personal experience at the time, one of the strong memories of the people who were following the events from Britain was the television footage of the temporary burial in a mass grave of the casualties from 2 Para at Ajax Bay by Chaplain David Cooper.

During the wars in Iraq and in Afghanistan the bodies of British service personnel were repatriated to Britain. Government data shows an increase in casualties in Afghanistan from 2008 reaching a height in 2009 and 2010. [36] When the intensity of battle in Helmand Province reached new heights the practice of

---

32 John Smyth, *In This Sign Conquer* (London: A.R. Mowbray and Co, 1968), p.306.

33 'Colonel the Reverend 'Sam' Davies (Glosters' Chaplain Korea)', thread on *British Militaria Forums* at < https://www.tapatalk.com/groups/britishmilitariaforums/colonel-the-reverend-39-sam-39-davies-glosters-39--t8557.html>, accessed 28 October 2022.

34 Associated Press Archive, 'CROATIA: REPATRIATION SERVICE HELD FOR 3 DEAD BRITISH IFOR TROOPS', <http://www.aparchive.com/metadata/youtube/205e9e9d240f984ba16517f58495caa2>, accessed 20 November 2021.

35 Lieutenant-Colonel David Vassalo RAMC (retd), interviewed by the author July 2021.

36 'British fatalities: Operations in Afghanistan', <https://www.gov.uk/government/fields-of-operation/afghanistanfatalities>, accessed 14 October 2022.

vigil services emerged. A vigil or memorial service was held in the late afternoon and attended by all who could on the base. It was a formal parade including a scripture reading by the senior officer present, a eulogy by a representative of the cap badge, prayers of commendation, and the Last Post. There were representatives from other nations, and in Afghanistan representatives of the Afghan Forces. At such ceremonies at Camp Bastion there could be thousands on parade. It was found that it was inadvisable for the coffins to be present in the heat of the day so later the ramp ceremony at the airhead took place late at night. This was essentially for the men and women of the casualty's own unit, their Commanding Officer and chaplain, when the body would be carried to the plane and loaded after a short ceremony ending with the chaplain facing backwards to the hold, to give a blessing before the tail gate was closed.[37]

Major Nigel Jordan-Barber was a rifle company commander with 3 Scots (the Black Watch) in summer 2009, a particularly bloody period for British troops in Afghanistan. Several 3 Scots soldiers died during the battalion's six-month tour of Musa Qala, Helmand Province. He described a ramp service he had taken part in for Gus Millar as 'one of the most contradictory and moving events I have experienced':

> His coffin was paraded past the battlegroup on to the tailgate of the aircraft which was to fly him home. Padre Duncan said some quiet prayers before the aircraft taxied away. I discussed it with some of my soldiers afterwards and they were very clear that although it wasn't a funeral we all felt we had taken part in a very spiritual event.

Jordon Barber also appreciated that Millar was very popular and his death came as a shock to most of his company. Being able to call on a padre who knew the deceased, and knew the soldiers, to advise him how to manage their grief, was of immense importance. He also commented: 'This is not mawkish sentimentality, but essential in my role as commander to make sure that they had the time and the resources to get their thoughts in order before they went back to their operational tasks'.[38]

This comment, which stresses the benefit to morale of such services, is relevant to the sometimes-controversial question of the effect chaplains have on morale, whether they are seen as a force multiplier – that is to say, an item or a support that magnifies the ability, firepower, or reach of a unit. Another occasion related

---

37 Andrew Totten, 'Contextual Issues: War and Peace' in Christopher Swift, Mark Cobb and Andrew Todd (eds.), *A Handbook of Chaplaincy Studies* (Farnham: Ashgate, 2015), p.220.

38 Riazat Butt, 'UK chaplains in Afghanistan: ordinary priests with an extraordinary flock', *The Guardian*, <https://www.theguardian.com/uk/2011/oct/05/uk-chaplains-afghanistan-priests-congregation>, accessed 14 October 2022.

by chaplain the Rev. Stephen Sharkey concerned the taking of a memorial service at a forward operating base which was coming frequently under fire. The service started peacefully but the base suddenly came under attack: 'I stared out of the side of my eye towards the officer in charge and the company sergeant major. They made no move.' He realised that the real decision on whether to continue the service was his. The service continued, with some troops falling out to man guns with supressing fire but the majority staying and carrying on. Later he considered that this instinctive decision had been correct as the service would have not had the same effect on the soldiers if it had been abandoned or continued later. However, he did consider that the service rendered the troops more charged and focused. 'It did prove to be a force multiplier'.[39]

An operating instruction sent out by the Rev. Andrew Totten to the chaplains of 16 Air Assault Brigade in July 2010 just before deployment is illustrative of the wide variety of services and religious input that were expected. Chaplains were expected to give spiritual support 'underpinned by religious services both military and denominational'. Pre-deployment and homecoming services were to be arranged and 'in addition to their daily devotions chaplains will lead at least one act of public worship each week'. Plans were to be made for Remembrance Sunday and Christmas and the 'religious elements which attach to the different stages of repatriation' were to be considered. Prayers and orders of service were to be made available for junior commanders to take services when the chaplain was unavailable and prayer books and collect cards (cards on which the regimental collect was printed) were to be distributed to all personnel.[40]

Chaplains with Prisoners of War

During the First World War few chaplains were captured and became prisoners of war compared with the Second World War. The Rev. Benjamin O' Rorke was one of several chaplains captured early in the war, in his case at Landrecies in August 1914 when staying behind the retreating British Army with an ambulance unit. He was repatriated in August 1915 in an exchange of prisoners. He had no opportunity to minister to fellow prisoners other than officers but for the last months of his stay he had been allowed to go to other camps and to the camp hospital to visit the sick.[41]

39   Andrew Todd, 'Chaplaincy in Contention' in Andrew Todd (ed.), *Military Chaplaincy in Contention: Chaplains, Churches and the morality of Conflict* (Farnham: Ashgate, 2009), p.9.

40   Jonathan Ball '"Oh Hear Us When We Cry to Thee": Liturgy in the Current Operational Context', in Todd (ed.), *Military Chaplaincy in Contention*, p.129.

41   Peter Howson, *Padre, Prisoner and Pen-Pusher: The World War One Experiences of the Revd Benjamin O'Rorke* (Solihull: Helion and Company, 2015), p.23.

The Rev. Harold Spooner was captured with two other chaplains of 6th Indian Division at the siege of Kut. Having survived a 600-mile trek and a five-day river voyage to Baghdad in which he witnessed appalling treatment of prisoners, he was dismayed to discover that he was not allowed to visit camps of other ranks despite repeated appeals to the Turkish authorities, and had to contain his ministry to his camp of officers and orderlies. Spooner suffered an intense nervous breakdown as a result of the atrocities he had seen as a prisoner of war and spent 16 years in a nursing home, eventually recovering and going on to a happy retirement.[42]

In the Second World War many more chaplains were taken prisoner, reflecting their increased presence in all theatres of war. By 1942 86 chaplains were listed as prisoners of war with another 38 listed as missing. Many of these had been captured by the Japanese and imprisoned in camps such as Changi and along the Burma Railway. The Rev. Eric Cordingly was a chaplain at both Changi and on the Burma Railway from the fall of Singapore until 1945. He described in his memoirs of camp life the camp chapel which had been previously a mosque for Indian troops and the services taken there with home brewed wine for Holy Communion and the problems of lack of food and many deaths from dysentery. Cordingly survived his time on the Burma Railway, unlike 45 percent of the prisoners forced to work on it in intolerable conditions. The Japanese captors on the Burma Railway went out of their way to prevent religious services taking place.[43]

In Europe, as chaplains were kept in camps for officers and not allowed to visit other ranks, there were often quite a few chaplains in each camp, who frequently occupied themselves with the setting up of educational schemes and lectures as well as taking services and pastoral duties. Airborne chaplain the Rev. Murdo McDonald, captured in North Africa in 1943, ended up in Stalag Luft 3 and was closely involved with the major figures in the Great Escape, although he felt that as a chaplain it was his duty to stay in the camp. The Rev. John King was captured at Dunkirk and spent five years as prisoner, leaving a detailed description of his captivity, including visiting camps and working parties.[44]

In the Korean War the Rev. Sam Davies in a Korean prison camp ministered in extremely difficult conditions, facing harsh punishment in solitary confinement and constant opposition to church services from the Chinese captors who insisted that he was using religious services for political activities.[45] He was the only one of the four captured UN chaplains to survive his imprisonment. Since the Korean War, thankfully there have been no mass imprisonments of British soldiers.

42   IWM 1/51/94, Papers of the Rev. Harold Spooner.

43   Eric Cordingly, *Down to Bedrock: The Diary and Secret Notes of a Far East Prisoner of War Chaplain 1942-45* (Norwich: Art Angels Publishing, 2013).

44   John H. King, *Thank you Padre* (privately printed, unknown date).

45   S.J. Davies, *In Spite of Dungeons* (London: Hodder and Stoughton, 1954) p.99.

Chaplains as Morale Boosters and Force Multipliers

Stephen Sharkey's account of the service under fire in Afghanistan, quoted above, is an example of how the chaplain's job is inextricably mixed with questions of their effect on morale.

We have seen how Great War chaplains were considered to be good for morale. General Sir Douglas Haig, appointed on 10 September 1915, considered chaplains vital for morale, not only in their role as providing material comforts and recreational pursuits, but in their preaching and direct influence on the troops. Michael Snape argues that Haig 'consistently sought to ensure his chaplains made a concerted and systematic effort to bolster morale the pursuit of victory, particularly among front line units'.[46] At a conference at Cassel in January 1916 Haig said: 'We must have large minded sympathetic men as parsons who preach the great cause for which we are fighting and can imbue their hearers with enthusiasm. Any clergyman who is not fit for this work must be sent home.'[47]

However simple this association of chaplains with good morale may have been to the generals, it was a difficult and ambiguous matter for the chaplains. Many were aware of the conflict between their position of men of God and their many faceted role, and the implications were resented. Rev. E.C. Crosse wrote extensively in his diary about morale. He realised that chaplains were considered important for 'improving general morale' by their pastoral and material care and sometimes their sermons and talks, and considered that religion was important, encouraging 'inner discipline', but did not equate this to instilling bellicosity or glorifying war under a religious banner. He considered that there were two very different types of morale, the 'fighting spirit' needed for battles and the 'spirit of endurance' needed to survive life in the trenches. He stressed that their religious and pastoral duties were uppermost in the minds of the chaplains.[48]

The early twentieth century historiography of chaplain literature, particularly that of Anglican chaplains, has been one of criticism, by such well-known contemporary observers as Robert Graves and Siegfried Sassoon, but also from historians such as Stephen Louden and Albert Marrin who have disparaged the 'Holy Grocery' and morale boosting aspects of military chaplains.[49] Perhaps because he was one of the most well-known and well-loved pares of the Great War, the Rev. G.A. Studdert Kennedy, has come in for much criticism in this area. Stephen Louden in his book *Chaplains in Conflict* is vociferous in his condemnation: 'Studdert Kennedy resolved the conflict between

---

46 M.F. Snape, *God and the British Soldier: Religion and the British Army in the First and Second World Wars* (Oxford: Routledge, 2005), p.96.

47 Snape, *Clergy under Fire*, pp.219-221.

48 IWM 8/20/1 The Papers of the Rev. E.C. Crosse.

49 Stephen Louden, *Chaplains in Conflict* (London: Avon Books, 1996); Albert Marrin, *The Last Crusade: The Church of England in the First World War* (Durham, N.C: Duke University Press. 1974).

the system of values proclaimed by Christianity and those engendered by the current view of patriotism almost invariably in favour of the latter',[50] and one of his biographers, William Purcell, commented that 'He seems at times to have allowed himself gladly to be used as a morale booster to an extent which would certainly have been regarded as improper in a chaplain of the Second War'.[51]

Louden described the talks given by Studdert Kennedy at the 4th Infantry School at Flixecourt as 'larded … with a fire eating bombast, which best calculated to boost the morale of the fighting men to spur them to the supreme sacrifice'.[52] The talks given by Studdert Kennedy at the end of a show which became known as the 'travelling circus' were remembered by the commanding officer, Colonel R.B. Campbell. He described how the talks 'never failed to get a wonderful response from his audience. Leaving them with their "tails up" and ready for battle'.[53] This has been seized upon as evidence of his overt boosting of military morale, but war correspondent Phillip Gibbs, who heard him at Flixecourt, described his speeches as talking of 'God, war and the meaning of courage', which gives a wider and more nuanced appreciation of the way in which Studdert Kennedy raised morale on these occasions.

In modern ideas and studies of chaplaincy there seems to be a change of emphasis in the role of chaplains as force multipliers which considers a wider definition of 'morale'. The question of the role, real or assumed, of chaplains as force multipliers, leads to the question of role tension in chaplains. In the second half of the twentieth century, Alan Wilkinson and Gordon Zahn explored role conflict and chaplains, the latter remarking that 'by his very presence the pastor in uniform represents a symbol of legitimacy … if it were not permissible for believers to take part in the war, would the priest be there?'[54] At variance with this perspective are the works of Michael Snape, Edward Madigan, and the present author, who have defended chaplains in studies which examine ministerial roles and effectiveness.[55] Wilkes and Gutkowski, in considering the role of modern chaplaincy, have stressed the tension between the chaplains as symbols of neutrality and peace, and the fact that they are an embedded part of the fighting force and can be seen

---

50 Louden, *Chaplains in Conflict*, p.61.
51 William Purcell, *Woodbine Willie, An Anglican Incident* (London: Hodder and Stoughton, 1962), p.105.
52 Louden, *Chaplains in Conflict*, p.61.
53 D.F. Carey, 'War Padre', in J.K.Mozley (ed.) *G.A.Studdert Kennedy by His Friends* (London: Hodder and Stoughton, 1929), p.129.
54 Gordon Zahn, *Chaplains in the RAF: Study in Role Tension* (Manchester: Manchester University Press, 1969), p.112.
55 Snape, *The Royal Army Chaplains' Department, 1796-1953*; E. Madigan, *Faith under Fire: Anglican Army Chaplains and the Great War* (London: Palgrave Macmillan); Parker, *The Whole Armour of God*.

as 'Instruments of the state'.[56] However, David Cooper was in no doubt after his experiences in the Falklands about the way in which chaplains are most of all important as providing Christian witness at all times: 'I have no doubt at all that we need good priests when we have a war, that we have a war priest who can talk sensibly about Christ and show Him in their lives'.[57]

Chaplains Working with Medical Services

Chaplains and medics have always worked closely together from the earliest days of military life. In the First and, to a certain extent, the Second World War, chaplains physically took part in medical procedures, acting as anaesthetists and bandaging limbs. In the Falklands Conflict there were chaplains aboard the hospital ship *Uganda* as well as at first aid post posts on land. At Camp Bastion, there were always several chaplains who were specifically assigned to the hospital and worked closely with the medical staff. Chaplains of different military services and different denominations worked closely together. David Vassalo, former consultant surgeon at Camp Bastion, described the support given to the medical teams, who were traumatised by their constant struggle with death and injury. He described their role as 'caring for the carers'.[58] Several chaplains have recounted occasions when they watched over a seriously injured man in the operating or ward and then were told that no more could be done and for the chaplain to 'take over' to administer the last rites and to pray for the patient and the medical team.[59]

The Reverend Paul McCourt Chaplain to the Forces (Volunteer), Roman Catholic Chaplain to 201 (Northern) Field Hospital (V)) wrote of his experiences:

> I arrived in Camp Bastion [in January 2012] to find my life as a priest would assume a vastly different appearance to the norm back home… Compared to visiting NHS hospitals where a chaplain may sometimes feel outside of the whole care structure, this environment by contrast seems to draw the chaplain to the very core of its existence. Staff here actively and generously draw me in and seek me out. It would seem that the chaplain is very much an integral part of the hospital's care structure, and my presence here is largely respected and warmly received by colleagues and patients alike.

---

56   Stacey Gutkowski and George Wilkes, 'Changing Chaplaincy: a Contribution to Debate over the Roles of US and British Military Chaplains in Afghanistan', *Religion, State & Society*, 39:1, pp.111-124.

57   Editorial, 'Falklands Recollections', p.15.

58   Lieutenant-Colonel David Vassalo RAMC (retd), interviewed by the author July 2021.

59   See for example interview with the Rev. Stuart Hallam, *Church Times*, 9 November 2010.

As a chaplain to the sick, the wounded and the dying I have found in them and in the staff who care so carefully for them a glimpse of the divine presence of God.[60]

Relationships with Commanders, Officers and Other Ranks

Chaplains have often been the sources of comfort and advice to senior army officers as with the Rev. Duncan and Haig in the First World War or the Rev. Freddie Hughes and Montgomery in the Second World War. Some commanders realise that the chaplain is often in a good position to gauge morale and to provide a moral compass both for officers and men. The Rev. Philip McCormack has studied the implications of asymmetric warfare on the intersection of legal justification for military action and the moral and ethical justifications. In modern warfare where the enemy is not bound by international legality, the legal parameters set by nations are not always an appropriate guide. He recounts the experience of a brigade chaplain sitting in on a planning meeting for an action in Afghanistan who was asked why he had said nothing during the meeting. He replied that they would not like what he had to say, and, when pressed, explained that the military planning had as its basis the consideration of what was lawful and not what was ethical or moral. He continued by stating that the war had been explained to the public as a moral and ethical war and that 'what often resonates with the public is the moral impact of an attack or incident and not the finely tuned balanced niceties of legal judgement'.[61] The ability of chaplains to sometimes tactfully challenge decisions and actions means that they can act as a moral compass to both officers and other ranks.

An example of the consequences when this fails to happen were seen in the failure of a chaplain in the Iraq conflict to speak out or intervene in any way with the ill treatment and torture of prisoners in British custody in Iraq. The judge who presided at the Baha Mousa Inquiry criticised the chaplain for not 'intervening immediately or reporting it up the chain of command'.[62]

In all wars men and women see death as a constant companion. Men and women facing death need the reassurance of the resurrection even when they are not overtly religious. The need to know their men becomes important in times of

---

60 Personal account by The Reverend Paul McCourt CF (V), Roman Catholic Chaplain to 201 (Northern) Field Hospital (V)), quoted in David Vassallo, 'A short history of Camp Bastion Hospital: part 2—Bastion's catalytic role in advancing combat casualty care', at <https://www.friendsofmillbank.org/downloads/camp_bastion_short_history_2.pdf>, accessed 28 October 2022.

61 P. McCormack, 'You've Been Silent Padre', in Andrew Todd(ed.) *Military Chaplaincy in Contention*, p.40.

62 *The Tablet*, 17 November 2011.

conflict. Padre David Cooper in the Falkland Islands with 2 Para did not often use the language of the church or liturgy. He spoke of:

> [The] willingness of the soldiers to put the interest of their friends before their own desire for personal survival – there was an obvious link between this and what Christ did but if he was to talk about it he would use not Church language, but the language they understood. In simple terms they were asked to be prepared to die.[63]

The chaplains in the Falklands conflict were very aware of having been close to, and having a good relationship with, their men that dated back to peacetime. As he was moving among the wounded at Bluff Cove, the Rev. Brooke of the Welsh Guards said: 'As I recognised and spoke to some of the injured, the value of being a pastor among men and of being known by them became blindingly obvious. Later, moving among the shocked survivors, the same message was brought home to me.'[64]

Bill Gates in Helmand, although a naval chaplain serving with the Royal Marines, emphasised a feeling common in many Army chaplains, that is the need to 'suffer with the men whatever happens'. He felt that an important part of his role in the battlefield area was to 'Help men coping with their friends dying ... they become aware of what is important'.[65]

The then Chaplain-General for HM Land Forces, the Ven. Stephen Robbins, spoke in the General Synod of the Church of England in February 2010: 'Chaplains and soldiers who witnessed slaughter asked a valid theological question: "What is God like, to let this happen"?'. He continued: 'But God was in Christ who made himself vulnerable, it is the God of love who is the motivation for the Armed Forces' Chaplaincy', explaining that soldiers were not natural-born killers and that they often sought forgiveness for what they had done. 'They might not queue up at the altar, but they did want hope of the resurrection when faced with their own death or that of friends'.[66]

Change and Continuity in Army Chaplaincy

The First World War was a steep learning curve for the chaplains. By the end of that conflict, 3,475 had served. It is generally accepted that chaplains had found a niche

---

63   *Church Times*, 6 November 1987.
64   *Church Times*, 31 December 1982.
65   Comments made by the Rev. Bill Gates interviewed for 'What It's Like Being a Commando Chaplain in Afghanistan', documentary available at <https://www.youtube.com/watch?v=HWyNKKKri10>, accessed 28 October 2022.
66   *Church Times*, 19 February 2010.

that went beyond both the purely material and purely spiritual and which involved them in a variety of roles, from base camps to field dressing units on the front line. It can be argued that in many ways, despite a century of continued war, change in the armed forces and change in armed forces chaplaincy, that some aspects of the chaplain's role have had a remarkable continuity. The 'ministry of presence' has always been considered important. Andrew Todd in his study of Army chaplains explained: 'Because the chaplain's key role is first of all to be present, he has the capacity to respond to the human needs of the military personnel – to see their need for sleep, a listening ear or physical contact and respond accordingly.'[67] This chimes with Studdert Kennedy's advice to 'Live with the men, go everywhere they go. Make up your mind that you will share all their risks and more if you can do any good'.[68]

The presence of chaplains on the front line, offering spiritual, material and sacramental support has been described by Padre Michael Peterson as 'a model of pastoral care for chaplains that still stands today... Today we refer to this model of care as the ministry of presence; and is taught at the very start of chaplain training.'[69] A former chaplain to a bomb disposal unit commented on the 'strong pioneering element to Army Chaplaincy for we are often confronted with new and challenging situations', and the fact that the pioneering work of padres in the in the First World War helped in twenty-first century situations: 'It was always an encouragement to consider other padres who had tackled their tasks with innovation and adaptability'.[70]

Another aspect of continuity had been the role of Chaplains at home bases, in war and peace. Chaplains in the First and Second World Wars provided spiritual and pastoral care of the troops on home duties or training to go overseas, often dealing with the problems of soldiers who went absent without leave and providing support for the families of casualties and fatalities. During the Second World War the 'Padre's Hour' was instituted, giving chaplains the opportunity to meet and discuss religious, moral, and contemporary matters in a relaxed atmosphere: it is still a feature of the chaplain's role today.[71] In war and peace, chaplains have a role to play in the moral and religious education of recruits, discussing the core values of the army: courage, discipline, respect for others, integrity, loyalty, and selfless commitment. Chaplains see it as very important to know the families of soldiers

67   Andrew Todd, 'Military Chaplaincy in Contention' in Andrew Todd (ed.), *Military Chaplaincy in Contention: Chaplains, Churches and the Morality of Conflict* (Farnham: Ashgate , 2013), p.3.

68   Letter from Studdert Kennedy to Mary Bailey Hardy quoted in D. Raw, *It's Only Me – A Life of the Rev. Theodore Bayley Hardy VC, DSO, MC 1883-1918* (Gateback: Frank Peters Publishing, 1998), p.1.

69   Email conversation with Major Mike Peterson, Course Resource and Development Officer CAF Chaplain School and Centre (all views his own).

70   Conversation with the Rev. John Durant, RAChD chaplain 2000-2013.

71   Comments made by the Rev. Bill Gates and Rev. Nigel Beardsley interviewed for 'What It's Like Being a Commando Chaplain in Afghanistan'.

well, by visiting and taking baptisms, weddings and funerals. The Army chaplain has the advantage of being able to visit and relate to his personnel at work, on exercises and training, and at leisure in barracks and messes.

However, in some ways the role of the chaplain has had to change and adapt to the changing technical developments throughout the century, the changes in British society from which Army personnel are drawn, and the changing role of Britain in global affairs. Female chaplains have been serving since 2002, and are an established part of the department. In 2004 a convergence agreement was signed which brought the Roman Catholic chaplains into a unified department with the Anglicans and other denominations.[72] The men and women of the British Army are drawn from a Britain that is multi-cultural, resulting in a proportion of recruits with world faith backgrounds. Mandeep Kaur became the first Sikh chaplain to the forces in 2005 and there are five World Faith Non-Christian civilian chaplains working across all the British Military Services. Today there are one full-time and two part-time Jewish chaplains. The government publication 'Guidance on Religion and Belief in the Armed Forces' sets out detailed instructions and information about the observance of different beliefs and religious customs.[73]

There is a continuing need for chaplains to be a listening ear to all. Today mental health problems are more openly acknowledged. Issues such as inclusivity, gender identity, hidden and open disabilities are matters that are spoken off more frequently than in the past. There is also a much wider understanding of the concept of moral injury, defined as 'the damage done to one's conscience or moral compass when that person perpetrates, witnesses, or fails to prevent acts that transgress one's own moral beliefs, values, or ethical codes of conduct'.[74] Brian Powers, Vann Fellow at Durham university and an ex-combatant in Afghanistan, has recently written a powerful piece about the moral injury that is bound to be experienced by serving soldiers and veterans of the as a result of the sudden withdrawal from Afghanistan: 'speaking as someone who studies moral injury I can say that the large scale collapse of our Afghanistan mission is likely to exacerbate moral trauma for the veterans of the conflict and bring morally injurious experiences back to the forefront of their minds.' [75] Two chaplains from 2 Para and 3 Para accompanied the troops in their recent attempts to evacuate people at risk in Kabul during Operation PITTING. Chaplains will no doubt be engaged in pastoral work surrounding this event and the memories it had raised for some time. When

72 'Roman Catholic Bishopric of the Forces'.

73 'Guidance on Religion and Belief in the Armed Forces', available at <https://assets.publishing.service. gov.uk/government/uploads/system/uploads/attachment_data/file/28127/guide_religion_belief.pdf>, accessed 17 October 2022.

74 'What is Moral Injury', at <https://moralinjuryproject.syr.edu/about-moral-injury/>, accessed 17 October 2022.

75 Brian Powers, 'Moral Injury and Afghanistan', at <https://vannfellow.wordpress.com/2021/09/03/moral-injury-and-afghanistan/>, accessed 17 October 2022.

discussing the effect of religious faith on a person's experience of action stress, the Rev. Andrew Hillier suggested that in fact, people with a strong religious faith may be more subject to moral injury.[76]

Chaplains of the United States forces were officially involved in the "Hearts and Minds" campaign in Afghanistan and Iraq, with a defined purpose and separate funding, but British Army chaplains had no formal role in dealings with the local Muslim populations, although informally they have acted as liaison and advisory roles involving local religious leaders. This role is not without controversy:[77] anecdotally, they have been asked on occasion to take part in intelligence gathering while engaged in liaison and hearts and minds work thus provoking an ethical dilemma for chaplains as they consider the results of such action, either as a force multiplier, or as the cause of deaths resulting from action taken on the information they provided. Another consideration is the fact that there are few enough chaplains to fulfil their primary spiritual and pastoral roles.[78]

However, much of the work carried out informally by British Army chaplains in these theatres has been low-key and considered beneficial; for example, chaplains have met with local people, distributed articles for use in Quranic worship and study and taken part in discussions with individuals and groups. In their comparison of the different role of American and British chaplains, Wilkes and Gutkowski state: 'If the chaplain's efforts result in "force protection", according to the US doctrine developed for chaplains working in religious support, then that is no breach of their neutrality nor of their fundamental status as non-combatants.'[79] The extent of the use of chaplains in these kind of roles is something which is a debate for the future.

The United Nations Security Council has adopted 10 resolutions on Women, Peace and Security (WPS) since 2000, in response to persistent advocacy from civil society. They guide work to promote and protect the rights of civilians, particularly women, in conflict and post-conflict situations. The United Kingdom is the penholder – that is to say, the member of the Council that leads the negotiation and drafting of resolutions on a particular council agenda item – for these issues in the United Nations so has been deeply involved in WPS and human security issues. The Ministry of Defence adopted Joint Service Publication 1325 in 2019 but it is rather silent on the role of chaplains being involved in what seems to be obvious areas for chaplaincy to be involved in.[80] Army chaplains have in any case been involved in promoting the human security agenda in all operations that they

76 The Rev. Andrew Hillier, interviewed by the author July 2021.
77 Gutkowski and Wilkes, 'Changing Chaplaincy', pp.113-116.
78 Gutkowski and Wilkes, 'Changing Chaplaincy', pp.113-116.
79 Gutkowski and Wilkes, 'Changing Chaplaincy', pp.111-124.
80 Ministry of Defence, JSP 1325 Human Security in Military Operations, 2019, available at < https:// assets.publishing.service.gov.uk/government/uploads/system/uploads/attachment_data/file/770919/ JSP_1325_Part_1_2019_O.PDF>, accessed 17 October 2022.

are engaged in as part of their role. This publication is now in the process of being reviewed, which will hopefully result in a clearer definition of the role of chaplains on issues that the United Nations sees as crucial to world peace and security.

Conclusions

Military chaplains have been active and present in all aspects of army life, save bearing arms. Throughout the last century there has been in many ways continuity in their roles even whilst the changing global circumstances and conditions have also ensured change. The expansion of academic study on chaplaincy has made space for many serving chaplains to pursue areas of academic research that have enhanced their understanding of their role. The Army continues to face security challenges globally due to a rise in the need for humanitarian relief as conflict and climate change feed the crises around the world. The chaplain's role can be to help members of the armed forces to deal with a complex level of ethical judgement in situations where there is no clear right or wrong, and to support them in their moral judgements, especially men and women with responsibilities making crucial decisions.

Sir John Smyth, in his overview of Army chaplaincy quoted a Second World War chaplain who saw his role in a way which still holds good today as: 'A link with home and a link with God – and through his own non-combatancy – a link with peace.' [81] Chaplains have provided spiritual support, pastoral care, and moral guidance to all, irrespective of religion or belief, so that many men and women serving in the British army in the last 100 years will have had occasion to say 'thank you padre'.

Bibliography

Archival Sources

Museum of Army Chaplaincy
 Papers deposited by Rev. P.R.C. Abram CVO.
Imperial War Museum
 IWM 1/51/94, Papers of the Rev. Harold Spooner.
 IWM 8/20/1, Papers of the Rev. E.C. Crosse.

---

81   Smyth, *In This Sign Conquer*, p.243.

Printed Primary Sources

Cordingly, Eric, *Down to Bedrock: The diary and secret notes of a Far East prisoner of war chaplain 1942-45* (Norwich: Art Angels Publishing; 2013).

Davies. S.J., In *Spite of Dungeons* (London: Hodder and Stoughton, 1954).

King, John H., *Thank you Padre* (privately printed, unknown date).

Milner-White, E, 'Worship and Services', in F. B. Macnutt, (ed.) *The Church in the Furnace* (London: McMillan, 1918).

Secondary Sources

Editorial, 'Falklands Recollections: Interviews with Revs David Cooper and Dereck Heaver' *R.A.Ch.D. Journal*, Vol.27 No.2, December 1982.

Gutkowski, Stacey, and Wilkes, George, 'Changing Chaplaincy: a Contribution to Debate over the Roles of US and British Military Chaplains in Afghanistan', *Religion, State & Society*, 39:1, (2001), pp.111-124.

Hamilton, Nigel, *Monty the Field Marshal, 1944-1976* (London: Sceptre, 1987).

Howson, Peter, *Britain and the German Churches, 1945-1950: The Role of the Religious Affairs Branch in the British Zone* (Martlesham: Boydell and Brewer: 2021).

Howson, Peter, *Padre, Prisoner and Pen-Pusher: The World War One Experiences of the Revd Benjamin O'Rorke* (Solihull: Helion and Company, 2015), p.23.

Louden, Stephen, *Chaplains in Conflict* (London: Avon Books, 1996).

Madigan, E., *Faith under Fire: Anglican Army Chaplains and the Great War* (London: Palgrave Macmillan 2011).

Marrin, Albert, *The Last Crusade: The Church of England in the First World War* (Durham, N.C: Duke University Press. 1974).

Parker, L., The *Whole Armour of God: Anglican Army Chaplains in the Great War* (Solihull: Helion, 2009).

Purcell, William, *Woodbine Willie, An Anglican Incident* (London: Hodder and Stoughton, 1962).

Snape, M., and Henshaw, V., 'Flanders to Helmand: Chaplaincy, Faith and Religious Change in the British Army 1914-2014', *Journal of Beliefs and Values*, 38 (2), pp.194-229.

Smyth, John, *In This Sign Conquer* (London: A.R. Mowbray and Co, 1968).

Snape, M.F., *The Royal Army Chaplains' Department, 1796-1953: Clergy under Fire (Studies in Modern British Religious History)* (Woodbridge: Boydell Press, 2007).

Todd, Andrew (ed.) *Military Chaplaincy in Contention, Explorations in Practical, Pastoral and Empirical Theology)* (London: Routledge, 2013).

Wilby, Timothy D., *Attitudes to War in the Church of England 1939 – 1983* (PhD Thesis, Durham University, 1987).

Zahn Gordon, *Chaplains in the R. A. F.: Study in Role Tension* (Manchester: Manchester University Press, 1969).

Newspapers

Church Times
The Guardian
The Tablet
The Times

Online Resources

Armstrong, Stephen, 'The Good Fight' *The Guardian*, 15 October 2005, available online at <https://www.theguardian.com/world/2005/oct/15/iraq.comment>.

Butt, Riazat, 'UK chaplains in Afghanistan: ordinary priests with an extraordinary flock', *The Guardian*, <https://www.theguardian.com/uk/2011/oct/05/uk-chaplains-afghanistan-priests-congregation>.

Ministry of Defence, JSP 1325 Human Security in Military Operations, 2019, available at < https://assets.publishing.service.gov.uk/government/uploads/system/uploads/attachment_data/file/770919/JSP_1325_Part_1_2019_O.PDF>,

Powers, Brian, 'Moral Injury and Afghanistan', at <https://vannfellow.wordpress.com/2021/09/03/moral-injury-and-afghanistan/>.

Vassallo, David, 'A short history of Camp Bastion Hospital: part 2—Bastion's catalytic role in advancing combat casualty care', at <https://www.friendsofmillbank.org/downloads/camp_bastion_short_history_2.pdf.

'British fatalities: Operations in Afghanistan', <https://www.gov.uk/government/fields-of-operation/afghanistanfatalities>.

'Colonel the Reverend 'Sam' Davies (Glosters' Chaplain Korea)', thread on British Militaria Forums at < https://www.tapatalk.com/groups/britishmilitariaforums/colonel-the-reverend-39-sam-39-davies-glosters-39--t8557.html>.

'Guidance on Religion and Belief in the Armed Forces', available at <https://assets.publishing.service.gov.uk/government/uploads/system/uploads/attachment_data/file/28127/guide_religion_belief.pdf>,

'Roman Catholic Bishopric of the Forces', at <https://www.rcbishopricforces.org.uk/royal-navy>.

'Royal Army Chaplains' Department Centenary' at < https://web.archive.org/web/20211217154522/https://www.army.mod.uk/news-and-events/events/2019/royal-army-chaplains-department-centenary/>.

'The Chaplains at Arnhem', at <https://www.paradata.org.uk/article/chaplains-arnhem>.

'Padre Gerry E. Weston MBE', at <https://www.paradata.org.uk/people/gerry-e-weston.

'What is Moral Injury', at <https://moralinjuryproject.syr.edu/about-moral-injury>.

Audio-visual Resources

Associated Press Archive, 'CROATIA: REPATRIATION SERVICE HELD FOR 3 DEAD BRITISH IFOR TROOPS', <http://www.aparchive.com/metadata/youtube/205e9e9d240f984ba16517f58495caa2>.

'What It's Like Being a Commando Chaplain in Afghanistan', documentary available at <https://www.youtube.com/watch?v=HWyNKKKri10>.

Index